UNIVERSITY OF NORTH CAROLINA AT CHAPEL HILL
DEPARTMENT OF ROMANCE LANGUAGES

NORTH CAROLINA STUDIES
IN THE ROMANCE LANGUAGES AND LITERATURES

Founder: URBAN TIGNER HOLMES
Editor: CAROL L. SHERMAN

Distributed by:

UNIVERSITY OF NORTH CAROLINA PRESS
CHAPEL HILL
North Carolina 27515-2288
U.S.A.

NORTH CAROLINA STUDIES IN THE
ROMANCE LANGUAGES AND LITERATURES
Number 274

IMAGES IN MIND: LOVESICKNESS,
SPANISH SENTIMENTAL FICTION
AND *DON QUIJOTE*

IMAGES IN MIND: LOVESICKNESS, SPANISH SENTIMENTAL FICTION AND *DON QUIJOTE*

BY
ROBERT FOLGER

CHAPEL HILL

NORTH CAROLINA STUDIES IN THE ROMANCE
LANGUAGES AND LITERATURES
U.N.C. DEPARTMENT OF ROMANCE LANGUAGES

2002

Library of Congress Cataloging-in-Publication Data

Folger, Robert.
    Images in mind: lovesickness, Spanish sentimental fiction and Don Quijote / by Robert Folger.
    p. cm. – (North Carolina studies in the Romance languages and literatures; no. 274).
    Includes bibliographical references.
    ISBN 0-8078-9278-5 (pbk.)
    1. Spanish fiction–Classical period, 1500-1700–History and criticism. 2. Lovesickness in literature. 3. Desire in literature. I. Title. II. Series.
PQ6147.S44 F65 2002
863'.095353–dc21   2002029995

Cover design: Heidi Perov

© 2002. Department of Romance Languages. The University of North Carolina at Chapel Hill.

ISBN 0-8078-9278-5

DEPÓSITO LEGAL: V. 4.791 - 2002

ARTES GRÁFICAS SOLER, S. L. - LA OLIVERETA, 28 - 46018 VALENCIA

TABLE OF CONTENTS

	Page
ACKNOWLEDGEMENTS	7
INTRODUCTION	9
CHAPTER I: A HORIZON OF EXPECTATIONS	19
1. Lovesickness in modern scholarship	19
2. Interpretive frames contemporary to sentimental fiction	27
a) Faculty psychology	27
b) The concept of lovesickness in the Latin West	33
c) Lovesickness in vernacular texts	41
d) *Remedia amoris*	51
3. Lovesickness and sentimental fiction	56
a) Love-as-sickness as a subject of sentimental fiction	56
b) "Psycho-analysis" and sentimental fiction	63
CHAPTER II: THE FIRST GENERATION OF SENTIMENTAL FICTION	82
1. 'Digno de perpetua membrança': *Siervo libre de amor*	82
a) *Bursario*	84
b) Guillaume de Deguileville's *Le Pèlerinage de la vie humaine*	95
c) *Siervo libre de amor*	106
2. 'Todas las cosas tienen dos entendimientos': *Sátira de infelice e felice vida*	132
3. 'Por aquella olvidança es causa la presente hobra': *Triste deleytaçión*	146
Final observation	167
CHAPTER III: THE SECOND GENERATION OF SENTIMENTAL FICTION	171
1. 'Nuevas leyes usays en amor': *Grimalte y Gradissa*	171
a) *Libro de Fiameta*	173
b) Flores's Fiometa	177
2. 'Si pudiese remediar su mal sin amanzillar mi onrra': *Cárcel de amor*	194
a) Opening icons: "La imagen femenil" and the prison as soul	201

	Page
b) Leriano's failed salvation	215
c) Nicolás Núñez's reading of *Cárcel*	227

EPILOGUE: 'Esto del morirse los enamorados es cosa de risa': Faculty psychology and lovesickness in *Don Quijote* 234

a) Don Quijote's *locura* 234
b) Lovesickness in *Don Quijote* 239

TEXTS CITED 249

ACKNOWLEDGEMENTS

THE rhetoric of acknowledgement demands exhaustive and lengthy lists of supporting institutions, grants and fellowships, scholarly exchanges with many colleagues, and mentors. My list is not long. Thus I am all the more indebted to those who helped me.

A publication grant from the Program for Cultural Cooperation between the Spanish Ministery of Education, Culture and Sports and the United States Universities was crucial in financing this book.

Ivy A. Corfis and Juan Carlos Temprano read earlier versions of this study. I am grateful to Florian Neumann for checking my translations from Latin and to Helmut Zedelmaier for looking at the first chapter, and for the source of encouragement he has been to me for many years. I owe thanks to an anonymous reader for NCSRLL. E. Michael Gerli's studies on sentimental fiction opened up perspectives for my own work, and his comments on my manuscript were invaluable. Without Steven Hutchinson's support I could not have pursued my investigations on this topic in the first place.

Carol Sherman from NCSRLL accompanied *Images in Mind* from manuscript to book with competence and good spirit.

Anna Larsson made this book possible by carefully reading my text, shaping its style and, no less important, by putting up with me when my excitement for love-as-sickness spilled over into everyday life. This book is dedicated to her.

INTRODUCTION

IN the last few decades, scholarship has broadened our understanding of the family of texts denominated as "sentimental romance," "novela sentimental," or "ficción sentimental" and their authors.[1] We know now that an amazing number of subtexts, genres, cultural practices and traditions constitute the "genetic make-up" of each individual text.[2] The metaphor of the literary artifact as a palimpsest seems appropriate because it calls attention to the writerly activity, the various levels of textuality, the evasiveness of

---

[1] As my analysis will show, the generic label "romance" in its modern meaning misconstrues the narrative structure and pragmatics of the texts under consideration; for opposing views see, for instance, Deyermond ("Lost genre") and Cull; Rohland de Langbehn reviews the prevalent views on the question of the genre's name (*Unidad genérica* 12-15). Though occasionally used in recent studies, today's critics agree that Marcelino Menéndez Pelayo's creation "novela sentimental" is misleading. In the following I will use the neutral and less restrictive term "sentimental fiction."

[2] See Alan Deyermond's impressive chart of the "relaciones genéricas" of the sentimental fiction (58). I will discuss the sentimental fiction scholarship in detail in my analyses of the individual primary texts. After submitting the final copy of my book to the NCSRLL, Antonio Cortijo Ocaña's *La evolución genérica de la ficción sentimental de los siglos XV y XVI: género literario y contexto social* (Colección Támesis, Serie A: Monografías 184. London: Tamesis, 2001) appeared. His study impressively shows that the possibilities of source studies for sentimental fiction have not yet been exhausted. He provides an invaluable contribution to situating sentimental fiction in a historical context. I see, however, no reason to modify the essential claims of the following book and my readings of the texts under consideration. Too late, I realized that I could have profited greatly from Julian Weiss' 1990 *The Poet's Art: Literary Theory in Castile c. 1400-60* (Medium Ævum monographs, New series 14. Oxford: The Society for the Study of Medieval Languages and Literature) in my attempt to reconstruct 15th-century reading habits.

the text, and by extension, the workings of language. In a more elusive way, the metaphor of the palimpsest also emphasizes the process of reading: sentimental fiction can be described as a dense web of entangled, faded readings, as a challenge to the reader. While the parameters of writing sentimental fiction and its textuality have been explored with great success, reading and readers have been largely neglected.[3] The following study is shaped by the conviction that special attention given to the reader will further our understanding of the texts and the individuals who produced them.

The advance in sentimental fiction scholarship that I propose is, as a matter of fact, a step back in terms of the history of literary criticism. Some of the most important contributions to reader-centered criticism were published in the 1970s. Objections were raised that only the determination of the authorial intention prevents the multiplication of fortuitous readings. Iser's concept of *repertoire* inscribed in a given text, Fish's and Chartier's *interpretive communities*, groups that share sets of reading/writing strategies, and Jauß's method of reconstructing common horizons of expectations compellingly dispel the modern critics' horror of the postmodern *anything goes*. Post-structuralist critics, like Paul de Man, on the other hand, observe that reader-response criticism as a hermeneutical method is "by definition, a process directed toward the determination of meaning; it postulates a transcendental function of understanding, no matter how complex, deferred, or tenuous it might be, and will, in however mediated a way, have to raise questions about the extralinguistic truth value of literary texts" (9). Even if we accept that no text escapes the play of the *différance* and the impossibility of establishing a stable center that conveys meaning, this does not devalue reader-centered hermeneutics as a tool for historical research. Medieval readers were well aware of the treacherous nature of the letter, yet strove to overcome textual indeterminacy in a

---

[3] John Dagenais's important *The Ethics of Reading in Manuscript Culture* demonstrates how a reader-centered approach is able to open new perspectives in an otherwise well-researched area of Hispanomedievalism; for the impact of Dagenais's book see the "Dialogue review" published in *La Corónica* 1997 (25.2; p. 237-47). Further reviews were written by Dorothy Severin and María Rosa Menocal. See also Seidenspinner-Núñez's 1990-91 plea for a reorientation of medievalist scholarship. In Alan Deyermond's bibliographical review of sentimental fiction scholarship after 1988 the question of the reader is virtually absent, both in a plethora of studies in recent years and as a perspective for future studies ("Estudio de la ficción").

process of active, "ethical" reading. *Rezeptionstheorie*, then, approximates the actual discursive formation that generated premodern literature.[4]

The reconstruction of horizons of expectations and *épistémès* of past cultures is, of course, a heuristic and hermeneutic fiction, but a useful one.[5] According to Hans-Georg Gadamer, the hermeneutical process necessarily involves the fusion (*Verschmelzung*) of past horizons of expectations and the interpreter's present horizons (*Wahrheit* 289-90; *Truth* 306).[6] Thus, hermeneutics cannot claim to unravel the "authentic" meaning that a premodern reader would infer in a premodern text. This limitation distinguishes Gadamerian hermeneutics from the author-centered and historicist interpretations and makes it,[7] despite the claim that it reaches a determinate meaning, an approach that shares the poststructuralist tenet that there is no definite, true interpretation, but only a momentary and revisable locking of an endless chain of interpretations.

Since the horizon of the interpreter is a constituent of the hermeneutical process, it may be helpful to explain my own experience as a reader of sentimental fiction. Already the expression "reader of sentimental fiction" holds an implicit interpretive assumption that shapes the reading experience of the modern critic. I could only become a reader of sentimental fiction because hispanomedievalist scholarship provided me with the organizational concept of "sentimental romance." This generic label largely determined my first selection of texts. In my research, however, *pace* Rohland de Langbehn,[8] I have found no convincing definition of

---

[4] Regarding the parallels between modern and medieval hermeneutics see Patrick J. Gallacher's and Helen Damico's introduction to *Hermeneutics and Medieval Culture* and the essays in this collection by Florence H. Ridley, Karl F. Morrison, Robert Worth Frank, Jr., and Chauncey Wood.

[5] Niklas Luhmann's *Systemtheorie* shows that any theory is only operational due to its "blind spot." This principle also applies to deconstruction, which has its main focus in the unraveling of the "blind spots" of truth-claiming discourses.

[6] Regarding the relation of Gadamer's "philosophical hermeneutics" and literary theory, see Weinsheimer.

[7] Friedrich Schleiermacher's proposition "to understand a writer better than he understood himself" (321) is, according to Gadamer, the fundamental problem of traditional hermeneutics (*Wahrheit* 180; *Truth* 192).

[8] So far, Rohland de Langbehn has accomplished the most ambitious and detailed attempt to describe the "Unidad genérica" of sentimental fiction (see also "Novela" and Antonio Cortijo Ocaña). Revealing of the intricacy of defining a unifying genre on the basis of content, form and structure is her concluding statement that "la ejecución del género analizado en muchos de los casos que se le adscriben

the genre "sentimental romance." The lowest common denominator among critics is that the texts of sentimental fiction, as Keith Whinnom puts it, are "short love-stories" (*Diego de San Pedro* 76; see also Deyermond, "Estudio" 29). Bracketing the vexing question of genre,[9] I decided to accept provisionally the implicit horizon of expectations and read the canonical texts labeled by modern scholars as "sentimental fiction."[10] I focused on the generally accepted "unifying" feature of the genre: the importance given to love. Having just finished a study on memory in medieval Castilian historiography, I was perplexed by the fact that the equivalent of the modern term "to love" is a rather odd semantic field: the lover of sentimental fiction uses the verb "to remember" or its equivalents when expressing his passion for his beloved.[11]

While it was obvious that the texts under consideration were somehow centered on the topic of love, I had the impression that the notion of love inscribed in these texts differed remarkably from our modern understanding. From my puzzlement as a modern

---

es meramente virtual [...]" ("Unidad genérica" 91). Ultimately, she provides a comparative structural analysis of a group of texts assembled by modern scholars under a generic label. I question that the genre of "novela sentimental," a *post hoc* construct of modern critics, had an equivalent among early readers in the sense that a set of specific rules of the genre shaped their horizon of expectations, whence it does not contribute a *historical* understanding of the texts under consideration.

[9] See Weissberger's incisive study of the invention of novela sentimental/sentimental romance and her plea to overcome the classificatory impasse, following the example of other branches of medievalism, by fusing "chivalric" and "sentimental" romance into one single category of romance ("Gendered Taxonomy").

[10] Gadamer describes understanding as an *"Einrücken in ein Überlieferungsgeschehen*, in dem sich Vergangenheit und Gegenwart beständig vermitteln"* ["*participating in an event of tradition*, a process of transmission in which past and present are constantly mediated"] (*Wahrheit* 275; *Truth* 290). Jauß also demands that the critic must be able "to justify his judgement taking into account his present position in a historical series of readers" ("Literaturgeschichte" 171 [my translation; the passage is omitted in Bahti's translation]).

[11] See, for instance, *Triste deleytaçión*: "forçado por el contínuo seguir d'aquella recordar," (18), "pues sigo ya tu memoria" (27), "que en sta dulçe gloria / d'amor que nos enlazamos / nunqua sea por vitoria, / mas juntos con la memoria, / siguiéndola l'alcançamos" (73), "la enamorada memoria de la triste senyora" (75), "que mi memoria, tanto ocupada en querer a ti" (80), "la memoria apasionada del E°" (83); the examples could be easily multiplied. Complementary to the notion of love as a continuous recollection is the idea that oblivion is the solution to the unhappy lovers' suffering, which is conveyed in Rodríguez del Padrón's *Siervo* (ed. Hernández Alonso, 168), *Bursario* (238), and F.A.d.C's *Triste deleytaçión* (ed. Gerli, 16) with the image of the Lethian water. The theme is repeated in Golden Age Literature in Jorge de Montemayor's *Los siete libros de Diana* where the wise Felicia cures the lovesick shepherd Sireno with a potion that causes oblivion.

reader arose an interest in the question of how a 15th-century reader could make sense of these texts. I tried to approach this issue by investigating what this reader's notion of love could have been. Among the many forms of love the Middle Ages knew–Christian love, *charitas*, love as friendship, "courtly love," merely carnal concupiscence, mutual love of superiors and subordinates as the glue of social formations and mediator of power structures–it was particularly the notion of love-as-sickness that attracted my attention. Besides my personal fascination with the topic, there were two particular characteristics of sentimental fiction's love-stories that made me suspect that lovesickness was pertinent to these texts: the disastrous emotional and physical effects of passionate love and the denial of a happy ending.

I discovered that a substantial number of widely read medieval and Renaissance medical writings treat lovesickness, or *amor hereos*. Furthermore, these treatises showed me that there existed a highly sophisticated pre-modern psychology, which modern scholarship denominated "faculty psychology." Faculty psychology clearly indicates that modern critics' projection of post-Cartesian "subjectivity" (the notion of a unified subject as a transcendental center of meaning) onto sentimental fiction is a blatant anachronism.[12] Going back to my specimens of sentimental fiction, I realized that these texts are larded with terms that would resonate to a reader with basic "psychological" and medical lore. Hence my "pre-conceiving [*Vorgriff*] of an expectable whole or regulative system" (Jauß, "Theory and Genres" 93-94; see also Gadamer, *Wahrheit* 275-90) of the series of texts I wanted to analyze, was the idea that sentimental fiction could be interpreted by early readers as explorations of cases of lovesickness using contemporary psychological concepts.

The obvious objection from author-centered critics will be (and actually was) that there is no proof that authors of sentimental fiction were sufficiently familiar with *amor hereos* and faculty psychology to justify my emphasis. Although there is, as I will point out whenever appropriate, significant evidence that they had more than basic

---

[12] In his enlightening *Vision, the Gaze, and the Function of the Senses in* Celestina James F. Burke construes the medieval "self," bringing together Lacanian gaze theory and faculty psychology: "In the medieval period the identity of the individual was thought to be constructed largely visually through a play of reflections between this person and a set of exterior models" (88).

medical knowledge, the very concept of horizon of expectation renders the *conscious* knowledge of the author irrelevant. De Man explains that Jauß's term "horizon," which derives from Husserl's phenomenology, "implies that the condition of existence of a consciousness is not available to this consciousness in a conscious mode, just as, in a perception, conscious attention is possible only upon a background, or horizon, of distraction" (12). To give an example, the majority of 20th-century literary works in the Western World are shaped by psychological concepts like "subconsciousness," "repression," "neurosis," etc., regardless of the authors' active knowledge of contemporary psychology or the "influence" of Freud's work; consequently, Freudian psychology belongs to the 20th-century reader's horizon of expectations.

The subconscious, collective nature of the horizon implies, according to De Man, that "it is, at first, nondifferentiated and unstructured; under the impact of the individually structured questions, as understood and identified by the historian-interpreter, it becomes aware of itself as background and acquires, in its turn, the coherence necessary for its organization and potential transformation" (14). The reconstructive and structuring activity of the critic entails that she is not only aware of the horizon but also, possibly, more knowledgeable than any actual reader contemporary to the historical texts.[13] This is, in the words of Catherine Gallagher and Stephen Greenblatt, "the core hermeneutical presumption that one can occupy a position from which one can discover meanings that those who left traces of themselves could not have articulated" (8).

Hence the present study is not an attempt to piece together an authentic medieval reader by means of a sort of ventriloquism; the "medical-sensitive reader" whom the reader of the following study will accompany is, I confess, I. On the other hand, in the re-construction of the horizons of expectations I have tried to supplement the fictitious "medical-sensitive reader", whenever possible, with the testimonies and traces of actual 15th-century readers, to mention particularly the writers-as-readers of sentimental fiction. Every interpretation is inevitably reductive; so is my choice to privilege the medical tradition in my explanation of sentimental fiction's horizon of expectations. I am convinced, however, that the approach I have

---

[13] I am not referring, here, to understanding in the Gadamerian sense.

chosen is capable of accounting for a significant number of the features of the texts studied, respects their alterity, and furthers a historical understanding.

In order to emulate a medical-sensitive early modern/late medieval reader of sentimental fiction, it is not satisfactory only to address the thematic aspects, i.e. the notion of love that the reader could recognize as underlying the texts. Since reading is an active process of producing meaning, it is imperative to take into account interpretive strategies and reading habits. I will show that faculty psychology suggests an alien epistemology, a "thinking in images" which translates in reading to a mental processing of texts into images, which are, in turn, the basis of literary re-creation. Complementary to the hermeneutical enterprise, then, is a poetics not centered in the creative authority of the writer but in the interpretive authority of the reader. In De Man's words, "one has to have 'read' the text in terms of poetics to arrive at a hermeneutic conclusion" (9).[14]

The diachronic change of horizons (*Horizontwandel*) is of crucial importance for Jauß's Rezeptionsästhetik. Jauß argues that the individual work is not intelligible as an expression of the prevailing convention of its time, but only as foregrounded against a horizon of previous readings or literary traditions. Even a work apparently "new" relates to subtexts that constitute a possible horizon of expectations of the readers.

> A literary work [...] does not present itself as something absolutely new in an informational vacuum, but predisposes its audience to a very specific kind of reception by announcements, overt and covert signals, familiar characteristics, or implicit allusions. It awakens memories of that which was already read, brings the reader to a specific emotional attitude, and with its beginning arouses expectations for the 'middle and end,' which can then be maintained intact or altered, reoriented, or even fulfilled ironically in the course of the reading according to specific rules of the genre or type of text. ("Literary history" 23)

Juan Rodríguez del Padrón's *Siervo libre de amor* is such an apparently new work in Castilian letters. It is the point of departure of

---

[14] De Man also calls attention to the fact that the publication series of the Konstanz school has the title *Poetik und Hermeneutik* (9).

the following analyses of sentimental fiction, not only because it is chronologically the first text in the series of sentimental fiction, but also because it favors the reconstruction of a horizon of expectations. Rodríguez del Padrón translated a medievalized version of the Ovidian *Heroides* into Castilian with the title *Bursario*; there is evidence that he was familiar with Guillaume de Deguileville's *Le Pèlerinage de la vie humaine*. Both texts were widely read in the Middle Ages, and we can assume that they shaped not only the literary horizon of the reader Rodríguez del Padrón, but also that of the readers of his *Siervo*. While *Bursario* reflects interpretive strategies of sentimental fiction, i.e. an exegesis of love silhouetted against the horizon of the medical notion of *amor hereos*, Guillaume's modelic allegory, by way of contrast, makes visible *Siervo*'s use of imagery and its technique of "psycho-analysis." The authors of *Sátira de infelice e felice vida* and *Triste deleytaçión*, the sentimental fictions chronologically closest to *Siervo*, were readers of *Siervo*. Their texts share motifs, narrative techniques, the strategies of constructing authority, and the central preoccupation of sublimating passionate love.

The first generation of sentimental fiction itself became a horizon for later authors like Juan de Flores and Diego de San Pedro. Hence the analysis of the first generation of sentimental fiction is the core of my study because it allows the description of a *Horizontwandel*. From the second generation of sentimental fiction I have chosen *Grimalte y Gradissa* and *Cárcel de amor*, two works that unfold, in diametrically opposed ways, the potential of meaning that is embedded in the first generation. In the successive readings of the individual texts, I continually revise my initial proposition that sentimental fiction gives an answer to the question of what happens when the consequences of *amor hereos* are played out in longer prose texts, thus engaging in a hermeneutical circle that helps to approach a 15th- or 16th-century reader's understanding of sentimental fiction.

The ultimate goal is to come to a historical understanding of sentimental fiction. Relating these texts to pragmatic, medical and psychological discourses, I hope to re-assign them a "locus in life" (*lebensweltliche Situierung*),[15] instead of dehistoricizing them as es-

---

[15] The hermeneuts of the Konstanz School draw on the theory of German *Wissenssoziologie* (most importantly Alfred Schütz and Thomas Luckmann) and its concept of the *Lebenswelt*.

capist literature, literary playgrounds, or expressions of an obscure *Zeitgeist* ("Waning of the Middle Ages," "prerrenacimiento").

In chapter one, from the most important Latin and Spanish medical writings, I reconstruct the concept of lovesickness, or *amor hereos*, in the context of faculty psychology. The basic type of premodern brain physiology assumes three adjacent and connected ventricles in the brain. These cavities are the seat of interior senses (imagination, judgment, memory) pertaining to the animal soul. The interior senses work upon the data conveyed by the exterior senses from which they generate mental images. This process results in "emotions" or *passiones*, which affect body and soul. The interior senses of the animal soul are ideally checked by the higher faculties of the rational soul. Medieval scholars and physicians considered passionate love a "brain disease." In the *philocaptio* the *vis estimativa* misjudges the image of a beautiful woman, resulting in an incessant recollection of her image. It is a psychosomatic disease with wide-ranging, even fatal consequences. Physicians devise a series of cures (*remedia amoris*), which aim at replacing or altering the enticing image of the beloved.

According to faculty psychology, "thinking" is not possible without images. In reading, a written text is translated into mental images, which are stored in the *vis memorativa*. In the process of literary creation a writer reenacts mnemonically stored previous readings and introduces these elements in his own "fiction." Given the fact that the images which are derived from sensory perception of empirical phenomena have the same ontological status as those derived from reading processes, the "clash" of diegetic levels, "fiction" and "reality," would not strike a contemporary reader as "metafictional" but conform to his reading habits and horizons of expectations.

In chapter two I argue that the rationale behind early sentimental fiction (*Siervo libre de amor*, *Sátira de infelice e felice vida*, *Triste deleytaçión*) is the protagonists' struggle with, and triumph over, the psychosomatic symptoms of lovesickness and its sublimation in constant, altruistic love. Addressing the readers in a cyclic narrative closure, the authors attempt to rehabilitate their frustrated lovers as memorable heroes of constant love and praiseworthy "authors."

In chapter three, I show that both San Pedro's *Cárcel* and Flores's *Grimalte y Gradissa* play out the fatal consequences of lovesickness. Whereas Flores creates the persona of the pathetic Grimalte, who unwillingly lays open the unredeemable outcome of *hereos*, San Pedro conceives of the persona of El Auctor, who presents himself as a reliable witness and capable chronicler of Leriano's heroic deeds. In both texts only the shrewd women, Gradissa and Laureola, who have the strength to resist the power of passionate love and courtly persuasion, escape the cataclysm of love, indicating a fading away of the discourse of ennobling courtly love.

In an epilogue I emphasize the central role that the parody of lovesickness plays in *Don Quijote*. The protagonist's creation of Dulcinea results from a lucid decision, which is, as it were, bracketed in his folly; his love is not crazy but unreasonable. Associating *Don Quijote* with the Enlightenment épistémè, it is the "unreason" within madness that is the target of derision and persecution.

CHAPTER I

A HORIZON OF EXPECTATIONS

1. LOVESICKNESS IN MODERN SCHOLARSHIP

FROM Greek and Roman antiquity, through the Middle Ages until the Renaissance and even after, lovesickness enjoyed a significant interest in medicine, theology, and, as I will show, in literature. In spite of this continuity, the meaning of the medieval *terminus technicus* for lovesickness, *amor hereos*, was already unknown to readers and commentators by the end of the 17th century (Lowes 491-95). With the emergence of the notion of romantic love in the 18th century, love-as-sickness fell utterly into oblivion. In 1905, in an often-overlooked pioneering study, Hjalmar Crohns made the first contribution of modern scholarship to the "history of love as a disease." Departing from the famous episode of Antiochus and Stratonice, documented by classic authorities like Appian, Lucian, and Valerius Maximus,[16] Crohns sketches the phenomenology of morbid love. He traces a genealogy of medical writers that includes Galen, Paul of Aegina, the Arabic authors Rhazes (al-Rāzī), Ibn al-Jazzār, Haly Abbas ('Alī ibn al-'Abbās) and Avicenna. Crohns also mentions the importance of Constantine the African's translations of Arabic sources and Arnald of Villanova's writing on *amor hereos*, and analyzes Bernard de Gordon's widely disseminated *Opus lilium medicinae*. While Crohns felt obliged to justify his topic with the historian's duty not only to report the "steady and valuable" but also the "ridiculous" (68), John Livingston Lowes realized only a decade later that the concept of lovesickness and the etymology of

---

[16] Ciavolella supplies a more comprehensive list of the Antiochus theme in world literature ("La tradizione dell'*aegritudo amoris*" 509-10).

amor hereos help our understanding of some obscure passages in medieval and Renaissance authors like Chaucer and Burton. He points out that the student of literature meets "the traces of *hereos*" at every turn and postulates a *"mutual* influence–a sort of osmosis" between medical writers and poets (52-53).

In spite of the perspectives Lowes's study opened for the history of medicine and literature, love-as-sickness was widely neglected thereafter. When, in his 1973 introduction to Diego de San Pedro's *Cárcel de amor* (*Obras* II), Keith Whinnom discussed the "sentimental world" of the author, he rebuked the historians' disregard for morbid love (13-15). And indeed, in the sixty years since Lowes only two contributions to the study of lovesickness had been made. In 1951 Lawrence Babb explored Renaissance ideas of passionate love in the context of contemporary humoral theory (128-42). [17] The only contribution to the medieval tradition was made by Bruno Nardi, who showed in 1959 how some medieval Italian poets used material from treatises on lovesickness.

However, soon after Whinnom's observation, with the new interest in cultural history and the scholarly controversy about sexuality sparked by Michel Foucault's *Introduction* to his *History of sexuality* (Smith 319-20), the subject of lovesickness attracted the attention it deserved from historians. In 1976 Massimo Ciavolella's monograph on the "mallattia d'amore" in Antiquity and the Middle Ages appeared. The introductions of Michael R. McVaugh to Arnald of Villanova's *Tractatus de amore heroico*, and of Ciavolella and Donald A. Beecher to Jacques Ferrand's *Treatise on Lovesickness* provide a fairly comprehensive picture of *amor hereos* in the medical tradition. [18] With Wack's translation and edition of Constantine's *Viaticum* I.20, and the glosses on this seminal text (*Lovesickness*), a corpus of the most important primary texts on the topic is now easily accessible.

The origins of lovesickness and the evolution of the concept have been traced and a genealogy of influential medical authors has been established. Furthermore, the supporters of the Hispano-Arabic origins of courtly love assert the influence of the Arabic theory

---

[17] The standard work on melancholy from Antiquity to the Renaissance is still the monograph by Raymond Kilbansky, Fritz Saxl and Erwin Panofsky.

[18] Also worth mention are the overview by Hans Schadewaldt, the collections of articles edited by Theo Stemmler, Beecher and Ciavolella (*Eros and Anteros*), Massimo Peri (23-41), and Michael R. Solomon (*Literature of Misogyny* 49-64).

of passionate love (Boase 62-75). Still, many of the ramifications of love-as-sickness and the cross-fertilizations with other discourses are yet to be explored.

In his attempt to systematize the love conceptions underlying medieval literature, Rüdiger Schnell argues that courtly love must always be seen in the light of "suspicious sexual love" (138). In order to be socially acceptable, "courtly literature" sublimates the physiological and psychological causes and effects of passionate love which medieval physicians describe (139-51). According to Schnell, the differences in the treatment of love in lyric poetry and longer narrative texts are not due to general discrepancies in the notion of love, but to the perspective an author adopts when observing the conventions and formal exigencies of the genre (128-29): the lyric poet's persona can limit the description of his relationship to his idealized, imagined beloved to a mere reflection of his emotional and mental state; since the authors of longer narrative forms have to show their protagonists in action, they tend to ironize "courtly love" or expose and criticize the illusion of the "love's fools."

Wack's study of lovesickness in the Middle Ages not only presents an important chapter in intellectual history, but also suggests the pervasiveness of morbid love and its relation to a broader cultural and social context:

> The *mal d'amour* was a socially recognized way of coping with love, hostility, and the inversion of gender-power relations. By suffering love as a disease, or by imagining himself to do so in poetry, the lover could alienate himself from the responsibility for this dubious desire and yield himself to its most intense degree. Passion could thus become a sign of 'noble love' and the 'feminine' state of illness be reclaimed into a masculine sphere of value. (*Lovesickness* 171)

As we have seen, modern scholars of lovesickness recognized the pertinence of the subject to literary criticism from the beginning. In the last decades the medical subtext in important medieval authors like Cavalcanti, Dante (Fontaine), Petrarch (Küpper), Boccaccio (Ciavolella, "La tradizione dell'*aegritudo amoris*") and Chaucer (Ciavolella, "Mediaeval Medicine"; Heffernan) have been studied. A 1979 study of the *remedia amoris* in Castilian letters by

Françoise Vigier indicated the profusion of medical lore in diverse literary genres ("Remédes"). However, even in 1989, Pedro Cátedra had to call attention to the fact that the repercussions of the topic of lovesickness in Hispanic literature are enormous, although the function of this topic has been treated deficiently or only as a basic element of particular works like *Celestina* (57). Cátedra's own study indicates how 15th-century scholastic natural philosophy discussed love and how this university tradition became the point of departure of literary creation in the form of *contrafacta* of disputations and repetitions. He shows that this academic tradition and its corollary in fictional texts took into account *amor hereos* as discussed by physicians (57-69).

Guillermo Serés attempts to integrate natural philosophy into a study of medieval and Renaissance lyric poetry inspired by Platonic ideas (*Transformación de los amantes*). He argues that the Platonic motifs of lost integrity and ideal resemblance of the lovers merged with analogous biblical passages in the topos of the transformation of the lovers. The lover embraces the mental image of his beloved with his senses to the point where the soul, which is a mirror in which he can see himself, only reflects the other person. If requited, he himself becomes a mirror for his beloved, resulting in a mutual transformation. This transformation transcends sensual love in intellectual contemplation and Christian love, *agape* and *charitas*.[19]

According to Serés, this (neo-)Platonic, mystic conception of love, which he equates with "courtly love," could be reconciled with the Aristotelian, naturalist account of perception. *Amor hereos* is the result of a failure to transcend wordly desire and the adherence to incessant cogitation of the mental image (*Transformación de los amantes* 69-74). Although Serés, basing his analysis of *amor hereos* on a deficient corpus of relevant medieval texts, overemphasizes the neo-Platonic subcurrent in medical tradition and natural philosophy, he gives some valuable examples of the topos of the transformation of lovers and of the failure of transformation in *cancionero* poetry and sentimental fiction (87-136).

Recently Michael Solomon made a case for an intriguing interplay between misogynist literature and medical discourse in Alfonso Martínez de Toledo's *Arcipreste de Talavera* and Jacme Roig's

---

[19] St. Augustine's ideas about "use" and "abuse" of physical beauty were instrumental in the evolution of this notion (Robertson 65-76).

Spill (*Literature of Misogyny*). Martínez de Toledo and Roig both perceived the upheaval of their time as the outcome of improper, pathological sexual practices. Treatises on lovesickness advised purging the patient's mind of harmful images of the beloved by distraction or by altering the positive image of the woman. Martínez de Toledo and Roig opted for administering this logotherapy in the form of written texts. According to Solomon, "antifeminist discourse [...] is at the heart of this therapy" (*Literature of Misogyny* 8). Solomon shows that prominent 15th-century authors were very well-versed in the medical discourse and that they employed this knowledge in their texts. In 15th-century Spain, learned conceptions of passionate love became widely disseminated to a broader public through vernacular handbooks (97-99). Roig and Martínez de Toledo, then, met the horizons of expectation of their readers.[20]

In this review of Hispanist studies on lovesickness Fernando de Rojas's *Celestina* deserves particular consideration, not only because of the quantity and quality of scholarship, but also because of the intertextual relationship between Rojas's masterpiece and sentimental fiction.

Textual borrowings in *Celestina* taken from sentimental fiction have been noted early (Castro Guisasola 183-85). Peter G. Earle included *Celestina* in the genre of sentimental fiction because "its central problem is a sentimental affair" based on a similar concept of love (90). Likewise, Edward Dudley claims that sentimental fiction and Celestina share "the matter of analysis of love itself", and the image of the *cárcel* ("Inquisition of love" 239-41). María Rosa Lida de Malkiel, on the other hand, underscores the uniqueness of *Celestina*. Yet in her monumental source study "Originalidad artística de *La Celestina*," we also find scattered references to sentimental fiction.

More recent scholarship tends to emphasize the parodic subversion of sentimental fiction in *Celestina*. Dorothy S. Severin sees Calisto as a parody of Leriano, protagonist of Diego de San Pedro's *Cárcel de amor*, who is reputedly the embodiment of the courtly lover ("Introducción" 29). According to Severin's reasoning, Rojas

---

[20] According to Gerold Hilty, there is, with the exception of one of the *Cantigas* of Alfonse the Sage and the *Libro de Apolonio*, little evidence of the motif of lovesickness in 12th- and 13th-century Spanish literature. A more meticulous study would unquestionably yield more substantial findings. Daniel L. Heiple refers to some examples in late medieval and Renaissance literature (61-63).

undertook no less than the writing of an anti-romance which "destroyed the literary antecedent" (38). Similarly, María Eugenia Lacarra identifies sentimental fiction as the predominant subtext of *Celestina*, a subtext which is parodically reflected in Rojas's text. "Esta parodia es total, no sólo de las historias sentimentales en su nivel anecdótico, sino que se extiende a sus personajes claves, amantes, intermediarios y padres [...]," and in particular, "la parodia del amor cortesano representado por el género sentimental [...]" ("Parodia" 13). Lacarra also points out that Calisto shares the amorous obsession of sentimental fiction's lovers. Illicit love is punished in sentimental fiction as severely as in *Celestina* (17). The paramount importance of obsessive love and its tragic outcome, however, contradicts the tenet of "total parody" of sentimental fiction. Severin's and Lacarra's assertion–that Rojas intended a parody of the love conception of sentimental fiction–rests on two premises: first, that *Celestina* subverts courtly love, and, second, that sentimental fiction perfectly reflects the "courtly love" underlying lyric poetry. While there is overwhelming evidence to sustain the claim that *Celestina* subverts idealizing forms of human love (Deyermond, "Text-Book Mishandled"; Martin 71-134; Severin, "Introducción"; Lacarra, "Parodia"; Corfis, "*Celestina* and the Conflict"; Castells, *Fernando de Rojas*; Burke, *Vision*),[21] it is untenable, as I will show in the following chapters, to describe the love conception of sentimental fiction as utterly idealizing and uncritical. It is, then, plausible to interpret *Celestina* as a parody of the pathos and rhetoricism of sentimental fiction,[22] and, at the same time, to acknowledge that sentimental fiction shares with *Celestina* a gloomy outlook on passionate love.[23]

Rojas, San Pedro, Flores and Rodríguez del Padrón have in common that they play out cases of obsessive love, which are en-

---

[21] For an opposing view see Castells ("Calisto and the imputed parody"), who argues that Calisto's behavior reflects *De amore*'s etiology of lovesickness. The conclusion that *Celestina* therefore conforms to the principles of courtly love is debatable, as are interpretations that recognize the discrepancies between *De amore* and *Celestina* and attest a parody, because Andreas presents a complex amalgam of idealizing, naturalist and moralist currents; see above.

[22] Which comes, in Genette's terminology, closer to "travestissement burlesque" than "parodie" (30).

[23] In 1536, Fray Francisco de Osuna expressed disapproval of the "amores" in *Celestina* and *Cárcel* (Weissberger, "Resisting readers" 176). This provides evidence that near-contemporary readers also acknowledged a shared conception of love.

capsulated in many pieces of lyric poetry. The denouements of their works are equally disastrous and the interest in showing the danger inherent in courtly love is equally paramount. Peter Cocozzella stresses the fact that 15th-century *cancionero* poetry, sentimental fiction and *Celestina*, each in its own way a *psychomachia*, share a concern for the exploration of psychic spaces and emotional dimensions of the subject. Given that psychological analysis and love phenomenology are at the heart of both sentimental fiction and *Celestina*, the love conception underlying *Celestina* promises to reflect on love in sentimental fiction. Even if we assume a parody of "sentimental love" in *Celestina*, it follows that Rojas had to project a recognizable and, to a certain degree, faithful image of "sentimental love" in his work (Genette 14-19).

It is, therefore, highly significant that various *Celestina* critics have noted the presence of lovesickness in the text (Green, "Artistic Originality" 26; Fraker, "Lida de Malkiel on *Celestina*" 179-80; Seniff; De Armas; Cátedra 68-69; Joset 260; Castells, "Mal de amores," "Calisto and the imputed parody," *Rojas and the Renaissance Vision*; Fraker, "Four Humors" 139-40, 145-51).[24] Moreover, studies by Michael Solomon, Miguel Garci-Gómez, Ricardo Castells and James F. Burke show that love-as-sickness is more than a marginal aspect in the rich intertextual net Rojas wove.[25] Michael Solomon opposes the widely accepted view of *Celestina* as an extended parody of courtly love.

> The ensuing bitextual encounter between the implications of *amor hereos* and those of 'humoral superfluity' permeate the first act, creating for the medical-sensitive reader an extensive parody of the way human beings attempt to mediate the pain and frustration wrought by unsatiated desire. ("Calisto's Ailment" 42)

---

[24] Fraker's study on the four humors, in particular, yields convincing evidence of the presence and importance of Galenic medical lore in *Celestina*.

[25] De Armas justly asserts that love-as-sickness is the rationale behind Calisto's disconcerting behavior, Celestina's intervention and Melibea's surrender, yet misconstrues lovesickness as a mere humoral disorder. Also worth mentioning here is Castells ("Calisto and the imputed parody"), who points out the centrality of lovesickness in *Celestina*, yet focuses on Andreas Capellanus's *De amore* without taking into account more pertinent writings on *amor hereos* and the broader context of faculty psychology.

He explains that these "medical-sensitive readers" would distinguish between humoral imbalance caused by superfluous semen and "real" *amor hereos* caused by the apprehension of a beautiful form. Sempronio's initial diagnosis of *amor hereos* and the adequate psychological cure is countered by Calisto's self-diagnosis of humoral superfluity which calls for expelling excess humor through coitus. "As the work progresses all the major characters begin to act around the axis of the counter-diagnosis" (Solomon, "Calisto's Ailment" 56). According to this interpretation, the author(s) of *Celestina* intended the disastrous end of the lovers and other main characters to prompt the reader to reflect on socially accepted patterns of sexual conduct (58).

In his recent monograph *Fernando de Rojas and the Renaissance Vision*,[26] Ricardo Castells takes up Miguel Garci-Gómez's contention that the anonymous first scene (*Auto*) of *Celestina* presents a dream of the lovesick protagonist Calisto ("El sueño de Calisto"; *Calisto*). Supported by a study of the treatment of lovesickness in fictional and nonfictional texts of the European tradition, Castells understands that Calisto's character is determined by his suffering from *amor hereos* and the resulting psycho-somatic effects. Like Solomon, he sees *Celestina* as related to the tradition of the *reprobatio amoris*.

Though not made explicit,[27] lovesickness is also an integral part of James F. Burke's reading of *Celestina*. He reasons that, according to premodern faculty psychology, in perception and cognition, sensorial data is combined with and transformed by previous "readings" and the mnemonic images derived from them ("Insouciant Reader" 35). Physical and mental health–intertwined with spiritual well-being–could be affected in two ways. Bodily sufferings, such as accidents, illness, or aging, could disturb or impede the mind's ability to process the sensory data in a beneficial manner. Alternatively, "the tendency of the *imaginativa* to evolve infelicitous combinations from the *sensibilia* and the possibility that the *estimativa* could become obsessed with such" (39), could produce treacherous *imagines*. Calisto and Melibea, Rojas's protagonists, are suffering from

---

[26] See also Castells's earlier studies ("El sueño"; *Calisto's dream*).

[27] In the context of premodern psychology, Burke focuses on the process of perception and cognition without indicating the possible medical reasons for the malfunction of the senses.

the latter "accident," *amor hereos*. Both lovers' disastrous negligence and unsound reactions to their surroundings are the result of the power of memory malfunctioning. In other words, the image of the revered person is associated in an infelicitous fashion with the treasures of the storehouse of memory, thus violating a principle of medieval education: the association of sense data with mnemonic images in an ethically advantageous way (41). "The literary text *Celestina*," Burke concludes, "which we as readers follow, becomes, then, a map of mis-readings of what were for the Middle Ages the two great ur-texts, the book of nature and the book of memory. Two principal signifiers, Calisto and Melibea respectively, are mistaken and mis-read within context, each by the other" (43). In his recent *Vision, the Gaze, and the Function of the Senses in Celestina*, Burke elaborates on this idea, suggesting "what [...] the author(s) of *Celestina* have done at the most basic level is to create a kind of personification allegory that presents in new form the drama of the fall through the senses, a descent facilitated by this earthly Celestina" (41).

It cannot be inferred, of course, from Solomon's, Castells's and Burke's analyses of lovesickness and its consequences in *Celestina*, that lovesickness is equally significant in *Celestina*'s subtext, sentimental fiction. Yet if we accept the idea that *Celestina*'s protagonists are somehow modeled on the lovers in sentimental fiction, the love-as-sickness theme might very well hint at the love conception underlying sentimental fiction. What is more important is that Burke's, Castells's and Solomon's original and insightful readings draw on interpretive frames contemporary to Rojas: the medical tradition and faculty psychology. These discourses merit a closer examination in order to establish how the writers of sentimental fiction conceptualized love and how they were understood by their readers.

2. Interpretive Frames Contemporary to Sentimental Fiction

a) *Faculty psychology*

Pre-modern psychology, the interplay of external senses, inner wits and higher spiritual powers, has been the subject of thorough investigation by Harry Wolfson, Murray Wright Bundy, E. Ruth Harvey, and others. In Castile, as early as the 13th century, we find the first systematic exposition of faculty psychology in vernacular language. J. Homer Herriot was the first to point out a comprehensive classification of the external senses ("sentidos de fuera") and the internal senses ("de dentro") in a 13th-century manuscript of the *Siete Partidas* (British Museum Add. 20787) which, in his opinion, reflects the earliest redaction of the encyclopedic Alfonsine law codification (270). Castilian medical writings of the 15th and 16th centuries like Francisco López de Villalobos's *Sumario de la medicina*, translations of older Latin texts like Lanfranc of Milan's *Chirugia maior* (fol. 27^r-27^v) or Brunetto Latini's widely read *Tresor* (18-19), confirm that on the Iberian Peninsula basic assumptions of scholastic faculty psychology were shared and accessible to a non-latinate public in a period that stretches at least from the 13th to the 16th centuries.

Students of the subject have called attention to the difficulty of describing faculty psychology as a coherent system. The terminology and phenomenology varies from author to author, and even within the writings of one author or a particular text we find inconsistencies. Bernardino Montaña de Monserrate's *Libro de la Anathomia del hombre* (Valladolid, 1551), certainly, is not a foundational or original text, yet it gives a suitable resumé of medieval and Renaissance positions on faculty psychology. It can also be considered representative of "popular" medical lore,[28] since the author proposes not only to be "vtil y necessario a los medicos y cirujanos que quieren ser perfectos en su arte [...]," but also addresses "a los otros hombres discretos que huelgan de saber los secretos" (fol. 1^r). The final part of the work consists of a dialogue between the *Doctor* and Luis Hurtado de Mendoza, the Marquis of Mondéjar. The physician interprets a dream of the Marquis in which he explains the different parts of the human body and their functions.[29] When the interpreter arrives in his exegesis at the human head, he faces

---

[28] Although the medieval and Renaissance theorists of faculty psychology share basic assumptions, individual authors do not agree on the terminology of the senses involved, their number and their precise functions. For a comparison with Avicenna's influential writings see the analysis of Wolfson (40-47). The similarities with Lanfranc (27^r-27^v) also demonstrate that Montaña de Monserrate does not express a genuine 16th-century conception, but elaborates common medieval medical lore.

[29] The dream and its explanation are an intriguing example of the textualization of an architectonical memory system: in his dream the Marquis visits a building filled with images. By means of exegesis, this mnemonic grid is superimposed onto the human body, facilitating memorization of the Physician's lessons.

the problem of explicating the function of the human brain. Though he and his inquisitive patron agree that this matter is "escura y muy confusa [...]," the Marquis reassures him that everybody, "si tiene algunos principios de filosofia [...]" (fol. 125ʳ), will understand it. The *Doctor* explains that the exterior senses "draw" ("debuxa") without categorizing the "figura de algun objecto exterior sensible como es el color; el olor, y el sabor, y otros semejantes objectos exteriores que se suelen sentir" (fol. 122ᵛ). They have the function of "representing" the "formas," or *species*, to the inner wits.[30] The question of how the external senses, sight in particular, convey the *species* to the inner senses was debated among medieval scholars. Against the Galenic idea of "blood rays," i.e. pneumatic vapor mixed with thin blood and sent out by the eyes,[31] stood the widely accepted notion of the *species in medio*, i.e. the continuous emanations of *species* from the object into the surrounding medium (Tachau).[32]

While, according to Montaña de Monserrate, the "ancient philosophers" ("filósofos antiguos") knew only three wits,[33] i.e. *imaginatio, estimativa* and *memoria*, physicians differentiate among five: "sentido comun, fantasia, ymaginatiua, extimatiua, y memoratiua" (fol. 122ᵛ).[34]

The common sense receives the first "impression" ("se imprime") of the "debuxos" which the external senses generate when stimulated by an object. The "forms" of the objects perceived are

---

[30] The question how the external senses, in particular sight, convey the *species* to the inner senses was debated among medieval scholars. Against the Galenic idea of "blood rays" sent out by the eyes, which was adopted by neoplatonic Renaissance theorists (Couliano 28-52), stood the widely accepted notion of the *species in medio*, i.e. the continuous emanations of *species* into the surrounding medium (Tachau).

[31] This concept was adopted by neoplatonic Renaissance theorists (Couliano 28-52).

[32] Regarding premodern theories of vision and perception and their continuity from the Middle Ages to the Enlightenment see also Burke (*Vision* 9-31).

[33] Some natural philosophers assume four powers, not differentiating between the two imaginative faculties. Thomas Aquinas, for example, argues in the *Summa* against Avicenna's tenet of a fifth power (vol. 11, p. 140; 1a. 78,4). Albert, on the other hand, differentiates in *De anima* between the two faculties, precisely in the same way Monserrate does (pp. 166-68; lib. 3, tract. 1, cap. 2).

[34] In all references to texts transcribed according to the norms established by the Hispanic Seminary of Medieval Studies of the University of Wisconsin-Madison, I eliminate the editorial mnemonics.

also imprinted in the fantasy ("fantasia").[35] In contrast to the common sense, which is only capable of representing objects while excited by the external senses, fantasy represents its object "segun que es absente [...]" (fol. 123ᵛ); it is, then, a retentive power that stores the sense impression temporarily after the object is no longer sensed by contact. The third interior wit, the "ymaginatiua", represents the external sensual objects

> no como presentes ni passados, sino como possibles entendiendo aqui por possibles los que no implican contradicion y mediante esta virtud podemos imaginar qualquier cosa possible aunque sea disparate, o como dizen chimera. (fol. 124ʳ)

Imagination is the power to transform sense impressions and create new images on the basis of previous experience and sense data. It is a compositive ("deliberative") imagination which breaks up images in order to forge composite, hybrid images, or to make up images of non-existent things (Carruthers, *Book of Memory* 53). Thomas Aquinas gives us this example: Imagination is capable of combining the "form" of gold and the "form" of "mountain" to the image of a golden mountain, which was never before seen (*Summa*, vol. 11, p. 140; 1a. 78,4).

Montaña de Monserrate locates the internal senses discussed so far in the first ventricle of the brain and describes them progressing from the front to the center. Abutting imagination, in the very middle of the brain, is judgment.

> Ay otra virtud que se dize estimatiua mediante la qual juzgamos de todo lo que se representa por las otras virtudes si es prouechoso o dañoso para nosotros, segun la manera como lo representan las otras virtudes, es a saber, o de presente, o en tiempo passado, o en tiempo possible que esta por venir, del qual conocimiento nasce el apetito sensitiuo de los animales para alcançar la cosa, o huyrla. (fol. 124ᵛ)

The *estimativa* is truly central in the working of the brain, inasmuch as it is concerned with images produced and retained by the neighboring internal wits, imagination and memory. Its function is to ex-

---

[35] Other authors use the term *imaginatio* to refer to the retentive imagination.

tract from the *species* what Latin texts call *intentiones*. In a treatise with the title *Kitāb al-najāt* Avicenna defines "intention."

> As for intention, it is a thing which the soul perceives from the sensed object without its previously having been perceived by the external sense, just as the sheep perceives the intention of harm in the wolf and to flee from it, which causes it to fear the wolf, without having been perceived at all by the external sense. (ed. Rahman 30; bk. 2, ch. 6,3)[36]

In *De anima* Avicenna specifies that the external senses are incapable of comparison and that it is, therefore, the function of the *estimativa* to extract "intentiones non sensatas, quae sunt in singulis sensibilibus" ("non-sensed intentions, which are in singular sensibles"; p. 21; pars 1, chap. 5, fol. 5ʳ). Upon these *intentiones* extracted from sensible *species* acts the orectic part of the soul (*pars animae appetitiva*).[37] The "apetito sensitiuo," to which Montaña de Monserrate refers, is divided into *appetitus concupiscibilis*, which, again in the words of the Castilian physician, incites one to "obtain a thing," and *appetitus irascibilis*, which provokes the opposite inclination, "to flee it."[38] The appetites in turn produce *passiones* in the heart, which result in the boost or reduction of vital spirit (*pneuma*), the vehicle of humidity and heat. Furthermore, as Mary Carruthers points out, Latin scholastics distinguish between the *estimativa* in animals, i.e. the instinct, and the human "*cogitativa* defined as conscious, though pre-rational activity" (*Book of Memory* 53). "And so what we call natural instinct in other animals," Aquinas explains, "in man we call cogitation, which comes upon intentions of the kind in question through a process of comparison" ("Homo autem etiam per quandam collationem. Et ideo quæ in aliis animalibus dicitur æstimativa naturalis in homine dicitur cogitativa, quæ per collationem quandam hujusmodi intentiones adinvenit"; *Summa*, vol. 11, p. 140-41; 1a. 78,4).[39] In his commentary on Aristotle's

---

[36] Some scholastic philosophers use the term "second intention" to refer to the relations established between sensual *species* and mental concepts (Myles 82-83).

[37] Carruthers explains that *intentiones* provoke an "attitude" or emotional "inclination" and "intensity" toward the image (*Craft to Thought* 124-26).

[38] Thomas Aquinas describes and classifies the "emotions" in great detail in his *Summa* (1a.2ae. 22-30). The counterpart to the sensory *appetitus* is the intellectual *appetitus* or *voluntas*.

[39] If not otherwise indicated, I have reproduced the English translations of the respective editors of the Blackfriars series.

De memoria et reminiscentia Aquinas differentiates between the activities of the soul.

> It is obvious that, when the soul directs itself to the phantasm, insofar as it is a form preserved in the sensitive part, then this is an act of the imagination or fantasy. Also the intellect is considering its relation to universals. If, however, the soul directs to the same phantasm in its aspect of being an image of something we heard or understood before, this pertains to the acts of memory. And because an image assigns an intention to a certain form, Avicenna rightly says that the memory receives the intention, and imagination the form apprehended by the senses. [my translation]

> (Sic igitur manifestum est quod quando anima convertit se ad phantasma, prout est quaedam forma reservata in parte sensitiva, sic est actus imaginationis sive phantasiae, vel etiam intellectus considerantis circa hoc universale. Si autem anima convertatur ad ipsum, inquantum est imago eius, quod primus audivimus aut intelleximus, hoc pertinet ad actum memorandi. Et quia esse imaginem significat intentionem quamdam circa formam, ideo convenienter *Avicenna* dicit quod memoria respicit intentionem, imaginatio vero formam per sensum apprehensam; 342; p. 97)

Albert, however, argues in *De bono* that the completed phantasm which is stored in memory consists of "form" and "intention": "The *intentiones* which memory preserves are not separate from the particular images [...]. Therefore, the *intentiones* are saved together with the image" ("intentiones, quas conservat memoria, non sunt absolutae a particularium imaginibus [...] intentiones simul cum imaginibus accipiuntur"; p. 251; 4.2.2; cf. Carruthers, *Book of Memory* 53-54).

From this it becomes clear that through the activity of the *estimativa*, which assigns an "intention" to the perceived and recollected *species*, the completed images become emotionally tagged. Since mental activities depend essentially on images, as I will explain in greater detail later, this also implies that imagination, memorization, recollection and rational "thinking" are essentially related to affects (Carruthers, *Book of Memory* 199-202).

Montaña de Montserrate, however, suitable to the interests of his interlocutor, focuses on the anatomical aspects of the internal wits. From the central ventricle harboring judgment he progresses to the cerebellum ("celebro menor") the site of the power called "memorativa."

> De la qual su obra y prouecho es conseruar en si todas las figuras alcançadas por qualquier de las dichas quatro virtudes, las quales no embargante que en aquel lugar no representan nada passandolas al celebro mayor representan la cosa segun el lugar donde se passan, es a saber, en el sentido comun por presentes, en la fantasia por passadas, en la ymaginacion por possibles, por manera que esta virtud sirue para acordarnos de lo que aprendemos. (fol. 124^v)

In this passage Montaña de Monserrate seems to conflate the internal wit memory, or sensory memory, and the higher "rational" faculty memory.[40] In other words, he refers to the power that stores memory images and he alludes to memory as the recipient of the knowledge accumulated in perception, imagination, cognition and intellection (Kolve 20). This is why Aquinas regards memory as part of prudence: "many functions of sensory psychology enter into prudence, and remembering is among them" ("unde multa quæ pertinent ad partem sensitivam requiriuntur ad prudentiam, inter quæ est memoria"; *Summa*, vol. 36, p. 62-63; 2a.2æ. 49,1). He thus points to the central importance of memory in premodern thinking. All of the internal wits are mnemonic tools with a different temporal dimension: they "recall" the present (*sensus communis*), the future (*imaginativa*) and the past (*memorativa*).

b) *The concept of lovesickness in the Latin West*

The complex interplay and delicate balance of the internal senses was, of course, prone to malfunctions. Thomas Aquinas points to the danger arising from an overreaction of the senses.

---

[40] This might be due to *auctores* like Constantine the African, who assigns memory to the human soul (Harvey 41). Avicenna, furthermore, distinguishes will, or *motiva*, which is moved by the *estimativa* (Harvey 46-47). In Triumphus Augustinus de Anchona's *Opusculum perutile de cognitione animae* (Bologna, 1503) this power is located in the very back of the third ventricle (Kolve 25).

> The material aspect is the physiological modification produced by the emotion of love, and this may be harmful when it is excessive; but that is equally the case with the operation of the senses, and of any other mental faculty whose functioning is accompanied by physiological modifications.
>
> (Quantum vero ad id quod est materiale in passione amoris, quod est immutatio aliqua corporalis, accidit quod amor sit læsivus propter excessum immutationis: sicut accidit in sensu, et in omni actu virtutis animæ qui exercetur per aliquam immutatione organi corporalis; *Summa*, vol. 19, p. 102-03; 1a.2æ. 28,5)

What is intriguing to modern thinking is the fact that love can cause permanent psychosomatic harm. In its pathological form, *amor hereos*, an ailment affecting mind and body, love became naturally the concern of medieval physicians.

The conception of love-as-sickness has its roots in 5th-century B.C. Greek Hippocratic medicine. Passionate love became a subject of the medical tradition with the writings of Galen (ca. 130-200). The study of lovesickness, properly speaking, was initiated by the Byzantine physicians Oribasius (325-403) and Paul of Aegina (fl. 650), whose descriptions of pathological love were adopted by Arabic physicians and inspired an ample treatment of the topic (Beecher and Ciavolella, "Introduction" 59-70). Constantine the African's versions of Arabic sources proved seminal for the reintroduction of the concept in the Latin West.[41] Constantine (d. ca. 1087), the most prominent representative of the Salneritan school, adapted Ibn al-Jazzār's (Ibn Eddjezzar, d. 979?) medical vademecum *Zād al-musāfir* (Wack, *Lovesickness* 31-50). Book one, chapter twenty of Constantine's *Viaticum peregrinatis* discusses love "qui et eros dicitur" which he defines as "a disease touching the brain. For it is a great longing with intense sexual desire and affliction of the thoughts" ("morbus [...] cerebro contiguus. Est autem magnum desiderium cum nimia concupiscentia et afflictione cogitationum";

---

[41] As Wack points out, medieval Christianity was receptive to the notion of erotic malady because passages of the Bible (the story of Amnon and Tamar and the refrain in the Canticles) could be read as references to *amor hereos*. Furthermore, in the image of the crucified Christ the ideas of "passionate love" and suffering coalesced. "Popular" concepts of lovesickness also connected with the medical tradition (*Lovesickness* 18-30).

186-87). [42] The malady is sometimes caused by "the natural need to expel a great excess of humor" ("multa humorum superfluitate expellenda"; 188-89).

> Sometimes the cause of eros is also the contemplation of beauty. For if the soul observes a form similar to itself it goes mad, as it were, over it in order to achieve the fulfillment of its pleasure.
>
> (Aliquando etiam eros causa pulchra est formositas considerata. Quam si in sibi consimili forma conspiciat, quasi insanit anima in ea ad uoluptatem explendam adipiscendam; 188-89).

Though Constantine is ambiguous in his assessment of the causes of lovesickness, i.e. humoral imbalance and apprehension of an enticing form, he is definite that "this sickness has more serious consequences for the soul, that is excessive thoughts [...]" ("hec infirmitas forciora anime subsequentia habeat, id est cogitationes nimias [...]"; 188-189). [43] His chapter on "amor eros" ends with a description of the *signa amoris* and a paragraph on the cures for lovesickness.

The importance of the *Viaticum* for the formation of a scholastic discourse on lovesickness can be gauged by the abundance of manuscripts that have come down to us, and the fact that it became instrumental in the education of physicians at universities (Wack 46-50). Being part of the medical university curriculum, the brief chapter on lovesickness sparked a number of commentaries. The earliest documented gloss on the *Viaticum*, dated by Wack at the last decade of the 12th century and before 1236 (51), was authored by Gerard of Berry, a Parisian physician. His widely read *Glosule super Viaticum* supplements Constantine's terse account of the causes, symptoms and cures of love with his readings of the Arabic scholar Avicenna (Ibn Sina, d. 1037).

---

[42] If not otherwise indicated, all subsequent English translations refer to Wack's edition.

[43] In *De coitu* Constantine clarifies that moderate sexual fantasies are necessary for human procreation: "Tria vero sunt in coitu: appetitus ex cogitatione fantastica ortus, spiritus et humor" ("Tres son los elementos que intervienen en el coitu: el deseo, producto de la fantasía imaginativa, el neuma y el humor"; 81-82).

LOVE THAT IS CALLED HEROS. This disease is called a melancholic worry by medical authors. It is indeed very similar to melancholy, because the entire attention and thought, aided by desire, is fixed on the beauty of some form or figure.

(*Amor qui heros dicitur*. Hec passio dicitur apud auctores sollicitudo melancolica. Est enim plurimum similis melancolie, quia tota intentio et cogitatio defixa est in pulchritudine alicuius forme uel figure desiderio coadiuuante; Gerard of Berry 198-99)

Gerard closely follows his source, Avicenna's *Canon medicinae* (fol. 190^v; lib. 3, fen 1, tract. 4. cap. 24), in associating "amor heros" with melancholy. However, he clarifies that these similarities are due to the fact that both the patient of melancholy and the patient of lovesickness suffer from a fixation of "attention and thought" on the beauty of an apprehended object.[44] Hence he eliminates the humoral disposition from his etiological discussion. Also missing is Constantine's passing reference to the Platonic furor sparked by a similar "form." Gerard thus prefigures the strictly naturalist position of Thomas Aquinas, who argues that "the impression of the sense-object on the sense goes with physiological change; that is why the intensity of the object of sensation can injure the sense" ("sensitivum patitur a sensibili cum corporis immutatione. Unde excellentia sensibilium corrumpit sensum [...]"; *Summa*, vol. 11, p. 16-17; 1a. 75,3). Gerard of Berry draws in his further analysis mainly from Avicenna's *Liber de anima* which gives him "the means, through faculty psychology, to relate mental and emotional conditions to physical states, that is, to specify their material basis" (Wack, *Lovesickness* 55). He consequently defines lovesickness as a *passio* that hampers the soul's faculties ("uirtutes impediantur"; Gerard of Berry 198).

The cause, then, of this disease is a malfunction of the estimative faculty, which is misled by sensed intentions into appre-

---

[44] From a philosophical point of view also Aquinas identifies the object as "causa amoris": "Sicut supra dictum est, amor ad appetitivam potentiam pertinet, quæ est vis passiva. Unde objectum ejus comparatur ad ipsam sicut causa motus vel actus ipsius. Oportet igitur ut illus sit propie causa amoris quod est amoris objectum" ("We have already shown that love is seated in the orectic faculty; and since that is a passive power, its object functions as the cause of its movement or action. Therefore that which is the object of love will properly be called the 'cause' of love"; *Summa*, vol. 19, p. 74-75; 1a.2æ. 27,1).

hending non-sensed accidents that perhaps are not in the person. Thus it believes some woman to be better and more noble and more desirable than all others.

(Causa ergo huius passionis est error uirtutis estimatiue que inducitur per intentiones sensatas ad apprehendenda accidencia insensata que forte non sunt in persona. Unde credit aliquam esse meliorem et nobiliorem et magis appetendam omnibus aliis; 198-99)

The *estimativa* does not properly extract the "intentions" of the person and misjudges her to be most beneficial and therefore desirable, discarding other sense impressions ("estimat cetera sensata non esse consimilia"; 198).[45] The estimative power commands the imagination "to fix its gaze on such a person" ("ut defixum habeat intuitum in tali persona"; 198-99). This, in turn, causes the *estimativa* to assign constantly positive *intentiones* to the image. Therefore, concupiscible appetite longs for this particular person, and instigates the amorous passion of the heart. The imagination's fixation is aggravated by the "spirit-consuming" activity of the *estimativa* which desiccates and cools the first ventricle where, according to Gerard, the imagination is located. In this "melancholic" environment the imagination is no longer able to rapidly produce "thoughts," yet provides ideal conditions for the formation of a durable image.

The most elaborate and ambitious commentary on the *Viaticum* was written around 1250 by Peter of Spain, later pope John XXII. His *Questiones super Viaticum*, which has come down to us in two versions, provides a scholastic treatment of the topic of morbid love based on the *Viaticum* and incorporating earlier contributions to the discussion.[46] In his introductory lines Peter classifies "AMOR QUI

---

[45] The external senses cannot err because they merely convey *species*. Yet, as Robert Myles points out (83), there are numerous, potentially improper "second intentions." In his study *Vision, the Gaze, and the Function of the Senses* Burke conjectures that the amorous obsession is due to the fact that the image received in the short-term memory of the *imaginatio* is not properly associated with images proporcionated by positive *habitus* in the long-term memory (59-60).

[46] Besides Gerard's *Glosule* Peter was evidently familiar with Giles's (Egidius) *Glose super Viaticum*, a text which has survived only in one copy (Wack, *Lovesickness* 74-82).

ET HEREOS DICITUR" as a disease ("MORBUS") of the brain (214).[47] He faces the problem of assigning the disease to a particular mental faculty ("virtus"), the testicles or, following the Aristotelian psychology, the heart. He concedes that there is a "passion of the heart" ("passio cordis") which he does not consider an ailment (218-19). Regarding authentic lovesickness he determines that it damages the estimative faculty, which affects the other internal senses in a chain reaction (216-17). His analysis of the process is reminiscent of Gerard's description. The *estimativa* judges, perhaps erroneously, "some woman or some other thing" ("aliquam mulierem an aliquam aliam rem"; 216-17) to be more beautiful than anything else. The *estimativa* commands the cogitative faculty, another aspect of judgment, to fix itself on the form of this object ("ut profundet se in formam illius rei"). *Amor hereos* is thus a suffering from "profundacio cogitationes" ("depressed thought"). On the basis of the apprehended form and the extracted *intentiones*, imagination then forms an image which affects the irascible and concupiscible faculties which have their seat in the heart (216-17). His assessment of *amor hereos* in version B of the *Questiones* is similar. The semiology of morbid love resembles melancholy "with a depression of thought in which the mind is transfixed because of beauty and an inclination toward the beloved" ("cum profunditatione cogitacionum in qua figitur mens propter pulchritudinem et dispositionem ad effectum"; 232-33). To the treatment of the question of which faculties are primarily disturbed by morbid love, Peter's Version B adds another layer: "the estimative faculty suffers in love and transfers its desire to the faculty of memory" ("virtus estimativa patitur in amore et mandat suum desiderium ad memorativam"; 242-43). He thus points to a fact important for my argumentation and only noted in passing by most modern scholars of the subject. Though most authorities emphasize imagination and judgment in the nosological discussion, memory is also intrinsically related to the phenomenology of pathological love.[48]

---

[47] Regarding the evolution of the Latin equivalents for the Arabic term "'iskh" from Constantine's "eros" to the commonly used "hereos" see Wack (*Lovesickness* 182-85).
[48] See for example Ciavolella ("Eros and the Phantasms of *Hereos*") and Beecher; students of memory, on the other hand, are well aware of the mnemonic power of erotic images (Bolzoni).

Constantine's *Viaticum* initiated a learned discourse on lovesickness in medieval Scholasticism. With the assimilation of faculty psychology, mostly indebted to Avicenna, the commentaries on the *Viaticum* displace its underlying Galenic conception, and establish *amor hereos* as psychosomatic suffering. It is a *passio*, an appetition of the senses, which causes bodily changes via the spirits emitted by the heart. The *virtutes* themselves are not damaged, but their operations are seriously disordered. Though the individual authors, Constantine, Gerard and Peter, differ in their assessment of the etiology, they agree that the patient of lovesickness suffers from continuous "cogitationes."

Despite the fact that it is a difficult task to determine direct influences of Constantine and his glossators (Wack, *Lovesickness* 105-08), it is indisputable that later physicians share basic assumptions about *amor hereos*. This is evident in the most representative texts of the school of Montpellier, together with Salerno, the center of scientific scholastic medicine. No later than the mid-1280s (McVaugh 11), the famous Montpellier physician Arnaldus of Villanova wrote a *Tractatus de amore heroico*. Like the Arabic authorities and Constantine and his followers, he defines *amor hereos* as "assidua cogitatio" about the desired "thing," which is fueled by the hope to obtain pleasure ("cum confidentia obtinendi delectabile apprehensum ex ea"; 46). The intensity of this "furious love," which overthrows the rule of reason, springs from the singular pleasure expected from coitus (47).[49]

In his treatise we also find a fairly comprehensive description of the physiological process the *philocaptio* involves. "The pleasure," Arnaldus explains, "caused by the perception of the beautiful object has the effect that the vital spirits, which are produced by the

---

[49] Analyzing Andreas's *De amore*, Wack argues that the lover is actually fantasizing, forming images about the realization of the desire, i.e. the sexual act ("Imagination"). In *The Romance of the Rose*, Love promises the Lover that "there will be a time when you will think that you are holding her, with shining face, quite naked in your arms, just as if she had become wholly your sweetheart and your companion" (Guillaume de Lorris and Jean de Meun 64). The medical texts, however, speak only about pleasure-promising *intentiones* constantly extracted from the image of a beautiful woman. While it is clear that the pleasure is related to expected sex, it cannot be inferred that the imagination, which is fixed on the "figura," carries out sexual fantasies. The *Romance of the Rose* also supports this position: "As a result of the beauty that you see, great joy will dwell in your heart; know, too, that by looking you will make your heart fry and burn" (63).

heart, multiply, heat up rapidly and spread all over the body" ("ex gaudio delectabilis apprehensi spiritus in corde multiplicati subito calefiunt, et calefacti subito [...] delegantur ad membra corporis universa"; 49-50). The *estimativa* is affected by the spirits radiating from the "inflamed heart." It is no longer able to resist the extreme heat which leads to misjudgment ("fallacia et errore"; 50) and initiates the continuous "cogitationes."

Carruthers reminds us that "cogitatio," the specific activity of the *estimativa*, cannot adequately be rendered as "thought" but rather must be understood as a process which combines images from memory's store-house with the newly formed images (Carruthers, *Book of Memory* 33-4; see also Burke, "Insouciant Reader" 36-39; Pietropaolo). This means that the "continuous thinking" about the beloved is conceived of as an incessant recollection. Arnald is most explicit in this respect.

> In this way, because of the fierce desire for the thing, its imprinted form is held firmly by the fantasy, and by way of memorizing it, it is continuously recalled.
> From these two there follows a third, that is, that from the fierce desire and recollection arises an assiduous impulse to thinking.
>
> (Quod propter hoc rei desiderium vehemens eius formam impressam phantastice fortiter retinet et memoriam faciendo de re continue recordatur.
> Ex hiis vero duobus nascitur tertium consequenter, oritur etenim ex vehementi desiderio et recordatione assidue cogitationis impulsus; 46-47)

Once the image produced by the imagination is tagged with intense emotions, it must be stored in the "hard matter" of memory, which is the only faculty capable of preserving mental images over a prolonged period. Thus, the persisting "thoughts" about the beloved draw on a durable and extremely powerful mnemonic image.[50] This is the particular problem the two lovers, Calisto and Melibea, face in *Celestina*. According to James F. Burke, the lovesick Calisto "has sunk into himself, into the chambers of his

---

[50] According to Bolzoni, by the 17th century ex-lovers as *loci* for images had become a commonplace of the *artes mnemorativae*, because of their mnemonic power.

imaginativa and *memoria* where he need do little else save contemplate the image of the beloved" ("Insouciant Reader" 40).

In the writings on lovesicknes by university-related physicians from Constantine to Arnald there is little evidence of key elements that might have made possible the synthesis of Aristotelian and Platonic love psychology which Guillermo Serés proposes (*Transformación de los amantes*). The authors under consideration give no importance to the pneumatic circulation of images. They also seem to adhere to the Aristotelian conception of *species* emanating from the object against the neo-Platonic, Galenic tenet of the externalization of pneumatic blood rays through the eyes. Ultimately, the latter theory also conforms with the etiology of *amor hereos*: the *species* incorporated in the blood circulation are converted into images once they reach the common sense (Couliano 29-30), initiating the process of incessant contemplation. With Marsilio Ficino's writings the mutual transformation of the lovers was incorporated into the medical discourse (Couliano 28-52), but earlier medieval and contemporaneous scholastics displayed a gloomy attitude toward sensual love.[51] Until the end of the 15th century the learned, latinate medical tradition provided little basis for a notion of love as an ennobling force as it was presented in poetry. In this, as I will show, the Latin texts on lovesickness do not differ significantly from vernacular writings on the topic.

c) *Lovesickness in vernacular texts*

Fernando de Rojas, who apparently projects medical views of *amor hereos* in *Celestina*, might very well have had access to Latin sources on the topic through his studies at Salamanca. The question arises, to what degree authors of sentimental fiction and, more importantly, their readers who did not enjoy this privilege, could have been familiar with the natural-philosophical and medical ideas about morbid love.

---

[51] The development of the moral philosophical discussion on sex until the 13th century has been studied by Michael Müller. He shows that the rigorous Augustinian position was moderated by 13th-century thinkers, yet only to the point of acknowledging pleasure as a necessary evil due to the postlapsarian deficiencies of man.

Bernard de Gordon, who reached the pinnacle of his medical career between 1283 and 1308, is arguably the most influential representative of the Montpellier medical school and a key mediator between scholastic conceptions of *amor hereos* and more "popular" lore (Cull and Dutton). Completed around 1305, his widely disseminated *Opus lilium medicinae* was printed in 1495 in Castile with the title *Lilio de medicina*. Gordon conceived of the *Lilio* as a practical, often simplifying manual devoid of theoretical speculation. His sketchy etiological analysis of *amor hereos* in the *Lilio* might have particularly appealed to medical laymen, and thus contributed to the proliferation of medical information about passionate love (Solomon, *Literature of Misogyny* 97-99). In book two, the *Lilio* describes "passiones" which can affect the human brain and suggests remedies. Following the Arabic tradition, Gordon treats diseases like "vértigo e scotomia," "litargia," "corrupción de la memoria," "congelación," "sueño profundo e non natural," "estupor," and "mania & melancolia" (2).[52] In this context he also discusses the "amor que se dize hereos" (p. 107, bk. 2 chap. 20). According to Gordon, lovesickness is a "worry" similar to melancholy ("solicitud melancónica"; p. 107, bk. 2 chap. 20),[53] caused by the love for a woman.

> **Causas.** D'esta passión es corrompimiento determinado por la forma e la figura que fuertemente está aprehensionada, en tal manera que quando algund enamorado está en amor de alguna muger e assí concibe la forma e la figura e el modo que cree e tiene opinión que aquélla es la mejor e la más fermosa e la más casta e la más honrrada e la más especiosa e la mejor enseñada en las cosas naturales e morales que alguna otra [...]. (p. 107, bk. 2 chap. 20)

The quote from Gordon specifically refers to the outcome of excessive "passion." The victim of this affliction judges the image ("figura") of the woman with whom he falls in love to be morally and physically perfect. This means that the *estimativa* apprehends the

---

[52] I refer to the edition of John Cull and Brian Dutton. A transcription of the 1495 *editio princeps* by Cull and Cynthia M. Wasick is also available on microfiche and in the *Corpus Médico*.

[53] The allusion to melancholy is merely a reference to Avicenna's *Canon* (fol. 190ᵛ; lib. 3, fen 1, tract. 4. cap. 24). Gordon does not give a humoral explanation.

object represented by the image to be most beneficial and therefore desirable. Accordingly, Gordon continues.

> E por esso muy ardientemente la cobdicia sin modo e sin medida, teniendo opinión que si la pudiesse alcançar, que ella sería su felicidad e su bienaventurança. E tanto está corrompido el juizio e la razón que continuamente piensa en ella e dexa todas sus obras [...] porque es en continuo pensamiento. (p. 107, bk. 2 chap. 20)

Gordon diagnoses *Amor hereos* as a defect of the "juizio" or *vis estimativa* which causes "continuous thoughts." Later on, he seems to contradict himself, asserting that lovesickness "es propria passión del celebro, e es por causa de la corrupción de la imaginativa" (p. 109, bk. 2 chap. 20). He is, however, fairly consistent in his argumentation, because he points out that the damage to the *estimativa* causes a chain reaction, which affects the other psychic powers and the whole body (p. 108, bk. 2 chap. 20). Gordon leaves no doubt about the gravity of the disorder: "La pronosticación es tal que si los hereos non son curados, caen en manía o se mueren" (p. 108, bk. 2 chap. 20).

It is evident that the 15th-century Castilian version of Gordon's *Lilium* offers the non-latinate reader a description of the etiology and effects of lovesickness which does not differ significantly from the ideas expressed in the texts from Constantine the African to Arnaldus of Villanova.

Francisco López de Villalobos, royal physician to the Spanish kings in the first half of the 16th century (Granjel 7-18), attests that Gordon was not disseminating knowledge confined to a narrow circle of medical doctors trained in universities and to those familiar with scholastic philosophy. In his *Sumario de la medicina* (Salamanca, 1498) he proposes a compendium based on Avicenna "con el qual ligeramente podra quien quiera que en la dicha sciencia tenga principios. Acordarse de las pesquisas que deue hazer en qualquiera enfermedad y de las formas" (fol. 1ᵛ). He uses rhyme, a mnemotechnical tool most convenient to neophytes in the *ars memorativa*, to achieve the "popularization" of his work. Like Gordon, he treats the "mal de amores que [...] llaman hereos" in the context of mental diseases like "memoria corrupta," "manja y melancolia" (fol. 3ᵛ).

> Amor hereos segun nuestros autores
> es vna corrupta imaginacion
> por quien algun hombre se aquexa de amores
> y en este ques hito de los trouadores
> sin ser lisongero dire mi razon
> sabed por muy cierto quel entendimiento
> jamas no se mescla en aquestas pendencias
> la imaginatiua y bestial pensamiento
> como es gran potencia y padeçe el tormento
> engaña consigo a las otras potencias. (fol. 3ᵛ)

Villalobos associates *amor hereos* explicitly with love as expressed in courtly poetry. He defines it as a damage of the imagination. However, reflecting the contemporary theoretical considerations on the collaboration of the inner wits, he relates imagination to the *estimativa*: "bestial pensamiento" refers to the specific activity of judgment and the loss of humanity because of "bestial" instinctive craving (Augustine, *De trinitate* XII,XI,16), "apetito sensitiuo" in the words of Montaña de Monserrate (fol. 124ᵛ). Villalobos asserts that the failing of the imagination and judgment affect the other powers. He underscores that *entendimiento*, the higher faculty of understanding, is not the cause of the illness. Then, he elaborates these points: Imagination induces the other wits to devote all "memoria y deseos y ojos/ y oydos [...]" to this "pensamiento." It impels the senses to consider the beloved "ser lindo y gracioso y ornado y honesto [...]." This judgment is flawed, however, "por falsos testigos tan falsa sentencia [...]." The consequences of the malfunction of the "pensamiento y la imaginatiua" are far-reaching: "perdio su juyzio sus fuerças perdio / perdio su razon su consejo y prudencia." The lover suffers from burning passion in his heart ("ardentissimo fuego") and insatiable desire: "siempre el deseo lo atyza [sc. el coraçón] y lo abiua" (*Sumario* fol. 3ᵛ-4ʳ).

Villalobos also bears testimony that a 15th-century reader considered *amor hereos* and its psychological implications pertinent to the understanding of literary texts; in other words, that effects and causes of lovesickness belonged to the horizons of expectation of "medical-sensitive readers" of fictional texts (Solomon, "Calisto's Ailment" 42). Villalobos adds to his translation of Plautus's *Amphitrion* (Calatayud, 1515) a commentary "para la declaracion [sic] de la postrera cena y capítulo desta comedia [...] para la doctrina y enseñamiento de los mancebos [...]" (487). First he explains briefly the function of the vital spirit which is produced in the heart and conveys heat and moisture to other parts of the body. The vital spirit is transported from the heart to the brain and there it is dehumidified, cooled, and "purifícase para poder usar las obras sensitivas [...]" (488). Connecting the brain with the rest of the body, the refined vital spirit, also called *animal spirit*, is essential for sensory processes (Babb 8-9). Villalobos then describes "un género de locura que se llama alienacion [sic]" (*Anfitrion* 489),[54] which affects the working of the body's spirits. An imbalance of the bodily humors pollutes the spirits operating in imagination and produces "la imágen [sic] falsa, causada segun la hechura y fuerza del humor que allí se pone [...]" (489). This mental image retained by imagination is highly pernicious, because it contaminates all thoughts which are, according to Villalobos, necessarily dependent on the formation of images (488-89): the "alienated" person has a fixed idea, a mental image with which he becomes obsessed.[55]

> Los enamorados son desta materia: que la imágen [sic] de su amiga tienen siempre figurada y fija dentro de sus pensamientos, por donde no pueden ocupar jamás la imaginacion [sic] en otra cosa; en esta imágen [sic] y en las cosas anejas y tocantes á ella, están trasportados y rebatados todas las horas; con ella hablan, della cantan y della lloran, con ella comen y duermen y despiertan [...]. (489)

He thus defines love of women as a subcategory of "alienación," a pathological fixation of the imagination. This means, if we remember Peter of Spain and Arnald of Villanova, an incessant recollection of a mnemonic image. Specific to lovesickness is that the image is based in the beloved and that the lover has yielded his will to her (Villalobos, *Anfitrion* 487).

---

[54] Arnald of Villanova refers with the term "alienatio" in *De parte operativa* to mental illnesses, and also discusses *amor hereos* in this context (Nardi 536).

[55] Babb shows that this can be the case in "melancholy delusions [which] are due primarily to the vitiation of the animal spirit and the substance of the brain by the melancholy humor or its vapors" (42). In a gloss to his translation of *Amphitrion* Villalobos glosses the expression "humor melancólico" to which Sosia attributes Alcumena's supposed fancies. Villalobos explains that melancholy, "humor terrestre y negro," obfuscates the senses, like dirt or soot clouds a fountain of clear water (473).

Villalobos's commentary is not only interesting because he applies the diagnosis of lovesickness found in medical treatises to a literary text, but also because he opposes the "amores sensuales" for women to the "amores intellectuales" for God (491). He assures his reader that he will not lose his mind ("aquí no receles de perder el seso [...]") through divine love, because "en estos amores ninguna imágen [sic] ni fantasma tienes formada ni figurada en la imaginacion [sic] ó fantasía [...]" (491). Only understanding ("entendimiento") is involved in the contemplation of God. Though this goes beyond the capacity of the human being, it does not exhaust the psychic resources. Thus, he alludes implicitly to the vicious circle intiated by *amor hereos*: the mental labor of the lower faculties of the sensitive soul (imagination, judgment and memory) consumes *animal spirit* which draws in turn on vital spirit, thus depriving the body of heat and moisture and producing even more pernicious humors (Babb 25).[56] However, this is not Villalobos's primary objection to "sensual love"; he implicitly condemns the moral transgressions of love and its effects on the rational soul.

The repercussions of love on the most noble part of the human soul also have a basis in natural philosophy. Most physicians implicitly refuse to treat the question of the effects of sensual love on the rational soul. Some of them state, like Montaña de Monserrate on several occasions, that they do not want to transgress into topics not of their expertise. The interplay between animal soul and rational soul, however, is an indispensable corollary to the medical discussion of *amor hereos*.

Arnald of Villanova emphasizes that it is the prospect of sexual intercourse that fuels "furious love," which corrupts the regime of reason (47). Thus passionate love is intrinsically related to lust and sexual pleasure, both of which had been condemned by theologians since the early days of Christianity (Müller, Michael). Likewise the neo-Platonic tradition, which recognized that love originates from physical beauty, would not condone untranscended sexual attraction, the failure of transformation to Christian love, that occurs in lovesickness (Serés, *Transformación de los amantes* 15-53).

Amor hereos must be disapproved, because it is not only socially

---

[56] Ficino considered the possibility of "ocular hemorrhage" which occurs when the lover looks excessively at his beloved, emitting pneumatic blood rays (Couliano 30).

disruptive but also intellectually unproductive. Continuous "thinking" about the beloved occupies the mind and presents an insurmountable obstacle for intellectual activity. Since the intellect depends on images supplied by the imagination,[57] the fixation on the form of a beautiful woman deprives the higher faculty of understanding of its raw material. Particularly for this reason, Jacopo da Pistoia condemns amorous passion in his 13th-century *Quaestio disputata de felicitate*, repudiating it as an "impendientia autem a veritatis speculatione" (qtd. in Nardi 522). There is, then, a straightforward explanation for the hostility toward passionate love on moral and philosophical grounds. There is, however, also a more complex model which takes into account the diversity of the human soul and its powers, a model which we will encounter in texts like *Siervo libre de amor*.

According to Thomas Aquinas, the soul does not suffer change nor is it moved directly; but it can be affected indirectly by the passions, which belong to the body-soul composite (*Summa*, vol. 19, p. 9; 1a.2æ. 22,1). The linkage between soul, the internal wits, and body is established through the "sensitive appetite" which in turn produces passions and causes bodily changes. Sensitive powers are connected with corruptible and corruptive bodily processes and material objects. For this reason it is paramount that the intellectual powers, i.e. the powers of the rational soul, oversee and rule them. "The intellectual powers," Aquinas emphasizes, "are superior to the sense powers and, therefore, guide and command them" ("potentiæ intellectivæ sunt priores potentiis sensitivis; unde dirigunt eis et imperant eis"; *Summa*, vol. 11, p. 102; 1a. 77,4).[58] The control over the sensitive soul is exerted by the practical faculty of the rational soul. "The practical faculty," Avicenna expounds, "is the principle of the movement of the human body, which urges it to individual actions characterized by deliberation and in accordance with purposive considerations. [...] But far from being passive and submissive this faculty must govern the other bodily faculties so that it may have excellent morals" (*Kitāb al-najāt*, ed. Rahman 32; bk. 2, ch. 6,4). It is a moral obligation that the "intellect" controls the senses and the resulting "emotions," which, in the words of Aquinas, "leads one towards sin insofar as it is uncontrolled by rea-

---

[57] I elaborate on this point below.
[58] My translation.

son; but insofar as it is rationally controlled, it is part of the virtuous life" ("passiones animæ inquantum sunt præter ordinem rationis inclinant ad peccatum; inquantam autem sunt ordinatæ a ratione pertinent ad virtutem"; *Summa*, vol. 19, p. 36-37; 1a.2æ. 24,2).

Aquinas acknowledges, however, that the sensitive appetite is not entirely controlled by the

> cogitative power under the direction of abstract reason (in the case of man), but also by imagination and sensation. We experience conflict between reason on the one hand and aggression and desire on the other when we sense or imagine a pleasure reason forbids or feel sad at something reason commands.
>
> (cogitativa in homine, quam dirigit universalis ratio, sed etiam ab imaginativa et sensu. Unde experimur irascibilem vel concupiscibilem rationi repugnare per hoc, quod sentimus vel imaginamur aliquod delectabile quod ratio vetat, vel triste quod ratio præcipit; *Summa*, vol. 11, p. 212-15; 1a. 81,12)

The rule of the rational soul over the emotions has a two-fold aspect to it. In order to be morally good the emotions must be voluntary. "They will be called voluntary to the extent that the will commands them, or at least does not check them" ("Dicuntur autem voluntariæ, vel ex eo quod a voluntate imperantur, vel ex eo quod a voluntate non prohibentur"; *Summa*, vol. 19, p. 34-35; 1a.2æ. 24,1). In Thomist thinking, however, will is secondary to intellect, which, as it were, counsels the higher orexis (*Summa* 1a. 82,3). From this it becomes clear that passionate love, as described in the medical tradition, has fatal repercussions for the spiritual well-being of the patient. *Amor hereos* produces impulsive passion toward a woman without the higher powers, will and understanding, intervening and exerting their moral obligations. Moreover, the defining feature of pathological passionate love is a continuous "thinking" (*cogitationes*) about the apprehended image of a beautiful woman. Given that Aquinas recognizes memory as part of the rational soul, "if memory is taken to mean a power to keep thoughts in mind [...]" ("si memoria accipiatur solum pro vi conservativa specierum"; *Summa*, vol. 11, p. 168-69; 1a. 79,6), it follows that *amor hereos* also implies a failure of the "intellectual" memory.[59]

---

[59] According to the *modistae*, J. Stephen Russel explains (21-28), the *intellectus*

The Thomist account of the intellectual soul connects with, in fact absorbs parts of, the Augustinian model of the human soul.[60] J. K. Walsh outlines the evolution of the conception of the faculties of the rational soul and studies some manifestations of how the theme was treated in medieval and Renaissance Spanish literature. According to Walsh, Books X and XI of St. Augustine's *De trinitate* were seminal for the conception of the tripartite rational soul in the Middle Ages. This patristic author conceives of the rational soul with its three parts (*memoria, intelligentia,* and *voluntas*) as a reflection of the Trinity. According to Walsh, St. Bernard basically reaffirms this conception, yet accentuates the aspect of tension and struggle between the psychic powers (2). Only balance and harmony between the faculties can ensure that the soul is directed toward the "memory," "understanding," and "love" of God. *Floresta de philósophos,* a 15th-century compilation from various sources, occasionally attributed to Fernán Pérez de Guzmán, refers to some "dichos" by Bernard regarding the powers of the human soul.

> 2066. En el anima son tres potencias: memoria, entendimiento, voluntad.
> 2067. Por la memoria debemos remembrar de Dios, por el entendimiento lo devemos ver e conoscer, con la voluntad devemos desear abraçarnos con el. [...]
> 2073. Non es costa de quantas son tan semejable a la alta sabiduria de Dios como el anima en que ay razon.
> 2074. La anima en que ay razon por la memoria e el entendimiento e por la voluntad siempre esta llegada e cosida con la alta Trinidad. (96-97)

The emphasis that is made here on the "upward" orientation of the rational soul is representative of various strands of scholasticism. Scholars influenced by Peripatetic, Platonic or Stoic thinking, agree that uncontrolled passions enslave man, depriving him of liberty and reducing him to an animal-like state (Canet, "Reflexiones

---

agens has the function of matching the sensory data to an "identity" (on the basis of previous experience), which is passed on to the *intellectus passivus.* Although the latter, a "difference engine" (Russel 22), is not prone to deceptions, the proper working of the mind depends on the mnemonic accuracy of the *agens intellectus* and the image provided by the interior senses.

[60] The connection between Aristotelian and Augustinan conceptions are also evident in the writings of prominent "Augustinians" like Bonaventure (Prentice).

filosóficas" 195). Theologians argue that the disorder which the internal wits suffer in the *philocaptio* and the resulting amorous *passio*, has a devastating effect on the soul's spiritual harmony, because the auxiliary sensitive powers do not fulfill their tasks. Aquinas qualifies the subversion of the hierarchy in which the "higher appetite is displaced by the lower" as a violation of the natural order, which "leads to fault (*peccatum*) in morality, in just the way that monstrosities are faults in nature" (*De anima* 415-16; bk. 3, chap. 16 {434a12-15}). *Amor hereos* is a perversion of "pure and simple" love, which becomes "evil when directed towards something which is not genuinely good" ("Et sic aliquis amor est malus, inquantum tendit in id quod non est simpliciter verum bonum"; *Summa*, vol. 19, p. 76-77; 1a.2æ. 27,1).

The patient's all-powerful desire is directed not toward God, but toward the woman who sparked the creation of the forceful mental image. Memory does not fulfill its task since it is involved in a "perverse meditation" (Fraker, "Lida de Malkiel on *Celestina*" 179) of the image of the beloved, causing the intellect to be severed from the storehouse of memory. The intellect fails in its task to distinguish the truly good and beautiful and contemplate it. Since the passion for the beloved implies the abjection of everything else on the level of imagination, understanding becomes "accidentally" obsessed with this image, neglecting "intellectual matters" important for spiritual well-being. The powers of the rational soul are dominated by the sensory faculties.[61] It is a state which is deemed an unnatural and sinful constellation. The human soul without harmony, the "razón" of the *facultates animi*, which makes man God's "image," is reduced to the level of an animal that follows its instinctive cravings. In *Celestina* the moral ruin of the ailing lover finds its emblematic expression in Calisto's display of sexual activity before Lucrecia; in medieval opinion, an act utterly removed from human behavior (England).[62]

The condemnation of passionate love from a theological point of view does not exclude the possibility of a sublimation in literature. The negative view of human love, perhaps, constituted part of

---

[61] With emphasis on the Neoplatonic tradition, Burke studies the conflict of wordly sensory perception and the intellectual transcendence of images toward the immutable realm of the Divine (*Vision* 9-31).

[62] See also Burke, who analyzes the references to Calisto's "bestiality" in *Celestina* ("Calisto's imagination").

the allure of a transformation of "bestial love" into ennobling *fin'amors*. However, a reader familiar with the medical writings which discuss *amor hereos* would focus on the disastrous psychosomatic effects. Despite the fact that the physicians refrain from transgressing the boundaries of their profession, he was bound to be aware of the serious implications passionate love has for the rational soul.

d) Remedia amoris

Medieval and Renaissance physicians and moralists naturally took an interest in devising *remedia amoris* (Solomon, *Literature of Misogyny*). Some medical authorities recommend sexual intercourse in the case of humoral imbalance caused by excessive semen (Solomon, "Calisto's Ailment" 43-51).[63] This position is reflected in some late medieval texts, in which lovesick characters like Calisto or *Triste deleytaçión*'s F.A.D.C. try to justify their sexual urge.[64] However, the Castilian polymath Alfonso Fernández de Madrigal (d. 1455), El Tostado, excludes humoral superfluity in his *Quaestio* about Judg. 16 ("Quomodo Sampson semper amabat mulieres philistinas") from "real" lovesickness.

> This passion, however, does not arise from the natural desire to expell superfluity caused by the tickling of the venereal heat, because this love could be purged with any woman. It originates in the apprehension of the form alone, because this form appears to him attractive, and no other woman, even though she is more beautiful, pleases him. All will be rejected because of the one who is loved in such a way.

---

[63] Constantine propagates this position in *De coitu* (120-125). He warns about the general dangers of coitus, desiccation in particular, yet also refers to other authorities: "Rufus vero ait quia coitus solvit malum habitum corporis et furorem mitigat, prodest melancolicis et amentes revocat ad noticiam et solvit amorem concupiscencie, licet concumbat cum alia quam concupivit" ("Sin embargo añade que el coito elimina la mala condición del cuerpo, mitiga el furor, viene bien a los melancólicos, devuelve la razón a los dementes y libera de la pasión sexual, incluso aunque las relaciones sexuales sean con mujer distinta a la deseada"; 126-28).
[64] The therapeutic effect of sex manifests itself in *Triste deleytaçión* in the contrast between E°'s frustration and psychosomatic suffering and A°'s behavior. The Friend is little affected by the symptoms of *amor hereos* because his desire is satiated by Mª; see below chapter II.

> (Ista autem passio fit non ex desiderio naturæ ad evacuandum superfluum propter titilationem caloris venerei, quia amor cum qualibet expleri potest, sed ex sola aprehensione formæ, quia illa forma videtur ei jucunda, et nulla alia mulier, etiam si sit nimis speciosa etiam plusquam illa, placebit. Omnes enim repudiabuntur propter illam quæ tali amore diligitur; qtd. in Cátedra 189)

In the 14th and 15th century, with the controversies about *species* (Tachau), lovesickness became increasingly associated with imagination and obsessive "thoughts" (Wack, "From Mental Faculties to Magical Philters" 14-15; Beecher). Consequently, humoral diagnosis and cures lost importance. Since *amor hereos* was mainly understood as a cerebral disorder of the internal senses which resulted in a suffering from ceaseless recollection, the *remedia amoris* could take the shape of an *ars oblivationalis*.[65]

This is precisely the interpretation that Harald Weinrich applies to Ovid's poem *Remedia amoris* in his study of the art of forgetting in world literature from ancient Greece to the present (*Lethe* 30-34). Ovid recommends a strategy of unlearning love, "dediscis amare" (line 553), using the techniques prescribed by the *ars memorativa*: the "patient" must mobilize or make up negative memories of the woman he wants to "forget" (l. 297-356).[66] Correspondingly, he must avoid familiar situations, places and objects, which could be associated with his passion, because memorabilia might recall the pernicious image. Ovid advises him to seek diversion in work and traveling (l. 150-224). He became an *auctor* for medieval writers who echo his *remedia amoris*. The physician Gordon, for instance, refers to Ovid when suggesting that the *enamorado* should be forced to alter the "image" of the woman he loved.

> Por ende búsquese una vieja de muy feo acatamiento con grandes dientes e barvas e con fea e vil vestidura, e traya debaxo de sí un paño untado con el menstruo de la muger, e venga al enamorado e comience a dezir mal de su enamorada, diziéndole que es tiñosa e borracha e que se mea en la cama e que es epilén-

---

[65] Ciavolella reports a 17th-century cure for lovesickness which attempted literally to liquify the hard matter of memory through exposing the brain to heat ("Eros and the Phantasms of *Hereos*" 82-84)

[66] The 15th-century *Tratado de amor*, attributed by a 16th-century reader to Juan de Mena, draws significantly from the Ovidian precepts, which are here twice introduced with the expression "vale para oluidar" (342).

> tica e fiere de pie e de mano e que es corrompida e que en su cuerpo tiene torondos, especialmente en su natura, e que le fiede el fuelgo e es suzia, e diga otras muchas fealdades, las quales saben las viejas dezir, e son para ello mostradas. (p. 108-09; bk. 2, chap. 20)

The *Lilio* also reflects Ovidian advice (Ovid, l. 484-86), when suggesting that the old love should be replaced, "forgotten," by loving other women: "E después fazle que ame a muchas mugeres por que olvide el amor de la una [...]" (Gordon p. 108; bk. 2, chap. 20). The patient should be occupied with work and exposed to emotional experiences. The cure that Gordon prescribes involves either influencing the ongoing imaginative and recollective process by associating the mental image with negative features which render it less desirable, or with providing new sensory input in order to replace the image which is troubling the mind (Eco 259-60).[67]

Before taking these drastic measures, Gordon appeals to the "reason" of the patient.

> E si es obediente, quítenlo de aquella falsa opinión o imaginación algund varón sabio de quien tema e de quien aya vergüença con palabras e amonestaciones, mostrándole los peligros del mundo e del Día de Juizio e los gozos del Paraíso. (p. 108; bk. 2, chap. 20)

The cure for lovesickness includes the exhortations of prudent men which "evoke" the dangers the patient is facing. In other words, the patient should be provided with "autoridades" which may fortify his treasure-house of memory by association with wisdom and images already stored there (Burke, "Insouciant Reader" 36-40; Carruthers, *Book of Memory* 33-34; Pietropaolo). Thus, the first step in the cure of *amor hereos* is to make the patient aware of the implications of his passion and encourage a process of recollection, reflection and auto-analysis.[68]

---

[67] The advice to beat the lover until he "stinks," is also based on the assumption that the greater physical pain will replace the amorous pain, making the lovers "forget" (Gordon 108; bk. 2, chap. 20).

[68] This is the strategy adopted by Andreas in *De reprobatione amoris*, the third book of *De amore* (286-325).

Giovanni Boccaccio's *Corbaccio* illustrates a successful cure for lovesickness that combines a variety of *remedia amoris*.[69] Traditionally, *Corbaccio* was regarded as a "serious" misogynist work. Robert Hollander has challenged this view, asserting that Boccaccio intended to write an ironic retort to his detractors. He relates *Corbaccio* to the Ovidian *Remedia amoris* which he equally qualifies as a subtle mocking of "dull readers" (37).

> Boccaccio's *Corbaccio*, like Ovid's *Remedia amoris*, is a witty work apparently aimed at saving suicidal disappointed lovers from their intended fates. In both cases, such concerns serve more as pretexts than as genuine concerns. (36)

Yet, if "most medieval readers of the *Remedia*," as Hollander admits, "took the work as a serious attack by a reformed lover" (36), then it is safe to assume that *Corbaccio* was equally perceived as a serious cure against the deadly threat of *amor hereos*. Instead of speculating on Boccaccio's genius that only the modern reader is able to appreciate, and recuperating the *intentio auctoris*, I prefer to adopt the perspective of a "dull reader." As such, I find in Corbaccio a narrator who, rejected and humiliated by a woman, ponders suicide. He falls into an exhausted sleep and "diverse forme" appear to his "virtù fantastica" (54; p. 13). He finds himself trapped in a somber valley that turns out to be a vagina. The deceased husband of his paramour appears and explains to him that

> love is a blinding passion of the spirit, a seducer of the intellect, which dulls or rather deprives one of memory, a dissipator of earthly wealth, a waster of bodily strength, the enemy of youth, and the death of old age, the parent of vices, and the inhabiter of inane breasts, a thing without reason or order, stifler of human liberty. (23)

> (amore essere una passione accecatrice dell'animo, disviatrice dello 'ngegno, ingrossatrice, anzi privatrice della memoria, dissi-

---

[69] Early readers associated Alfonso Martínez de Toledo's logotherapeutic *Arcipreste de Talavera* (Solomon, *Literature of Misogyny*), better known since the 1498 incunable under the subtitle *Corbacho*, with the Boccaccian *Corbaccio*. Impey suggests that *Corbaccio* was the source of the transformation of the Aborintio in *Triste deleytaçión* ("Contraria" 150-51); furthermore, she associates E°'s mental and emotional turmoil projected into this allegory with the medical notion *amor hereos* (153).

patrice delle terrene facoltà, guastatrice delle forze del corpo, nemica della giovanezza e della vecchiezza, morte, genitrice de' vizi e abitatrice de' vacui petti, cosa senza ragione e senza ordine e senza stabilità alcuna, vizio delle menti non sane e sommergitrice dell'umana libertà; 193; p. 49)

The narrator's interlocutor was sent by divine grace as a healer. His task consists of reinforcing the lover's memory and appealing to his reason.

> You must know, therefore, that a shrewd doctor cannot always heal every illness or every patient with sweet-smelling ointments, since there are many illnesses and many patients who do not respond to these and who require foul-smelling remedies if they wish to be led back to health, and if there is any sickness which one may wish to purge and cure with foul words, arguments, and demonstrations, ill-conceived love in a man is one of them, because in a short time a foul word has more effect on the scornful intellect than a thousand decent and pleasant persuasions poured into the deaf heart through the ears over a great length of time. (52)

> (Dei adunque sapere né ogni infermità né ogni infermo potere esser sempre dal discreto medico con odoriferi unguenti medicato, per ciò che assai sono di quelle e di quelli che nol patiscono, e che richeggiono cose fetide, se a salute si vorrano conducere. E se alcuna n'è che con vocaboli, con argomenti, con demostrazioni puzzolenti purgare e guarire si voglia, il mal concetto amore dall'uomo è una di quelle; per ciò che più una fetida parola nello 'ntelletto sdegnoso apodera in una piccola ora che mille piacevoli e oneste persuasioni, per gli orecchi versate nel sordo cuore, non faranno in un gran tempo; 389-90; p. 106-07)

The bulk of *Corbaccio* is made up of a misogynist diatribe that aims at dispelling the positive image of the woman. Upon awakening, the narrator is cured of his "ill-conceived love." *Corbaccio*, the text itself, becomes a *remedia amoris* capable of exhorting and treating men in similar situations.[70]

---

[70] In the conclusion the narrator addresses his "little work" admonishing it to be useful to those "who, with eyes closed, set out without guide through unsafe places [...]" (77). By means of this anthropomorphization the book becomes an authorial voice that finds another expression in Alfonso Martínez de Toledo's *Arcipreste de Talavera*.

Serious or not, Boccaccio wrote a (probably fictionalized) autobiographical account of a case of *amor hereos*. He combined a realistic story with a psychoanalysis by means of imagination. Had the author not chosen to allow his narrator/lover a "happy end," and played out the destructive potential of passionate love, he would have created what modern critics call a "sentimental romance."

3. LOVESICKNESS AND SENTIMENTAL FICTION

a) *Love-as-sickness as a subject of sentimental fiction*

José Luis Canet Vallés has analyzed Andreas Capellanus's treatise *On love* in the context of the 12th-century reception of Aristotelian philosophy. He argues persuasively that it can be seen as the first "scholastic summa" on the topic of love ("Reflexiones filosóficas" 208). Similarly, Mary Wack emphasizes the impact of natural philosophy in *De amore*. "Salernitan theories of imagination allowed Andreas to couple the sexual psychology of the new science with the principles of rhetorical invention to generate the lovers' dialogues" ("Imagination" 102). The traditional view of Andreas's *De amore* as a codification, as it were, manifesto, of courtly love has been qualified in recent scholarship.[71] Winthrop Wetherbee, for instance, pointed out that the philosophical background of the 11th century, Stoicism, Hermeticism and Platonism, contributed to the "formulation of an idea implicit in many love-lyrics: that at its heart the natural bent of our emotion, though aroused by carnal and subjective motives, reveals the traces of a primordial state of psychological integrity in which human and spiritual feeling were one" (49). *De amore*, the Aristotelian "summa," however, certainly exercised a considerable influence on later writers, and, more importantly, shows that natural philosophy and medical discourse were instrumental in the "discovery of love" in the 12th century (Dinzelbacher).

In spite of the attacks of Robertson, Benton and Dronke, among others, and the ongoing debate about the origins and concretizations of courtly love, a consensus seems to have been reached

---

[71] Toril Moi provides a useful synopsis of the prevalent readings of *De amore* in recent scholarship (13-17).

that courtliness and chivalry were essential for aristocratic self-representation, and hence the claim to social superiority and power.[72] In his survey of critical approaches to courtly love, Roger Boase observes that key features of troubadour lyric poetry "are incomprehensible without reference to the Graeco-Arabic medical tradition" (124). Schnell goes one step further when recognizing that medieval literature used medical psychological symptoms to depict a variety of love relationships; it was up to the reader to interpret the *signa* and decide which kind of love was displayed (25-26). A medical-sensitive reader, like Villalobos faced with *Amphitrion*, would diagnose a case of *amor hereos*, where lovers express their longing.

Given the continuity of medieval psychology and medicine, it is conceivable that the idea of *amor hereos* as a psycho-somatic phenomenon fueled and haunted diverse amorous literary manifestations which took shape in specific socio-economic, intellectual and aesthetic contexts. Glossing on Bernard de Gordon's exposition of *amor hereos* Couliano suggests that

> the erotic syndrome only represents the medical semiology–of necessity, *negative*, since we are in the realm of psychosomatic pathology–of the courtly love glorified by the 'faithful.' Indeed, they seem to use every means not only [sic] to escape that baneful infection but, on the contrary, *to catch it*. Quite rightly, mention has been made of 'semantic reversal,' a reverse valorization of the pathologic symptoms described in the Greco-Arab *materia medica*. (21)[73]

In light of Couliano's argument it is instructive to reconsider the somewhat irritating conclusion of Juan Alfonso Baena's prologue to the *cancionero* compiled by himself. After reproducing the Alfonsine prologue to the *Estoria de España* about the functions and benefits of history for princes, Baena embarks on an apology for aristo-

---

[72] C. Stephen Jaeger's recent study puts the novelty of courtly love into a historical perspective. He argues that ennobling erotic, non-sexual love was an essential part of aristocratic self-representation. However, from Antiquity until the end of the 11th century it was restricted to men.

[73] Since the ennobling power of love depends on an act of self-mastery (Jaeger 117), *amor hereos* certainly presents the ultimate challenge for the virtuous lover. Pointing out the importance of the notion of *amor hereos* in Spanish *cancionero* poetry, Elena Carrillo recently suggested a contamination of the medical tradition with a religious current which exalts sickness as a means of spiritual purification (168).

cratic "sports." Literature is the most profitable of noble diversions. History books provide edifying and instructive *exempla* and invigorate the mental faculties. Finally reaching the topic of lyrical poetry in his exposition, he claims that also "el arte de la poetría e gaya ciencia" endows its practitioners with "avisación e dotrina" (74). This "science" requires understanding, subtle *ingenium*, bookish erudition, personal experience and courtesy. Baena's description of the ideal poet culminates in the claim

> otrosí que sea amador, e que siempre se precie e se finja de ser enamorado; porque es opinión de muchos sabios, que todo home que sea enamorado, conviene a saber, que ame a quien deve e como deve e donde deve, afirman e dizen qu'el tal de todas buenas doctrinas es doctado. (74)

What is striking here is that Baena demands that the courtly poet should feign to be in love, if he happens not to be so. This can be interpreted as an indicator of the lack of sincere feeling in *cancionero* poetry. However, given that Baena's prologue is couched in naturalist terminology, I suggest instead that "fingir" be read in this context as "imagine." The poet could create a mental image which emulates the effects of a "real image."[74] Thus, the aroused imagination and its psychosomatic corollary become a locus for poetic creativity, and the poetic images form the basis for ennobling intellectual activity. Feigned love's "real" images bring into being the discourse of courtly poetry which, as Julian Weiss convincingly argues, is firmly "rooted in the here and now, constructed from a position of strength, and populated by fictions of aristocratic masculine power" (242-43). "The phenomenon of courtly love," Couliano ventures, "results from a warped purpose that brought about a shift of emphasis concerning the concept of *health* as defined by medical science at the time. Through this *Umwertung*, the gloomy equilibrium of psychic forces recommended by learned treatises was transformed into a sickness of the intellect, whereas, on the contrary, the spiritual sickness induced by love ended by being extolled as the real health of body and soul" (21). However, the poetic *Umwertung* was by no means irreversible and the medical notion of *amor hereos*

---

[74] Glossing on this passage in Baena's prologue, Julian Weiss makes the astute observation that "to feign" is derived from the Latin *fingere*, which also means "to create" (240).

could resurface at any time, emphasizing in another "semantic reversal" the destructive power of human love.

Particularly in the second half of the 15th century, when love became associated with imagination and magic, emblematically in the *Witch Hammer*, a negative view of passionate human love prevailed (Wack, "From Mental Faculties to Magical Philters"; Beecher). With the waning of Jewish-Arabic medical lore in the 15th century, the consequential "reflujo de la escolástica" (García Ballester 9), and the popularization of the naturalist conception of love (Solomon, *Literature of Misogyny*), the Iberian Peninsula participated in this trend.

It has been pointed out that changes in attitudes toward love in the second half of the 15th century also affected lyric poetry in Spain. María Isabel Toro Pascua claims that due to the assimilation of naturalist thinking, poets depict the intrusion of *amor hereos* and display a markedly gloomy attitude toward passionate love (cf. Grieve xiii-xvi). María Eugenia Lacarra contends that "la ficción sentimental exponía de forma narrativa lo que la poesía lírica encerraba en la expresión amorosa instantánea" ("Parodia" 12). Yet Lacarra's equation of courtly love and love in sentimental fiction dismisses the effects of the narrativization of love themes. Unlike lyric poetry, prose texts with amorous themes, Schnell reminds us (128-29), did not present the lyric I in a state of fleeting emotional excitement, but had to play out in a narrative the consequences of the *philocaptio*.[75]

It comes as little surprise, then, that particularly in sentimental fiction the authors make no attempt to sublimate the moral paradoxes the lover faces (Gascón Vera, "Ambigüedad" 132, 136), and display a critical, ironic attitude toward courtly love (Dudley, "Inquisition of love" 235-36; Corfis, "Sentimental Lore" 159-71).[76] Two important book-length studies go one step further: Patricia Grieve argues that in sentimental fiction the paradoxes of *cancionero* poetry are played out, resulting in frustrated or violent, destructive love (115); Marina Brownlee, on the other hand, under-

---

[75] Grieve acknowledges that "poetic paradoxes" of the courtly love lyric played out in prose result in destruction and violence (115), yet does not account for the underlying culturally and historically specific (physio-)psychology of love. Leonardo Funes denies even the possibility of comparing the "love ideologies" in lyric poetry and narrative prose forms (336).

[76] Rohland de Langbehn points out that we do not find explicit, verbal irony in sentimental romance: "El nivel irónico no se realiza mediante recursos del estilo discursivo, sino de las situaciones y acciones" (*Unidad genérica* 82).

stands the genre as a radical subversion of traditional, idealizing forms of love (*Severed Word*). Antony van Beysterveldt polemically asserts that the sentimental fictions of Juan de Flores present the "*mise au point* chocante y brutal" of the 15th-century revision of the interactions between men and women as it was propagated by the courtly "religion of love" ("Revisión" 10).

Recent scholarship supports the idea that it is necessary to consider the alterity of love conceptions in the analysis of important texts of 15th-century Spain. Cátedra's study of the scholarly discussion of love and the literary adaptations of naturalist theory demonstrates the importance of premodern ideas about love for the evolution of new literary genres in the 15th century. Solomon shows how lovesickness and medical and moral theological discourses are interspersed in Castilian misogynist literature (*The Literature of Misogyny*). The same author makes a case for a medical reading of *Celestina* ("Calisto's ailment"). Similarly, Burke contends that pathological love and malfunctioning memory result in a "map of mis-readings" by the protagonists which a contemporary reader of *Celestina* would recognize (43). Hence, there is sufficient evidence that some 15th-century literary texts are imbued with precise medical lore and that this knowledge was integral to the horizons of expectations of at least part of the audience.

As I pointed out earlier, it is highly significant that the medical subtext is so manifest in *Celestina*, a work which also maintains distinctive intertextual relations with the genre of sentimental fiction regarding the notion of love. Cátedra, moreover, analyzes Juan Rodríguez del Padrón's *Siervo libre de amor* against the backdrop of the scholastic discussions on love and the naturalist medical conception of love-as-sickness (143-59), hinting at the importance of this discussion for the canonized texts of sentimental fiction.[77] The

---

[77] Fraker ("Lida de Malkiel on *Celestina*" 181) points out that the anonymous *Question de amor*, a text included by Whinnom in the corpus of sentimental fiction (*Spanish Sentimental Romance* 69-70), expresses explicitly the medical conception of *amor hereos*; in the *Egloga* recited by Flamiano, Quiral provides a definition of passionate love:

> Es cosa que nace/ de la fantasia
> y ponese enmedio/ de la voluntad
> su causa primera/ produze beldad
> la vista langendra/ el desseo la cria
> sostienela biua/ penosa porfia
> dale salud/ dudosa esperança
> ni alla donde esta/ nunca entra alegria. (111)

relevance of the premodern conception of mental processes and the impact of lovesickness on sentimental fiction has also been underscored by Canet. He considers the process of falling in love (the origins, development, causes and effects) not only the primary theme of sentimental fiction, but also the central point of the structure (228). He recognizes the *enamoramiento* as a psychic torment caused by a malfunction of the imagination. The individual texts, he argues, are variations on this theme. Canet provides a catalogue of criteria that define sentimental fiction as a genre.

> Lo importante es mostrar cómo una persona (hombre o mujer) que vive en una situación 'normal' (casada felizmente o soltera, noble de buena posición, etc.), a causa de la pasión amorosa es capaz de llegar a situaciones 'anormales' o extremas por su propia voluntad (abandonar casa y amigos; perder su estatus social; deshonrarse a sí y su familia; e incluso destruir su alma y cuerpo). Es decir al confundir el 'objeto amado' con el 'Sumo Bien' o la 'suma felicidad', las potencias anímicas del enamorado aceptan el dictamen de la voluntad, basando en un juicio erróneo de la estimativa. (233)

He adds that love is not seen as an art, but as a "passion" that attacks the individual, becoming a furor that affects the actions of the victim and his social life and mental health (233-34). The authors of sentimental fiction pay particular attention to the psychic condition of the characters. "Es más importante mostrar," according to Canet, "los sentimientos internos de los enamorados y sus contradicciones que la consecución del amado/a" (234). Since sentimental fiction tries to illustrate the pernicious outcome of the process of falling in love, it strives, for the sake of didactic authority, to present itself as a "real story" (234).

Building on the suggestions of Cátedra and Canet, I will analyze in the following chapters how sentimental fiction depicts the process of falling in love and its disastrous consequences. In the discussion of medical texts I have been arguing that memory is of paramount importance in the *enamoramiento*. The patient of *amor hereos* experiences continuous recollections of the beloved's image. Sentimental fiction not only explores the lover's emotional world and his motivations (Gerli, "Toward a Poetics"), but also the struggle between the psycho-physiological urge to satisfy the desire and the necessity of overcoming lovesickness. The *remedia amoris*, as advised in medical texts, aim at disrupting the ceaseless recollection of the lover. The cure, therefore, heeds the precepts of the "art of forgetting" as espoused by Ovid and medieval medical texts. Since the *ars oblivationalis* uses mnemonic techniques like the "overcrowding" of *loci* or the manipulation of images (Eco 259-60), the strategies of learned memory are reflected in sentimental fiction in varying aspects: in the attempt to persuade the lover by using the commonplace knowledge that the storehouse of memory offers,[78] and in the effort to transform the obsessing image into a less compelling or even repugnant one.

According to Canet, the psychic powers of the *enamorado* accept the regime of will based on an erroneous judgment of the *estimativa* which causes serious repercussions in social relationships and everyday life (233). The ultimate consequence of *amor hereos* is, as the medical and theological texts teach, the physical and moral destruction of the lovers. Based on this premise, the typically disastrous denouements of sentimental fiction are perfectly explicable as conforming to the expectations of the readers familiar with the concept of *amor hereos*. They would consider the patient of *amor hereos* doomed from the beginning. The connection between love and death in sentimental fiction, emphasized by Patricia Grieve (112-14),[79] has a basis in contemporary medical discourse.

Since passionate love was, increasingly in the last decades of the 15th century, regarded by important sectors of society as morally and ethically unacceptable (Solomon, *Literature of Misogyny*; Ciavolella, "La tradizione dell'*aegritudo amoris*" 498; Wack, "From Mental Faculties to Magical Philters"; Beecher), we can assume that there was an interpretive community critical and sensitive of love-as-sickness. These readers would interpret the texts of Spanish sentimental fiction as *exempla* or, as it were, case studies of *amor hereos*.

---

[78] Ivy A. Corfis ("Sentimental Lore") demonstrates that sentimental fiction, particularly the early texts, which explore essentially the psychological dimensions of love affairs, are imbued with intertextual references, i.e. memories of previous readings of *auctores*.

[79] Cvitanovič argues that the "ideal" love in sentimental fictions can only find consummation in death, making "la presencia de la muerte [...] una constante en la novela sentimental" (*Novela sentimental* 26).

b) *"Psycho-analysis" and sentimental fiction*

Virtually all scholars of "sentimental romance" have noted (Dudley, "Inquisition of love"; Whinnom, *Diego de San Pedro* 76; Canet; Prieto 35; Cocozzella, "Thematic Unity" 192; Grieve 23; Herrero 753; Gerli, "Towards a poetics", Gerli, "Revaluation" 115; Rohland de Langbehn, "Desarrollo" 71-72; Deyermond, "Relaciones genéricas" 47) that the primary focus of the texts grouped under this generic heading lies on the exploration of the emotional processes underlying and caused by "amorous captivity." In the context of medieval psychology and medicine this means that the "authors," either pseudo-autobiographical narrators like Rodríguez del Padrón's *Siervo* or first-person "eyewitnesses" like the narrator in *Cárcel*, reflect on their suffering from *amor hereos* in terms of psychic powers. As we have seen, lovesickness affects not only the vegetable soul (danger to physical health) and the sensitive soul (malfunction of perception and cognition), but also the rational soul (threat to spiritual well-being). The inner wits involved in the *enamoramiento*, the struggle and lack of equilibrium between the higher faculties understanding, will and memory, present an important dimension in the analysis of emotional sufferings. The question arises how a medieval author could textualize a "psycho-analysis."

To approach this issue we can again turn to faculty psychology. The significance of memory and imagination for the medieval *épistémè*, and therefore literature, can hardly be overestimated. Following the argumentation of Kolve (8-38), Horst Wenzel asserts that medievalist literary theory must conceive of or reconstruct a "poetics of visualization (of images and metaphors) [...] a poetics of reminiscence/remembering and representation" ("Poetik der Visualisierung (der *imagines*, der Bilder und Metaphern) [...] eine Poetik der Erinnerung und Vergegenwärtigung [...] "; 395).

The medieval practice of visualizing "incorporeal things" and picturing "corporeal similitudes" had a profound impact on some manifestations of medieval literature. Sylvia Huot, for instance, analyzes a 13th-century Italian manuscript of troubadour lyric, which illustrates the "importance of the visual imagination in the medieval appreciation of literature" (3). The illustrations in this manuscript present an intriguing case of the visualization and allegorical narrativization of lyric poetry with a mnemotechnical, didactic purpose.

The practice of visual mapping of texts is also attested and recommended by influential medieval rhetoricians. "The *imagines* as persons, objects, and actions bring before the mind's eye an *imaginaria visio*, as Matthew of Vendôme, calls it" (Kelly, *Medieval Imagination* 29). V. A. Kolve's study of the "imagery of narrative" in the first five *Canterbury Tales* indicates that in late medieval literature contemporary conceptions of memory and imagination shaped the reading habits and interpretive frames of the audience. He also shows that these faculties played a crucial role in literary composition (32-40). "Imagination is," according to Douglas Kelly, "a fundamental feature of the conception of art prevalent from the twelfth to the fifteenth century" (*Medieval Imagination* xv). "Appropriate visual representations gave access to ideas and sentiments which ultimately defied rational scrutiny and analysis. [...] In this way epistemology joined with rhetoric to become poetry" (29).

The epistemology to which Kelly refers is 11th-century philosophy, which drew heavily on Stoic, Hermetic and Platonic conceptions (Wetherbee 46). These philosophical notions were incorporated into the tradition of courtly poetry. However, with the assimilation of Aristotelian thought the epistemological basis was transformed, eventually altering the conception and appraisal of courtly love. This does not mean that imagination lost its crucial role for literature; on the contrary, the 15th century in particular witnessed a heightened interest in imagination–now, however, under the sway of naturalist thinking.

Juan de Mena, Castile's most celebrated quattrocento poet, shows that philosophical and medical lore were not only a remote subtext of literary texts of the epoch, but could shape contemporary conceptions of literary composition. Mena's *Coronación*, written between 1438 and 1440, is dedicated to Íñigo López de Mendoza, Marqués de Santillana, commemorating his conquest of Huelma in 1438. Mena's work is most noteworthy for the encyclopedic glosses the author supplied to the narrative poem. The commentary cannot be reduced to a mere display of erudition or didactic tool, but emulates the hermeneutic procedures an ideal reader would employ, according to Mena. In *copla* CXI the poet declares that he does not want to depict the torments women have to suffer in the Inferno of the river Acheron, yet cautions his readers not to make "ligera contemplación" (219). In the gloss he elaborates on that line.

> Quiere dezir esta copla que deue hombre las cosas que son encargadas de tener al juyzio del leedor que se deuen ver e catar con estudio sotil e memoria reposada e ojo atento e contemplación prolongada, por-que sepa el estilo de la escritura e la entención e propósito del que la ordenó, quál fue e a qué fin se endereça, así lo malo como lo bueno, lo bueno para en ello perseuerar e lo malo para apartarse d'ello. (221)

The reader is supposed to look, judge and contemplate "las cosas," in other words, to visualize the poetic images. The dark passages, *integumenta*, trigger a recollective process in which the present texts becomes associated with previous readings ideally stored in memory.

Moreover, Mena's glosses reflect the author's familiarity with philosophical knowledge,[80] which he deemed relevant for the reader. The main conceit of *Coronación* is the quest of the author's persona for Thessalian Mount Parnassus. After a journey through a Danteësque Hell and several perils, he reaches the mountain of wisdom, home of the Muses. As he comes within reach of the peak, the splendor of wisdom and his reaction to it defy his means of expression. He makes a "esclamación coadjutoria a los sentidos por-que puedan de lo que en ella se contiene escreuir según parece" (304). He invokes Orpheus's lute to inspire his "five senses" and then addresses them directly.

> ¡Ved, sesos interiores,
> por dónde començaremos
> las fazañas y loores
> de nuestros antecessores,
> o qué orden les daremos,//
> pues que fueron colocados
> por sus fechos estremados
> e muy grandes marauillas
> en aquel rencle de sillas
> que da vida en los pasados!
> (310-11; st. CXXXII)

---

[80] In his studies, Mena obviously also became acquainted with scholastic medicine. The line "La mi sangre que alterara" of stanza CXXII is accompanied by a gloss that explains the alterations of body liquids due to a passion affecting the heart (271-72).

In the gloss he explains that the "sesos o potencias interiores" are necessary to describe the marvels of the mountain. He goes on to describe with remarkable erudition the five senses, "seso común, ymaginatiua, fantasía, extimancia e memoria" (311), and their working. He also supplies an illustration that bears quoting in full.

> Yo veo arebatar a vn lobo vn cordero, esto//sólo faze el ver que es seso exterior, después que estas especias son entradas por el ojo fasta la frente, que es célula del seso común, judgo que el lobo es pardo no es el cordero, e el cordero es otro cosa que el lobo, después que estas especias entran adelante en la cabeça a la otra célula, que es llamada maginatiua, e aquélla no faze saluo recologirlas e tenerlas, e después tómalas de ally. La tercera potencia que está más adelante, que es llamado fantasía, e ésta ordena de aquel lobo e cordero, vn lobo, medio lobo e medio cordero, e otros desuarios tales, ca aquél es su officio. Después viene la quarta potencia o seso interior, que es llamada estimatiua, e de aquellas especias o formas pasadas por los sentidos saca ella vnas intenciones, assí como porque vido leuar el lobo al cordero judga ella vna intención como que deue hauer enemistad entre el lobo y el cordero, e aqu'ésta es dicha intención e éste es su officio de la estimatiua. La quinta potencia e seso interior es dicha memoria e ésta está en el fin de la cabeça, que es el celebro, e su officio d'ésta es retener las formas e intenciones pasadas por los otros sesos, e en quanto faze el officio del retener es dicha memoria en quanto se miembra d'ello es dicha reminiscençia. (313-14)

Mena's gloss is intriguing for several reasons. It is, as Herriot pointed out, a testimony for the treatment of the inner senses in Spanish literature (274-76). Then, more importantly, Mena accounts rather precisely for the function of the inner senses in poetry. In a gloss to line four ("de nuestros antecessores") he specifies: "pensad, potencias e sesos interiores, e usad de vuestros oficios por-que demos orden a las fazañas e loores de los fechos de los passados" (315). He refers here, first, to memory which harbors the "fechos", and, second, assigns to the inner senses the task of *dispositio*, of structuring ("orden") in rhetorical terms.

The starting point for the gloss, however, was the difficulty of finding the right "expression" for the beauty of the mountain. The faculty which is responsible for the creation of images is, according to Mena, "fantasía." Fantasy is capable of combining the *species* of the wolf and the lamb to a chimera, and other "silly things." Mena describes the specific function of fantasy in more detail.

> La tercera potencia o seso interior es fantasía, el su oficio d'este seso es conponer las formas o especias que están ayuntadas en la maginatiua a [sic] faze ellas d'ellas por fantasía semejança, que la maginatiua tiene en sí forma de oro e de aquella forma faze la fantasía, e conpone vn monte dorado o otra cosa semejante o de otras especias que están en la maginatiua faze la fantasía chimera o ycoceruo, es a saber conpone vna semejança de animalías de estranyas fechuras que no crio naturaleza. (312-13)

It is clear that this faculty is paramount in the creation of literary imagery. Mena proudly names the sources for his knowledge on the working of the inner senses "E aqu'estas cosas dichas pruéualas Aristótiles en el tercero *De anima*, e Santo Tomás sobre él" (314-15). This reference is not, as Herriot suggests (275), spurious. Herriot rightly points out that there are only four internal senses in the Thomist conception of the sensible soul. However, this indicates only that Mena was also acquainted with the Avicennan medical tradition. There is evidence that Mena had firsthand knowledge of Aquinas's commentary on *De anima*. Aristotle makes the following distinction (*De anima* 427b14-16):

> But that phantasia and opinion are not the same is clear. For the first state is up to us, when we want: for it consists in composing [something] in front of our eyes–just like, in recollection, things are positioned and an image is composed. Forming opinions, however, is not up to us: for it is necessary that it asserts what is false or true. (317-18)

Thomas clarifies this passage:

> **The state** of phantasia **is up to us, when we want,** because **it is** in our power to form something that appears (*apparens*) before **our eyes,** so to speak–such as golden mountains or whatever we want to appear. This is plain in the case of people who remember **and** form for themselves **images** of things, which they see at will. (*De anima* 325; bk. 3, ch. 4)[81]

---

[81] The phrasing in Thomas's *Summa* is nearly identical: "Mediam inter æstimativam et imaginationem, quæ componit et dividit formas imaginatas, ut patet cum ex

Thus, Mena's *Coronación* not only points to the existence and practice of a poetics of visualization and remembering, but also hints at the most important expression of its epistemological basis in philosophical discourse.

Harvey indicates that the writings of Thomas Aquinas mark a paradigmatic shift in medieval faculty psychology (53-61). [82] In *De memoria et reminiscentia* Aristotle asserts that it is not possible to think without an image and also that "memory, even the memory of objects of thought, is not without an image" (48-49; 449^b). This Aristotelian idea was adapted and elaborated by Thomas Aquinas. In his comment to *De memoria et reminiscentia* Aquinas repeats Aristotle's position (91-92; 311-15). In his gloss to *De anima* (432a3-10) we read: "Instead, **when one** actually **contemplates** (*speculatur*) anything, one must **at the same time** form **a phantasm** for oneself. **Phantasms** are likenesses of **sensible things,** but they differ from them in that they **exist** outside of **matter** [...]" (*De anima* 391; bk. 3 ch. 13). He expresses the same idea in the *Summa*. "The body is necessary for the activity of the intellect, not as the organ through which it acts, but in order to supply it with its object; for images stand in relation to the intellect as colour in relation to the sight" ("Dicendum quod corpus requiritur ad actionem intellectus, non sicut organum quo talis actio exerceatur, sed ratione objecti; phantasma enim comparatur ad intellectum sicut color ad visum"; vol. 11, p. 12-13; 1a. 75,2). Thomist-Aristotelian epistemology is firmly grounded in the theorem that knowledge is based essentially on perception. In other words, the intellect is even dependent on sense

---

forma imaginata auri et forma imaginata montis componimus unam formam montis aurei quem nunquam vidimus" ("Somewhere between instinct and imagination, a power which composes and divides imagined forms, as when from the image of gold and the image of mountain we compose the single form of a golden mountain which we have never seen"; vol. 11, p. 140; 1a. 78,4).

[82] St. Augustine had emphasized the hermeneutic and expressive superiority of figurative language (Robertson 52-64). Hence images, which participate in and trigger the anamnesis of ideas, are also crucial in the other important brand of late medieval thinking. The reception of Aristotelian psychology could build on a long ecclesiastic tradition which underscored the importance of images. Saint Gregory's letter 13 to the bishop of Marseille was fundamental in this respect: "What the literate learn by reading the Scriptures, the illiterate learn from images, because in these also the ignorant see what they should observe, in these the illiterate read. Therefore, the people read primarily images" ("Nam quod legentibus scriptura, hoc idiotis præstat pictura cernentibus, quia in ipsa etiam ignorantes vident quid sequi debeant, in ipsa legunt qui litteras nesciunt. Unde et præcipue gentibus pro lectione pictura est"; col. 1128).

impression and images while "thinking." [83] This "thinking," however, is only possible because the "intelligibles are preserved in the mind, in the form of symbols or similitudes in the sensory memory" (Harvey 59). "Thinking" is, then, conceived of as a "small-scale composition" (Carruthers, *Book of Memory* 34) which is based on the images stored in memory, re-presented by the imagination, and judged by the *estimativa*. This is precisely the notion we find in the *Tratado del alma*, written in the 16th century by the celebrated Spanish humanist Juan Luis Vives.

> Cuando al espíritu se ofrece un objeto simple y sin composición, si está presente, la imaginación recibe la figura misma que se ofrece a los sentidos; si está ausente, v. gr., cuando se habla de él en una conversación, si es cosa de las que caen bajo los sentidos y está impresa en la memoria, la fantasía reproduce su forma, tomada de la memoria misma. Si es un objeto que no puede ser conocido por los sentidos, el ser o no ser, de una o de otra manera, es la mente quien la infiere con la razón, y la fantasía quien inventa su imagen, tomada de las cosas que ya conoce; así, por ejemplo, cuando representa a Dios, a los ángeles, nuestras mentes y otros objetos análogos. (57; bk. 2, chap. 1)

In perception, imagination receives the *species* of the present object. Images can also be cued by linguistic tokens and retrieved from memory. In "thinking" of *abstracta* or non-empirical entities, the intellect relies on images instigated by "reason" on the basis of previous experiences, which are necessarily stored in memory. Vives clarifies that the Thomistic-Aristotelian principle of "ut pictura cogitatio" is not limited to "tangible" objects. In his commentary to *Amphitrion*, in which he exposes the etiology of lovesickness, Villalobos also subscribes to this view.

> Ca en el espíritu que está en aquella parte de los sesos que sirve á la imaginacion [sic], represéntanse imágenes de las cosas que se piensan, así como en un espejo claro se representan los bultos y figuras de las cosas que se ponen delante. Que si tú piensas en caballos, es porque en la imaginacion [sic] tienes entonces formadas las imágenes de aquellos caballos, et si piensas

---

[83] As Robert P. Prentice shows, Thomas is in his Aristotelianism not only representative of the Dominican tradition. Also Bonaventure, commonly related to Augustinian thinking, couches his "psychology of love" in Aristotelian terms.

en la mar ó en la tierra, en las mercadurías ó en la guerra, allá tienes dentro plasmadas las imágenes de todas estas cosas; y como allí están hechas las imágenes, así las piensas [...]. (488-89)

When "thinking" of a horse or merchandise, the intellect can fall back on images saved in the storehouse of memory. Also thinking of "war" in terms of images does not, at first sight, strike the modern mind as exceptional since the concept will immediately call forth a visualization of previously experienced scenes of war. However, what is important here is that this visual representation of an *abstractum* is inevitably tropic. If we evoke an image of two knights engaged in single combat on a battlefield, this image signifies the concept in the form of a synecdoche. However, the image is only a vehicle for thinking since there is, as Vives shows, no essential link between signifying image and signified "thought." Imagination, therefore, is relatively free in choosing the components of the image. Relatively, because it is limited by pragmatic concerns. In other words, it is crucial to create efficient images which can be the basis of thought processes.

In his commentary to *De memoria et reminiscentia*, Aquinas addresses the question of how something not observable "in singularibus" could be transformed into an image.

> Memorabilia are accidentally intelligibles, which cannot be apprehended by man without fantasy. That is why what is subtle and spiritual we can least remember. Easier to remember is what is crude and sensual. If we want to memorize some intelligible thoughts more easily, it is necessary that we tie them to other phantasms, as Cicero teaches in his Rhetoric. [my translation]
>
> (Per accidens autem memorabilia sunt intelligibilia, quae sine phantasia non apprehenduntur ab homine. Et inde est quod ea quae habent subtilem et spiritualem considerationem, minus possumus memorari. Magis autem sunt memorabilia quae sunt grossa et sensibilia. Et oportet, si aliquas intelligibiles rationes volumus memorari facilius, quod eas alligemus quasi quibusdam aliis phantasmatibus, ut docet *Tullius* in sua *Rhetorica*; 326; p. 93)

In this quote Aquinas refers to the widely read *Rhetorica ad Herennium* (III 16, 28-40). The text was erroneously ascribed to Cicero, becoming thus the most important authority for artificial memory in the Middle Ages. As I have been arguing, the images stored in memory fulfill an important role in all mental processes. The condition of efficacy, then, applies to all images, making the *artes memorativae* pertinent to the analysis of premodern imagery in general. The alterity of medieval "thinking in images" lies not in the employ of images, but in the fact that images are not merely associations that may or may not be evoked in mental processes; images were epistemologically essential. That is the reason why memory and imagination had to educated, giving rise to an art of memory and imagination.

In the *Rhetorica ad Herennium* Aquinas could find a basic principle for the formation of mnemonic images: "what we most admire, is imprinted best in memory. We admire, however, what is new, unusual and exceptional" ("ea quae admiramur, magis memoriae imprimantur. Admiramur autem nova praecipue et insolita [...]"; *De memoria et reminiscentia*, 96; 332). What Aquinas has in mind here is the formation of so-called *imagines agentes*. The efficacy of these images is based on the principle that memory best grasps what is of extreme beauty, "sensuality," violence and strangeness.[84]

While it is easy to understand why these images are readily remembered, their "agency" seems rather alien to the modern mind. Aristotle proposes in *De memoria et reminiscentia* that in order to reconstruct a sequence in time it is necessary to remember a small-scale model for the time-lapses (57-59; 452^b). In the context of Aristotelian epistemology, then, memory based on images is *in nuce* narrative.[85] In *Confessiones* X,8 Augustine gives an account of the final step in his search for God. He reaches the "fields and spacious palaces" of his memory, where treasures of "innumerable forms" are to be found. Some of his memories have to be excavated; "other things rush out in troops" and offer themselves to the recollecting soul-searcher who interacts with his memories ("quaedam catervatim se proruunt et, dum aliud petitur et quaeritur, prosiliunt in medium quasi dicentia: 'ne forte nos sumus?'"; p. 94-95). These

---

[84] Glossing on the *Rhetorica ad Herennium*, Albert the Great expresses this principle most articulately in *De Bono* (p. 248; 4.2.2).
[85] Sylvia Huot also suggests "a possible narrative expansion of a poetic image" ("Visualization" 6), which is at the same time a mnemonic image.

memories, images and thoughts beyond the control of the unified, monadic self have been confined by post-enlightenment philosophy and psychiatry to the realm of the pathological and insane. Yet they were an integral part of the medieval and Renaissance phenomenology of the soul and considered essential in thought and reminiscive processes. The *imagines agentes* were considered instrumental for the "learned memory."

They "function," according to Carruthers, "like icons in a computer program in that they set in motion a task, the associative procedures of recollection" ("Poet as Master Builder" 882). So when Villalobos suggests the creation of an image of "war" this could, by way of metonymic transposition, take the shape of a figure, like Juan de Mena's "madre Belona" in *Laberinto de fortuna* (st. 13). Taking the associative process one step further, this figment of the poet's imagination could in its quality as an "agent image" very well enrapture the poet's persona and take him on an imaginative, possibly allegorical journey (Burke, "Interior journey"). Since mental images are not only at the heart of imagination but also of memory and thought processes, the boundaries between "realistic" and "phantastic", between conscious, waking thought process and dreamlike vision, are fluid (Lynch 64). Sudden transitions in literary mode, from "mimetic" to "fantastic", do not violate the principle of verisimilitude.

Giovanni Boccaccio offers an instructive example of the permeability of "reality" and "fiction" on the common meeting ground of imagination in one of his least innovative, yet most important works for the 14th and 15th centuries: *De casibus virorum illustrium*. This text, completed in 1373, was translated toward the end of the 14th century into Castilian (Naylor, "Introduction"; "Pero López"; "Sobre la traducción"), according to the testimony of Fernán Pérez de Guzmán in his *Generaciones y semblanzas* (15), by his uncle Pero López de Ayala. In his dedication to Mainardo de Cavalcanti the narrator explains that while he was pondering to whom to dedicate his work "occuritque primus Gallus Sicamber" (4). Ayala renders this passage with "me paresçe que veo delante mj a vn Rey de galia llamado por nonbre canbrio" (fol. 1[v]). The Castilian version, which emphasizes the visualization of the author's memories, captures paradigmatically the structure of *De casibus*. The author, dwelling on the topos of the "fall of great men," experiences the apparition of famous personalities from the stock of collective (literary) memory or his personal experience.

As Anthony Grafton points out, the narrator's "imaginative interaction" with classical authors can be found in the texts of humanists like Petrarch and Machiavelli. His explanation of this encounter between reader and classical author as a metonymic "allegory" of a particularly humanist way of intensive reading is supported by the text he analyzes (179-81). Boccaccio's conflation of diegetic levels, which entails the encounter of the reader/writer with memories and previous readings, on the other hand, must be related to a traditional, very medieval style of reading and composing.

In Boccaccio's *De casibus* "coming to mind" must be taken literally. At the beginning of book six, when the narrator wants to resume his task after a rest, Fortuna appears and reproaches him. A similar situation opens book eight. Reflecting about indolence ("pereza"), the narrator falls asleep. After waking up he wants to continue writing but is overcome anew by weakness and lies down again.

> E ahe que me paresçio que venja no se de qual partida vn omne [...] E estando asi comjgo conosçi que era françisco petrarca mj señor [...] E por ende ove mayor vergüença asi commo aquel que me sentia non digno de paresçer antel E despues estando vn poco catandome asi commo con vna cara desdeñosa & esperando que diria començo el hablar. (fol. 212ʳ-12ᵛ)

In both examples the narrator is in a state of physical exhaustion, which he expressedly distinguishes yet approximates dream-like situations. In this condition of *vacatio*, a severance or distancing of the soul from the body (Couliano 49), his imagination is highly activated and out of control of what we call today the "subject." Thus, the images are not only unintentional but also *agentes*. These autonomous images easily transgress the border from the diegetic universe into the *hic et nunc* of enunciation.

De casibus reflects on the process of poetic creation in a way that some critics would term metatextual. However, imagination, not writing, is the object of this reflection. Imagination mirrors imagination. It is, therefore, more precise to speak of a metaimaginative layer in *De casibus*. Boccaccio illustrates the tension between imagination and actual textualization–that is, the transformation of images into a narrative. In a culminating scene, "algunos querellosos" appear in Boccaccio's study and complain of *not* having been considered by the author (fol. 274ʳ). This paradox illustrates very well that in the Middle Ages, writing was not an act in which the authorial subject disposed freely of the elements that would make up his composition. The author must confront, sometimes even fight, the images evoked by his contemplation. In *De casibus* "fictional" characters invade the world of the "author"; yet it is Boccaccio who is ashamed to "appear before" Petrarch. He might as well have been "sucked" into an imaginary space, becoming a character, or *actor*.[86] At any rate, 15th-century readers familiar with works like Boccaccio's *De casibus*, Boethius's *De consolatione* or Mena's *Coronación* would not have labeled the narrative techniques of sentimental fiction, for instance the gemination of *el autor* in character and "author," as experimental or innovative. On the contrary, these texts conformed with their horizons of expectations.

After this digression into the Thomist-Aristotelian epistemology and poetic imagination, the initial question of how a 15th-century writer could conceive of a "psycho-analysis" of an ill-fated love affair has a simple answer: it would be *entirely* an imaginative-reminiscive quest. The model of medieval imagination which I have been tracing is capable of accounting for some of the features of sentimental fiction which have intrigued the critics. For instance, San Pedro's *Cárcel de amor* is, according to Bruce W. Wardropper, "starting from an obvious allegory interpreted in all its details, passes on to an allegory none the less real for being less obvious" ("Allegory" 42) For this reason, "one wonders whether Macedonia is not as fantastic a place as the Prison of Love, and whether Leriano, Laureola, and the courtiers are not the figments of a dream" (43). Wardropper concludes that "the *Cárcel de amor* has to be interpreted, then, as a vision in which there is an easy transition from allegory to reality" (44). While I agree with his astute observation that *Cárcel* as a whole can be read as a "vision," I would caution against describing this vision as "dreamlike."[87] Moreover, the opposition

---

[86] "The important consideration for the author," as Kelly points out, "is the idea that provides characterization and context; the representation in *matière* is an Imagination combining idea and substance, no matter how 'realistic' it may appear. The Imagination may include the reader himself or his projection into the author's experience" (*Medieval Imagination* 38).

[87] Whinnom ("Introducción II" 52) and Brownlee (*Severed Word* 164) also argue against interpreting *Cárcel* as a dream. I discuss the problem in detail in chapter three.

between "allegory" and "reality" does not prove pertinent in the light of contemporary conceptions of imagination and literary creation. Kathryn L. Lynch shows that medieval psychology regarded dreams as a phenomenon not categorically distinct from other perceptive processes (64). A poet might use a dreamlike setting because it provided a "realistic" explanation for an increased activity and independence of the imagination and visionary power (65).

Critics, though, all too easily identify any medieval vision with "dreams," since the dream is one of the few states of mind modern psychology has set aside for "autonomous," "agent" imagery. However, even in cases where the text explicitly introduces an "allegorical" dream sequence, like in *Visión deleytable* by Alfonso de la Torre, it is too reductive to consider dream and vision as mere vehicles to make a transition to allegory in which the author could use "indiscriminately false figures" (Salinas Espinosa 907). A medieval author hardly had to resort to these ruses to "justify" the introduction of allegory, or more precisely "imagery." On the contrary, the post-Thomist epistemology suggested, if not required, the transformation of ideas into images. Thus, the shift that we witness in texts like *Cárcel de amor* is not a puzzling leap from "mimesis" to "allegory," but a smooth transition in narrative or imaginative mode, comparable to the blending of third-person narration with direct speech.

In sentimental fiction the medieval theory of imagination, a conception of morbid love indebted to the medical tradition, and the broader framework of faculty psychology are interlaced. As Wack has argued, the aroused imagination of the person suffering from lovesickness becomes rhetorically productive ("Imagination" 109). A first-person narrator typically depicts his personal involvement in an unhappy, morbid love affair. Whether this account has an authentic autobiographical basis or is entirely fictitious is of secondary importance. The author would, conforming to the epistemological frame of which he and his readers could dispose, emulate and actually (re)create an imaginative quest. The narrator initiates a contemplative process in which he remembers and imagines the external circumstances, the story, and the internal struggle in his soul effected by the *philocaptio*.

As we have seen, the faculties of the soul are the conceptual building-blocks of the "psyche." They are, therefore, also analytical categories in the description of a mental disorder like *amor hereos*.

Faculty psychology is also capable of providing a detailed vocabulary of "emotions" or *passiones* (Thomas Aquinas, *Summa*, 1a.2æ. 22-30). Hence, the textualization of the internal phenomenology of a case of *amor hereos* could take the shape of composing ("agent") images of will, understanding, desire, and other agents in the psychic drama. From this point of view, the "allegorical" figures, prosopopoeia, imaginative landscapes and buildings in sentimental fiction from Rodríguez del Padrón to Nicolás Núñez are as "real" as the image of the beloved,[88] as "real" as the author who imagines himself exploring his soul.[89]

I have said that it is in the logic of contemporary epistemology to analyze the *enamoramiento* in terms of faculty psychology and to visualize the psychic struggle in the form of images of the involved powers. This does not, however, preclude the possibility of an allegorical reading of individual texts of sentimental fiction. Chandler Rathfon Post has included texts of sentimental fiction in his classic study of medieval Spanish allegory. Though frequently appearing in the footnotes of recent studies, his study is outdated and serves as a mere repository of the usage of imagery and "personification" in medieval Spanish literature. The vast and in many aspects diverse scholarship on allegory agrees on discarding the presence of images as a sufficient reason to qualify a text as an allegory. Allegory can be imposed on any text, if the reader is ready to assume behind the surface meaning a secondary, though more essential, "allegorical" meaning. This procedure, *allegoresis*, is characteristic of medieval Biblical exegesis and rhetoric (Freytag 22-38), and, as Northrop Frye has noted, of critical comment on poetic imagery in general (89).

Aside from the reader's will to *allegoresis* there are textual indicators which establish a consistent secondary level of meaning in which the elements are coherently connected. Constituent of allegory is the existence of such a coherent allegorical meaning that goes

---

[88] "Following the path of contiguous relationships," Roman Jakobson points out, "the realist author metonymically digresses from the plot to the atmosphere and from the characters to the setting in space and time. He is fond of synecdochic detail" (92). In sentimental fiction we find an inward digression to "metonymic details" of the lover's suffering.

[89] Kolve analyzes the illuminations of a 15th-century French manuscript of *Consolation of Philosophy*, which depicts the author Boethius in his auto-therapy interacting with prosopopoeic images (38-40).

beyond the surface meaning (Freytag; Harms and Speckenbach; Quilligan; Tuve; Michel). [90] However, "allegorization is," cautions Paul Michel, "the ultima ratio of the exeget, which should only be employed if it is otherwise impossible to find the point of a text" ("Allegorisierung ist die ultima ratio des Exegeten und soll erst angewendet werden, wenn einem Text anders keine Pointe abgewonnen werden kann"; 541). [91] Thus, instead of postulating allegory as an essential or accidental generic feature of sentimental fiction it seems prudent to analyze the individual texts, attempting to find their "point." After all, as Michel reminds us, it is the difficulty or opaqueness of a text or passage that triggers *allegoresis* (501). The alterity of a text, which the modern reader perceives due to his different habits of thinking, does not necessarily justify the conclusion that a text has "deeper" significance to the audience for whom it was intended.

In most texts of sentimental fiction we do not find a "sacred pretext," which is, in the words of Maureen Quilligan, allegory's "original treasure house of truth" (98). However, there is what Quilligan calls a "repository of ideas" (98), a subtext, which a medical-sensitive reader would recognize without resorting to the ultima ratio of *allegoresis*. Faculty psychology and the medical conception of *amor hereos* make it possible to account for most of the imagery and its meaning. In other words, "understanding" stands in these texts for the faculty of understanding, which is a factor in the phenomenology of passionate love. It is a constituent of the "surface level" of the text, and there is no need to infer a deeper, allegorical meaning. There is, as Marina Scordilis Brownlee recognizes, a fundamental difference between the imagery in Dante and sentimental fiction (*Severed Word* 12-15). In Dante's *Commedia* the imagery of the diegetic universe must be allegorically transcended; by contrast, in sentimental fiction the images do not require a hermeneutic effort, because there is no "deeper" meaning behind the signifying images. In other words, for a contemporary reader the faculties of the soul, their activity and struggle, are signified, not

---

[90] In Mena's *Laberinto*, for example, the imagery can be explained in terms of medieval epistemology (Burke, "Interior journey"), yet lends itself also to an allegorical reading as a *figura* for an "agenda [...] of national unity" (Hutcheson 49).

[91] Raymond D. Di Lorenzo, for instance, shows that much of Jacobus de Cessolis's 14th-century "chess allegory" is perfectly explicable as imagery constructed according to medieval mnemotechniques.

symbolized. They do not require interpretation because they are directly understood (Todorov 73).

What appears, then, to the modern critic as a subversion of Dantean allegory, an unreconciled disassociation of signifier and signified, could be seen by 15th-century reader versed in faculty psychology as a rather straightforward representation of psychosomatic *realia*.

Another argument against the presence of allegory in sentimental fiction is that the individual authors do not exploit the polysemic potential of the elements of the "pretext" in order to generate narration on the surface level and coherence on the allegorical level (Quilligan 26). On the contrary, analysis of the imagery of sentimental fiction will reveal that the "prescribed reading" (Chartier, *Texts* 157-58), the way an author tries to condition the interpretation of his text, attempts to avoid polysemy by providing only minimal ekphrasis and limiting the range of action of the personifications. The images used are, with the exception of *Cárcel de amor* and, to a lesser degree, of *Siervo libre de amor*, predominantly what is usually termed *abstracta agentes*. Some of them might be called *abstracta loquentes*. If we take into account the ontological status of the faculties signified in the discourse, it becomes clear that the *facultates animi* are not abstract concepts based on a synthesis of discrete phenomena. They are not mental categories which are empirically not observable, but organic realities of the human mind, like "brain," or "synaptic activity." Schnell points out that medieval people frequently considered personification "allegories" as real (380). Regarding sentimental fiction, the belief in the reality of concepts of will or understanding is partially derived from prevalent neurophysiological models. Medieval psychology describes the faculties as concrete entities with a certain degree of independent agency. For this reason, it is more adequate to use the term *imagines agentes* instead of speaking of *abstracta agentes*.

As we have seen, the process of forming mental and literary imagination involves the retreat to mnemonic imagery. Michel points out the striking parallels between locational mnemotechniques and allegory (549-51).[92] From the point of view of the

---

[92] Carruthers defines locational memory systems as "any scheme that establishes a set of ordered, clearly articulated, and readily recoverable background locations into which memory 'images' are consciously placed" ("Poet as Master Builder" 881-82).

mnemonist, allegory contributes to easy memorization of the contents associated with the images and the narrative it establishes. From the point of view of the writer, the *ars memorativa* provides the tools for the invention of striking, moving images. For this reason, we can expect to encounter in sentimental fiction images which are, to a greater or lesser degree, formed and arranged according to the precepts of *artes memorativae*.

However, the parallels between *ars memorativa* and allegory are not primarily due to the mnemotechnical function of allegory, but to the fact that the formation of images, as we have seen above, always involves interaction between the inner senses, imagination, judgment and memory. In Mena's *Coronación* the poet's persona declares that he wants to spare his reader a description of the torment women have to suffer, but not without "exortando que no fagas / del tal linie de plagas / ligera contemplación" (p. 219; st. 111). In his glosses Mena, who made extensive use of mnemotechniques in *Laberinto de fortuna* (Burke, "Interior journey"), explains the diligent reader's task (*Coronación* 221). The reader looks at and contemplates the image evoked by the poem. He must relate it to images stored in his memory in order to appreciate the poetic qualities, discover the "authorial intention," and draw moral profit from the reading. Mena refers here to a process of "rumination" in which a written text is decomposed and incorporated beneficially into the reader's own memory (Carruthers, *Book of Memory* 156-88). This reading process also involves the actualization of earlier reading experiences (Pietropaolo 206; Burke, "Insouciant Reader" 36-37).

So, if we consider the authors of sentimental fiction for a moment as readers who textualize an imaginative-reminiscive analysis of cases of morbid love, we can provide a contemporary theoretical framework for some of the narrative peculiarities of the genre. In his examination of cases of lovesickness, the author draws on contents stored in memory. He evokes similar or associated imagery based on previous readings, using the material memorized in previous readings as settings for their own re-creation. This practice, according to Kolve, is at work in Chaucer's *House of Fame*.

> It seems to me to concern [...] a process of intellectual recall and imaginative response [...]. In effect, we are shown a poet remembering a poem he has read as a series of pictures, by way of

creating a new poem that describes those pictures as though they were real. (42)

As Wenzel points out, the distinction between personal and foreign experience is marginal in medieval literature (223). This is, as I have argued, partially due to the epistemology of reading and writing where the personal and the foreign, the real and the fictitious, collapse in the notion of essentially imaginative thought and memory processes. The assimilation of bookish experience to "authentic" autobiographical experience has a profound impact on the practice of writing, particularly autobiographical or pseudo-autobiographical writing. A narrator, for instance, telling a love story he personally, "really" experienced or invented, could refer to the exemplary love story of Tristan and Iseult. His own story could be modeled on the subtext he experienced by reading, or he could even introduce "foreign" characters in his narration, granting them the same ontological status as his beloved and himself.

The protagonists of sentimental fiction suffer from *amor hereos*, a state of frenetic imagination and reminiscence which implies permanent access to memory images. This disease can be countered, according to the physicians, by activating the treasure house of memory. Hence, not only do the characters adduce *exempla* and associated narratives, but the author also grounds his narration on related subtexts evoked by the reminiscive process. Some of the metafictional experimentations and linguistic subversion of idealistic amatory codes in sentimental fiction (Gerli, "Metafiction"; Blay Manzanera, "Metaliteratura"; Brownlee, *Severed Word*; Haywood, "Narrative"), indeed, have originated as a projection of the *autor* into psychic spaces or imaginatively reenacted subtexts like Guillaume de Deguileville's *Le pèlerinage de la vie humaine*, Boccaccio's *Fiammetta* or San Pedro's *Cárcel de amor*.[93]

The appearance of "autonomous characters" from Flores's *Grimalte y Gradissa* to Unamuno's *Niebla* can be interpreted as an unfolding of a tradition in Spanish literature (Gillet). This approach, however, blurs the fundamental difference between modern literary

---

[93] The "metaficional" dimension has also a rhetorical facet. The intertexual relations can be seen in the context of topical invention: as an outcome of the imaginative immersion and reenactment (*augere* and *minuere*) of *copia rerum et verborum* of the topos "disastrous affairs of passionate love" (Bornscheuer 81-82).

techniques and medieval literary practice. By conflating diegetic levels and diegesis, modern writers like Unamuno, Borges, García Márquez and other authors of Magical Realism produce an ontological and metafictional vertigo in their readers (Thiem). The ontologization and textualization of the imaginary in sentimental fiction, however, was not a defamiliarization *avant la lettre*, but, on the contrary, corresponded to contemporary horizons of expectations and literary practices.

Approaching sentimental fiction from the angle of the contemporary epistemological basis does not highlight the innovative quality and originality of these texts, but contributes to a better understanding of their alterity.

CHAPTER II

THE FIRST GENERATION OF SENTIMENTAL FICTION

1. 'DIGNO DE PERPETUA MEMBRANÇA': *SIERVO LIBRE DE AMOR*

SINCE Marcelino Menéndez Pelayo's seminal work, Juan Rodríguez del Padrón's *Siervo libre de amor* has been considered a prototype of Spanish sentimental fiction (*Orígenes* II, 13-21). It was first seen and studied as an important, though primitive, evolutionary step in the development of the genre.[94] In the 1970s and early 1980s *Siervo* attracted a remarkable number of critics who analyzed the text in its own right (Whinnom, *Spanish Sentimental Romance* 28-32). Although Rodríguez del Padrón's work was treated by Brownlee (*Severed Word* 89-105) and Grieve (*Death and Desire* 1-24) in their important monographs on sentimental fiction, interest in *Siervo* has recently ebbed. However, in E. Michael Gerli and Joseph J. Gwara's 1997 collection of "Studies on the Spanish Sentimental Romance (1440-1550)," Gerli's article on the "Old French Source" of *Siervo* shows clearly that Rodríguez del Padrón's unwieldy text cannot be overlooked in the project of "Redefining the genre" (hence the programatic subtitle of Gerli's and Gwara's anthology).

In my analysis of *Siervo* I will show that the issues treated for decades by *Siervo* scholarship are still worth discussing. Moreover, I contend that some essential questions are yet to be raised. *Siervo* has been analyzed principally in terms of textual coherence, unity,

---

[94] Reviewing older studies on *Siervo*, Cocozzella suggests that these assessments of the text regard it "as a promise rather than a fulfillment, as an imperfect stage in the evolution of the genre rather than a substantial accomplishment in its own right" ("Thematic Unity" 189). Lida de Malkiel, for instance, emphasizes the echoes in Diego de San Pedro's "superior" writings ("Influencia" 17-18).

and narrative closure. Other issues were the author's intention and the notion of love he projected into his work. In my analysis I will address all of these topics. Yet, diverging from traditional approaches, I will not focus on the writer Rodríguez del Padrón, but on the writer as reader and the readers of his text.

Rodríguez del Padrón authored a text apparently novel and revolutionary in Castilian letters. Most scholars deemed the sources and precursors that sparked the creation of *Siervo* a key to its interpretation. Six main *loci* of inspiration have been established: the Italian literature of the trecento, chiefly Dante's *Divina Commedia* (Andrachuk, "Italian Influence"; Brownlee, *Severed Word* 89-105) [95] and Boccaccio's *Elegia di Madonna Fiammetta* (Menéndez Pelayo, *Orígenes* II, 3-12; Weissberger, "Habla el auctor"); Castilian and Provençal lyric poetry (Cvitanovič, *Novela sentimental* 117-18; Prieto 14); French chivalric romances (Lida de Malkiel, "Vida y obras" 323-24); medieval "tratadismo" reflecting academic disquisition on the subject of love (Dudley, "Inquisition of love" 233-34; Cátedra 143-59); the medieval tradition of Ovid's *Heroides* (Impey, "Literary Emancipation"; Impey, "Ovid"; see below); and, lately, Guillaume de Deguileville's *Rommant des trois pèlerinages* (Gerli, "Penitential Tradition" 100-01; Gerli, "Old French Source"). [96]

These sources and comparative studies have yielded evidence that Rodríguez del Padrón was influenced by a substantial number of authors and traditions. Most scholars, though, are not satisfied with describing the intertextual matrix, but claim a principal "source." They assert that a mastertext is capable of elucidating Rodríguez del Padrón's intention and the meaning of his *Siervo*. The multiplication of intertextual echoes in *Siervo* in particular, and the "generic relations" of sentimental fiction in general (Deyermond, "Relaciones genéricas"), cast some doubt on the hermeneutic and interpretive value of the construction of an increasingly complex textual genealogy. The most obvious conclusion which can be

---

[95] Reviewing these studies, Irene Zaderenko rejects a Dantean subtext and claims *Historia troyana polimétrica* as an influence of *Siervo*.

[96] Also worth mention is Deyermond's attempt to relate sentimental fiction to some influential Latin medieval authors like Augustine, Boethius, Abelard, and fictional autobiography ("Relaciones genéricas"). Gerli points in a similar direction ("Penitential Tradition"); see below. Nepaulsingh sees *Siervo*'s structure as essentially determined by the medieval tradition of the Wheel of Fortune (161-73).

drawn from the sheer number of literary antecedents of *Siervo* is that Rodríguez del Padrón was a very well-read man.[97]

Hence, further investigation must look at Rodríguez del Padrón as a reader. Since reading and writing are governed by the same conditions of meaning (Culler 50), the author-as-reader Rodríguez del Padrón arguably provides, in addition to actual traces of readings of his work, the best model for a potential contemporary reader of *Siervo libre de amor*.

From this point of view, two of the aforementioned "influences" are of particular interest: Rodríguez del Padrón's version of Ovid's *Heroides* and Guillaume's *Pèlerinages*. The translation and continuation of the *Heroides* provides a rather detailed protocol of Rodríguez del Padrón's appropriation of his source material; it documents 15th-century reading habits. The reminiscences of the *Pèlerinages* in *Siervo* also show, on one hand, how the reader/writer Rodríguez del Padrón imaginatively and mnemonically transformed a subtext. On the other hand, Guillaume paradigmatically exercises medieval writing and reading. By way of contrast, his text is perfectly suited to illustrate the peculiarities of *Siervo*'s imagery.

a) Bursario

The 12th century, which has been termed *aetas ovidiana*, made Ovid's *Epistulae Heroidum* a basic text of the medieval literary canon. Ovid authored twenty-one highly erotic epistles by famous female characters of ancient mythology addressing their absent lovers. Embedded in explanatory prologues (*accessus*), rubrics, glosses and other commentaries, they were read in the Middle Ages as exemplary texts that demonstrate legitimate, "good" love. One of the earliest translations of the complete *Heroides* into the vernacular was done by Juan Rodríguez del Padrón. The author of *Siervo libre de amor* rendered the Ovidian letters into Castilian with the title *Bursario*.[98]

---

[97] This is one of the functions of the list of authors in Rodríguez del Padrón's address to Gonzalo de Medina: he presents himself as an erudite man (*Siervo* 156), but does not indicate his sources (Lida de Malkiel, "Vida y obras" 343-44). It is a signal to the readers that they must read this text carefully, associating it with their own previous readings.

[98] Rodríguez del Padrón did not include letter XV ("Sappho Phanoni"). This passage is also omitted in the majority of Latin medieval manuscripts of the *Heroides* (González Rolán and Saquero Suárez-Somonte 26-27, n. 51).

Rudolph Schevill (116) and Charles E. Kany (49-50) acknowledged that we owe thanks to Rodríguez del Padrón for making the *Heroides* part of Renaissance fiction. Yet the quality of his version has been criticized. The main objection is that he treated his source loosely, translating many passages very freely or erroneously (Paz y Meliá xxx; Schevill 115-16; Lida de Malkiel, "Padrón: vida y obras" 336; Gilderman, *Rodríguez de la Cámara* 115; Impey, "Ovid" 284, "Literary Emancipation" 306).

Olga Tudorică Impey also labels Rodríguez del Padrón's translation "a careless, slipshod piece of work, as if he considered it, from a linguistic point of view, little more than an exercise" ("Literary Emancipation" 306). However, in her fundamental studies she points out the paramount importance of the *Bursario* for the evolution of Spanish amatory prose. Impey demonstrates that the *Bursario* depends linguistically on the 12th-century partial translations of the *Heroides* incorporated in the Alfonsine chronicles. Furthermore, she contends that the hermeneutic and ideological principles of Alfonse X and his collaborators determined Rodríguez del Padrón's own literary production. "Alfonso's concept of love, as well as the accompanying ethical values that allow marriage and love to coexist harmoniously, left a deep imprint on Juan Rodríguez's literary letters" ("Ovid" 290). Impey sees in the *Bursario* not an humanistic *aemulatio* of the author Ovid, but a medievalizing yet productive transformation of Ovidian eroticism. She agrees with the majority of *Bursario*'s critics in judging the three epistles which Rodríguez del Padrón added to his version of the *Heroides* a literary endeavor with significant impact on the genesis of *Siervo* and the evolution of the genre of sentimental fiction ("Literary Emancipation"; Gilderman, *Rodríguez de la Cámara* 116; Prieto 28-30). According to Impey, Rodríguez del Padrón's three "original" letters prefigured *Siervo* in thematic focus ("amor mesurado"; "Literary Emancipation" 309), narrative technique (narrative intermezzo, "psycho-allegorical debates"; 308-9, 312-13), conception of characters ("passive," "sentimental hero," "maiden who loves with decorum"; 310, 313) and plot configuration ("novella-like plot"; 308).

Brownlee ascribes an equally important role to Rodríguez del Padrón's *Bursario* (*Severed Word* 37-57). She gives Rodríguez del Padrón the merit of creating "the kind of interpretive polysemy that is at the root of his recuperative reading [...]." She sees a "dismantling of the medievalizers' reductive positivism in terms of true and foolish love" (55). He frees the *Epistulae Heroidum* from medieval "emprisonment" and transforms them "in such a way as to recuperate their original epistemological value as novelistic discourse" (10). Rodríguez del Padrón achieves this, according to Brownlee, by creating with his *Bursario* a "counterfeit" of the medieval hermeneutic paratexts that framed the *Heroides*. From this perspective, his introduction and didactic rubrics are deliberately unconnected with the letters, generating inconsistencies. This "makes the allegoresis if not derisory, unconvincing at the very least" (51).

It is patent that Brownlee's and Impey's diametrically opposed interpretations hinge on their respective readings of the *Bursario*'s introduction and rubrics. These paratexts, however, cast into the frame of contemporary reading habits and interpretive strategies, suggest a different assessment of the innovative quality of the *Bursario* and the literary practice of its author. Tomás González Rolán and Pilar Saquero Suárez-Somonte, latest editors of the *Bursario*, point out that "si exceptuamos el título que J. Rodríguez da a su obra, *Bursario*, todo lo demás que se halla en el prólogo responde exactamente al canon de los *accessus* medievales" (34). John Dagenais elaborates in an insightful article on the function of the medieval *accessus* tradition in the *Bursario* ("Rodríguez del Padrón's Translation"). From his study it becomes clear that Rodríguez del Padrón's short prologues to the letters are not, as Impey ventured, "summaries of chapters taken from the *General Estoria*" ("Ovid" 288). Dagenais demonstrates that the Castilian *Bursario* derives from the *Bursarii*, an early 13th-century Ovid commentary ("Rodríguez del Padrón's Translation" 120-127). Thus, what Impey recognized as a particular Castilian tradition of Ovid reception, which explains the "decorous love" of sentimental fiction, was part of the common European heritage. Brownlee's tenet of the deconstruction (*Severed Word* 52) of the hermeneutic paratexts by Rodríguez del Padrón and the counterfeit nature of his *Bursario* is also challenged by Dagenais's conclusions. He argues that "the Middle Ages was able to live with the yawning gulf between what the letter of the text seemed to say and what the commentary said it said" ("Rodríguez del Padrón's Translation" 137).

Both Impey's and Brownlee's appraisals emphasize the *Bursario*'s importance as an evolutionary step in the apogee of Spanish letters in the Golden Age. On the contrary, Dagenais's research corroborates Lida de Malkiel's viewpoint that the *Bursario*'s prologue is a "verdadero repositorio de modos de pensar medievales" ("Vida y obras" 336, n. 23). However, what is meant by her as censure, grants, according to Dagenais, an insight into "general medieval reading techniques outlined in the academic prologues as part of the medieval program for co-opting classical authors, such as Ovid, and adapting their works to Christian values" ("Rodríguez del Padrón's Translation" 119, n. 2). Juan Rodríguez del Padrón, indeed, proves a careful reader and interpreter of the Latin *Bursarii*.

In his translation of the *Bursarii*, he renders an explanation for the title.

> E por quanto este tratado es llamado por su semejable propiedat BURSARIO, avemos de saber por-que es llamado asý. Segúnd la propiedat del vocablo, bursario es derivado o ha naçimiento de *bursa*, vocablo latyno que quiere dezir en nuestro romançe bolsa; por-que asý como en la bolsa ay muchos pliegues, asý en este tratado ay muchos oscuros vocablos y dubdosas sententias; y puede ser llamado bursario, por-que es tan breve compendio, que en la bolsa lo puede hombre llevar; o es dicho bursario, por-que en la bolsa, conviene a saber, en las çélulas de la memoria deve ser refirmado con grand diligençia, por ser más copioso tratado que otros. (65)

This passage has prompted interpretation of "Bursario" as "pocket novel" (Gilderman, *Rodríguez de la Cámara* 115) or "cartero o correo" (Lida de Malkiel, "Vida y obras" 336, n. 23). These reductive readings, however, reveal their authors' unawareness of the "modos de pensar medievales." Dagenais indicates that "the association of 'memory' and 'bag,' and textual commentary certainly antedates the *Bursarii*" ("Rodríguez del Padrón's Translation" 123). He quotes Peter of Poitiers's compendium *Historiae in Genealogia Christi*, a widely read school text, as a possible source. Nevertheless, the source of inspiration is difficult to pinpoint, because "bag," particularly "money pouch" (*sacculum, marsupium*) as a metaphor for memory was a medieval commonplace (Carruthers, *Book of Memory* 34). Glossing on Hugh of St. Victor, Carruthers explains that the content of the treasure house of memory "must be classified according to a definite, orderly scheme," in the way a money-changer separates and organizes coins in his money-bag (81-

82). The *Bursario* has a simple classificatory scheme, a "pouch" with two compartments.

> La materia d'este tratado es de amor líçito e illíçito, honesto y deshonesto, cuerdo y loco. La intinçión suya es loar a unas de amor lícito y honesto, asý como a Penalope, que amó a su marido Ulixes; y a otras repprehende de amor deshonesto [...]. (66)

Accordingly, the love expressed in the Ovidian letters is catalogued as legitimate/honest and illicit/dishonest.[99] This is apparently achieved through an interpretation which strikes modern critics as rather violent, yet reflects the medieval practice of "ethical reading," which implied a reaction to the text with praise, *laus,* or blame, *vituperium* (Dagenais, *Ethics of Reading* 16).

The "yawning gulf" between the letter of the *Heroides* and its commentaries (Dagenais, "Rodríguez del Padrón's Translation" 137) shows that there is much more involved in the "memorizing" of the epistles than the mere storage of contents. The prologue passage quoted above underscores the text's copiousness of "muchos oscuros vocablos y dubdosas sententias" which must be committed to memory (Rodríguez del Padrón, *Bursario* 65). The *integumenta* hidden under the surface of the Ovidian letters are the real interest of the commentator. The discovery of this truth requires a meditative process, a "ruminating" in which the new input is "digested" and incorporated into the *copia memoriae* (Carruthers, *Book of Memory* 164-69). This is what the prologue of the *Bursario* means when claiming that the reader must "reaffirm" the *Heroides* "with great diligence" in the "chambers of memory," in order to make it "a text more copious than others" (66).

The *Bursario* is a testimony of how a reader, Rodríguez del Padrón, literally transformed the *Heroides* into a "richer" text. With his translation he appropriated the Ovidian epistles mnemonically. It has already been noted that he took great liberties in his version. This is partly the result of his low proficiency in Latin and the difficulty of the *Heriodes*, but also indicates a conception of

---

[99] Mena's *Tratado de amor* has the same binary classificatory schema as the *Bursario*: "E amor otra ves se subdivide en dos partes; la una es en amor liçito e sano, la otra en no liçito e insano. Amor sano & líçito e honesto es aquel que viene por intervenimiento de matrimonio conjugal" (334).

"authority" different from the modern understanding. It is misleading to consider his addition of three letters of his own to Ovid's text a forgery.[100] The value of the *Heroides* does not lie in the "original" letter of the text. The text of the "author Ovid" is a product of the interpretive, mnemonic activity of his readers,[101] whence it is only a short step to the creative rewriting of the source. Rodríguez del Padrón used the "materia" of the *Heroides* to create his own heroic letters,[102] as he understood and interpreted them. Through this expansion of the subtext he became indeed the *auctor* of the *Bursario*, the person who augments (*augere > auctor*) a canonic text (Müller, Jan-Dirk, "Auctor" 18).

Since the three supplemental letters of the *Bursario* are the outcome of Rodríguez del Padrón's reading of the *Bursarii* it will be helpful to look at the paratexts of the *Bursario*. The general prologue and the introductions to the individual letters are meant as an aid to the reader, and, therefore, reflect the (proper) way of reading the *Heroides*. The *accessus* states that the usefulness of the letters resides in having "leydo este tratado, ayamos notiçia de las maneras diversas de amar" (66). The *Bursarii* differentiates between only two manners of love (the "materia"): "amor líçito e illíçito, honesto y deshonesto" (66). Impey contends that Rodríguez del Padrón propagates, like Alfonso X, the coexistence of wedlock and decorous love as the only legitimate form of love ("Ovid"). Nevertheless, the introduction to letter III praises Briseyda, the "amiga" of Archiles for her chastity "por-que no quería conoçer syno a Archiles que primera-mente amó" (80). According to the commentary to letter V, it is the intention of the *actor* to chide Oenoe for her illicit love, "loco amor," "por-que amó a Paris, seyendo moço. Ca los tales, como dicho es, suelen ser inconstantes" (96). Felis (letter II) is also accused of "loco amor, ca loca-mente amó, pues que amó a su huesped" (72). In the last two examples, it is the danger of loving men of whom, under the circumstances (one too young, the

---

[100] He also supplemented letter XIX with a poem by Pero Guillén, followed by an allegoresis (198-202).

[101] According to Jan-Dirk Müller ("Auctor" 21), the *intentio auctoris* refers to the meaning or intention of a text which is derived from the assembly of signifiers. It is only indirectly connected with the actual writer.

[102] Impey lists the reminiscences of the Ovidian *Heroides* in Rodríguez del Padrón's letters ("Ovid" 288-89; "Literary Emancipation" 307-08, n. 9).

other a guest), [103] constancy cannot be expected, which qualifies the respective relations as "loco amor." [104]

It becomes clear that the opposition underlying the judgments of the "actor" is not adulterous vs. matrimonial love, but loyal, "true" (*honesto*) vs. fickle, "false" (*dishonesto*) love. In short, the *Bursario* presents first-person accounts of love affairs as exemplary inquiries into the nature of love, which is either classified as "good" or "bad." In his continuation of the *Heroides* Rodríguez del Padrón drew on the *locus* he "invented" in the *Bursarii*.

In his first letter, "Carta de Madreselva a Mauseol" (229-35), the heroine writes in the fashion of the *Heroides* to her absent lover. [105] Madreselva, daughter of Hercules, was robbed of her reign of Scotland ("Caledonia") and thrown into prison by her uncle Aritedio. The reader can infer that she is accused of violating the laws of the country by loving Mauseol. In a narrative analepsis, Madreselva recounts how her maid Creta brought the news about the trial Mauseol faced for his crime. When Adelfa, Madreselva's mother, pleaded for the execution of Mauseol, Artamisa, daughter of the sorceress Çirça, opposed her. She claimed that Mauseol had violated her and that her honor could only be restored by marrying the offender. Artamisa won the case, married Mauseol, and the two of them left for Antiopia. The rest of Madreselva's *carta* consists of a complaint about Mauseol's infidelity, finally begging him for an answer she will never receive.

As various critics have noticed, there are obvious structural and thematic parallels between Madreselva's *carta* and later sentimental fictions. None of them, however, has looked at the letter in light of

---

[103] The Old Woman in the *Romance of the Rose* counsels against loving a "foreign traveler, for his heart is as flighty as his body, which lodges in many places" (Guillaume de Lorris and Jean de Meun 234). The fact of having fallen in love with a stranger is also at the heart of Fiammetta's tragedy.

[104] They are violating the first of *Los diez mandamientos de amor*:

En tal lugar amarás
do conoscas ser amado;
no serás menospreciado
de aquella que servirás.

(Rodríguez del Padrón, *Obras completas*, ed. Hernández Alonso 321).

[105] Lida de Malkiel points out that Rodríguez del Padrón's tale has nothing in common with the legend of Artemisa and Mausolus ("Vida y obras" 330). She identifies some echoes of Seneca, which she judges, with her usual contempt for Rodríguez del Padrón, a source of "ínfimo valor" (331).

the prescribed reading of the hermeneutical apparatus that the *Bursarii* suggests to its readers.

The first *carta* is not preceded by an explanatory rubric. Impey has taken this as an indication that Rodríguez del Padrón "gives up his docent stance [...]" ("Literary Emancipation" 308). The reader, however, who has read and committed to memory twenty letters following an orderly scheme, hardly needs more instruction. He will seek to determine by what kind of love Madreselva is driven, and if this love is true and laudable or blameworthy and unfaithful. Naturally Rodríguez del Padrón had in his recreation of the heroic letters more liberty than in his version of the *Bursarii*. In the latter the reader must carry out the hermeneutic operations to conquer the chasm between the Ovidian letter and the moralizing frame. As a reader who had already performed this task, Rodríguez del Padrón projected the notion of love which he shared with his contemporaries into his own letters.

Madreselva evokes in her letter the beginning of her love for Mauseol.

> Aquel listado día de nuestra primera conoçençia, quando, vista la tu tan fermosa demanda como trayas de vengar por armas las biudas offendidas damas, y las faleçidas, robadas de su fama, restituyr por sabiduría, no fuy yo sola la que tú forçaste de su libre alvedrío, por te hazer saber la secreta fuerça que me hazías durante la real fiesta, en fyn de los bayles armenios y danças tebanas. (233)

She underscores the impact of the first *sight*. Mauseol appears to her as a benefactor of the female sex and as a wise man. Hence the mental image formed of the handsome youth is associated with positive *intentiones*. Madreselva receives this "first" impression at a royal festivity in an aroused emotional state. This further contributes to the formation of a powerful mental image. As a result she and various other ladies of the court lose their "free will." Madreselva describes in this passage a *philocaptio*, and the readers of her letter would most certainly recognize it as such.

Already at the beginning of her letter she shows one of the most conventionalized *signa amoris*, which is also evidently associated with the semiology of *amor hereos*. Rhetorically positioned to catch the reader's attention, she emphasizes at the beginning and at the end of her letter that she is composing it at night.

> Quien bien ama vençe el sueño, y ningúnd trabajo le es por vençer. Asý Traçia, que amava sobre los nueve peligros, e Tisbe, bien amando, vençió en velar al velante Píramo. Llamo y no respondes, mesquina, y duermes. ¡Tú amas, y puedes dormir! (229)

Her address to Mauseol is meant as an accusation. He is not suffering, at least in the imagination of Madreselva, from sleeplessness.[106] This, however, would prove that he also "loved well." Madreselva also hints at the reason for her nightly restlessness. "E aun sy deçendes a la Vestigia infernal, yo te desampararé, contemplando en mucha tristura en nuestro caso tan affortunado [...]" (230). In a hyperbolic expression she assures Mauseol of her everlasting loyalty, relating it to contemplations, which are here synonymous with *cogitationes* caused by lovesickness. Mauseol's marriage to Artamisa, on the other hand, shows that he is not a loyal lover. Madreselva's love is "honesto" while Mauseol's is "dishonesto." The reader will recognize that the "intention of the author" is to praise Madreselva for legitimate love: she shows symptoms of a *philocaptio* and has chosen a lover she could expect to reciprocate her love. Madreselva is, of course, not praiseworthy for suffering from *amor hereos*. She makes clear that she was condemned "syn quebrantar la fe a la casta Diana [...]" (230). Her love is good love because she does not succumb to the temptation to satisfy her sexual desire. It is a "courtly love" in which lovesickness is sublimated in ever loyal and passionate ennobling love.

In Rodríguez del Padrón's letter from Troylos to Breçayda and her answer to him the implicit debate about the sincerity of the lovers is played out. In the rubric the author explains that he wants to complete the account of "Dites y Dayres, disponedores de Troya" (235).

> E por dar fyn y complimiento a lo que la dicha estoria nos ha recontado, queremos vos mostrar la carta embiada por Truylos sobre este hecho a Breçayda, la qual Ovidio naso puso en su libro de las Epístolas de las dueñas, comiença asý (236).

---

[106] Boccaccio's Fiammetta adduces the same topos in her diatribe against treacherous Pamphilo: "¿O por ventura sin ninguna recordança de mí muy suavemente duermes?"(*Libro de Fiameta* 178).

Rodríguez del Padrón associates his recreation of the *Heroides* with his reading of another celebrated medieval text, the apocryphal Troyan History of Dares and Dyctys. [107] However, the topic is still the nature of love.

> Nyn fallo razón alguna por donde yo de ty olvidado sea, o me devieses trocar por Diomedes, al qual yo soy çierto que amas, salvo sy con tus dulçes palabras, con affecçión de amar demostradas, que tu me dezías, por donde me tenías a ty tan costreñido y animado, eran infintosas y falsas, captelosas y malas. (236)

Troylos argues that the only explanation for the fact that his lover has forgotten him, or stopped incessantly remembering him, is that her love was feigned from the beginning. The same theme appears twice in his short letter.

> Mas no hizo aquí menester el agua del dicho río Lete, ni alguna otra cosa de aquellas que prueva su poderío, aquella [108] çedula a quien es recomendada la reminiçençia de la capaçidad, salvo la movible y no estable voluntat tuya, y la poca firmeza del tu falso coraçón. (238)

His complaint is clearly cast in terms of faculty psychology and the phenomenology of *amor hereos*. His image was never firmly stamped into the chamber of her memory. Her will is not conquered by the positive judgment of the *estimativa*, but vacillating and fickle. The heart, in the true lover emitting ardent pneuma, is false.

In her answer Breçayda tries to counter Troylos's charges by proving her true passionate love and loyalty.

> La voluntad me requiere antes de la escriptura dar la escriviente mano a la aguda espada; la razón lo desvía diziendo: primera-mente deva salvar la fama en tan grand fortuna. [...] Batallan los sentidos, vençen las partes de mí. (239)

---

[107] Lida de Malkiel hints at Benoît de Sainte-Maure, Guido de Columnis (Guido delle Colonne) and Leomarte as possible medieval sources of the exchange between Troylos and Criseyde ("Vida y obras" 332).

[108] I suggest an emendation to "a aquella."

She displays in this embryonic psychomachia the psychic conflicts typical of the sufferer of passionate love. Will, disturbed by intense emotions, battles with Reason. Reason, in turn, tries to regain control: "¿Qué pensaré, que la sentible passyon me rrobó mi discreción?" (239). She calls her beloved Troylos ("desseado Troylos") her "membrança sola" (239).

There are more indications of her "true" love.

> ¡Ay! que sy bien sopieses quántas vegadas por me dar a ty engaño la noche, desdigo las velas y guardas del campo, e sola me toma el gallo cantante [...] por-que faleçida de mi pensamiento, maldiziendo mi ventura, es por fuerça de me retraer, y retrayda, me dar a la secreta contemplaçión, en lo qual me toma el sueño, y en toda la noche no me parto de ty que siempre quería que durase! (245)

Like Madreselva, Breçayda spends her nights sleepless with "secreta contemplaçión." Her letter attempts to dissuade Troylos's distrust in her loyalty and in the sincerity of her love.

To sum up, the inscribed reader of the *Bursario* is an exeget of love. He has to determine if the love expressed by the narrators is feigned or true. Rodríguez del Padrón's additional letters to the *Heroides* suggest that true love is essentially constant love.[109] The constancy of love is related to the phenomenology of lovesickness. It is, however, a passionate love that sublimates the temptations and dangers of *amor hereos*. The *Bursario* is one of *Siervo libre de amor*'s many subtexts, one of the readings the author reworked in the creative process. It is of little surprise that scholars of Rodríguez del Padrón recognize elements of *Siervo* in his letters. Scholarship, then, has so far accomplished the identification of the *Bursario* as a source of *Siervo* and as an evolutionary link between classic models and sentimental fiction. Still, the *Bursario* is capable of teaching the modern reader something more interesting: a premodern way of making sense of a text. It attests a reading habit that obliges the reader to analyze the notion of love, to interpret the *signa amoris*, according to the binary opposition of legitimate and illicit love.[110] The same operations are not necessarily required

---

[109] As Vigier reminds us ("*De Arte Amandi*" 170), Andreas Capellanus cherishes the idea of unique and faithful love in *De amore*.

[110] Dudley claims that the genre sentimental romance can be defined as "in-

from the reader of *Siervo de libre de amor*, as the many perceptive interpretations by modern critics demonstrate. Yet doing so will result in a reading closer to contemporary conditions of meaning and horizons of expectations, thus shedding new light on some of the puzzles of *Siervo*.

b) *Guillaume de Deguileville's* Le Pèlerinage de la vie humaine

Following Alan D. Deyermond's suggestion of tracing the origins of sentimental fiction to a broader medieval intellectual heritage ("Relaciones genéricas"), E. Michael Gerli relates Juan Rodríguez del Padrón's *Siervo libre de amor* to the penitential tradition.

> *Siervo* becomes both a confession of sin and an act of contrition in which a novice penitent describes his voluntary atonement while seeking absolution from a superior before taking perpetual vows. ("Penitential Tradition" 95)

His thesis is essentially based on the biography of the author. He conjectures that Gonzalo de Medina, the explicit recipient of *Siervo*, "was, in fact, Rodríguez del Padrón's immediate ecclesiastical superior and that [...] the author addressed his chronicle of contrition to him just prior to making his religious profession" (95).[111] Yet *Siervo*, in the form which has come down to us, does not chronicle the contrition of the Siervo, reason's recovery of control, and the narrator's ultimate conversion.[112] Hence Gerli concludes that

---

quiries into the nature of love, a search for a test by which the authenticity could be proved" ("Inquisition of love" 238).

[111] Andrachuk had earlier exposed the same line of argumentation ("Missing Third Part"). Little is known about the life of Rodríguez del Padrón (Hernández Alonso 9-14). The connection between his biography and his authorial activity is but a conjecture.

[112] Though pointing rightly to *Siervo*'s connection with the penitential tradition, Gerli's argument is overstated and reductive. Gerli does not convincingly explain why Rodríguez chose this particular form of "confession." He does not account at all for the intercalated *Estoria de dos amadores*. The readers' attention is not geared toward penance in the literal sense but to a casuistry of love. Nepaulsingh notes that Medina is addressed not only as a superior, but also as an equal and friend. Rodríguez del Padrón's fictional 16th-century biography indicates that the author of *Siervo* was not primarily perceived as a penitent sinner but as a martyr of love; see below.

Siervo is only a fragment, lacking a third part which would have completed the penitential process.

According to Gerli, *Siervo*'s pertinence to the penitential tradition is further substantiated by the fact that Rodríguez del Padrón modeled his text after Guillaume de Deguileville's *Le Rommant des trois pèlerinages*. Guillaume, a Cistercian monk at the monastery of Chaalis (b. ca. 1294-95; Clasby xiii-xiv), is the author of three dream-visions with the titles *Le Pèlerinage de la vie humaine*, *Le Pèlerinage de l'âme*, and *Le Pèlerinage de Jhesuchrist*. The sizeable number of extant manuscripts, translations into Dutch, German, English and Spanish, attest to the popularity of Guillaume's writings. [113] Gerli recognizes three central motifs taken from Guillaume in the *Siervo libre de amor*: the nightmare-vision, the allegorical descent into the Valley of Despair, and the liberation by the Ship of Religion ("Old French Source" 10).

> Rodríguez del Padrón assimilates so completely these three key images from the *Pèlerinage de la vie humaine*, which contribute an orderly structure and closure to the French work, it is probably safe to infer that *Siervo* went on to follow Guillaume's model and has, hence, come down to us in an incomplete manuscript. Ostensibly lacking the portrayal of the path *Entendimiento* announced in the *Primer título*, it is reasonable to postulate that an absent third part of *Siervo* [...] did indeed exist, and that it illustrated the narrator's boarding of the ship and his journey to Jerusalem. (10-12)

While I agree with Gerli that Rodríguez del Padrón was most likely familiar with Guillaume's dream-vision, [114] that, indeed, he had *Le Pèlerinage de la vie humaine* in mind when composing the *Siervo*, I contend that *Siervo* cannot be seen as a calque on the *Rommant des trois pèlerinages*. On the contrary, the analysis of Guil-

---

[113] Gerli infers from this fact that the man responsible for the Spanish version (Toulouse: Henry Meyer, 1490) was a Franciscan, and "that work must have been particularly valued in Franciscan spiritual and religious circles" ("Old French Source" 7). However, the prologue of the *Pilgrimage of Human Life* explicitly addresses laymen (3). Clasby lists an impressive quantity of early print editions of Guillaume's writings (xxxv-xliv).

[114] Gerli also points out that Rodríguez del Padrón was a rather educated man who almost certainly had access to extensive book collections ("Old French Source" 4). There is also evidence of French influence in his choice of motifs and linguistic borrowings (4-5).

laume's work reveals profound differences with *Siervo*. In other words, it shows the selective criteria of the reader Rodríguez del Padrón and his reworking of the invented material.

First, it is essential to determine what Rodríguez del Padrón's actual French "source" was. Gerli argues that in *Siervo* Rodríguez del Padrón closely followed the *Pèlerinage de la vie humaine*, except that in the encounter with Grace at the shore of the Sea of the World he conflated the "*Vie* with the figure of Synderesis as she appears in the *Âme*, probably seeking to economize on Guillaume's sprawling work" (16). With this argument Gerli tries to corroborate his thesis that at the climax of the complete *Siervo* the narrator would have embarked on the spiritual journey toward Jerusalem and his profession in the Franciscan Order.

In Guillaume's *Vie*, Conscience, *Siervo*'s key character according to Gerli, is but an allusion. The Pilgrim encounters Penance in full allegorical array. She explains to him what happens to the heart of the sinner which is a "dirty pot full of filth" (30). [115]

> Because of this great filth, a worm finds nourishment in there. It is conceived and born there, nourished and brought up inside it. {2160} This is the worm of conscience, and it seems to have teeth of iron, for it is so cruel and wounding, so gnawing and biting, that if there were no one who could beat it, strike it and kill it, it would never stop gnawing until it had killed its master. (30)

After crushing the sinner's heart with her mallet (Contrition) she promises to avenge him on the worm: "I strike it and stun it, I beat it and I kill it" (30). This worm killed by Penance can hardly be, as Gerli suggests ("Old French Source" 12), the Synderesis/Conscience which Rodríguez del Padrón chooses to guide the *Siervo* to salvation. It is not convincing that in his emulation of the *Vie* he picked one detail from the *Âme*, replacing Grace, the truly central image not only in the *Vie* but also in theological terms. In all likelihood, Rodríguez del Padrón was not even familiar with the so-called *Rommant des trois pèlerinages*. From the eighty-two extant manuscripts of Guillaume's writings only some twenty-two contain all three pilgrimages (Clasby xv). Also, his translators and

---

[115] All quotations are taken from Clasby's translation for reasons explained below.

early editors showed a definite preference for the *Vie* (Clasby xxxv-xliv).[116]

Rodríguez del Padrón had no reason to supplement the *Vie* with elements of the *Âme*, for he had with the *Vie* a perfectly coherent and conclusive text at hand. Yet an attentive reading of the *Vie* shows that Gerli's suggestion to see this text as the origin of the imagery and allegory in *Siervo* is misleading.

After having read *Romance of the Rose*, the narrator, who introduces himself as a monk of Chaalis, dreams that the image of city of Jerusalem appears in a mirror in his cell. He is moved by this image to go to the Holy City. The new pilgrim is provided by Grace with the appropriate apparel. Throughout the journey he holds on to the image of Jerusalem in a mirror set atop the Staff of Hope. He is baptized and introduced to the sacraments. Memory, his maidservant, carries the Armor of Virtue which he is incapable of sustaining himself. After some perils he arrives at a fork in his path. Now he must choose between the path of Idleness and the path of Labor. Misled by his body, he follows the path of Idleness. Being assaulted by the Vices, he is not able to cross over to the other path, from which he is separated by the thorny Hedge of Penitence. He is rescued by Grace, who gives him an ABC prayer to the Virgin. Baptized once more in the waters of Repentance, the restoration of his original vision continues as he arrives at the Sea of the World. He meets Heresy and chases her away. He is carried away by Youth until their flight is interrupted by Satan and Tribulation. The Pilgrim clings to his staff and reaches the shore where he meets Grace once again. They await the arrival of the Ship of Religion. He enters the ship, where he encounters a plethora of figures like Charity, Obedience, Discipline, Voluntary Poverty, Abstinence, and many more. Suddenly he is approached by Old Age and Infirmity, both sent by Death. Finally, they arrive at the Holy City. After being stripped naked, he is able to enter. Just as Death is about to end his life, the sound of the abbey clock ringing for matins awakens him.

---

[116] Also the Spanish translation (*El pelegrinage de la vida humana*. Toulouse: Henry Meyer, 1490) by the Franciscan Friar Vicente Mazuelo is a version of the *Vie*. This text was edited by Maryjane Dunn-Wood (Diss. U of Pennsylvania, Ann Arbor: U Microfilms, 1985). Mazuelo based his edition on a late French prose revision carried out by an unknown clerk of Angers for Jeanne de Laval around 1465 (Dunn-Wood, "Guillaume" 259). For this reason, I base my analysis on the edition of Clasby, which represents the earlier, more popular version (written 1330-31) of Guillaume's *Vie*.

From this summary it becomes clear that penitence and conversion are *not* the principal theme of the *Vie*. The Pilgrim fails to penetrate the Hedge of Penitence and is saved by Grace. Guillaume presents his narrator by means of his prologue as the alter ego of a monk.[117] The boarding of the Ship of Religion, conversion, is not the climactic moment of the narration but just another step toward the real culmination of the dream-vision, i.e. the arrival at the Heavenly City.

Reading the *Siervo* as chronicle of contrition and penitence only makes sense if related to the real biography of Rodríguez del Padrón. However, the *Vie*, his "source," is most certainly not an autobiographical text. It is, as Eugene Clasby points out, "an account of what Augustine calls *peregrinatio* (*De doctrina christiana*, I, iv, 4), the journey of the soul seeking to return to its homeland" (xix). The allegorical dimension of the *Vie* lies precisely in the transcendence of the imaginary, though real, story of the Pilgrim's journey toward the plane of human existence in general. Bearing in mind these differences, in particular the *Siervo*'s (pseudo-)autobiographical and the *Vie*'s allegorical orientation, Gerli's tenet of a missing third part of *Siervo* must be reassessed (Haywood, "Narrative" 14-15). It is obvious that the connection between the two texts is very loose until the moment the respective ships arrive. Therefore, it is not to be assumed that Rodríguez del Padrón would follow his source more closely in the final section, sending his Siervo on the Ship of Religion bound for Jerusalem. On the contrary, the narrative logic of the *Vie* requires a breakdown of the analogy exactly at this moment. Guillaume's Pilgrim does not find salvation on the Ship of Religion because the Heavenly City cannot be reached in this life. The death of the protagonist could not be a denouement for the "temeroso amador" Rodríguez del Padrón, who promises his friend/equal/superior Gonzalo de Medina an account of his own "caso" (Rodríguez del Padrón, *Siervo* 155).[118]

What, then, is the pertinence of *Le Pèlerinage de la vie humaine* to the reader of *Siervo libre de amor*? According to Gerli, Rodríguez del Padrón "meticulously plundered certain key moments, elements, and images [...]" ("Old French Source" 6): the nightmare vi-

---

[117] The title of the German translation is *Die Pilgerfahrt des träumenden Mönchs* (Clasby xliii).
[118] All quotations are taken from the edition by Hernández Alonso (*Obras*).

sion, the allegorical descent, the arrival of the Ship of Religion. More importantly, we must add to these motifs lady Memory, who is responsible for the Pilgrim's virtue, [119] and the guiding image atop the Pilgrim's Staff of Hope. The Pilgrim holds faithfully to his staff with the image of Jerusalem, which ultimately guides him to spiritual perfection. The image that guides and drives the worldly lover Siervo is a mental one: the *imago* of his unidentified beloved. Both Siervo and Pilgrim are loyal in adoring the image initially impressed on their souls. [120] The *Vie* is essentially a tale of education. The initial love for the Heavenly city is only perfected after a lifelong apprenticeship and many errors and deviations. *Vie* and *Siervo* share the basic metaphor of life as a quest for a state of perfect, redeeming love.

The topic of "good love" is not pervasive on a thematic level in Guillaume's dream, yet it appears at a crucial moment in the text. In the very first lines of the *Vie* the narrator declares that while he was awake he had "read, studied, and looked closely at the beautiful *Romance of the Rose*" (3). He assures his readers that this was what moved him most to have his dream. In the Pilgrim's encounter with Reason we learn what his meditation on the *Romance of the Rose* revealed to him. Reason warns the pilgrims.

> Unbridled anger and violent rage make me leave the house they dwell in. Carnal love drives me out completely and makes me leave immediately. You can see this plainly in the *Romance of the Rose*. (14)

The reader Guillaume saw in the *Romance* a veiled *reprobatio* of carnal love and he encourages his reader to see his dream-vision inspired by it. [121] Sylvia Huot describes the *Vie* as a rewriting which systematically transposes "erotic allegory into religious allegory, replacing rationalism and naturalism with Christian doctrine" (*Medieval Readers* 224). [122] It might very well be regarded as an imagi-

---

[119] See below.
[120] See below.
[121] In Íñigo López de Mendoza's *Proemio e carta* directed to the Constable of Portugal, the *Romance of the Rose* is acknowledged as an *ars amatoria*: "el Roman de la rosa, donde, commo ellos dizen, el arte de amor es tota inclosa [...]" (215).
[122] Huot explains that in the reworking "important issues raised in the *Rose* are re-examined, but in a less provocative format, and with less ambiguous conclusions" (*Medieval Readers* 223). She conjectures that Guillaume's initial appraisal of

native reenactment of the *Romance of the Rose*. The gap that separates the *Vie* and the *Romance* indicates to what degree Rodríguez del Padrón, in turn, transformed the texts he had in mind when rewriting the *Vie*. It is important, however, to acknowledge that the three texts, *Romance*, *Vie* and *Siervo*, treat the same *matière*; they are inquiries into the nature of love and quests for the right kind of love.

Possibly the most important lesson the reader of Guillaume's *Vie* can apply to the *Siervo* is not one of structure, motifs or intentions, but one about the very process of "reading" imagery.[123] It is not a coincidence that the *Pèlerinage* has attracted distinguished scholars of medieval allegory; Guillaume's text is an exemplary demonstration of the allegorical use of images. In book one the Pilgrim meets one of the many personification allegories.

> I found her most astonishing. In one hand she had a mallet and in the other a stout bundle of switches, thin and green and supple. She held a broom in her mouth, between her teeth, and this astonished me even more. {2030} She held it delicately and she did not seem any the less wise for it. If someone else had held it like this, people would have thought she was out of her mind. She spoke first to the people and she spoke very wisely. Her broom did not keep her from speaking or preaching. (28)

The Pilgrim cannot identify her at first. Her array also does not make sense to him. Only by way of conversation does he gradually begin to understand.

> I am called Penance, warden of the hidden isle. {2050} I make people lay aside all uncleanness before they enter naked. Therefore, I carry with me a mallet, a bundle of switches and a broom. With the mallet I break and bruise and wring the human heart with contrition when it is hardened and full of old sins. I soften it and make it weep and lament, sigh and grieve. (29)

---

the *Rose* and his rejection in the 1355 recension may be due to the fact that Guillaume based his first version on an expurgated manuscript and his revision on an uncensored version (228).

[123] Most students of *Siervo* apply the term "allegory" indiscriminately to the text's imagery. Herrero, for instance, proposes to study the "allegorical structure" of *Siervo*, yet treats thematic coherence in order to determine the attitude toward "courtly" and "Christian" love expressed therein.

She uses the mallet to crush the heart of a sinner which is "like a great earthen pot, filled with a foul and stinking liquid" (29). This filth nourishes the worm of conscience, which is finally killed by Penance and her mallet. Starting with the metaphor of a "filthy heart," Guillaume creates a chain of metonymically related images that leads from dirt to pot, mallet, broom and worm. The whole ensemble of images explains allegorically the function and importance of penance. On his pilgrimage the narrator is confronted with systems of images to be studied and interpreted. He and his readers must learn to reveal the truth hidden behind the signs (Hagen). Guillaume's contemporaries assigned to this allegorical use of images heuristic and expressive superiority (Robertson 52-64), and mnemonic efficacy (Hagen 5).

The personification allegories of the *Vie* are not only conversing, they are very much *imagines agentes*. On the path of Idleness the Pilgrim is assaulted by frightening old crones, among them Envy.

> The other old crone was holding a spear full of human ears that were pierced {8220} and skewered on it. She pointed one end towards me and she had the other end between her teeth, together with a red, bloody bone she was gnawing on like a dog. A hook was fixed to the iron of the barbed spear. It was made for piercing and hooking pilgrims. The old crone acted very fiercely. (111)

In its use of abhorrent details Envy, like most of the figures of the *Vie*, ideally illustrates the precepts of the medieval Art of Memory. The full meaning of the image is revealed only after interpreting the riddle-like descriptions and the iconographic details. The agency of the images is not only a mnemonic one. For instance, Detraction seizes the Pilgrim with her teeth, knocks him down, and stabs a lance in his body. Treachery strikes his belly with a knife and dagger (118). The dreamer and the reader of the dream-vision are engaged in a violent hermeneutic struggle with the images they encounter.

The main difference in the use of imagery the reader notices, coming from the *Vie* to the *Siervo*, is that in the *Siervo* there are no *imagines agentes* in the two aspects just described. Furthermore there is little, if any, interpretive activity required from the reader.

The imagery of the *Siervo* is heterogeneous. After having been rejected by his lady, the narrator engages in a "contemplaçion" in which he finds himself in a "escura selva." He arrives then in the Garden of Fortune, where he sees three trees: a green myrtle, associated with Venus, a green olive tree, associated with Minerva, and a white poplar, associated with Hercules (166-67). These trees mark the beginning of three paths, "que son tres varios pensamientos" (166). Already in the introduction the narrator had established that these paths correspond to the three faculties of the rational soul, which are in turn related to the time of loving and being loved (Heart/Memory),[124] the time of loving and not being loved (Free Will), and the time of neither loving nor being loved (Understanding) (154). As the narrator walks, the grass, the trees and other plants, a nightingale and other singing birds change in appearance and behavior according to his gloomy mood (166-67). After the debate with his faculties and the intercalated *Estoria de dos amadores*, the Siervo moves along the narrow path of Understanding, passing the "great Alpes of his thoughts" and the dark valleys of his "primer motus." He arrives at the fringes of his "esquiva contemplaçión." He loses his way. He asks "montañeros," who ridicule him. Savages do not respond. Birds are silenced by his presence (203). From the top of the trees he looks for a settlement. Finally, he reaches the seashore where he encounters the vessel of Synderesis (207).

Herrero claims that an "extended allegory," presented in clusters of images, forms the "poetic backbone" of *Siervo* ("Allegorical Structure" 752). Some of the images to which he refers, indeed, have a secondary meaning: the garden, the trees, and the corresponding paths. Yet this meaning is assigned to them by convention. No hermeneutic effort is required from the narrator or the reader. The garden is presented right away as the Garden of Fortune. The fact that it is a garden is not allegorically transcended. There is also no reason to relate the olive tree to the path of not loving and not being loved, other than the fact that it *symbolizes* Minerva and wisdom.

Herrero points out that the Siervo's itinerary describes his emotional and mental development ("Allegorical Structure" 755). Certainly, the *Siervo*'s journey through the imaginary landscape is

---

[124] Regarding the dual nature of "heart" as bodily organ and faculty of soul, see below.

the "poetic backbone" of the text. In other words, the journey is the organizing metaphor of Siervo's psychic conflict. If the existence of a continued metaphor is a constituent feature of allegory, we may by the same token call *Easy Rider* an allegory. However, the discrepancy between Rodríguez del Padrón's use of imagery and the kind of medieval allegory we have seen in Guillaume's *Vie* is palpable.

It is important to acknowledge that *Siervo*'s vision is not entirely allegorical. As a matter of fact, there are only a few *res significativae* (things that signify other things) in the text. The narrator maps an imaginary topography composed of elements known from everyday experience. Except for casual information about color and brightness, the description is minimal. He merely names the objects that he encounters on his journey. The description of nature has chiefly the function of expressing the emotional state of the narrator. The pathetic fallacy, however, does not change the fact that no secondary, allegorical meaning is assigned to the things: the bird is a bird, the mountain is a mountain, and nothing else.

In Guillaume's *Vie* we have seen that it is the corporeality of things that sets the allegorical process in motion, both hermeneutically and narratively, mostly by means of metonymical expansion of an image. In *Siervo*, rich ekphrasis and descriptive details are conspicuously lacking. This cannot be explained in terms of narrative economy. It is obvious that the narrator seeks to minimize the corporeality of the images invoked in his account. He repeatedly labels them explicitly as mere thoughts: "escura selva de mis pensamientos" (165), "tres caminos, que son tres varios pensamientos" (166), "faldas de mi esquiva contemplaçión" (203), "Alpes de mis pensamientos" (203), "árbores de mi escura maginança" (207).

Besides these empirical images, Rodríguez del Padrón introduces Heart/Memory, Free Will and Understanding as interlocutors of the narrator. The introduction designates them as the "tres partes del omne" (153). Furthermore, at the pinnacle of the narrator's despair he blames his "çinco sentidos" who surround him, mourning (173).[125] A medieval reader would identify these figures without a second, allegorizing, thought as faculties of the rational

---

[125] In the modern editions, the first personification speaking to the Siervo is usually identified as "La discreción." I think that the first speech must be attributed to Syndéresis; see below.

and animal soul, respectively.[126] In contrast to Guillaume, who created predominantly *abstracta agentes*,[127] Rodríguez del Padrón introduces only personifications of an individual's concrete faculties. Again, there is no need or possibility to regard them as *res signicativae*. The reader has no choice, to give an example, but to attribute to an image presented as "mi libre alvedrío" the meaning "the narrator's higher orectic faculty." After all, if the reader has only a rudimentary knowledge of faculty psychology, the personifications of *Siervo* do not create an opaqueness which ultimately triggers *allegoresis* (Michel 501).

Regarding the "images" of the Siervo's faculties, the effort is manifest not to endow them with a "body" which could become the starting point for a chain of allegorizing associations and interpretations (Michel 473). They are devoid of any physical attributes, reduced to mere voices. Hence their interaction, unlike the very physical struggle of the personification allegories with Guillaume's Pilgrim, is not more than a dialogue, or, in the case of the five senses of the animal soul, an unarticulated expression of emotion.

To sum up, in the vision presented by Rodríguez del Padrón in the *Siervo,* the reader familiar with the sprawling imagery of Guillaume's *Pèlerinage* is consistently signaled to focus on the *sensus literalis*.[128] The narrator promises to Gonzalo de Medina "la muy agria relaçión del caso, los passados tristes y alegres actos y esquivas contemplaçiones, e innotos e varios pensamientos [...]" (155). In other words, he proposes to explain his very personal state of mind, affected by an individual amatory experience that is presented as real. To be sure, there is a layer of deliberately crafted opaqueness in the *Siervo*. Yet the "oscuros vocablos y dubdosas sententias" (Rodríguez del Padrón, *Bursario* 66) of this text owe their existence to rhetoric and linguistic artistry and, probably, to the inscription of a reading *à clef* (Impey, "Enigmas"). However, there is no indication of a veiled allegorical meaning in the text. *Siervo libre de amor* is

---

[126] After the *Estoria de dos amadores* the narrator addresses his "esquivo pensar" (202). I consider this invocation a rhetorical figure, not a personification.

[127] Reason and Memory in the *Vie* are not the individual Pilgrim's faculties, but concepts important to Man in general.

[128] Andrachuk suggests that "Ricardo" in the list of *auctores* in the *Siervo* refers to Richard of St. Victor, an authority for an anagogical interpretation of the Scriptures ("Italian Influence" 48, n. 13). However, given the absence of respective textual markers, this passing reference will certainly not engage the reader in an *allegoresis*.

conceived as a "realistic vision," an autobiographical protocol of a lover's psychic tribulations.

This characterization of *Siervo*'s imagery is, of course, not pertinent to the denouement of the narration, i.e. the Siervo's encounter with Syndéresis. Here we find elements that call for hermeneutic, allegorizing operations: a prosopopoeic figure that cannot be identified easily and unequivocally, a rather elaborate ekphrasis, an interaction between narrator and personification. The analysis of this complex image will be part of the following reading of Rodríguez del Padrón's *Siervo libre de amor*.

c) Siervo libre de amor

We possess only a few documents of the later life of Juan Rodríguez del Padrón's *Siervo libre de amor* in Spanish letters (Lida de Malkiel, "Influencia").[129] However, the anonymous *Vida del trovador Juan Rodríguez del Padrón*[130] attests to the author's popularity in the second half of the 16th century.[131] Rodríguez del Padrón appears in the *Vida* as a member of the high Aragonese nobility.

> Así en las guerras que ubo como en los actos y exerçiçios de caballería se aventajaba a todos, y en la buena gracia, gentileza y discrecion les excedía; por las quales gracias fue muy conocido, famoso y estimado, y de muchas damas muy favorecido. (383-84)

Even the Castilian queen falls for him. She initiates a liaison without disclosing her identity, but Rodríguez del Padrón confides in a friend. Ultimately, this violation of the law of secrecy rouses the queen's ire and leads to Rodríguez del Padrón's exile. In Paris the French queen, too, falls in love with the Aragonese gentleman. Af-

---

[129] Lida de Malkiel overlooks the most interesting reading of *Siervo*, i.e. Dom Pedro's *Sátira de infelice e felice vida*; see below. Furthermore, there exist strong intertextual relations between *Siervo* and the anonymous *Triste deleytaçión*; see below.

[130] The authenticity of the *Vida* published by Pedro José Pidal in 1839 was disputed until the recent discovery of two extant manuscripts (Whinnom, "Pidal vindicated"; Garcia).

[131] Only a decade after the composition of *Siervo*, Dom Pedro praises its author as "Juan Rodrigues, poeta moderno e famoso" (*Sátira* 137 [gloss]). All quotations of *Sátira* are taken from the edition of Luis Adão Fonseca.

ter the affair becomes public, he attempts to flee to England. He is killed on the way to Calais by some French knights.

The *Vida* is ostensibly not based on Juan Rodríguez del Padrón's biography. It is a fictitious account extrapolated principally from his *Siervo libre de amor* (Menéndez Pelayo, *Orígenes* II, 19).[132] There is a strong tendency in modern scholarship to emphasize the subversion or rejection of the notion of love as expressed in traditional *cancionero* poetry. However, the modern reader is well-advised to keep in mind that this important testimony of an early reading of *Siervo* presents the author of the text as an epitome of the courtly lover-poet and martyr of love.[133]

Pedro M. Cátedra discerns in *Siervo libre de amor* an "opción por una actitud polémica en contra de las concepciones naturalistas del amor [...] para acogerse a una concepción propiamente cortés y poética" (143-44). From this statement I infer three arguments which point to the line of investigation I will pursue. First, *Siervo* explores and contrasts different conceptions of love. Second, the naturalist discourse about love is an important subtext of *Siervo*; the reader cognizant of faculty psychology finds abundant evidence to explain Siervo's amatory quandaries in terms reminiscent of *amor hereos*. Finally, as a piece of literature heir to the tradition of lyric love poetry, *Siervo* sublimates and transcends the naturalist notion of love.[134]

The introduction to *Siervo* informs the reader that the following "tratado" consists of three parts, which are symbolized ("figurados") by three paths and three trees which stand for the three parts of man: Heart ("coraçón"), Free Will ("libre alvedrío") and Understanding ("entendimiento"; 153).[135] The first part (green myrtle/*coraçón*) treats the time of "good love" ("bien amar"; 154). The second part (white poplar/Free Will) refers to the time of "loving well" and not being loved. The third part (green olive/Understanding) corresponds to the time of neither loving nor being loved. Ac-

---

[132] Nicolás Antonio, in his *Bibliotheca Hispana Vetus*, and Fernando de Lucena, 15th-century translator of *Triunfo de las donas*, regarded the legendary liaison of Rodríguez del Padrón and the queen as a historical fact (Hernández Alonso, "Introducción" 14).

[133] Rohland de Langbehn remarks that the anonymous author of *Triste deleytaçión*, who was evidently familiar with *Siervo*, presents Rodríguez del Padrón "expresadamente como campeón de las mujeres" (*Introducción* 29).

[134] I consider my article about memory in *Siervo libre de amor* superseded.

[135] All quotations are taken from Hernández Alonso's edition (*Obras*).

cording to this introduction, the "siervo entendimiento" follows the latter path "después de libre, en compañía de la discreçión" (154).

The term "tratado" used in the introduction has led some critics to read *Siervo* as a didactic text emulating the Latin genre *tractatus* (Cvitanovič, "Tratadismo"; Andrachuk, "Prosa y poesía" 62; Andrachuk, "Italian Influence" 49; Weissberger, "'Habla el auctor'" 206-13). This view was convincingly rejected by Whinnom ("*Autor and tratado*") and Dagenais ("Rodríguez del Padrón's Translation"), who demonstrated that in the 15th century "tratado" did not designate a specific didactic genre. Dagenais argues that "*tratado* is used to call attention to itself, to alert the reader that the author is taking some position vis-à-vis the tradition of academic (and generally moralizing) commentary in the work" ("Rodríguez del Padrón's Translation" 136). Hence, the appearance of the term "tratado" alerts the reader that the first of *Siervo*'s paratexts is not an introduction to the work, but an interpretive commentary very much in the vein of the *accessus* to the *Bursario*'s letters (Lacarra, "*Siervo*" 151-52).

The main text of *Siervo* is presented as an epistle from the author-persona Juan Rodríguez del Padrón to Gonzalo de Medina. In this letter the narrator gives his addressee an introduction to the narration that follows. This "second prologue" contained in the letter is preceded by a section which establishes a classificatory scheme of the kinds of love to be found in the letter and gives an overall interpretation of the text. Vera Castro Lingl observes the change from the markedly impersonal tone of the first prologue to the second. There is also a change in names from "Rodríguez de la Cámara" in the "primer título" to "Rodríguez del Padrón" which the author uses to refer to himself at the beginning of the second preface ("Back to the text" 49-50). This, together with the "necessity of a second introduction," makes her "wonder if the same person is responsible for both introductions" (50). To the evidence noted by Castro Lingl we must add discrepancies between the epigraphs and the text. The portion of the text overwritten with "DE BIEN AMAR Y SER AMADO" (Rodríguez del Padrón, *Siervo* 154) contains the author's address to Medina in which he explicitly designates himself as a "temeroso amador," suffering from unreciprocated love (155). Under the same heading he also summarizes the entire love affair. Oddly dissimilar to the pronounced autobiographic character of the main text, the title to the *Estoria de dos amadores* refers to

"EL DICHO JOAN RODRÍGUEZ" (174). The first harangue is attributed to "La discreçión" (158).[136] In the section to which the title refers, the speaker is first Syndéresis addressing the author-persona ("¡O mi buen señor [...]" 158-59);[137] then, within one and the same sentence, the *auctor* assumes the narrative voice in order to introduce a poem by *Coraçón*.

> No dubdo yo [sc. discreçión], si tú no vienes en condiçión que hazes con él [sc. amor] perpétua [sic] paz, sin más contender, que la furia de aquel no te sea merçed, y merçed dolor perdurable, cuyo pavor, si[n] más pensar [sc. yo, el auctor], forçó luego mi coraçón a dezirme esta cançión. (159)

This section is also of particular interest because it coincides with the first prologue in identifying Syndéresis as *Discreción*: "por donde siguió [sc. el entendimiento], después de libre, en compañía de la discreçión" (154).

In short, there is substantial evidence that the first prologue and other paratexts in the only manuscript of *Siervo* are not authored by Rodríguez del Padrón. Do these portions of the text therefore reflect an early reader's understanding of *Siervo*? Does it give the modern student of the work valuable interpretive clues? The answer to these questions is yes, but not in the way most critics have seen it.

Hans Ulrich Gumbrecht shows that there existed a tradition of "double prologues" in late medieval Castilian literature. He argues that these prologues relate differently to the following text, thus unfolding a hermeneutical space (894). In the second prologue the author seeks to give a specific introduction to the text (900). The first prologue, on the other hand, locates the text in an "adequate field and genealogy of knowledge" and calls for an allegorical reading of the text which attempts to avoid potential polysemy (895-96). In the case of the *Siervo*, the first prologue is situated in the tradition of academic commentary (Dagenais, "Rodríguez del Padrón's Translation" 136) and the discussion of amatory matters (Cátedra

---

[136] According to the editor Hernández Alonso, this "heading" appears in very small letters and barely legible at the margin of the manuscript (*Siervo* 158, n. 38).

[137] See below. I refer with "Syndéresis" to the image presented by Rodríguez del Padrón as opposed to the theological concept of habitual conscience ("synderesis").

143-44). If the main text of *Siervo* is indeed preceded by a "double prologue," we can expect a diverging introduction in the second prologue.

Hence the question of the authorship of the first portion of the preface is only secondary. It is, however, of chief importance to acknowledge that the interpretation given by the first prologue may not be determined by an accurate reading of the text but by the hermeneutic apparatus provided by the "field of knowledge." In analyzing and relating the first prologue and the paratexts which map the text, we must bear in mind that they may reflect an attempt to domesticate an unwieldy text. In any case, students of *Siervo* must be cautious in interpreting the headings and the first prologue's affirmation that *Siervo* was intended to be a "tratado" with "tres partes principales" (153). Also the affirmation that freed Understanding is guided by *Discreçión* at the end (154) must be subjected to a critical analysis of the text. The *Bursario* is a perfect example of the gulf that can separate the commentary and the letter of the text. The prologue's obvious obsession with the number three, the concern for symmetry and clear-cut narrative closure, do not buttress the asseveration that *Siervo* is a fragment, missing a third part, in which the redeemed narrator follows the path of loving and not being loved.[138] Similar to the texts studied by Gumbrecht, the second prologue, in which the author-persona introduces the reader to the text, suggests a diverging reading of the text.

In the author-persona's preface, at the moment of enunciation, he presents himself unmistakably as a lover on the path of loving and not being loved: he is a "temeroso amador careçiendo de los bienes que me induzían amar" (Rodríguez del Padrón, *Siervo* 155); he is now in a position contrary to loving and being loved ("Yo aver sido bien affortunado, aunque agora me vees en contrallo"; 156). At the insistence of Gonzalo de Medina, he promises "la muy agria relaçión del caso," i.e. an account of his love affair (155). He proposes to follow the "style" ("estilo") of some "antigos" like Homer, Ci-

---

[138] The older debate about the completeness of *Siervo* is summarized by Fernández Jiménez; see also Deyermond ("Estudio preliminar" 15, "Estudio de la ficción" 5). Gerli ("Old French Source") and Castro Lingl ("Constable") made the most important contributions to the question in recent years. Based on a minute comparison of *Siervo* and *Sátira*, Castro Lingl shows that the Constable of Portugal reworked a manuscript of *Siervo* much like the text that has come down to us, which makes it unlikely that the extant version is incomplete.

cero, Horace "no por que yo sea honrrador de aquellos, mas pregonero del su grand error, y siervo indigno del alto Jhesús" (156). Some critics have seen the last sintagma of this declaration as reflecting Rodríguez del Padrón's decision to renounce wordly love and join the order of the Brothers Minor (Andrachuk, "Function" 28, "Missing Third Part" 179, "Italian Influence" 49; Nepaulsingh 163; Gerli, "Penitential Tradition" 99). Yet a series of quotes from other texts presented by Castro Lingl shows that "his statement seems to represent a recurrent motif used by his contemporaries and predecessors, and reflected the writers' attitude towards mythology and their need to reconcile it with their faith" ("Back to the text" 51). Moreover, the author-persona does not reject the "ficçiones" of ancient and medieval authors. On the contrary, he declares that he himself follows their example.

> Ficçiones, digo, al poético fin de aprovechar y venir a tí en plazer con las fablas que quieren seguir lo que naturaleza no puede sofrir, aprovechar con el seso alegórico que trahe consigo la ruda letra, aunque pareçe del todo fallir; la cual si requieres de sano entender, armas te dizen contra el amor; ni porque mi tratado a mí se endereçe en obras mundanas o en fechos de amores, por él te amonesto que devas amar, o si amas perseverar; que en señal de amistad te escrivo de amor, por mí que sientas la grand fallía de los amadores y poca fiança de los amigos; e por mí juzgues a tí amador. (156)

The author-persona's *ficçión* is not "natural" or mimetic. He suggests to Medina that the account of his vision can be read allegorically. However, every text, the "ruda letra," is potentially allegorical; the narrator introduces his work as a text obviously not allegorical ("pareçe del todo fallir"). He continues to suggest not *allegoresis*, but an exegesis of love: the text must be read with "sano entender" in order to provide "arms against love." Medina is inscribed in the prologue as a reader very much like the readers of the *Bursario*: he is supposed to recognize the type of love, and approve or reject it. Similar to the reader of the exchange between Troylos and Criseyde in the *Bursario*, he has at hand the author-narrator's version of the amatory conflict and a letter by his beloved ("te dirá la su epístula"; *Siervo* 157).

Siervo's second prologue does not bluntly reject love, which in its various manifestations is truly paramount for the medieval mind.

The question is what kind of love he promises to battle or to alleviate. The author-persona does not primarily address Medina as a superior or inquisitor but as a friend and equal "en bien amar" (154). Both the author-persona and Medina are lovers whose feelings are not requited. The second prologue promises *remedia* against this kind of love.[139]

Again, there is no outright rejection of love; on the contrary, Medina should be a constant lover ("por él te amonesto que devas amar, o si amas perseverar"; 156). The author-persona presents his "case" as an example which will demonstrate to his friend the great mistake of lovers like him ("la grand fallía de los amadores"; 156). Analyzing the author-persona's story, Medina will realize that he is already a real lover on the path of loving and not being loved ("e por mí juzgues a tí amador"; 156). The second prologue, then, does not persuade Medina to renounce love but to persevere on his path. The author-persona's account is intended to provide him guidance on this course, by way of illustrating the dangers, mistakes and remedies of love.

In the sequel the reader learns about the beginnings of the narrator's liaison with a most beautiful and noble woman ("grand fermosura e desigualdat de estado"; 157). He also emphasizes the exchange of looks and the solitary, sad *cogitationes*: "me dava a la grand soledat, maginando con tristeza" (157). Yet, even though the circumstances for a *philocaptio* were given, the narrator did not contract lovesickness immediately.

> Formado consejo de mis çinco sirvientes, luego prendí por señora, e juré servidumbre, non discordando parte de mí salud, esa que es madre de todas virtudes, con temor de lo pasado, que contrastava lo por venir diziendo: [...]. (157-58)

Similar to the "feigned" love Baena suggests to the courtly lover,[140] the narrator of *Siervo* deliberately chooses to inflict *amor hereos* on

---

[139] Lacarra points out that *Siervo* is a "reprobatio amoris" and "remedium amoris," yet relates the rejection of love to the religious and spiritual conversion of the author-persona and Rodríguez del Padrón ("*Siervo*" 153). In note three of the same article (150), she announces a study on the influence of Boccaccio's *Corbaccio*, which is, as I have argued, essentially a "weapon against love."

[140] See above chapter I.

himself with the help of his interior senses.[141] From the perspective of a physician like López de Villalobos, this description reflects a widespread misperception of passionate love.

> Los enamorados tienen ajena la imaginacion, y la voluntad con ella; y con todo esto, ha venido en costumbre de la gente que á los otros desvariados llaman locos, et á estos no, sino galanes; y la causa de su manifiesto error nació y tuvo principio de ver que en los amores cada uno entra por su voluntad propria y por su proprio querer [...]. Y no embargante que entre por su propria voluntad, ya despues que está dentro, enfermo está [...]. (*Anfitrion* 489)

Rodríguez del Padrón, however, not only presents the protagonist's *philocaptio* as a sane decision but exalts it, by having it sanctioned by a venerated referee. He states that the "mother of all virtues" and a "part of his health" do not object. In the margins of the manuscript this entity, which assumes the voice, is identified as "La discreción" (158, n. 38).[142] The author of the first prologue had identified Syndéresis as "discreçión" (154). Indeed, Syndéresis appears in the final section of *Siervo* as a "dueña ançiana, vestida de negro, y siete donzellas" (207-08), which can be interpreted as the seven virtues.[143] It is not too far-fetched, then, to identify the narrator's first interlocutor as Syndéresis, who initiates the vision part of *Siervo* and brings it to a close. Syndéresis first blames the narrator for

---

[141] Rodríguez del Padrón was evidently familiar with the concept of love-as-sickness. In the poem *¡Ham, ham, huíd que ravio!* we find a hyberbolic reference to *amor hereos*; the speaker presents himself as transformed into a dog (ed. Hernández Alonso, *Obras* 329-30), suffering from lycanthrophy (Gilderman, "Apoteosis" 40). Dom Pedro adapts the phrase "çinco servientes" from *Siervo*, apparently referring to the external senses (*Sátira* 102).

[142] Dante's description of his own *philocaptio* in the *Vita nuova* is imbued with medical lore; however, instead of condemning his amatory captivity, he presents himself as a modelic courtly lover, revalorizing the corruption of health as a "reasonable," ennobling decision: "E avvegna che la sua imagine, la quale continuatamente meco stava, fosse baldanza d'Amore a segnoreggiare me, tuttavia era di sì noblissima vertù, che nulla volta sofferse che Amore mi reggesse sanza lo fedele consiglio de la ragione in quelle cose là ove cotale consiglio fosse utile a udire" ("And although her image, which continually stayed with me, gave Love its strength to rule over me, it was nevertheless of such noble power that at no time did it allow Love to rule me without the faithful counsel or reason, in those things where such counsel was useful to heed"; 48-49).

[143] See below.

giving up his inborn, natural liberty ("libertad que en tu naçimiento te dio naturaleza [...]"; 158) and not following her. Nevertheless, as the introduction to her sermon indicates, she does not entirely condemn the lover's decision. Reciting a vituperative poem against love composed by him earlier, she argues that the lover cannot expect a positive outcome. Unless he makes "perpetual peace" ("perpétua [sic] paz"; 159) with love, he will suffer "perpetual pain" ("dolor perdurable"; 159). In other words, Syndéresis advises the lover to accept Love's reign and embrace his feelings with good will.[144] He will then achieve the desirable emotional state Aquinas describes in his *Summa*. In order to be morally good, emotions must be voluntary (vol. 19, p. 32-33; 1a.2æ. 24,1) and checked by Understanding (vol. 19, p. 36-37; 1a.2æ. 24,2); the final goal for the lover is balance and peace between *voluntas*, *ratio* and *passiones*, represented in *Siervo* by *Libre albedrío*, *Entendimiento* and *Coraçón*.[145]

Coraçón supports this counsel: "fazed paz con el amor" (Rodríguez del Padrón, *Siervo* 160). The newly captured lover resumes the relation of his love affair. In spite of progressively positive responses in a nonverbal exchange, the Siervo has not made his peace with Love. He is saddened by the impossibility of expressing his "intrínseco fuego" openly (162). Violating Love's rules, he confides in a friend who encourages him to send her a letter. His letter/poem is received with benevolence, and a meeting is arranged. The joy of the Siervo turns to despair when he is betrayed by his friend, who incites the lady's ire. However, the Siervo's passions, "los primeros movimientos que son fuera del humano poder" (164), remain unchanged and rage out of control. He retires to a deserted place and engages in an incessant reminiscive and imaginative process: "todos días remenvrándome lo pasado, me dava a la siguiente contemplaçión" (165).

---

[144] The last of Love's arrows that pierces the Lover's heart in the *Romance of the Rose* "is Fair Seeming; it does not allow any lover to repent of serving Love, no matter what woes he may suffer." It is anointed with an unguent: "Without the sweet ointment I would have been dead and in an evil plight" (Guillaume de Lorris and Jean de Meun 56). After the *philocaptio* is completed the lover makes his peace with Love, becoming his loyal vassal.

[145] According to Diego de San Pedro's *Sermón*, in an evidently courtly context, the "most important consideration is that he [sc. the lover] is suffering in a good cause. He should think of the excellence of the lady who has caused his passion; if he is unhappy it is because that is her wish, and he should be glad to suffer for her sake" (Whinnom, *Diego de San Pedro* 89).

In this *contemplaçión*, the Siervo wanders through the "dark jungle of his thoughts" ("la escura selva de sus pensamientos"; 165) until he arrives at the Garden of Fortune. In the Garden he finds three paths, which he designates as "tres varios pensamientos" (166). In the bark of the trees he finds carved his *mote*: "INFORTUNE" (167). He is unfortunate (because his love is not reciprocated), in Fortune('s garden), and he is without fortune because he has not yet made up his mind. In this state he experiences a transformation: "fue alterado fuera de mí" (167). In an exteriorization of his psychic conflict the three faculties of his rational soul emerge.

Free Will rushes down "la desçiente vía, que es la desperaçión" (167). He appeals to Understanding to follow him with the prospect of guiding him to the Elysian Fields where the river Lethe flows. In the waters of this river the "furioso amador," the lover suffering from painful memories, can find "olvidança, solo reparo" (168). In his response Entendimiento warns the Siervo about the dangers of the Underworld. The Siervo is mistaken in expecting to achieve the "gloria" through suicide. Desperate lovers suffer only pain in the Underworld (169).[146]

> Sé yo bien cierto que antes del quarto çerco donde penan los que mueren por bien amar, te será vedado el paso; ca serás luego arrastrado de las guardas de aquel donde penan los infortunados que por fuir los peligros de la sinisestra fortuna, más quisieron morir que padeçer y bevir; donde no es mi voluntat de pasar, ni seguir tu dañada compañía. (171)

Entendimiento's objection aims, after all, not at the passage to the underworld which every mortal must inevitably undertake. On the other hand, Siervo's intention to commit suicide will result in disaster because he will not reach the fourth circle where those suffer who died for "good love" ("bien amar"). He will be condemned to the region of those who tried to escape their sinister fortune and did not live and suffer. From Entendimiento's reasoning we can infer that "bien amar" means constancy also in unhappy love. Even the real lovers suffer in the otherworld; suffering is an essential part

---

[146] After the Castle of Jealousy has been erected, the Lover of the *Romance of the Rose* emphasizes that Hope is essential for the true lover's valor (Guillaume de Lorris and Jean de Meun 91).

of love. Entendimiento refuses to accompany the Siervo on the path of desperation, which is not the path of "good love." After the harangue, it departs on the "angosta senda, la qual es la vida contemplativa de no amar" (166).

Free Will is not satisfied with Understanding's answer and calls *Coraçón* who is far away in the temple of Athena. It answers that it is not in possession of its liberty, since Siervo has pledged servitude to his "muy generosa señora," and "que su voluntat no era de jamás aquella desviar a que[e]l arbor de Venos, deesa de amores, bien amando le demostrara" (172). Heart/Memory is, then, eternally in a prison of love, the temple of Pallas Athene; it judges this captivity "good love" ("bien amando").

According to Herrero, the narrator, "engrossed in his pain, [...] enters into his own soul and finds himself to be a divided being" ("Allegorical Structure" 753). A careful reading of *Siervo*, however, reveals that the narrator has projected himself into an imaginary landscape that reflects his emotional state and the choices open to him in his love relationship. The imagery presented by the author-persona is a (psycho-)analytical tool.

In accordance with the contemporary psychological model, the lover conceptualizes his psycho-emotional conflict in the form of the somewhat autonomous faculties of the soul. As we have seen, the peculiarity of his *philocaptio* lies in the fact that he is not a victim of a malfunction of his interior senses, but deliberately chooses to serve his lady. Consequently, he turns in his *contemplaçión* to the rational soul and its faculties which are ultimately responsible for his current state. Free Will, Understanding and Heart are integrated into his vision. The first prologue is correct in designating them as the "tres partes del omne" (153). In the Middle Ages the heart was frequently considered the seat of memory (Carruthers, *Book of Memory* 9). It is also central in the phenomenology of amatory passion, since the *appetitus concupiscibilis* produced by an enticing mental image results in a boost of humid, hot *pneuma*.[147] Therefore, heart as a metaphor for memory expresses the psychosomatic emotional impact of the continuous recollective process the lover undergoes.[148]

---

[147] See above chapter I.

[148] Vives underscores the crucial role the heart plays in thought processes: "De aquí dimana que el estado y hábito del corazón influya no poco en el pensamiento y

As the first prologue states, the three faculties are associated with three different paths. Nevertheless, it is crucial to acknowledge that the paths presented by the narrator-persona are *not* the paths of loving and being loved, loving and not being loved, and neither loving nor being loved. The Siervo has his vision at a moment in his life when his love is not reciprocated. The path of "loving and being loved" does not exist at this moment and cannot be presented as an option in the Garden of Fortune. He has three choices. He can follow Free Will on the way of "desperation" and suicide, hoping to achieve the eternal "gloria" of the lovers or relief from this amatory pain. Understanding rejects this option because it means the ruin of the Siervo, who can only expect to suffer eternally among the fainthearted "infortunados." Entendimiento follows the narrow path of not loving and contemplation. Again, for the Siervo, in the grip of his passion, this is not really an alternative. Entendimiento recommends that he endure the pain of love in order to join the ones who died for good loving (Rodríguez del Padrón, *Siervo* 171). A similar "solution" is proposed by Memory who is "bien amando," dedicated to never forgetting the beloved.

The Siervo standing in the Garden of Fortune must make a resolution; that is why he calls Free Will "guardián de los caminos" (167). At the end of the faculties' speeches they depart on the three paths; the narrator is deserted "de libre alvedrío, apartado del entendimiento, desapoderado del coraçón [...]" (172). He has not physically moved in the Garden of Fortune, nor did he accept any of the solutions presented to him.[149] Once more, he rages against love: "forçado me fue maldezir al alto Cupido, fijo de la deesa, la fadal disposiçión de la triste ventura, e la causa porque yo avía de falleçer por amar [...]" (172). He recites a poem "por maldiçión" of his lady. It is quite obvious that he has not followed the counsel of Syndéresis; he has not made his peace with love.

He enters a stage of psychic chaos: his spirit is about to leave him. His "çinco sentidos", the interior senses, are in complete dis-

---

la inteligencia; por eso se llama a los hombres 'cuerdos', o al contrario 'no cuerdos' o insensatos; [...] A veces hasta se ha tomado el corazón por inteligencia misma, y así leemos en las *Sagradas Escrituras*: 'Del corazón provienen los pensamientos' [...]" (p. 80; bk. 2, ch. 6).

[149] After the *Estoria de dos amadores* we learn that his thoughts ("pensar") were inclined to follow the path of "perdiçión" (202-03). The narrator himself has not moved.

array, circling him and moaning (173). In this life-threatening crisis he remembers happier times when his love was reciprocated. The reader familiar with the concept of *amor hereos* is not surprised that these memories only aggravate the suffering. Death is approaching, invoked by the Siervo himself.

> ¡O regurosa y mal comedida muerte, deseosa de mí! [...] ¿por qué así no te plase que yo deva morir por la más leal señora que bive, según que te plogo de otorgar al digno de perpetua membrança Ardanlier, hijo del Rey Creos de Mondoya e de la reina Senesta? (173-74)

Only now does he observe the physicians' precepts against the devastating, incessant *cogitationes*. *In extremis* he activates a different memory. In the transition to the *Estoria de dos amadores*, he evokes again the motif of the "perpetua membrança", now contrasting the hell of incessant memories the patient of lovesickness suffers with memories invested with markedly positive meaning: Ardanlier is presented as an exemplary and memorable figure.

Ardanlier, son of the king Creos, falls in love with Liessa, the daughter of the Lord of Lira. Together with Ardanlier's educator Lamidoras, they decide to flee from Creos who opposes their relationship. In a journey through Europe Ardanlier proves himself a chivalric champion. Among the many women who fall in love with him is Yrena, daughter of the French king. She gives him the key to a bracelet symbolizing her amorous captivity. After having helped the Emperor, and after many perils, Ardanlier and Liessa arrive in the Galician city of Padrón, where a secret palace is carved in a rock. There they live happily until Creos finds the entrance to the subterranean palace. In Ardanlier's absence he kills the pregnant Liessa. When Ardanlier arrives he discovers his dead lover and learns from Lamidoras the circumstances of his father's terrible deed. He refrains from seeking revenge by himself. After writing a letter to Yrena in which he reports the tragic events, he commits suicide. Lamidoras delivers the letter to Yrena and spreads the news all over Europe. The kings and the emperor vow to punish Creos. Meanwhile, Yrena travels to Galicia and devotes her life to the memory of Ardanlier and Liessa. She orders the construction of a precious tomb for the two lovers. Lamidoras dies soon after his mission and is buried in the first chamber of the tomb. After her death, Yrena is buried in the second chamber. Afterwards, the palace becomes enchanted and can only be conquered by the most loyal lover. After many years and many frustrated attempts by the most noble men, Macías penetrates the tomb, and the spell is broken. The tomb/palace opens miraculously three times a year and becomes the center of a pilgrimage of love.

The *Estoria de dos amadores* apparently clashes in many aspects with the frame narration, with its convoluted prose, prosimetrum form, use of imagery, narrative ruptures and inconclusiveness. Thus, it serves to highlight the Siervo's chaotic state of mind. Yet the contrasts naturally raise the question of narrative coherence of the *Siervo libre* and the function of the *Estoria*. Some students of *Siervo* point out the disparate dimensions of the *Estoria* in the context of the work and the poor integration of the tale (Lida de Malkiel, "Vida y obra" 323; Hernández Alonso, "Introducción" 54, "Rodríguez del Padrón" 16). Nevertheless, the majority of critics acknowledge the importance of the *Estoria* as an *exemplum* to the Siervo and the reader. Opinion, however, is divided as to whether to see the *Estoria* as a negative or positive example to the Siervo.

To address this problem it is advisable to clarify what the author-persona understood by "exemplo" (Rodríguez del Padrón, *Siervo* 197). According to Peter von Moos, an *exemplum* is in the first place a *memorabile*. It has multiple functions and does not necessarily present the solution to a problem, but may as well present it (x-xi); the meaning of the *exemplum* depends on the context and ultimately on the reader's interpretive frame of reference.[150] The medical-sensitive reader realizes that *Siervo*'s *exemplum* temporarily alleviates the narrator's amorous *cogitationes* and their noxious psychosomatic consequences. The author-persona's recollective and associative process is obviously triggered by Ardanlier's violent death. However, the *exemplum* as a whole does not provide him with a solution because his love affair is by no means comparable to Ardanlier and Liessa's story. However, the *Estoria* can shed new light on

---

[150] Dom Pedro uses Ardanlier as an *exemplum* of a desperate lover who prefers death to a long, painful life without the beloved: "queriendo ante muerte açellerada que larga vida con ansia e con tormento" (*Sátira* 39). From his summary of the *Estoria de dos amadores*, the character of Yrena and the crucial tale of the establishment of the commemorative cult are conspicuously absent. The *exemplum* is used in this context by the lovesick and unreliable narrator (see below); hence it does not shed light on the meaning of the *Estoria* in *Siervo*.

his own quandary and help him to restate his initial question: "why can I not die for the most loyal Lady alive?" (174).

The opening paragraph of the *Estoria* describes the nature of Ardanlier and Liessa's love.

> E las fuerças del temor acreçentava[n] en los coraçones de aquellos las grandes furias del amor a tal son, que[e]el gentil infante, ardiendo en fuego venéreo, que más no podía durar el desseo [...]. (Rodríguez del Padrón, *Siervo* 174)

Given the ardent, passionate love of Ardanlier, he behaves in a remarkably reasonable way. He leaves his kingdom well provided with riches and faithful servants. His chivalric prowess is not affected at all by his passion. He creates a sumptuous palace for himself, his wife and their offspring. Ardanlier, then, has his passion well under control. He embodies the paradigm not of the courtly lover but of the caring husband.[151]

A disturbing element in this picture of ideal chivalric love is Ardanlier's relationship with the princess Yrena. Their liaison actually represents the strain of courtly love in the *Estoria* (Weissberger, "'Habla el auctor'" 231). Yrena is also passionately in love with Ardanlier ("muy apassionada"; *Siervo* 176). In secrecy, "con pavor de Liessa" (176), she orders a golden bracelet with a lock "en señal de buen amar" (176) and gives the key to the bracelet to Ardanlier.

> Rogándole por gentileza que en su menbrança le pluguiese de la cativar y tomar en prisionera con sus valientes manos, pues con la amorosa vista la avía cativado; e que promessa hazía [al] alto Cupido, hijo de la deesa, a las reliquias leyes venéreas, nunca jamás trocar la invención, ni soltar de la figurada prisión su cativo coraçón, hasta que al señor de las llaves pluguiese abrir y librar de la pena a la padeçiente Irena. (176-77)

Ardanlier does not hesitate to accept the compromise: "no tardó cumplir su mandamiento" (177). After Liessa's death it becomes clear that the *philocaptio* was mutual. Ardanlier confesses in his last letter: "desque entendida la firme fe tuya; siempre ardí en intrínseco amor de ti, por fuir la deslealtat, ella ni tu sabidoras [...]" (187). This declaration of love strikes Castro Lingl as "awkward

---

[151] Impey calls Liessa a "spouse-like beloved" ("Ovid" 292).

and, more importantly, senseless for Yrena [...]" ("Back to the text" 57). Also Deyermond argues that there is a contradiction between Ardanlier's confession to Yrena and his rejection of her love by way of voluntary death ("Punto de vista" 81-82). Finally, against textual evidence of Ardanlier's "ardent" passionate love for Yrena, Lacarra associates Ardanlier and Liessa with "el amor venéreo" and Yrena and Ardanlier with "el amor cortés idealizado" ("*Siervo*" 164). However, only Ardanlier's passionate love for Yrena and loyalty to Liessa makes him and the *Estoria* truly an *exemplo*.

In his European quest Ardanlier makes many friends.

> E bolando su fama en pregón de las obras, vino en requesta de la famosa y linda hermana del rey de Almaçia, e la gentil Alexandra, hija del grand duque Vitoldo, y otras infantes damas que venían en su espera, atendiendo el fin de la nombrada empresa que traía por amor de Liessa, no pensando que voluntad fuesse jamás servir la señora que servía. (Rodríguez del Padrón, *Siervo* 177)

He captures the hearts of many women who do not really believe in his consummate dedication to Liessa. In his letter to Yrena he expresses the fear of succumbing to the temptation.

> E ya solo pavor he de mí, predicarse de mí tan gran crueldat, ¿¡e cómo es de consentir yo ser amado y no amador de tal presionera de mí!? ¡O desseada Irena! (186)

He argues that he cannot follow his feelings for Yrena because she herself would have to judge him "desleal" (187). His suicide, then, is not motivated by despair over the death of his beloved, but by the fear of disloyalty, born of passionate feelings for another woman. Ardanlier is capable of controlling his passions; he is a "reasonable" lover who does not just follow his appetites. Hence it is significant that in his vow to Yrena he addresses not Venus, but Minerva, the goddess of Wisdom (187). He is a loyal servant of his lady, not because he is madly in love, but in spite of his ardent love for another woman. His suicide is the ultimate act of loyalty and *bien amar*.[152]

---

[152] The importance of loyalty in the *Estoria* has been acknowledged by most students of the *Estoria de dos amadores* (Lida de Malkiel, "Vida y obras" 323; Gilderman, *Rodríguez de la Cámara* 105; Impey, "Ovid" 293; Grieve 21).

The theme of love transcending death is repeated in the *Estoria* by Ardanlier's thirteen dogs, his teacher Lamidoras and, most importantly, by Yrena's course of action after Ardanlier's suicide. Together with the letter, she receives the key to her bracelet, and is thus figuratively released from her amatory captivity.[153] Since the person of her obsession has perished she is also actually free. Yet she chooses to remain a loyal lover. Of course, the nature of her love changes because Ardanlier and the possibility of fulfillment of her desire have disappeared. Her change in attitude is expressed by her "conversion" to "la muy clara Vesta, deesa de castidat" (191). Like Ardanlier she sublimates her carnal passion in loyal service to an unattainable beloved. She becomes a "siervo libre de amor."

The *Estoria* presents "bien amar" as a conflation of the themes of love, loyalty and memory.[154] Yrena converts the secret palace which was consecrated to the goddess of love into a temple of Vesta and establishes a commemorative cult. A tomb is erected with an epitaph that epigrammatically expresses the *Estoria*'s exemplarity.

> EXEMPLO Y PERPETUA MEMBRANÇA,
> CON GRAND DOLOR,
> SEA A VOS, AMADORES,
> LA CRUEL MUERTE DE LOS MUY LEALES
> ARDANLIER Y LIESSA,
> FALLEÇIDOS POR BIEN AMAR,
> [...]
> DESPIERTEN DEL GRAND SUEÑO, E SUS MUY
> PURIFICAS ANIMAS
> POSSEAN PERDURABLE FOLGANÇA. (197)

---

[153] Since the object of a passionate obsession is a memory, Ardanlier's death does not mean the end of her passionate love; Garci Sánchez de Badajoz evokes the theme:
> La forma vista y amada
> la memoria recibió,
> y su puerta se cerró
> con fe de amores sellada;
> sellada de tal manera,
> que su estoria
> nunca pueda en la memoria
> despintarse, aunque ella muera.

(cit. Serés, *Transformación de los amantes* 72-73).

[154] In Dante's *Vita nuova* and Petrarch's *Rime* the lover remains faithful to the memory image of the deceased beloved; see Castells (*Rojas and the Renaissance* 18-19).

"Perpetua membrança" is at the same time the condition for and the reward of loyalty. This is what constitutes "bien amar." In qualifying Ardanlier and Liessa's souls as "puríficas," the *Estoria* unmistakably places the lovers in a desirable location of the underworld, i.e. the fourth circle, which Entendimiento had assigned to those who die for "bien amar" (171). Yrena becomes a follower of theirs.

> La qual, muy apassionada por su falleçimiento, en membrança contínua de aquellos, siguió después en tan áspera vida a los dos amadores, por los librar de las penas, que, por continuaçión de los años, el affanado spíritu ovo dexar forçado la compañía del muy generoso cuerpo, que oy día reposa por gloria y fama en el medio tinel del segundo albergue. (198).

From the fact that Yrena wants to soothe their pain, it cannot be inferred that they are punished in Hell or Purgatory.[155] There is no need for Yrena and her followers to do penance for the sinners' souls. Penance is most certainly not of interest in the *Estoria* because Ardanlier committed suicide to avoid a sin against the precepts of good love.[156] Yrena's task is to commemorate the lovers and guarantee their afterlife in the collective memory, thus easing their pain until Judgment Day, after which they can enjoy eternal freedom ("perdurable folgança").[157]

Of course, perpetual memory can only be achieved if Yrena's commemorative service is prolonged after her death. She converts the secret palace into a *lieu de mémoire* and becomes part of it with her own burial. The palace/tomb turns into the Mecca of a pilgrimage of love. Hyperbolically underscoring the importance of loyalty,

---

[155] Nepaulsingh argues that what Yrena, the pilgrims, and the narrator believe to be Paradise is, actually, Hell; this contrasts with the "true vision of Synderesis" (163-64); see also Herrero ("Allegorical Structure" 755). Since there is no indication of Penance in the *Estoria*, his opinion rests on the mistaken premise that Syndéresis can be identified unequivocally as Penance.

[156] Herrero's contention that Yrena and her maidens have become nuns ("Allegorical Structure" 761) and Dolz-Ferrer's claim that Yrena can be allegorically interpreted as representing the superior path of neither loving nor being loved are untenable. The hierarchical arrangement of the tomb, with Ardanlier and Liessa in the first chamber and Yrena in the second, clearly shows that they professed the same "religion," indicating the superiority of the couple in love matters.

[157] As numerous studies in the last years demonstrate, commemoration was of paramount importance to the medieval cultures. Commemoration established a "real presence" of the death and communion between the commemorating community and their ancestors (Oexle).

the sepulcher becomes enchanted, and can only be penetrated by the most loyal of lovers. For many years the most noble men's attempts are frustrated until, finally, Macías, the famous poet and the epitome of the martyr of love, conquers the tomb "por su grand gentileza, lealtat, destreza y grand fortaleza" (199). In a surprising twist, the narrator establishes a link between himself and the enchanted tomb of the now-mythic lovers.

> De la qual [sc. de la cámara], en señal de vitoria, el buen gadisán [sc. Maçías] tomó nombradía [158] y todos aquellos que d[e]él desçendieron, de los quales yo siendo el menor, rico del nombre de ser de los buenos; e sólo heredado en su lealtad. (202)

At the end of the *Estoria* the narrator resurfaces to inscribe himself in a genealogy of loyal lovers. Furthermore, the figure of Macías is also significant because he provides a "real life" paradigm of achieving *perpetua membrança*: via his poetry Macías sublimated and transcended his own love quandaries, creating a literary *persona* which was honored and remembered by posterity (Martínez Barbeito).[159]

At the end of his evocation of the *Estoria de dos amadores,* the author-persona remembers his heritage of loyal loving. However, the *Estoria* does not serve as an *exemplum* answering the Siervo's initial question. It does not address the issue of whether suicide is a solution to his amatory problems. It was the only solution for Ardanlier, because otherwise he would not have proven a loyal lover. It was not a solution for Yrena, whose suicide would have been an act of despair. It is obvious that loyalty is at the heart of "buen amar" in the *Estoria*. Furthermore, all the main characters in the *Estoria* lay the foundations of their own "perpetua membrança": Ardanlier with his suicide and letter to Yrena, Yrena with the construction of the temple and her commemorative service, Macías with his prowess and his literature. On the other hand, the desperate Siervo in the Garden of Fortune is inclined to suicide because he wants to forget his pain; he will be forgotten not only by his estranged beloved but also by posterity, because his disloyalty is not

---

[158] The narrator alludes here to the author's family, the De la Cámara.

[159] Weissberger notes that Rodríguez del Padrón relies on the reader's familiarity with Macías's biography ("Authority Figures" 257).

memorable. Particularly because the narrator's case can be contrasted with Ardanlier's story on every point (Andrachuk, "Function" 34), the *Estoria* provides him with orientation. The question for the Siervo is now no longer how to regain the lady's favor or end his pain, but how to prove his loyalty and transform it into *perpetua membrança*. The author-persona's course in the last section of the *Siervo* is directed by these maxims.

The Siervo awakes from his dreamlike state ("la fabla que pasado entre mí avía [...] como de un grave sueño") and is still filled with "furia de amor" (202). Yet he obviously has changed his "pensar," which he pleads to turn back from the "deçiente vía de perdición" and follow the "muy agra senda donde era la verde oliva, consagrada a Minerva, qu[e]el entendimiento nos enseñava quando partió airado de mí" (202-03). In his description of the Garden of Fortune the narrator had labeled this path of Minerva as "la vida contemplativa de no amar" (166). Entendimiento, however, advised against desperation and suicide instead of "padeçer and bevir" (171). We also must remember that Ardanlier invoked Minerva when revealing his love to Yrena (187). The narrator himself is uncertain about the whereabouts of Entendimiento and the right path to take. After his paralysis in the Garden of Fortune, he begins to move swiftly in the imaginary landscape. He asks birds, "montañeros," and "fieros salvajes" for direction; he is only ridiculed by them. He recites a long piece of poetry in which he underscores his natural freedom:

> Aunque me vedes así
> cativo, libre naçí
> Cativo, libre naçí,
> y después, como sandío,
> perdí mi libre alvedrío,
> que no so señor de mí. (203)

He insists that he is not slave of love.

> Por ende digo y porfío
> que por servir leal mente,
> no soy siervo, mas sirviente (204)

In this insistence in his free will and his deliberate loyal service, he recalls the origins of his love when he decided to accept "servidumbre" with the conditional consent of Syndéresis (158). Connecting with the *Estoria de dos amadores*, he evokes Macías toward the end of the poem.

> No sé qué postremería
> ayan buena los mis días
> quando el gentil Maçías
> priso muerte por tal vía. (207)

This passage seen in isolation is ambiguous: Macías died because of love, or he captured ("priso") or defeated love through his loyalty; it can be read as a glorification of Macías's loyal love or a rejection of his example. Brownlee, for instance, sees in this passage a distancing of the narrator from his famous ancestor ("Generic Status" 638). Yet, in the light of the *Estoria de dos amadores* which openly celebrates Macías as a loyal lover and the shared preoccupation about posterity ("postremería") it is safe to assume that Macías is evoked here as a modelic forerunner. In the continuation of the poem we see the author-persona emulating Macías.

> Por ende, en remembrança
> cantaré con amargura
> cuidados y maginança,
> *cativo de mi tristura*. (207)

In commemoration of his literary forebear he himself has become a poet, singing about his sorrow and "imaginations." He is no longer in the grip of his passion, but a prisoner of his sorrow ("cativo de mi tristura"), because his free decision to be a servant of an ungrateful lady implies sadness and suffering.[160] The poem therefore marks a step in the author-persona's sublimation of his unhappy love affair.

So far the narrator has moved in his imaginative quest through a wilderness where he found only animals, peasants, savages who show no compassion. Moreover, they can hardly be considered a

---

[160] According to Impey, the key to the "comprensión del proceso amoroso del amante que de siervo de amor se convierte en sirviente, y de sirviente en siervo libre de amor; que pertenece a la amada, pero no del todo; que es cativo, pero no del amor sino de su propia 'tristura'" ("Poesía y prosa" 182); see also Hernández Alonso (*Rodríguez del Padrón* 22-23).

worthy audience for his love story. Now the narrator is moved into the highest trees of his "dark imaginations" in order to "devisar algún poblado" (207), a place of civilization (207). In another rapid shift, he finds himself at the shore of "the big sea" (207), where he has his anagnorisis with Syndéresis.

The identification of the figure of Syndéresis has inspired critics of *Siervo libre de amor* to rather diverging interpretations. Some recognize Conscience in its aspects of habitual conscience (Nepaulsingh 163; Andrachuk, "Function" 32; Impey, "Poesía y prosa" 181) or the worm of conscience (Gerli, "Old French Source" 12). Others see in her Prudence (Fernández Jiménez 187; Impey, "Poesía y prosa" 181), a representation of a priest (Andrachuk, "Missing Third Part" 177), of Penitence (Cátedra 146), of Gonzalo de Medina (Hernández Alonso, *Rodríguez del Padrón* 18, 40; Vigier, "Fiction épistolaire" 240; Zaderenko 288) or even of the Arthurian fairy Morgaine (Gilderman, "Apoteosis" 49). Considering the consensus about the identification of other images in *Siervo*, such as Entendimiento or the White Poplar, this disagreement is significant.

This variance on how to identify Syndéresis is not only due to the "abrupt" ending of the text; also a contemporary reader could find indicators of more than one meaning of the image. In other words, the final pages of *Siervo* must be read allegorically.[161] In contrast with the narrator's preceding vision, the appearance of Syndéresis, her ship and its crew is described in considerable detail. This, together with the fact that she is not identified immediately by the narrator, encourages the reader to engage in an interpretive activity.

The "ruda letra" of the text is the logical starting point for the interpretation of the picture. Syndéresis has been rightly associated with the scholastic concept of conscience. In the *Summa* Thomas Aquinas discusses the question of whether synderesis is a special faculty or a habitus (1a. 79,12). In this context he gives a concise description of the function of synderesis: "synderesis is said to incite us to good and to deter us from evil in that through first principles we both begin and judge what we find" ("synderesis dicitur instigare ad bonum et murmurare de malo, inquantum per prima principia procedimus ad inveniendum et judicamus inventa"; vol.

---

[161] See above.

11, p. 188-90; 1a. 79,12). In Aquinas's thinking synderesis is a habitus of the first principles of practical reason; these universal principles lead the practical intellect in discerning good from evil, guiding man's actions toward the good and renouncing the evil (Delhaye 112-14).

This Thomasian concept lends itself to interpretations which emphasize the importance of the penitential tradition and the final departure on the path of Understanding. However, the medieval concept of synderesis is more complex. The Franciscan school connects synderesis with the orectic faculties and will. Bonaventure sees it as a natural appetite for the good which can be obstructed by the violence of a passion (Delhaye 111). A reader approaching *Siervo* with this conception discerns in the narrator's encounter with Syndéresis a restoration of Free Will.[162]

As Nepaulsingh points out (163), there is also the influential tradition of the commentaries on Jerome's exegesis of Ezekiel, which was incorporated into the *Glossa Ordinaria*.[163] Jerome interprets Ezekiel's vision as a listing of the psychological faculties (Delhaye 107). The man symbolizes reason, the bull the concupiscible, the lion the irascible, the eagle synderesis, here understood as the source of moral judgments. "It [sc. Synderesis] is properly illustrated by the eagle who does not mingle with the other animals, and can pounce down upon them. It is the 'spirit' that speaks for God in us through indescribable groanings" ("quam proprie aquilae deputant, non se miscentem tribus sed ipsa errantia corrigentem... Hic est spiritus qui interpellat pro nobis gemitibus inenarrabilibus"; qtd. in Delhaye 107, n. 10). Like reason, synderesis has the function of checking the lower appetites. This image of the eagle hovering above the struggling faculties and then swooping down on them could explain its absence in the confrontation of the narrator with the principal faculties of his rational soul.

---

[162] Compare Vives's description of *voluntad*: "La facultad que realiza este fin [sc. desear el bien] es, en los brutos, un apetito sensual; en el hombre la voluntad. Es ésta, por tanto, 'aquella facultad o fuerza del alma por la cual deseamos lo bueno y aborrecemos lo malo, con la razón por guía'; esta guía en los animales es la Naturaleza. Ha, pues, en la voluntad dos actos: la propensión o adopción del bien y el odio al mal. Privación de ambos fines se da cuando la voluntad inerte no se inclina a ninguna de las dos partes" (p. 96-97; bk. 2, ch. 11).

[163] The *Glossa* was composed by various authors in the 12th century and became an important authoritative text (Delhaye 107, n. 10).

What the theological concepts of synderesis have in common is the idea that a superior instance corrects a malfunction of the psychic faculties, be it Understanding, Will or Judgement, [164] guiding man back onto the right path of God. Yet *Siervo* is not a theological *tractatus*. I have been arguing that Syndéresis emerges at the beginning of the Siervo's vision, advising him not to renounce his passionate love but to make "his peace" with love. Syndéresis is absent in the debate between the faculties and his erring through the imaginary landscape. Like the eagle swooping down on the other animals, she reappears when Entendimiento and Coraçon and, above all, the *exemplum* of Ardanlier, Yrena and Macías have directed the author-persona toward a solution: the lover has to endure love's pain in order to prove his loyalty; he must willingly accept amatory servitude without hope of remuneration from his lady. Since synderesis is the faculty that checks a misdirected will, Syndéresis, an image that embodies conscience, is the ideal figure to bring the account of the frustrated love affair to a "happy end." She will repeat her advice to the author-narrator, who is now ready to accept her counsel. *Siervo*'s Syndéresis is, then, an image in which the reader has to mingle his theological and psychological knowledge with the conventions of courtly love. The medical-sensitive reader realizes that *Siervo* is a tale of deliberate *philocaptio*, resulting in serious mental disorder and final triumph over *amor hereos* by way of restoring the equilibrium and dominance of the faculties of the rational soul. Like his forerunners Ardanlier and Yrena, the author-persona has mastered the ultimate challenge for the true lover, transforming the destructive force of love into a source of ennoblement and moving from confusion to spiritual health in spite of his suffering (Lynch 78). [165]

Rodríguez del Padrón could have achieved this resolution of the lover's emotional and mental conflict by simply introducing synderesis as a voice admonishing the protagonist. Nevertheless, the

---

[164] Augustine qualifies synderesis as a faculty of judgement (Delhaye 113).

[165] According to Cátedra, the "ovidianismo" of *Siervo* consists of maintaining "la posibilidad relativa de eliminar la pasión y de ser libre dentro de la misma servidumbre" (152). Schnell, on the other hand, underscores the importance of perseverance in the tradition of courtly love: "Gefangenschaft des Liebenden bedeutet hier also nicht Unterwerfung des Geistes unter die Herrschaft des 'Fleisches', sondern im Gegenteil Zwang zum Verzicht auf rasche sexuelle Erfüllung, Zwang zum Ausharren in einem aussichtslos erscheinenden Liebeswerben, Zwang zur Niederwerfung 'niederer' sinnlicher Triebe" (36).

Syndéresis in *Siervo* is described with many details, which signal the reader not only to see in her habitual conscience or Prudence, but to explore another, allegorical layer of meaning.

Impey notes that *Siervo*'s Syndéresis evokes not only the theological synderesis but also Philosophy and "discreción" ("Poesía and prosa" 181). The association of the image of the "dueña anciana, vestida de negro" with Philosophy and Prudence is primarily due to the presence of seven maidens, which recall the seven liberal arts and the seven virtues, respectively. If we agree with the first prologue in identifying Syndéresis as *Discreçión* or Prudence (154),[166] we have to answer the question of why this figure is presented as "señora mastresa" (207).

A reader of Cicero's *De inventione* knows what Prudence teaches.

> Wisdom is the knowledge of what is good, what is bad and what is neither good nor bad. Its parts are memory, intelligence, and foresight. Memory is the faculty by which the mind recalls what has happened. Intelligence is the faculty by which it ascertains what is. Foresight is the faculty by which it is seen that something is going to occur before it occurs.
>
> (Prudentia est rerum bonarum et malarum neutrarumque scientia. Partes eius: memoria, intelligentia, providentia. Memoria est per quam animus repetit illa quae fuerunt; intelligentia, per quam ea perspicit quae sunt; prudentia, per quam futurum aliquid videtur ante quam factum est; p. 326-27; bk. 2, 160)

Dom Pedro, Constable of Portugal, a contemporary reader of *Siervo*,[167] obviously had this passage in mind when describing the "three faces" of prudence as "memoria o recordacion de las passadas cosas, consideraçion de las presentes, providençia o para lo porvenir" (*Sátira* 102-03).

Frances Yates pointed out that the Middle Ages gave Antiquity's conception of *memoria* an ethical turn and related, even identified it with Prudentia (20-21, 54). The designation of "mastresa" in

---

[166] The Constable of Portugal presents Prudence as "*señora e prinçesa*" of the other virtues (*Sátira* 50); in a gloss, he characterizes her in a way that could very well apply to Syndéresis: "prudençia determina quales son las cosas convenibles para proseguir, e quales para desechar" (51); see below.

[167] See below.

the *Siervo* also brings to mind the well-known Ciceronian *dictum* in which he calls "historia vero testis temporum, lux veritatis, vita memoriae, magistra vitae, nuntia vetustatis" ("History, which bears witness to the passing of the ages, sheds light upon reality, gives life to recollection and guidance to human existence"; *De oratore* p. 224-25; bk. II, 36). If we follow this chain of associations, we see that Prudence is Memory, Memory is History, and History is *maestra*. Hence Prudence is History and Memory, and the three of them are *maestras*.

The Synderesis/Memory figure in *Siervo*, which appears accompanied by the Seven Virtues, might very well be inspired by Guillaume's *Pèlerinage de la vie humaine*, where Lady Memory carries the Pilgrim's Armour of Virtue. With the presentation of Syndéresis as an image that evokes Understanding, Will and Memory, Rodríguez del Padrón achieves a sophisticated allegory of the reconciliation of the alienated three faculties of the rational soul; because of its difficulty, a medieval reader would certainly regard it as artistically satisfying (Robertson 54).

More importantly, the author-persona's anagnorisis with this embodiment of Historia/Prudentia/Memoria not only answers aesthetic demands, but also establishes the narrative closure of the entire text. Syndéresis goes on land "por algunos reparos, refrescos, afferes, en ardit y deffensa de sus enemigos" (Rodríguez del Padrón, *Siervo* 208).[168] It is surprising that she comes not to rescue the author-persona, but in search of "material" that can help her in her fight against her enemies. From the author-persona she demands his "aventuras" (208). The next logical step is the author-persona's account of his love affair ("recuenta"; 208), establishing a circular narrative closure (Hernández Alonso, *Rodríguez del Padrón* 40; Vigier, "Fiction épistolaire" 240; Grieve 22; Deyermond, "Estudio preliminar" 15).[169] In other words, she will re-

---

[168] Cátedra observes that "como en el caso del *Siervo libre de amor*, en tantas piezas del género los padecimientos concretos de los enamorados constituyen un *exemplum* que funciona como alimento de la argumentación [...]" (158).

[169] The eighth of Rodríguez del Padrón's *Diez mandamientos de amor* suggests that the narration of the caso has itself a therapeutic function:

> De bevir sólo recrescen
> grandes males sin medida,
> y, la fama destruida
> d[e]aquellos que lo padescen;
> tristeza, poco saber,

ceive the actual text, *Siervo libre de amor*, and the text will become *historia*.[170]

As Hernández Alonso (*Rodríguez del Padrón* 18, 40) and Vigier ("Fiction épistolaire" 240) point out, Sindéresis, the fictionalized first recipient of the author-persona's text, also represents Medina, the addressee of the text and its actual first reader. This is why Rodríguez del Padrón can assure Gonçalo de Medina that he will find "weapons against love" in his text (156); he will receive the "digested" supplies ("reparos, refrescos, afferes, en ardit y deffensa de sus enemigos"; 208) which the author-persona provides to Sindéresis/Historia. History is nurtured by exemplary cases like the one *Siervo libre de amor* presents. The memory and contemplation of these *historias* are essential for Prudence, which is the ultimate profit that Rodríguez del Padrón promises to his readers.

The readers, on the other hand, are critical in accomplishing a narrative closure, because their reception of the text redeems the hapless lover as an exemplary figure. For the author-narrator, the literarization of his real-life (?) love affair means that he makes himself known as a loyal lover. Like Ardanlier with his letter to Yrena, and Macías with his poetry, Rodríguez del Padrón lays the foundations of his own "perpetua membrança."

2. 'TODAS LAS COSAS TIENEN DOS ENTENDIMIENTOS': *SÁTIRA DE INFELICE E FELICE VIDA*

Dom Pedro, Condestável of Portugal (ca. 1429-1466),[171] composed the now-lost Portuguese version of his *Sátira de infelice e felice vida* as early as 1447 (Gascón Vera, *Don Pedro* 75); he complet-

---

                      desesperación, olvido
                      pensamiento desavido,
                      causan el seso perder.

(*Obras*, ed. Hernández Alonso 326-27).

[170] Syndéresis/Memoria arrives in a big ship which can be seen as a representation of the chambers of memory (Knape). Furthermore, it is a metaphor for poetic imagination (Lynch 38), representing the composition of the text. As in the case of Syndéresis, there is no agreement on the allegorical meaning of the ship. Cátedra (149), for instance, sees it as a representation of Entendimiento, while Andrachuk ("Italian Influence" 54) and Gerli ("Old French Source" 10) identify it as the Ship of Church.

[171] Gascón Vera traces the biography of Pedro and provides bibliographical references to the substantial literature on Pedro's role in 15th-century Iberian political history (*Don Pedro* 7-32).

ed the Castilian version around 1453.[172] In the canon of sentimental fiction *Sátira* is chronologically the second text after Juan Rodríguez del Padrón's *Siervo libre de amor*. While *Siervo*, in its quality as a "prototype" of sentimental fiction, attracted considerable interest, *Sátira* was widely neglected, if not scorned by scholars. We owe the first significant study on the text to Elena Gascón Vera, who dedicated a chapter of her 1979 monograph on the Constable to *Sátira* (*Don Pedro* 75-109). She interprets *Sátira* as a didactic work which represents a psychic conflict between passionate love and rational control within the framework of courtly love (84). In 1986, E. Michael Gerli pleaded for a "revaluation" of *Sátira* as an innovative text and important step in the evolution of the genre. He discerned a "fundamental subversion of the medieval narrative esthetic—we perceive action conceived for the sole purpose of producing and sustaining emotion" ("Revaluation" 115). Yet until now, Gerli's appeal has only prompted a few scholars to direct their attention to the text. Marina Scordilis Brownlee calls attention to the extensive glosses with which Pedro framed his *Sátira* (*Severed Word* 106-27). She contends that the author, with his metalinguistic commentary, deliberately subverted the lyric structure of the text and replaced it with novelistic discourse (116).[173]

Opposing Gerli and Brownlee, Guillermo Serés recently demonstrated that *Sátira* is essentially medieval in structure and content. He analyzes the rhetorical structure of the text and its descent from the medieval *accessus* tradition, the *artes dictaminis* and Ciceronian rhetoric ("Ficción sentimental"). Serés also proves that in his extended glosses Pedro drew on Alfonso Fernández de Madrigal's mythological compilation *Las diez qüestiones vulgares*, which he transformed according to traditional narrative conventions ("Pedro de Portugal").[174]

---

[172] According to Gascón Vera (*Don Pedro* 75) and Luis Adão Fonseca (x), Pedro wrote the Castilian version between 1449 and 1453. Serés suggests as *terminus post quem* of the Castilian version of *Sátira* 1453, the date of the composition of Fernando de Madrigal's *Las diez qüestiones vulgares*; he argues that Pedro needed the Tostado's extracts in order to complete his glosses ("Pedro de Portugal" 977).

[173] Brownlee's chapter in *The Severed Word* is based on an earlier version published as an article ("Untranscendent vision"). Besides the studies reviewed here, Gascón Vera's article "Ambigüedad en el concepto del amor" is also partially pertinent to *Sátira*.

[174] In his latest contribution Serés labels *Sátira* a paradigmatic text of a Castilian humanism "sui generis" ("Llamada ficción" 12-13).

At first sight, *Sátira* is hardly an attractive text. The highly rhetorical style, sentimental pathos, exuberant commentaries, prosimetrum form, extended prosopopoeia and minimal plot make it impenetrable to the reader used to the conventions of modern narrative forms. Nevertheless, scholarship's preference for works of sentimental fiction which are less derivative and opaque than *Sátira* is by no means justified. *Sátira* is a rich repository for the study of medieval reading habits, intertextuality and notions of *auctoritas*. Moreover, if we consider the exploration and hermeneutics of amatory quandaries a critical feature of sentimental romance, *Sátira* is arguably the most typical text of the genre. As I will demonstrate, it also illustrates, more clearly than any other text of the canon, the impact of *amor hereos* on sentimental fiction. Finally, Dom Pedro's reading of *Siervo libre de amor* in his *Sátira* corroborates my interpretation of the final portion of Juan Rodríguez del Padrón's work.

While students of Juan Rodríguez del Padrón's *Siervo libre de amor* have focused on the sources and models of the text, they have largely neglected the most important testimony of a contemporary reading: *Sátira de infelice e felice vida* by Dom Pedro, Condestável of Portugal. Only recently, Castro Lingl showed the close intertextual ties regarding introduction, structure, title, use of mythology, the beloved, the reason not to commit suicide, and the closure ("Constable"; see also Deyermond, "Estudio preliminar" 16; Haywood, "Narrative"). "Dom Pedro," she contends, "purposefully designed his *Sátira* as a commentary in order to blame, as well as praise, Rodríguez del Padrón's *Siervo*" (78). However, it is worth reconsidering Dom Pedro not as a critic of sorts, who tried to resolve *Siervo*'s striking ambiguities, but as a contemporary of Rodríguez del Padrón, who shared his reading habits.

Like *Siervo*, *Sátira* is an autobiographical account of frustrated passion for an anonymous lady. The narrator, an "adolescent" between 14 and 18 years of age (*Sátira* 21-22), presents himself as captive in the figurative "carçel" of amatory servitude. In a soliloquy he blames Fortune for his suffering, invoking her response to his charges. Instead, Discretion appears and advises him to give up his desperate quest. Convinced, the speaker is silenced and leaves his retreat on horseback. After a ride in a trance-like state, he finds himself in a flourishing orchard where he encounters a group of noble ladies, the "colegio de las virtudes" (53). Seven of them, the three theological and the four cardinal virtues, approach him. Prudence, the "*señora e prinçesa de aquellas*" (50), declares that they have been sent to defend the blameless lady against the lover's insults. Praising the lady's physical beauty, her moral excellence and insuperable virtues, Prudence argues that the lover should welcome his fate of having fallen in love with the most perfect woman. The lover objects that his beloved cannot be really virtuous because she has not taken pity on his suffering. The incriminated Piedat responds to his allegations, but does not succeed in convincing him. He takes the disappearance of the virtues as a sign of his victory in the debate. More desperate than ever, the lover curses the day he fell in love. In the last portion of the text, he contemplates, with sword in hand, whether to end his life or to wait for a possible answer.

Gerli observes that "besides some actual textual allusions to the *Siervo libre*, the *Sátira* derives its overall allegorical structure, thematic strain of sentimental complaint, and autobiographical analysis of the emotions from Rodríguez del Padrón's work" ("Revaluation" 111; see also Menéndez Pelayo, *Orígenes* II, 24-25). Yet, considering the "more theoretically and humanistically orientated literary sensibility" of Dom Pedro, he comes to the surprising conclusion that "the *Sátira*'s debt to Rodríguez del Padrón's *Triunfo de las donas* is considerably greater than to the *Siervo libre*" (111-12).[175] Nevertheless, as Castro Lingl demonstrates ("Constable"), a more detailed comparison between *Siervo* and *Sátira* shows a significant intertextual connex that sheds new light on both works.

Don Pedro evidently accepted Rodríguez del Padrón as an *auctoritas*; in the gloss to "Cardiana," the protagonist of *Triunfo*, he lauds "Juan Rodrigues, poeta moderno e famoso" (*Sátira* 137). Since he mentions Ardanlier in *Sátira* and gives a précis of the *Estoria de dos amadores* in a gloss (38-39), it is obvious that he was familiar with *Siervo libre*. As Gerli notes ("Revaluation" 108), the author-persona's erring and encounter with the virtues is reminiscent of Siervo's imaginative journey. Both protagonists experience a vision in a near-death state. They find themselves in a grove, where the grass they walk on wilts under their feet (*Siervo* 166; *Sátira* 49). They finally encounter seven maidens and Prudence. In addition,

---

[175] Serés also refers to *Triunfo* when suggesting that "Rodríguez del Padrón le [sc. a don Pedro] facilita el 'habla de los poetas', el *cortex*, el 'texto', en definitiva" ("Pedro de Portugal" 981).

there are numerous textual echoes of *Siervo* in *Sátira*. *Sátira*'s author-persona, for instance, presents himself as a "siervo" (4). We find an allusion to the captured heart (*Siervo* 176-77) and Rodríguez del Padrón's *canción* "Aunque me vedes así / cativo, libre naçí" (203): "coraçon, que de libre fuesse cativo e subjecto [...]" (*Sátira* 33). The examples could easily be multiplied.

The most intriguing intertextual relation between the two texts lies in Pedro's adaptation of *Siervo*'s image of Syndéresis. *Sátira*'s narrator is first addressed by Discretion, who did not object to his servitude for five years because the lover still had some hope.

> Mi discreçion que çinco años avia tenia puesta una impla delante sus ojos, çiega, enmudesçida en mis congoxas, ravias e dolor pestilençial, consintia, conosçiendo o pensando que alguna color de esperança por remedio o reparo e fyn de mis males me siguia. Mas agora que me veya despoblado e solo de toda esperança, consejo e remedio, mas por faser lo que devia que por contrastar mi infinito querer contra mi quexosa comenco [sic] desir [...]. (34)

We remember that *also* in *Siervo*, Discretion/Syndéresis is the narrator's first interlocutor. She also conditionally consents to the *philocaptio* ("non discordando parte de mi salud, esa que es madre de todas las virtudes, con temor de lo pasado, que contrastava lo por venir diziendo: [...]"; Rodríguez del Padrón, *Siervo* 157-58).[176] While in *Siervo* Discretion is presented as an external power, i.e. in its manifestation as Synderesis/Prudence, in *Sátira discreçion* appears as a faculty of the narrator's disturbed mind.[177] Her advice, to renounce the amatory service ("muevante a desquerer desesperaçion syn reparo, e crueldat muy continua"; *Sátira* 41), associates her more closely with *Siervo*'s Entendimiento, who also rejected the path of desperation, for similar reasons, and embarked on the "angosta senda, la qual es la vida contemplativa de no amar" (Rodríguez del Padrón, *Siervo* 166).

Siervo's encounter with Syndéresis is obviously the basis for the confrontation between *Sátira*'s lover and the "colegio de las virtudes." I have been arguing that the image of Syndéresis embodies

---

[176] See above not. 46.
[177] Regarding the role of *amor hereos* in *Sátira* and the reliability of the narrator see below.

and evokes Conscience, History/Memory and Prudence.[178] For this reason, she is presented as a figure apart from the seven maidens which we can safely identify as the Seven Virtues presented by Pedro of Portugal. For reasons I will explain below, the author of *Sátira* focused on one aspect of Rodríguez del Padrón's "señora mastresa" (*Siervo* 207), i.e. Prudence, "*señora e prinçesa*" of the Virtues (*Sátira* 50). Hence he had no reason to create a character apart from the seven Virtues. *Sátira*'s Prudence does not seek to convince the lover of the futility of his amorous obsession; on the contrary, she considers the loyal service of the lover a source of ennoblement. I take this as an indication that the earliest known reader of *Siervo* interpreted the text not as an allegory of religious conversion and renouncement of human love, but as a tale of the "sentimental education" of a loyal courtly lover.

In short, it would be an overstatement to call *Sátira* a calque on *Siervo libre de amor*. Yet it is obvious that in *inventio* and *dispositio* the Constable of Portugal drew considerably on *Siervo*. From the explicit reference to Juan Rodríguez del Padrón and the easily discernible intertextual ties between the two texts we can infer that the author of *Sátira* expected his readers to be familiar with *Siervo libre de amor*. At any rate, in the following analysis of *Sátira*, it is advisable to follow the example of a medieval reader who would associate the *Sátira* with his previous reading of *Siervo*.

Dom Pedro dedicates his work to his sister, queen Isabel of Portugal. In the mold of the *accessus* tradition he explains the biographical background and the topic of his work.

> Verdad sea que, aquexado de amor que en la mas perfecta del universo me fizo poner los ojos, e ally no acatando lo venidero, aprisionar el coraçon e los mis çinco servientes en carçel perpetua colocar, yo començe de escrivir, e, escriviendo, declarar mi apassionada vida, e las muy esclaresçidas e singulares virtudes de la señora de mi [...]. (*Sátira* 4)

He alludes to the *philocaptio* and clearly indicates that he is suffering from passionate love. He proposes a chronicle of his passion which also treats the virtue of his lady. This dual "biographical" aspect, he continues, explains the title's "de infelice e felice vida" (4-5).

---

[178] See above.

In his designation of "Sátira" he concurs with Mena's and Santillana's notion of the term (Gerli, "Revaluation" 109; Serés, "Ficción sentimental" 35-37).

> Satira, que quiere dezir reprehension con animo amigable de corregir; [...] e yo a ella primero loando, el femineo linage propuse loar, a ella amonestando como siervo a señora, a mi reprehendiendo de mi loca thema e desigual tristeza. (*Sátira* 5)

The reader realizes that it is the *intentio auctoris* to praise the female sex, represented by his señora. On the other hand he labels the lover's concern and his despair as "loco." Hence the Constable establishes the opposition *laus/vituperium* (Serés, "Ficción sentimental" 35), and, at the same time, he suggests to his readers an interpretive duality regarding the lover's and his faculties' discourse and the narrative voices which represent his lady. In other words, the prologue designates the author-persona as an unreliable narrator.[179] *Sátira*, then, is a text that requires an attentive reader who is able to discern the narrator's errors and madness. This ideal reader is Isabel of Portugal, who has the required "discreçion" and "ingenio" (*Sátira* 8).

> De lo qual no sortira pequeña salud e autoridat a la subsequente obrezilla mia. Ca, segund dixe, muchos deffectos contener. Sera muy neçessario que la suma prudencia vuestra emiende aquellos, e los yerros suyos con amigable correçion los re-prehenda e, reprehendida e emendada, sea digna de algund loor, o a lo menos no digna de reprehension. (8)

Authority is displaced from the writer to the reader through the latter's "emendations" and corrections. As Dagenais has demonstrated (*Ethics of Reading*), this appeal cannot be discarded as an exordial topos. Pedro is probably not envisioning a physical rewriting of his work. Earlier in his dedication he alludes to the mental activities involved in literature: "exerçitar el ingenio, asayar el entendimiento,

---

[179] Deyermond discusses the question of unreliable narrators in sentimental fiction ("Punto de vista" 71-75). However, among his criteria that ought to inspire the reader's skepticism he does not include the mental impediment the narrators face due to lovesickness and the fact that in some specimens of the genre, like *Sátira* and *Triste deleytaçión*; the epistolary form implies a perlocutive intention, possibly distorting the version of the love affair the narrator presents.

confirmar la memoria en cosas virtuosas, utiles e honestas [...]" (4). It is precisely this mental glossing that the Constable expects from his reader. The text itself needs this supplementation because his "madness" is projected into the author-persona's discourse.

This narrator, of course, is not capable of comprehending his own madness. It is the prudent reader who makes the *Sátira de infelice e felice vida* a "satire" by way of judging the text and adducing *auctoritates*.

> Et, por tanto, la fize no autorizada de los grandes sçientificos varones e, en algunos lugares, escura, porque la vuestra muy llena industria sabera de quales jardines salieron estas flores mias, e a la escuridat dara lumbre e claridat muy luziente. (8)

Since *Sátira* is a text that relies on the collaboration of the reader, it is vulnerable to abuse; it needs protection.

> Suplico que de las caninas e venenosas lenguas, mas habiles a reprehender que a loar, la libre, deffienda e ampare, e le acresçiente titulo de honor e de auctoridat, dando lugar a los sçientes que la miren e castiguen con ojos amigables e amoroso açote, e atapando las bocas de los simples o ponçoñosos retractadores no osen de la morder e llagar de enerboladas llagas. (8)

The ignorant and malevolent reader will revile the errors of the text; the prudent and benevolent reader will regard the "deffectos" as an opportunity to exercise his mental faculties, conferring on it "honor" and "authority."[180]

However, the Constable is not overly confident in the competence of his readers.

> Ffize glosas al texto [...]. [...] Movido quasi por neçessidat, lo propuse fazer, considerando, syn ello, mi obra paresçeria desnuda e sola, e mas causadora de quistiones que fenesçedora de aquellas; ca, demandando quien fue esta, o quien aquel, que es esto, o que es esto otro, no fenesçerian jamas demandas a los ignorantes, e aun en algunas cosas a los sçientes seria forçado rebolver las foias. (9-10)

---

[180] According to Dagenais, "praise accrues to the author in direct proportion to the amount of emendation readers carry out upon his text" (*Ethics of Reading* 25).

First neglected by students of the text, [181] the glosses Pedro provided to his own text recently became the focus of *Sátira* scholarship. Brownlee observes that the glosses are often "unhelpful" (*Severed Word* 111). Serés considers their main function to provide and demonstrate "cierto saber erudito" ("Pedro de Portugal" 978). Both observations are correct, yet fail to acknowledge that the Constable only textualizes a common medieval practice for the convenience of his readers, as he explains.

The text is a tool to exercise the memory ("confirmar la memoria"; *Sátira* 4). Hence, unlike modern forms of critical commentary, the glosses are not necessarily intended to explain or interpret the text. In the concluding paragraph of *Sátira* the Constable emphasizes once more the reader's task to "activate" the text. He baptizes his text "*Argos*" (10). In this image the sentinel's eyes represent the glosses to the text. They are blind until the hand of the capable reader, in this case Isabel of Portugal, opens the pages and eyes: "reçebid esta indigna sierva vuestra que, besando las manos reales, goze de la muy desseada vista" (10).

The introduction to *Sátira* creates a hermeneutical space akin to the prologues of *Bursario* and *Siervo*. The author projects different notions of love into the text, which the reader is supposed to discern and judge. *Sátira*'s prologue is most explicit in labeling the author-persona's concern and reasoning as reprehensible. In the first chapter this narrator is in a situation reminiscent of *Siervo*, having fallen from his beloved's grace.

> Estava retraydo de humana compañia, mas non de cuydados, anxias, congoxas e ravias era solo. De males, tristezas, daños y varias contemplaçiones no menos afligida que seguida veya la triste vida mia [...]. (*Sátira* 18)

Isolated from human companionship, he is plagued by memories and "contemplaçiones." He rages against Fortune, whom he blames for his amatory quandaries. Like Siervo before his encounter with Syndéresis, he has not accepted his fate. [182] It is a state of profound despair which is symbolized in *Siervo* as the "vía de perdición"

---

[181] Paz y Meliá included only a few samples of the glosses in his edition of *Sátira*. Gascón Vera (*Don Pedro*) and Gerli ("Revaluation") overlook them.

[182] Fortune is only evoked, not personified, in both texts.

(203); *Sátira*'s prologue refers to it as blameworthy "desigual tristeza" (5).

At this point the author-persona's *discreçion* emerges, reprimanding his suicidal thoughts. She argues that, unlike legendary lovers such as Ardanlier or Pyramus, he would die in vain, forgotten: "tu moriras por aquella que de tu bien una sola hora non tiene memoria" (41). She instructs her "siervo" (35) to abdicate his passion. The author-persona has no objection to her reasoning. The introduction, however, has warned the reader against accepting the narrator's "loca thema e desigual tristeza" (*Sátira* 5). *Discreçion* did not oppose the lover's passion for five years; she is responsible for his present suffering and might still be hampered by his passion. The lover's immediate consent does not make her more trustworthy.

Indeed, Discretion's counsel has no effect on the lover's pain. He flees from his mansion on horseback and falls into a stupor, that recalls Siervo's "contemplación" after the betrayal of his friend (*Siervo* 165). *Sátira*'s vision is decidedly "realistic." After a journey over mountains and valleys, the narrator arrives at an orchard reminiscent of Siervo's Garden of Fortune. Yet it is a garden without symbolic imagery. It is only an idyllic place, a *locus amoenus*, which contrasts with the author-persona's despair and presents an adequate setting for the encounter with the virtues. These are presented as stately ladies. Seven of the personifications of the virtues approach the author-persona and identify themselves as the three theological and four cardinal virtues of his lady. Prudence, the most excellent of them all, points out to the author-persona that they are of divine origin: "nos somos aquellas que del Dios uno e trino avemos proçedido" (53). This puts her and her entourage in a position superior to the lover's incriminated Discretion. In a *descriptio puellae* Prudence evokes the physical beauty of her lady. Then she praises her insuperable moral and intellectual virtues. Hence she evokes an *imago* composed of a beautiful form and alluring *intentiones*. Prudence argues that there is every reason to fall in love with this perfect woman.

> Et, por tanto, conosçe que tu libre voluntad derechamente se contenta, e con mucha causa e razon se proferio de sofrir aquello que en las ardientes llamas venereas e de la desesperaçion sufre. (132-33)

The author-persona, however, is not willing to accept his suffering. He denounces his lady's lack of compassion (135). Pity answers to these charges against her. She alleges three reasons why the lady cannot be blamed for her "cruelty." First, love cannot be forced (138).

> La otra, por no dar fe a tus palabras e a tus ignominiosas penas que, pero te viesse poco a poco acabar la vida, pensava que dolençia natural tan desigual pena fasia passar e sofrir. (138)

Piedat raises the suspicion that it is not the lady's indifference, but a "natural disease" that is at the heart of the lover's suffering. The third argument is even more intriguing.

> Quando agora tu discreçion e entendimiento, poniendo delante ty las desesperaçiones e infinitos males que te siguen, a tu voluntad refrenar ni contrastar no puede, que fuera de ti e de la desaventurada vita tuya? Sy della sentieras muestra del desseado reparo, por el qual tu discreçion obedesçiera, çiertamente lo que sientes no sintieras, porque dolorosa fin e inhumana muerte a tu angustioso bevir e a tu deseo syn esperança mucho ha que ovieras fallado. (138-39)

If the lady had requited the lover's desire, then his discretion would have given up its resistance against Will, aggravating his passion with fatal consequences. The lady's "cruelty," then, is ultimately an act of pity. The full meaning of Piedat's reasoning becomes clear only in the lover's retort.

> Pues de pensar que mis dolores innumerables dolençia natural los causava, voluntad çiega con crueldat e no conosçida razon lo costriñia pensar pues mi mal es possible, accaesçido a muchos que por amores murieron, e a otros que la sombra de la raviosa muerte padesçieron e sintieron. Como avino al de piadosa e perpetua recordaçion *Antioco*, que la muerte menos temia, que no la tardança della, et que, de gustar el fiero trago, de la pavorosa muerte estava mas çercano que de bevir gozosa vida. (145-49)

With reference to Antiochus, the most famous case of lovesickness,[183] he counters two of Piedat's accusations at a time. He is not

---

[183] See above chapter I.

suffering from just any disease, but from *amor hereos* caused by his lady, whence he has to explain how he could sustain the disease for five years: "que entonçe ni agora no muera, no es de presuponer menos amar que los otros que de semblante passion fenesçieron, ca yo naturalmente no bivo, mas bivo por grande milagro" (149). It is, to say the least, a weak argument.

Furthermore, with Antiochus's example he seeks to counter Piedat's argument that a "reparo" would exacerbate his medical condition. In a gloss to "Antioco" the Constable summarizes the well-known episode. Antiochus tries to conceal his love for his stepmother. After the physician (here called "Leptino"; 147) has diagnosed *amor hereos* "Selenco" (Seleucus) tries to save his son's life: "el amor paterno vençio la filial vergueña e resçibio el andando la su madrastra por muger forçosamente" (149). The author-persona implies that, as Seleucus's "pity" saved Antiochus life, so could his beloved's pity save his life.

Yet the *exemplum* can be turned against him. The truly exemplary figure in the episode is not Antiochus, but his father and his unselfish love. Every fairly educated reader knows that it is not the paternal love that cures Antiochus, but the sexual intercourse with the woman. The same reader is also very well aware that *amor hereos* is not disinterested love but ultimately aims at the fulfillment of the desire.[184] The author-persona is at great pains to dissipate this impression: "es venido [sc. el querer], e no con esperança de gualardon o merçed [...]" (150); "la libre voluntad fue causadora, e no otra provechosa esperança [...]" (150); "assy, sin esperança de toda merçed, de todo gualardon e benefiçio, me fizo tomar e faze mantener este mi querer maldito e honesto e leal amor [...]" (150). Notwithstanding, the rationale behind his complaint and his rage is the still-frustrated hope for a "galardón." It is obvious that his argumentation is flawed.

---

[184] See above chapter I. Antony Van Beysterveldt claims that the 15th-century feminist debate in Castilian literature led to a general "sexualization" of the "idealistic" conception of courtly love ("Revisión de los debates feministas" 11). The same critic argues that in Diego de San Pedro's novels a "new theory of love" is born which rejects the traditional idealistic and "masochistic" notion of courtly love: the *galardón* which the lover implores from his lady would ultimately culminate in "posesión carnal de la amada" ("Nueva teoría del amor" 78); see also Whinnom ("Introducción" 42) and below chapter III. Although Van Beysterveldt's teleological perspective is untenable, he rightly acknowledges the conflation of idealistic and "carnal" notions of love in 15th-century Castilian letters.

The *colegio de las virtudes* disappears without having changed the lover's mind: "Assy que claramente conosçi que, vençidas, de mi se partieron [...]" (153). He is once again mistaken. Still in the grip of *amor hereos*, deserted by the virtues, he perseveres in his "loca thema e desigual tristeza" (5).

He evokes his *philocaptio*.

> Maldito sea el dia en que primero ame, la noche que, velando syn reçelar la temedera muerte, puse el firme sello a mi infinito querer! Et jure mi servidumbre ser fasta el fin de mis dias! (154)

The lover is not cured, nor has he learned anything from the debate with the Virtues. The very fact that he rages against his fate proves that his "servidumbre" was conditional, that he is not a genuinely loyal lover. He thus violates the most important consideration for the courtly lover, according to Diego de San Pedro's *Sermón*: the perfect lover must embrace his suffering with patience, even joy, because it is for a good cause: "deve el que ama templarse y suffrirse, porque en tales casos quien buscare su remedio, hallará su perdición" (*Obras completas* I, 175).[185]

The *Sátira*'s author-persona realizes that his problem is oblivion: "e non solo dire que despues de la muerte por recordaçion non bevire, mas no dubdo que en la vida por muerte de olvido e de descuydo muero" (155). Still, unlike Siervo, he not a free slave of love but a suicidal prisoner of his despair.

> E yo, sin ventura padesçiente, la desnuda e bicordante espada en la my diestra mirava, titubando, con dudoso pensamiento e demudada cara, sy era mejor prestamente morir o asperar la dubdosa respuesta me dar consuelo. La discriçion favoresçe e suplica la espera, la congoxosa voluntad la triste muerte reclama, el seso manda esperar la respuesta, el aquexado coraçon, gridando, acusa la postrimeria. (174)

The closing paragraph adds a startling twist to the previous narration. So far the author-persona has underscored his despair and disillusion; in the main text there has been no indication that the narrator solicits or anticipates a response. Gerli assumes that he is

---

[185] Rohland de Langbehn holds that the genre of sentimental fiction illustrates and narratively unfolds what San Pedro prescribes in his *Sermón* (*Interpretation* 30).

waiting for a sign from his beloved ("Revaluation" 109). However, Queen Isabel is the inscribed recipient of *Sátira*. To her, Dom Pedro avows "amor inmutable" in the preface (8).

> Que no solo las leyes de naturaleza, mas aun las del amor que ante me avia la exçellençia vuestra en mi mas bara fortuna, aveys assy perfecta e complidamente guardado, que no solo por palabra e por escripto yo lo remerçio continuamente a la vuestra perfecçion, mas aun en las mis entrañas esta sellado e esculpido vuestro serviçio se anteponer a toda otra cosa mundana. (3)

The hyperbolic praise, the use of the seal metaphor,[186] and the promise of loyal servitude allude to the "imprint" of a mental image in the *philocaptio* and courtly forms of love. This, of course, does not mean that the Constable confesses an incestuous passion for his sister. In the same way the lover of *Sátira* is a persona of the author, Isabel is a persona of the unnamed beloved. The author-persona swore loyal service to his beloved yet rejected her virtues and her judgement. The actual author pledges perpetual dedication to his lady, too. Unlike the author-persona, however, the Constable does not question the beloved's virtues and reject her counsel. On the contrary, he subjects his *Sátira* and explicitly the author-persona's course of action to the judgment of Isabel's insuperable wisdom, "conosçiendo vuestra muy singular discreçion e natural ingenio sobrepujar a toda prudençia e artifiçial industria" (8). In contrast to the author-persona's despair and indictment of the beloved's Piedat, the Constable expresses the hope that Isabel's intervention, her "amigable correçion" (8), might bestow admiration upon him and his work. In his *Sátira* the Constable presents himself as a failed courtly lover. However, "reprehending" the author-persona and "correcting" and disseminating the text, Isabel will redeem the author as a constant, voluntary, and docile *sirviente*.

Sátira, then, buttresses Julian Weiss's contention that the "servitude" of the courtly lover exploits women as a source of male power (242-44). With his self-presentation as an abject, frustrated lover and the turn to Queen Isabel as a foundation of his authority,[187] the

---

[186] The author-persona uses the same metaphor when remembering his *philocaptio*: "puse el firme sello a mi infinito querer!" (154).

[187] According to Moi, "by dominating the word, he [the courtly lover] gains phallic power that contradicts his seemingly humble stance towards his lady" (24).

Constable of Portugal perfectly illustrates that he is "more interested in the display of his own desire than in his lady" (Weissberger, "Politics of *Cárcel de Amor*" 320).

In the Constable of Portugal's *Sátira* we find considerable thematic and structural borrowings from Rodríguez del Padrón's *Siervo*. *Sátira* also emulates *Siervo* in establishing the closure of a narration of amorous quandaries in suspension by means of a circular reference to the initial moment of the creation of the text. Similar to *Siervo*, in *Sátira* the literary process, the composition of the text and presentation to the audience, effects a narrative closure and sublimates the destructive force of *amor hereos*. It is a transformation of reprehensible silent despair and oblivion into praiseworthy literature and memory, of pathologic amatory servitude into male power.

3. 'POR AQUELLA OLVIDANÇA ES CAUSA LA PRESENTE HOBRA': *TRISTE DELEYTAÇIÓN*

"If it belongs to any literary genre," Gerli suggests, "*Triste deleytaçión* belongs to that of the sentimental romance" ("Introduction" 8). A précis and short characteristic of the text shows that his reluctant classification is all too prudent.

Written after 1458,[188] *Triste deleytaçión* is the third text of the canon of sentimental fiction. It pertains to the first generation of the genre which, according to Regula Rohland de Langbehn, essentially evaluates courtly love ("Desarrollo de géneros literarios" 76).[189] Only one manuscript of the work has come down to us (Ri-

---

[188] According to Gerli ("Introduction" 8), Riquer dates the composition between 1458 and 1467. Riquer, however, only points out that the "alma negra" (*Triste deleytaçión* 117), who he identifies as the Countess of Luna, was still alive at the time when the action of the work takes place. Hence the presence of the Countess in Purgatory suggests 1467 as *terminus ante quem* of the composition. Blay Manzanera puts forward a date of composition in the 70s or early 80s ("Dinámica espacio-temporal" 188). Based on an occasionally speculative reading à *clef*, Gómez-Fargas seems to suggest vaguely that the text was written before 1472, the end of the Catalan Civil War (121).

[189] In 1971, Rohland de Langbehn grouped *Triste deleytaçión* together with *Siervo* and *Sátira* (*Interpretation* 21). Later she tentatively associates *Triste deleytaçión* with the works of San Pedro and, particularly, Flores ("Desarrollo de géneros literarios" 67-69; *Unidad genérica* 45-46). Deyermond locates *Triste deleytaçión* "a caballo" between the first generation (*Siervo* and *Sátira*) and the "obras clásicas del género" ("Estudio preliminar" 17). Corfis points out that *Triste deleytaçión*, contrasting with the works of Flores and San Pedro, shares with *Siervo* and *Sátira* the abundance of quoted *auctoritates* ("Sentimental Lore" 154).

quer 33; Rohland de Langbehn, "Introducción" 41). It is attributed to a certain F.A.D.C. Martín de Riquer ventured that behind these initials stands Fra Artal de Claramunt, Comendador of La Guardia.[190] Though his conjecture was supported by Rosa María Gómez-Fargas (106-08), the question of authorship remains unresolved, because Artal did not leave further writings which might corroborate Riquer's speculation. However, from the linguistic features of the text and reference to historical personalities, it can safely be inferred that the author was Catalan. This author composed a work that differs significantly in length from other texts labeled as sentimental fictions.[191] He recounts a tale of an unfortunate liaison between a lover (Enamorado) and his lady (Señora), which is intertwined with the story of the lover's friend (Amigo) and the beloved's stepmother (Madrastra). The protagonists are referred to generally with the *chiffres* E°, S^a, A° and M^a.

The Enamorado is captured by the vision of a beautiful lady. His attempts to establish an amorous relationship are at first frustrated. He confides in a friend and suggests that he court the lady's beautiful stepmother. At the sight of M^a, A° also falls in love. While the Friend's love is reciprocated by the Stepmother, the Lover remains rejected by the Lady. Using a ruse to gain the Señora's favor, he joins the Prince's army and leaves the city. In a letter the Señora confesses her anxiety and implores his return. The erroneous news that he was killed in battle makes her realize that she feels passionate affection for the E°. She swears that she will retire to a nunnery if she is not able to marry him. Upon his return, the Lover is assured by the Friend of his Lady's love. However, the Lady is still plagued by shame and fear. A servant informs S^a's father of the liaison between A° and M^a. Attempts to kill A° fail. The Señora finally capitulates, and the lovers decide to avenge the betrayal. They meet and pledge their mutual love and exchange pleasures. An old

---

[190] Riquer thinks that the "F" (=Fra) hints at a member of the military orders (56). According to Rohland de Langbehn's interpretation ("Introducción" 69), the narrator joins the order of Saint John in the concluding portion of *Triste deleytaçión* (122). Recently, Rohland de Langbehn has ventured that the author could have been Alfonso de Córdoba, the lover of Catalina de Sandoval who, like M^a, was murdered by her jealous husband (*Unidad genérica* 45). All quotations are taken from Gerli's edition.

[191] According to Whinnom (*Diego de San Pedro* 76), the only consistent formal criterion which distinguishes the sentimental fiction from other "genres" is that it is short.

woman spies on their rendezvous and reports it to the authorities who in turn notify the Husband of his wife's betrayal and his daughter's dishonor. In light of the Husband's violent character, they decide to separate until his rage is tempered. The Husband, however, has his wife executed. The two friends depart for Barcelona. E° tries in vain to reestablish contact with his beloved. He learns that she has fulfilled her oath and has entered a convent. His passion unchanged, he too becomes a member of a religious order and begs news from his Señora.

This rather complex plot is further complicated by what Rohland de Langbehn calls "excursos" in her helpful descriptive summary ("Introducción" 51-69). The lover's *philocaptio* is followed by a debate between Reason and Will. E° and A° have a dialogue in verse about E°'s problems. A lengthy discussion between the Señora and her God-mother (Madrina), which Impey describes as a "doctrinal para las doncellas enamoradas" ("Doctrinal"), prepares the Lady for her relationship. E° and S^a exchange several letters before their first date. The narrator inserts a *planctus* in Catalan directed against Fortune after the Friend's escape to Barcelona. Finally, a long, versified allegorical journey of the narrator through Lover's Hell, Purgatory, and Paradise precedes his decision to enter a religious order.

Triste deleytaçión is written in prosimetrum form, using poetry not only to emphasize the emotions of the characters, but also as a vehicle of allegorical and "realistic" narration. Although the text is chiefly a compound of novelistic discourse, romance, vision and allegory, it assumes on occasion the form of an epistolary novel or a drama.[192] The convoluted syntax and the vexing shifts in point of view set further hurdles for the reader.[193] The narrative voice oscillates between an impersonal third-person perspective and an involved narrative I. Particularly intriguing is, to use Impey's expression, the "superimposición de *yos*" ("Doctrinal" 193): "la primera persona no es prerrogativa exclusiva del protagonista: en numerosas ocasiones la Señora, el Amigo, la Madrastra la emplean en sus epístolas y a veces, aunque brevemente también en la na-

---

[192] Fernando Lázaro Carreter considers *Triste deleytaçión* a precursor of the Spanish drama (68-70).

[193] As Impey points out, there is the possibility that the linguistic difficulties of the text result from the author's conscious attempt to create an ambiguous and enigmatic text ("*Contraria*" 159-60).

rración" (193). The narrative voices of the E° and F.D.A.C. are frequently indistinguishable.

Triste deleytaçión, in short, is a messy piece of literature. Hence it attracted primarily the attention of specialists of cluttered texts, i.e. scholars of sentimental fiction. After Riquer's pioneering 1956 study, which introduced *Triste deleytaçión* to a broader public and suggested a reading *à clef* (an approach recently also adopted by Gómez-Fargas), it was not before the 1980s that two critical editions realized by Gerli and Rohland de Langbehn instigated the scholarly debate.

Rohland de Langbehn asserts that "para el autor el relato como tal no tiene importancia primordial [...] no intenta la creación de personajes y de su historia, sino que éstos sólo sirven como trasfondo para las materias didácticas que contiene el libro" ("Introducción" 15). Impey elaborates on the didactic nature of *Triste deleytaçión*, calling attention to the importance of the Señora's conversation with the Madrina. In particular the secondary plot of the Amigo's and the Madrastra's erotic adventures appear as "dramatized projections" of the situations which the Madrina censures in her counsels ("Doctrinal" 219). The notion of love that nurtures her advice and imbues *Triste deleytaçión* is derived from Boccaccio's *Fiammetta* and Piccolomini's *Historia de duobus amantibus* (229-30). Impey's interpretation of the intercalated "doctrinal" in *Triste deleytaçión* is supported by Castro Lingl, who sees in the Madrina not the S^a's Godmother but a Midwife. In the dialogue with the Lady the Midwife dispenses "expert advice and help in female-orientated problems" ("*Triste deleytaçión*'s Madrina" 14), which accounts for the realism (if not cynicism) of her discourse, and some details in the plot (M^a's adulterous behavior, A°'s wound, the report of the case to the authorities; 21). Complementary to these studies of the didactic dimension of F.A.D.C.'s work is Françoise Vigier's analysis of the intertextual relation of *Triste deleytaçión* with Andreas Capellanus's *De arte amandi*. Vigier points out that the *precepta amorosa* expressed by Voluntad in the debate with Razón are directly inspired by Andreas while the *Doctrinal* presents a feminine, more practical counter-model of amorous conduct, possibly resulting from the contamination with the Ovidian conception and the courtly tradition ("Le *De Arte Amandi*" 171-72). Most recently, Impey focused on the allegory of the palace Aborintio which Razón presents in her debate with Voluntad ("Contraria"). Besides reconstructing a dense matrix of possible sources and models, her study makes an important contribution to an understanding of the poetics underlying *Triste deleytaçión*. In the Aborintio portion the archetype of the Labyrinth organizes a series of Petrarchist *contraria*.[194] In turn, this passage foreshadows the plot development on the primary diegetic level of *Triste deleytaçión*. According to Impey, the persistent use of *contraria* is the most salient and distinguishing feature of the text (162).

As with so many medieval texts which are presented as didactic works, the seriousness of *Triste deleytaçión*'s instruction is disputed among modern scholars. Rohland de Langbehn perceives an ironic tone in the last section of the narrator's allegorical journey, the erotic Paradise ("Introducción" 21). Gerli goes further in describing *Triste deleytaçión* as an "anthology of the medieval literature of love written with tongue very often firmly in cheek" ("Introduction" 14). He underscores the innovative character of the text which "at once incorporates and transcends the conventions of courtly love, offering a complex and surprisingly candid view of human emotions" (17). Brownlee sees in *Triste deleytaçión* a subversion of traditional modes of expression: she observes in the text an "axiological divergence effected by two distinct chronotopic milieux (novella and romance)" (*Severed Word* 128). This leads ultimately to an inversion of the Dantean etiology, in that the behavior in life is not rewarded properly in the afterlife (138). The hybrid discursive nature of *Triste deleytaçión* is also the subject of a study by Blay Manzanera. In her analysis of the narrator's allegorical journey through the Afterworld she substantiates Brownlee's conclusion,

> El análisis de la 'Ventura que allo el E°' demuestra que en su transcurso asistimos a la desmitologización del amante cortesano y la afirmación de unos nuevos usos amorosos más acordes con los nuevos tiempos. ("El más allá" 147)

Elsewhere, Blay Manzanera studies the *coplas de disparate* in *Triste deleytaçión* and shows other elements of humor in the text, claiming that F.A.D.C.'s transitional work prefigures literary modes of the Renaissance ("Humor"). In another article the same author

---

[194] However, Impey doubts a direct influence of Petrarch ("Contraria" 161, n. 19).

studies the space-time structure of *Triste deleytaçión*. She discerns a blurring of the border between allegorical and "realistic" chronotopes ("Dinámica espacio-temporal" 190). The open-endedness of the text has the effect that "el autor modernamente dejará por completo en sus manos [sc. de los lectores] no sólo la evaluación de unos hechos, sino incluso de la propia eficacia de su creación" (196).

While I differ with Blay Manzanera in designating the involvement of the reader a sign of the modernity of *Triste deleytaçión*,[195] I agree with her that the reader plays a critical role in the process of literary creation. Far from breaking the pattern established by *Siervo* and *Sátira*, *Triste deleytaçión* inscribes itself in a narrative tradition in which the closure of the text is realized through a cyclic reference to the reader and the initial moment of the writing of the text. In my analysis I contend that *Triste deleytaçión* coincides with the two earlier specimens of sentimental fiction in its amatory hermeneutics and the underlying concept of *amor hereos*. In accordance with Gerli, Brownlee and Blay Manzanera, however, I will show that in the "realistic" story of *Triste deleytaçión* no endeavor is made to sublimate carnal love, resulting in an unintentional subversion of earlier amatory fiction and prefiguring the works of Flores and San Pedro.

Similar to paratexts of *Siervo* and *Sátira*, *Triste deleytaçión*'s prologue does not provide the modern reader with a cogent, helpful introduction to the main text, but poses some puzzling questions. The narrator states that he learned about an "auto de amores," "[v]enido a conocimiento mío, ahunque por vía indirecta [...]" (*Triste deleytaçión* 1). He deems this *auto*, in which a virtuous lady, a gentleman,[196] a friend and the stepmother of the maiden are involved, memorable: "quise pora siempre en scrito pareçiesen" (1).

He explains why he does not provide a denouement to the affair. "Es verdat que si la fin destos amores en la presente hobra no se muestra, la causa fue no aplicar fiçión, por ser más obligado en tal

---

[195] Elsewhere, Blay Manzanera speaks of "rasgos incipientes de heterología y heterofonía" in *Triste deleytaçión* ("Metaliteratura" 56).

[196] There is also the possibility that the narrator is veiling his own involvement in the *auto*: If the friend can be a friend of himself ("de sí mismo amigo"), his friend the narrator ("de mí [...] amigo") can also be a friend of himself. If the narrator is a friend of himself, he might be referring to himself with this phrasing in the third person ("de mí como de sí mismo amigo"; 1).

caso a la verdat que al amigo [...]" (1). From this it can be inferred that F.A.D.C. was not an eyewitness to the events but gathered his information through an oral account (maybe a poem), or by reading about it.[197] *Triste deleytaçión*, at any rate, is based on a narrative subtext. The reader also understands that the case F.A.D.C. wants to preserve for posterity and proliferate in writing is particularly important for two reasons: On one hand, it deals with extraordinary matters ("la strema voluntat de la S^{ra} donzella y del E^o ajuntamiento de gran amor"; 1); on the other hand, it is a true "non-fictional" story. The truth of the story is further underscored by the open-endedness of the text (Blay Manzanera, "Dinámica espacio-temporal" 194-95). The narrator, then, presents *Triste deleytaçión* as a true, memorable tale, i.e. an *exemplum*. This *exemplum* is inserted in a rhetorical context. It is intended to persuade the audience.[198]

> Por que si aquella S^a de quien soy [...] por nueva fantasía le fuesen absentes mis deseos, fatiguas y danyos, por aquella olvidança es causa la presente hobra liendo non solo a ella buelba en la elecçión primera, mas a todas las hotras stimadas senyoras que de grand sangre tyenen ábito de sclareçido renonbre las aga de ingratitut delibres, ajuntándolas en huno con aquéllos que por bien querer les avían la principal fin de amor ofrecido. (1)

The narrator introduces the *exemplum* of the two couples as an argument or reminder for all Señoras to be loyal to their first love. He addresses in particular his own beloved, whose mind is, or might be, occupied by a "new fantasy," i.e. captured by the mental image of a new lover. The narrator insinuates here that the following tale shows, *in bono* or *in malo*, the necessity of loyal love. At the same time he underscores that the particular value of the text lies in its conformity to historical facts. It is this tension, between exemplarity and lived experience, between romance and novella as Brownlee calls it, that characterizes *Triste deleytaçión*. There is also, as I will show, an unreconciled tension between F.A.D.C.'s assertion to be a faithful chronicler of an "auto de amores" and his personal agenda to preserve or regain his lady's love.

---

[197] Glossing on the prologue of *Triste deleytaçión*, in which the author declares that he found an "auto de amores" (1), Lázaro Carreter speculates that F.A.D.C. based his novel on an ephemeral theatrical piece (69).

[198] See above n. 70 (chapter II).

The narrator presents himself as man of advanced age, [199] devoid of any amorous thoughts: "[a]partado de toda pasión de amor por la edat que la speriencia me negava, que caminar por sus deleytosas sendas no me dexava" (*Triste deleytaçión* 2). One day he is caught by the sight of a beautiful woman.

> Ansí andando descuydado y fuera de toda fatigua que enogar me pudiese, alçé los ojos, no en fin de ser preso ni de amor tomar a ninguna, do vi en una ventana una tan linda e fermosa donzella al grado y voluntat mýa tanto conforme, que sy Dios a otra más perfiçión dar le quisiera fuera forçado quedar vanaglorioso. (2-3)

After the *philocaptio* he shows signs of lovesickness. He retires to his chamber to recover from the mental tribulations, but this only aggravates his passionate *cogitationes*, "porque las ynmaginaçiones y pensamientos contrarios a sus deseos sin compasión ofenden más a quien es de consolaçión digno" (3). Similar to Siervo's resolution, he decides after a "secreto razonamiento" to accept the amatory servitude (3).

A dispute between Reason and Will reenacts the narrator's psychic struggle. Reason admonishes Will that "[l]a nueva speriençia de amor al vuestro virtuoso bivir grave impedimiento pone" (3). Will, who is obviously an *alter ego* of the lover, [200] denies that he is in love and challenges reason's competence to judge his passion: "otras pasiones que de amor seguir y desear se pueden [...]" (5). He fails to deceive Reason, who diagnoses *amor hereos*. [201]

> Sto es conoçido y visto por verdaderas esperiençias, porque el dormir non vos plaze, ny el comer vos contenta, los bienes no vos son caros, el reposo vos ofiende, el gozo vos causa pena, los sospiros vos deleytan, los pensamientos vos matan, l'alegría vos desdenia, la soledat vos demanda, la muerte tenéys por vida; si esto no fuese amor, pues ponerle vos el nonbre. (5)

---

[199] This is another instance where F.A.D.C. conflates his person with the E°'s. There are indications in the text that E° is a young man: his inexperience in love matters (*Triste deleytaçión* 12-13) and his military service.

[200] While Razón is a mere voice, Voluntad is invested with bodily features: "disimulados gestos" (3), "cabeça baxa" (4); and Will is suffering from the symptoms of *amor hereos* (5).

[201] Vigier mentions in passing that the *signa* listed by Razón relate to the medical tradition ("Le *De Arte Amandi*" 163).

Furthermore, Razón points out that Will's passion affects his thinking: "por querer vuestro entender terná turbio, dexa el tal juyzio a mí, a quien ste caso propiamente es atribuýdo" (7). Reason accuses Will of not having fulfilled its duty to check the judgments of the inferior faculties and the resulting appetites.

> E vos ¿no sabéys que sin pasar por las potençias y sentidos nuestros la libertat encadenar no se puede? Y ¿qué vos sóys la postrera, aziendo vuestras operaçiones segunt el juyzio fecho por el entendimiento, el qual dexa las más vezes la mejor y más prinçipal parte de todas por la menor y más inútil; y esto no por querer suyo, mas mandado vuestro? (8)

To this Voluntad replies that it is driven by the hope for the "delicious fruits" of love ("la sperança sus deleytosos frutos"; 8). Love is dangerous, but there is always the hope of belonging to the elected ones ("scogidos").

> E con sta sperança de ser de los scogidos, se ponen a la ventura aquéllos que suyos se dizen. Y aun yo conformarme con ellos, quando mi voluntat terná por bien pasar con deleyte las penas que su merçet por provar mi firmeza me dare. (9)

Razón is not convinced that Voluntad will be able to enjoy the fruits of love. Women shrink from reciprocating love out of fear for their reputation (10) and fickleness of their affection (14). Will, however, insists that it is worth the risk.

> [S]abe que los ojos, permitiéndolo Fortuna, me yzieron conoçer una senyora de tanta disposiçión en valer y belleza que su nonbre, en dando en boca de las más cortesanas, a mucha virtut las inclina. (10)

It is a reflex of the reason of the *philocaptio*: a woman, her *imago* to be more precise, is judged extremely beautiful and "beneficial."[202] Will is blinded and does not recognize the danger of misjudgment and describes love as an ennobling force (10-11). The two adversaries adduce historic and literary *exempla* of disastrous and fortunate lovers to buttress their respective positions (11-12).

---

[202] See above chapter I.

Razón argues that Will is not experienced enough to recognize the lady's "senyalles en ella que claramente muestran amaros [...]" (12); she also claims that Will is too ignorant to follow the *ars amandi* ("de amor sus condiçiones innoráys [...]"; [12]). This argument is countered by Will with a list of *signa amoris* and precepts of love which culminates in a definition of love reminiscent of Andreas Capellanus's *De Amore* (32-34; Vigier, "Le *De Arte Amandi*" 163-64).

> Que otra cosa es amor sino inmoderada forçíbol, scondida privación y deseo grande de abraçar la querida cosa. [...] Será amor, si lo entiendo, una pasión naçida del cuerpo y alma; tiene por fundamento el coraçón y por difinación el pensamiento, y por duraçión el sentido; causada de fermosura tal como aquélla qu'el día pasado con gran liberalidat me dý. (*Triste deleytaçión* 13-14)

In a final attempt, Razón describes an allegorical Palace of Love, called Aborintio, which she regards as "falso y sufístiquo" (15). Once the lover drinks from the water of forgetfulness the Palace is transformed into an Erotic Hell. In other words, once the lover is rid of the incessant amorous memories he will realize his error and the destructive force of love. With another allegorical description celebrating the merits of his Lady, Will signals that Razón's persuasion has not succeeded. Upon recovering from his "visión terrible," Eº realizes that he is suffering from passionate love, "forçado por el contínuo seguir d'aquella recordar" (18).[203]

He fails to establish a relationship with Sª by way of an epistle. She angrily responds:

> [No] sea la causa a vuestras fingidas pasiones ny piadosa scritura satisfazer, mas mi fama peligrosa de perder. [...] Vuestros deseos son puestos em parte que más en sus deleytes que a otra fin virtuoso tienen respeto [...]. (20)

---

[203] Blay Manzanera acknowledges that Eº suffers from the *aegritudo amoris*, yet does not elaborate on this insight ("Más allá" 140). Analyzing the Aborintio allegory, Impey observes: "Los caóticos *contraria* sugieren la insanidad [sc. *amor hereos*] que se describe en los tratados de medicina medieval [...]" ("*Contraria*" 153). She acutely associates the title *Triste deleytaçión* with a quote from Bernard de Gordon's *Lilium*: "Amor est mentis insania miserrimam delectationem omne tristabile videtur sibi delectabile" (153).

Echoing the debate between *Sátira*'s lover and the Lady's virtues, [204] S^a fears that E°'s passion is feigned and that he wants only to solicit improper *deleytes*.

At this rejection he falls in a state of despair. A° immediately recognizes the source of his depression: "conoçió que desconoçimiento d'amor devía ser causa [...]" (21). He engages the E° in a versified dialogue that partly mirrors the debate between Razón and Voluntad. E° first denies. After some reasoning he finally admits his amorous suffering. A° tries to help: "dio al E° el mejor consejo que posible le fue para quitarle la pena que tenía" (23).

> Que con liberalidat
> fuyréys donde stá ella,
> por que no tengáys querella
> de su jesto ni beldat;
> serviréys a otra dama
> por amores,
> y trocadas las pasiones
> el pensamiento desama.
> Vernéys a comunicar
> con hútilles compañýas
> que saben tales fantasías
> se pueden remediar,
> [...]. (23)

He also gives dietary tips ("fuyt de salsas y vinos") and recommends warfare and hunting (24). The Friend reproduces in detail the cure medieval physicians recommend against *amor hereos* (Vigier, "Remèdes" 167-68). [205] This is also patent in A°'s misogynist diatribe which aims at dispelling S^a's positive image (24-25). The logotherapy is unsuccessful; S^a's image still reigns in E°'s mind.

> Quien tiene más sentimiento
> de su singularidat
> dispone la voluntat,
> da byda al pensamiento;
> que solo ver el su jesto
> s'enalcança
> el bien hútil sin tardança,
> deleytable y onesto. (25)

---

[204] See above.
[205] See above chapter I.

He solicits his friend's help in conquering S^a, suggesting that A^o court S^a's Stepmother (26). A^o falls instantly in love.

While the Friend's love is well-received by M^a, alleviating his pain, only one idea ("ymaginaçión") prevents E^o from ending his life.

> Que la husança de las discretas senyoras es tal que con desfavores y desdenes pruevan la firmeza y amor de las personas que aman, por que en las eleçiones que azen no yer[r]en. (26)

He joins the Prince's army and parades in symbolically changed attire in sight of S^a before his departure. He interprets her change in gestures and complexion as a sign of her affection (27). Nevertheless, he is suffering more than ever from *hereos*, which now also affects his body: "constreñydos los espéritos, amorteçido cayó del caval[l]o" (27). In a letter S^a assures E^o that she is now convinced of his constancy ("firmeza"; 28). Warfare and separation from S^a should contribute to his cure, but he has taken precautions not to forget her (*desamar*): "contemplando infinidas vezes en la figura que de su S^a en hun pergamino pintada trayá" (30). The Lover enters a state of delusions, typical of the advanced stage of *amor hereos*.[206] He has another breakdown ("cayó en el suelo amorteçido"; 30). The painted "ymajen" becomes alive and declares that his love is reciprocated (30-31). In the meantime S^a is equally plagued by her passion, experiencing visions. In her aroused imagination ("visión tan spantable"), E^o pays her a visit in her chamber (35).

Upon E^o's return, A^o reports that in his absence S^a's "senyales y autos" assured him that his desire is reciprocated: "el deseo della era promto al querer suyo; qu'el E^o con la sperança del galardón sin más le fueyron sus males" (36). This passage indicates what kind of "deleytosos frutos" (8) and "deleyte" (9) Will indistinctly referred to in the debate with Reason, as the motivation for his amatory servitude. Since the Lady has already demonstrated her pity in her letters, it is clear that the "galardón" he expects is not only compassion, but passion.

Yet S^a is still troubled by Shame,[207] "atormentada de amor y temor determinar no sabía" (37). At this moment the Madrina en-

---

[206] I discuss in detail the connection of *amor hereos* and melancholic hallucinations in my analysis of *Grimalte y Gradissa* (chapter III).

[207] In Vergüença's oration we find another diagnosis of *hereos* with a list of symptoms (37).

ters and engages Sᵃ in a long discussion which takes up a quarter of the total length of the manuscript and constitutes the central portion of the text (fols. 66ᵛ-120ʳ of 194 fols.; Impey, "Doctrinal" 195).

Madrina's doctrine has been studied diligently by Impey. According to Madrina, Sᵃ should be careful in choosing her lover. Most importantly, he must be wealthy. Mature men of choleric or sanguine temperament are preferable ("Doctrinal" 197-98). Once the *doncella* has selected the right man, the most important principle for her is that she must be loyal under all circumstances (190). According to Impey, the main purpose of the *Doctrinal* is to teach the ladies how to keep their lover, cure him of new love and regain his favor (203).[208] At the end of the conversation Sᵃ recapitulates the lesson she has learned. She emphasizes particularly the importance of absolute loyalty.

> Me tenéys demostrado [...] enpués d'aver scogido la senyora no devrié ser variable, mas que deve para siempre morir y bivir con el primero amor [...] y cómo por ser firme en un amor sea por los honbres de más reputación y senyoras tuvidas en mayor stima, qu'es la cosa que la senyora d'estado más que ninguna deve mirar; [...] la mujer de bien sea obligada de bivir con su enamorado o marido virtuosamente [...]. (68)

The *Doctrinal* concludes with Sᵃ's promise always to obey Madrina's advice: "é delibrado con diligençia seguir l'opinyón de vuestra merçé toda mi vida" (68).

The conversation constitutes a long digression, inserted at a moment when the reader is anticipating a resolution of the erotic tension between E° and Sᵃ; in narrative terms it is, to say the least, anticlimactic. The *Doctrinal* is only very loosely connected with the narration of E°'s, Sᵃ's, A°'s and Mᵃ's story.[209] While it appears plausi-

---

[208] Blay Manzanera suggests that the author deliberately contrasted the colloquial style of the *Doctrinal* with the high register typical of sentimental romance in order to create comic effect ("Humor" 75-76). It appears only natural, however, that a shift in discourse from sentimental fiction to pragmatic didactism effects a stylistic change. If we follow Castro Lingl's argumentation ("*Triste deleytaçión*'s *madrina*"), Madrina, a midwife, belongs to a different strata of society with its own sociolect.

[209] Rohland de Langbehn acknowledges that the conversation between Madrina and Sᵃ does not complement the main action; she vaguely relates the *Doctrinal*, among other "excursos," to the "intención amatoria que forma el núcleo de la acción" (*Unidad genérica* 39).

ble that the Sª seeks counsel before selecting a partner, it is striking how unconnected Madrina's advice and the conversation as a whole are to the preceding narration. The qualities Madrina requires from the ideal lover are not an issue in *Triste deleytaçión*; we do not know anything about Eº's lineage, his wealth, his age and humoral disposition. Sª does not really have a choice because she already feels passionate love for Eº and no alternative has been mentioned. Furthermore, the insistence on the Lady's steadfastness and devotion to the husband or lover are misplaced and of no relevance to the narration. Mª and Aº, whose course of action might be influenced by Madrina's advice, are not present. "Sólamente el lector que lee toda la novela," Impey perspicaciously observes, "es capaz de apreciar el peso de los consejos en el argumento (*histoire*), el lugar que ocupan en la trama (*récit*), y la relación que tienen con la realidad histórico-social que los generó" ("Doctrinal" 206). In other words, the *Doctrinal* is directed to the readers, among them F.A.D.C.'s fickle lady. Hence Madrina's wisdom is tailored to the needs of the author: he might be the man described by Madrina, and his lady might need a reminder to be loyal to F.A.D.C., her "first love." The author, then, uses the suspense created by the story of Sª and Eº to pursue his personal agenda with the *Doctrinal*.

The fact that the lengthy indoctrination of Madrina does not affect Sª's course of action at all shows that the *Doctrinal* does not contribute to the development of the *récit*.

> Y la senyora donzella, quedando con intençión de confirmar su voluntat con aquél que amor por buen grado días avía tenía librado, mas empachada aun de Vergüença, no osava ny podía mostrar el amor grande que a su enamorado tenía. (68)

Although the *Doctrinal* is a direct address to the reader, it provides a valuable clue for the interpretation of the story and the manner in which it is interpreted by F.A.D.C. One of the criteria Madrina postulates in choosing the right lover is his sincerity.

> Seas çierta que quando tú berás qu'el enamorado tuyo que razón le causa temor si no con gran fuerça en más d'aquestas dos cosas: la primera, miedo de perder la Sª que ama; la otra será de no verla. Y más: le dará razón fuerça de poder desimular y limitar el amor y deseo suyo [...]. (39)

Already in her first letter to E°, S ͣ had ventured the misgiving that the Lover only feigns his love (20). [210] Madrina's counsel reveals that "true love" is essentially "unreasonable love." Hence the debate between Razón and Voluntad is critical in the evaluation of the E° as a lover and potential partner. The rejection of Reason proves that his motives are sincere and that his love will be constant. Of course, Madrina does not recommend choosing a man who has contracted a fatal disease, as described by contemporary physicians. As in *Siervo*, we see here the projection of a controlled passion which in *Triste deleytaçión* is characterized by the semiology of *amor hereos*. For this reason, the various narrators and protagonists pay great attention to the symptoms of lovesickness. It is, after all, only the reader who witnesses E°'s interior struggle, his physical suffering and S ͣ's amorous delusions. I venture that E°'s and S ͣ's authentic passionate love appealed to F.A.D.C.; the exemplarity of their story is founded in their realistic suffering from lovesickness.

Amor hereos also plays a significant role in the story's development after the *Doctrinal*. M ͣ convinces S ͣ to give in to E°'s advances. A rendezvous is arranged. "Mas stava conçertado entr'el[l]as no librasen de pena en aquella sazón el bien y no bienaventurado de[l] E°, por ser donzella su S ͣ" (72). The two women are aware that the lovers' ultimate goal is sexual intercourse. Yet in the case of S ͣ, who is a virgin, they must refuse because the dishonor would be revealed sooner or later. This tension between sexual desire and practical reasons underlies the following exchange of love letters. While E° appeals to the "piadat" of his Lady (72), she is concerned about her "fama" (73). In her letters S ͣ reverts to courtly rhetoric: "Como dixistes, arto sóys satisfecho por aver fecha tan buena eleçión, que amando a mí me scogestes por senyora vues-

---

[210] The theme is repeated in one of S ͣ's letters that precede their last rendezvous: "Es çierto que los más enamorados, por un boluntario deseo regidos, fingiendo se muestran delante de quien enganyar desean un querer sin lealdat, una amor sin afiçión; con desimulados jestos declaran por diversos modos aquéllas por ellos ser amadas [...]" (75-76). This preoccupation is expressed in countless texts which analyze love. In the *Romance of the Rose*, for instance, Resistance's anger is only softened when it becomes clear that in the Lover there is "neither dissimulation nor disloyalty" (77). Villalobos explains that "algunos grandes señores que toman los amores por su pasatiempo, y para disimular con ellos los grandes negocios que andan urdiendo, sábenlo tan bien hacer, que quien los viere jurara que están dentro [...]" (*Anfitrion* 489); see also Rodríguez del Padrón's *Triunfo de las donas* (96-97).

tra" (75). After E° renews his threat to commit suicide (77), S^a yields to him: "yzieron que pusiese antes mi honrra que vuestros deseos en olbido [...]" (78). When the four lovers finally have their reunion the ladies abide by their plan.

> E asý, tomadas las magníficas senyoras del primo e segundo e terçio amor, que sin contraste atorgaron a ellos todos aquellos benefiçios que a ellas dar era posible, salvo aquél que la S^a a su E° negava, que aze absente de toda congoxa al que bien ama. (80)

While A°'s psycho-somatic pain is alleviated through coitus, E° is denied this "therapy" which apparently would free him of "toda congoxa." However, he has high hopes for their next encounter.

> La amable S^a, de razón y grado forçada, sintiendo la voluntat del amante, no menos dispuesta que la suya deseava aquel deporte que consuella el pensamiento de amor travajado. [...] No dudava la noche siguiente en efeto inprosperidat pareciere. (81)

Yet the Vieja, who has eavesdropped on their tryst, betrays them; M^a is killed at the order of the cruel husband, S^a is confined to a sister's house, and the two friends flee. E°'s desires are still unfulfilled.

> Y asý no fue marabilla el diligente enamorado no ser contento solo de la primera ny segunda vez por ver a su senyora sperimentar su ventura, mas la terçera quiso tentar por ver si la suerte le cupiera por más afetados travajos acoger sus deseos. (90)

On his way to her he falls again into a delirium caused by the woes of love: "navegando en el tempestuoso mar de amor [...] le fue supliendo al demasiado querer suyo la tal ventura [...]" (90). The "ventura que alló el E° yendo a ver a su senyora" is an allegorical poem of 156 stanzas (Rohland de Langbehn, "Introducción" 56). The preceding portion was narrated by an impersonal voice; now the protagonist recounts in first person the adventures with which Love wants to try his loyalty.

> Quando más quiso mostrar
> amor el su gran poder,

> fue quando quiso provar
> las fuerças del desear
> del mi constante querer. (90)

The narrator arrives at an inhospitable plain, "altura, ynabitable e dura" (91). He witnesses how three lovers have to suffer for the infidelity committed in their lifetime. One of the ladies warns him about woman's inconstancy, particularly when the beloved is absent (99). E° defends the female sex, pointing out the loyalty of his lady (99-101). After some wandering the narrator is captured, stripped of his clothes and humiliated by a group of sailors. The ship is stranded and the narrator is freed. He confesses to the "dios de amor" and makes his testament (107-08).[211] Another group of sailors under the banner of Cupid arrives, addressing him as a suicidal lover: "¿Do es aquél que amando / quiso padeçer su vida?" (108). They are attacked and the victorious "jente guerrera" brings E° to the Hell of Love. Here M^a's husband and the treacherous crone are being punished for their sin against Love (111-12). The narrator learns that those also suffer in Hell who showed cruelty in matters of love, or feigned love (114). E° is tried, and the Judge finds him innocent.

> Pues no lo fallo en libro
> scrito ningún pecado
> contra amor aver fecho;
> pues el que no á errado
> no puede ser condenado,
> sy no nos defrauda el drecho. (114-15)

E° then is transported to Purgatory, where the indifferent do penance.

> Vibieron con poca gana
> a Venus de çelebrar,
> y con sperança vana
> desdenyaron a Diana;
> más tienen de traspasar. (116)

---

[211] A reader familiar with the *Romance of the Rose* will acknowledge here another proof of the lover's loyalty: "I make my confession to you before I die, O Love, as do all loyal lovers, and wish to make my testament here [...]" (Guillaume de Lorris and Jean de Meun 93).

A white bird, an angel, foretells that the E° will earn a "seat" of love, praising his and his lady's loyalty ("lealdat"; 117-18). The narrator finally arrives at the Palace of Love and his soul is filled with joy ("Por do mi alma sentía / tanta deleytaçión"; 119). He beholds a "triunfo d'amores" (121), in which a great many lovers, among them prelates and members of diverse religious groups, partake (120-22). With the enumeration of religious orders the E°'s *Ventura* ends.

According to Gerli, "even the most cautious reader [...] can find himself at pains to distinguish the anonymous author's cunning parodic intent until he finally arrives at the Lover's Paradise at the end of the work, where a spirit of fun clearly prevails" ("Introduction" 14). Blay Manzanera has underlined the carnavalesque elements in the *Ventura*, whence she infers that *Triste deleytaçión* is a text "de naturaleza transicional en el cual, a las puertas del Renacimiento, se da cabida al *homo facetus* [...]" ("Humor" 78). Brownlee's thesis of the subversion of the Dantean etiology and transition to novella discourse in *Triste deleytaçión* is founded on the discrepancies between the story of E° and Sª and the narrator's experiences in the Afterlife (*Severed Word* 128-41). These discrepancies lie at the heart of all of these interpretations of *Triste deleytaçión* as a parodic or subversive text.

While I agree that the insertion of the *Ventura* creates a rupture in *Triste deleytaçión*, I venture that it is not created by a conscious attempt to ironize. Similar to the *Doctrinal*, the *Ventura* is strategically placed. After the tragic events, when the E° has just announced that he will make a final attempt to satisfy his desire, F.A.D.C. once more takes advantage of the reader's heightened attention not to advance the story, but to present a digression which is self-contained and largely unrelated to the narration.

The *Ventura* glorifies the E° as a perfect lover and takes up the theme of the disastrous consequences of female disloyalty. This appears ironic because the E° is a clumsy and unheroic, though loyal, lover, and Sª has not shown any signs of infidelity. On the contrary, she has entered a nunnery, fulfilling a vow of loyalty given to E° (*Triste deleytaçión* 80). It is, however, important to realize that the *Ventura* is in perfect accordance with the aspirations F.A.D.C. expresses in the prologue and in the *Doctrinal*. The *Ventura* is another instance of the "superimposición de *yos*" (Impey, "Doctrinal" 193). F.A.D.C. portrays himself here as a loyal lover and desirable companion and reminds his readers once again of the dangers of disloyalty. The presence of comic elements in the *Ventura* does not discredit his serious attempt to persuade his beloved.[212] Moreover, if he is indeed a member of a religious order, the inclusion of clerics in the concluding Triumph of Love is a convincing argument to curry his Lady's favor.

After his vision, or "contemplaçión" (122), E° learns that S° has entered a convent. Impressed by her loyalty ("vista tanta lealdat"; 122) he joins an order too. His feelings are unchanged

> Mas sy por el pensamiento
> fuelgo en ver su presençia,
> no menos me da tormento
> quando me da el sentimiento
> reqüerdo de su absençia. (122-23)

In the conclusion of *Triste deleytaçión* E° addresses his S°, imploring a letter and underscoring his devotion to her in spite of his religious status (123). Blay Manzanera notes that in the last portion of the text the confusion of narrative voices is total.

> Nos preguntamos si quien profiere estas palabras es el E°, la dama que le contesta, o el propio F.A.D.C., que vuelve a retomar la palabra fundiendo su mensaje con el del E°. ("Más allá" 146)

The same scholar of *Triste deleytaçión* points to the most intriguing trait of the text.

> En cualquier caso la historia queda inconclusa –tal y como se anunciara en el prólogo–, abierta a una resolución feliz, la cual dependerá en última instancia, del logro perlocutivo del autor (146).

The end of *Triste deleytaçión* connects, indeed, with the prologue, particularly with a passage that absolutely conflates F.A.D.C.'s and the lover's concerns.

---

[212] Blay Manzanera studies in particular the *coplas de disparate* which the pirates use to scorn E°. She also regards the narrator's "martyrdom" as "*contrafactum* irónico del martirio de Cristo en la pasión [...]" ("Humor" 55). E°'s "passion" might very well be interpreted as part of a rite of initiation which involves the novice's humiliation. As many pieces of *cancionero* poetry show, the use of religious motifs, the passion included, is not necessarily parodic.

> Por que los leydores de mi dolor y tristura, constreñidos por innumerables suplicaçiones, inclinan ad aquél que sobre los enamorados tiene infinida fuerça, buelva la S^a donzella y E° en aquel stado y ser de bien querer que en la mala aventurada despedida los avía dexado. (*Triste deleytaçión* 2)

Since there was no indication that E° and S^a are not in a state of mutual "good love," it is probable that F.A.D.C. speaks here on his own behalf. His love is no longer reciprocated. It is the reader's task to restore the couple's bliss. This can be effected by the supplications of the female audience, whom F.A.D.C. addresses in the prologue; ultimately, however, only his lady can bring about the "narrative closure." For this reason Blay Manzanera is definitely accurate in asserting that

> en consecuencia, la obra se encerraría en una especie de círculo finito y quebrado, entre cuyas fisuras se permitiría novedosamente la participación del lector, que adquiere de esta manera un papel funcional en el desenlace de la trama. ("Dinámica espacio-temporal" 195).

The participation of the reader, however, in the process of literary creation and the cyclic movement in the narrative closure is not an innovation of *Triste deleytaçión*; I have demonstrated that Rodríguez del Padrón and the Constable of Portugal employ the same techniques. Yet there is something unique about the rhetorical strategy of *Triste deleytaçión*. The "logro perlocutivo" of the reader (Blay Manzanera, "Más allá" 146) depends on the rhetorical efficacy of F.A.D.C. The question is, then, whether F.A.D.C. is able to convince his audience of his worthiness as a lover.

I have been arguing that he pursues a double strategy in *Triste deleytaçión*. On one hand, he seeks to persuade his readers in his lengthy digressions about the necessity of female loyalty and his own merits as a lover. On the other hand, he presents the story of E° and S^a as an *exemplum* relevant to his own case. Since we have neither knowledge of F.A.D.C.'s identity nor his biography, we can only speculate on the basis of the textual evidence. Bearing in mind that F.A.D.C. adopted the persona of the E° in the *Ventura* and that the narration, surprisingly (Blay Manzanera, "Más allá" 146), does not shift back to prose which is the medium for the narration of the "realistic" story in *Triste deleytaçión*, it is safe to assume that F.A.D.C.'s voice is involved in the whole of the concluding portion of the text. From this it can be inferred that F.A.D.C. and his friend E° are both members of a religious order and that they are both separated from the women they love loyally.

More importantly, F.A.D.C. insists on the virtuousness of the lovers E° and S^a. After their love affair has taken an unfortunate turn, he intervenes to assure the right interpretation.

> Mas a tú, maldiziente, a quien mis dichos yo buelvo, que sengunt opinyón del que arías tú juzgado, abastarte debría de lo que dos se contenta, que es del perfeto querer, pues que fue entre ellos confirmado. (86).

Obviously he considers E°'s love exemplary. We have seen that he takes great pains to demonstrate that E°'s love is "real love," a passion that affects body and soul. He insinuates that he himself, like his alter ego E°, is madly and truly in love–and equally sexually frustrated.

The prologue shows that F.A.D.C. hoped that the presentation of a real-life *exemplum*, which would be recognized by the audience as such, would win him perlocutive momentum. The address to the "maldiziente," however, indicates that he was aware of the dangers of this strategy. A reader inclined to the tradition of courtly love poetry may accept that the *aegritudo amoris* can be sublimated into loyal love and become the basis of a stable relationship; in spite of the authorial intervention in the digressions, the medical-sensitive reader will see in *Triste deleytaçión* an *exemplum* of the socially, morally and medically destructive force of *amor hereos*.

Similar to Rodríguez del Padrón in *Siervo*, and the Constable of Portugal in *Sátira*, F.A.D.C. attempts to transform his abject condition into empowering courtly servitude by vampirizing the authority of his envisioned female audience. Yet contrary to his predecessors, he demonstrates a real interest in his lady (Weissberger, "Politics of *Cárcel de Amor*" 320), which leads to the juxtaposition of novelistic and idealizing, courtly modes of literary expression. I think that the fissure of the discourse is not only discernible for the modern critic, but that it was also apparent to the contemporary reader. It is an interesting speculation that the text's fall into oblivion might have been the result of *damnatio memoriae* of an author who accidentally, and probably unsuccessfully, exposed the mechanics and the weakness of male power. At any rate, it is hard to imagine that his contemporaries and early readers could have remembered F.A.D.C. as the epitome of the courtly lover, like the "trovador Juan Rodríguez del Padrón."[213]

FINAL OBSERVATION

This long study of the three short specimens of first-generation sentimental fiction provides substantial evidence for shared thematic and structural features: *Siervo, Sátira,* and *Triste deleytaçión* are examinations and evaluations of the protagonists' love quandaries; in the analyses they imaginatively reenact the struggle of the soul's faculties. A critical subtext of this psycho-analysis is the concept of *amor hereos.* The rationale behind early sentimental fiction is the protagonists' struggle with, and triumph over, the psychosomatic symptoms of lovesickness and its sublimation in constant, altruistic love. Addressing the readers in a cyclic narrative closure, Rodríguez del Padrón, the Constable of Portugal, and F.A.D.C. attempt to rehabilitate their frustrated lovers as memorable heroes of constant love and praiseworthy "authors." Although these results might lend themselves to yet another definition of the genre of sentimental romance,[214] I consider it more appropriate to reflect on and go beyond my initial hermeneutic proposition.

The horizons of expectation I tried to reconstruct are medieval faculty psychology and the medical notion of love-as-sickness; the task was to emulate the interpretive tools and parameters of a contemporary medical-sensitive reader. A crucial issue that I have not addressed in my readings is the pragmatic context. What purpose did early sentimental romance serve? In other words, and more consistent with my approach: Why would readers take interest in these texts? Although answering these questions would go beyond the scope of the present study, some speculations on the basis of scholarship on related literary discourses may direct the course for further studies.

---

[213] See above.
[214] Haywood shows further narrative and structural parallels between the three texts I discuss above ("Narrative").

Solomon argues in his *Literature of Misogyny* that Martínez de Toledo with his *Arcipreste de Talavera*, and Jacme Roig with his *Spill*, use misogynist discourse as a logotherapy against passionate love, or *remedium amoris*. In both cases the subtext, *amor hereos*, is the raison d'être of a didactic or therapeutic text. *Cancionero* poetry, on the other hand, which is also closely, and in a way similar to sentimental fiction, linked to the medical discourse, fulfills the function of courtly entertainment, evasion and social distinction or ennoblement. All of these aspects must be taken into account in a reconstruction of the pragmatics of sentimental romance. It is important to realize, however, that the inherent inconsistencies of the texts analyzed so far make it unlikely that they could fulfill these functions: love is presented as an ennobling force, yet the narrative expansion of cases of lovesickness unleashes the destructive potential of passionate love. They can hardly be considered didactic texts, *in bono* encouraging the reader to follow the protagonist's path to ruin, nor as negative *exempla* because of the intended glorification of constant, passionate love. Moreover, only a very few manuscripts of the early sentimental works survived; none of them reached a broader audience after the introduction of the printing press in Spain. However, from this it cannot be inferred, as many of sentimental fiction's critics do, that the earlier texts are only imperfect precursors in a process of artistic perfection in late medieval literature. It appears more instructive to ask to which degree they reflect the epistemic constellation of the historical period in which they were conceived.

In his *Eine Geschichte der spanischen Literatur*, Hans Ulrich Gumbrecht provides a theoretical model that is able to account for the "fascination" of sentimental fiction. He argues that in the Late Middle Ages Castile experienced a breakdown of collective horizons of meaning, which led in the 15th century to the emergence of subject-centered roles of meaning making (80-174). This implied a newly-established dichotomy between awareness of the body and consciousness; the nascent subjectivity is reflected in the literature of the epoch by the fascination for the subjectivity of the other.[215] While the chivalric novels enabled the reader to transcend his

---

[215] The term "literature" is misleading in this context, since Gumbrecht maintains that a fully developed subjectivity is *conditio sine qua non* of literature (*Eine Geschichte*).

everyday life into a sphere of heroic deeds and exotic countries, sentimental fiction allowed the exploration of the "interior" of experiences (195-96). Gumbrecht rightly points to the novelty and modernity of the interest in the individual psyche, yet he does not deal with the alterity and strangeness of the psychic space as presented in early sentimental fiction. The reader is confronted not with a unified unbodily subject, but with an ensemble of psychosomatic faculties in disarray. It might have been the transgression into the exalted or a diseased state of mind, depending on the perspective of the reader, that fascinated readers and writers of early sentimental fiction.

Moreover, Gumbrecht's contention that sentimental fiction is essentially escapist, which he shares with scholars like Funes (340), requires further scrutiny. The emotional distress described in sentimental fiction is not, as contemporary medical treatises clearly indicate, perceived as "fantastic;"[216] on the contrary, anybody could succumb to the power of passionate love, so the case studies of sentimental fiction were certainly of interest to the reader.

Finally, we must consider the "practical" concerns of early sentimental fiction. The motif of the author-persona's "perpetual remembrance" plays a crucial role in these texts. Given the prominence of "La idea de la fama en la edad media castellana," as Lida de Malkiel has called it, it is safe to assume that the authors of first-generation sentimental romance envisioned their literary afterlife as lovers and writers. What is more, they tailored their texts to very specific audiences: Gonzalo de Medina, Isabel of Portugal, F.A.D.C.'s beloved and a small group of readers/listeners the authors would expect to have access to their manuscripts. Hence in early sentimental romance the epistolary form is not mere form, but reflects its original rhetorical purpose. The epistolary frame remains essentially unchanged in later sentimental fiction. However, the advent of the

---

[216] The Castilian noble Suero de Quiñones wore an iron collar every Thursday as a sign of his "prissión de una señora" (Rodríguez de Lena 84). In 1434, king John II allowed him to defend his celebrated *Paso honoroso* in order to free himself of his amorous captivity. One hundred and eighty lances were broken, killing one knight and injuring many more. The spectacle was recorded by the royal secretary Pedro Rodríguez de Lena in a highly complex legal document. Unfortunately the text does not indicate if Suero only fulfilled a vow, or hoped to cure his lovesickness through martial exercise. In any case, the anecdote shows that *amor hereos* was considered a real and even socially acceptable phenomenon.

printing press in Spain produced a medial situation in which the author addressed a diffuse readership and created a paradigm of literary communication which was essentially one-directional. I venture that the radicalization of the notion of passionate love and the shift from autobiographical introspection to third-person psychoanalysis in Juan de Flores's *Grimalte y Gradissa* and Diego de San Pedro's *Cárcel de amor*, the subjects of the following chapter, is due less to changing mentalities than to pragmatics.[217]

---

[217] Severin presents a case study of the impact of medial change in some of San Pedro's writings ("Diego de San Pedro").

Chapter III

THE SECOND GENERATION OF SENTIMENTAL FICTION

1. 'Nuevas leyes usays en amor': *Grimalte y Gradissa*

JUAN de Flores composed *Grimalte y Gradissa* most likely between 1480 and 1485 (Matulka 458; Waley, "Introduction" 11-12). [218] Two 15th-century manuscripts of the text are extant. [219] The first, and until modern scholarship took an interest, only edition of the text, of which only one copy survives (Waley, "Introduction" 60-61), was realized by the German printer Heinrich Botel in 1495 in Lérida (Matulka 453; Waley, "Introduction" 11). [220] The modest success of *Grimalte y Gradissa* is mirrored in older scholarship (see for example Menéndez Pelayo, *Orígenes* II, 58), which conceded more importance and attention to Flores's "international bestseller" *Grisel y Mirabella*. Recently, however, *Grimalte y Gradissa*'s complex narrative structure has intrigued scholars, yielding some penetrating studies.

In 1983 Barbara Weissberger related *Grimalte y Gradissa* to the transition from oral culture to print culture. She pointed out that in the text we find various self-conscious authors, characters and readers ("Authors" 66). By way of merging fiction and reality Flores ex-

---

[218] Regarding the identity of Juan de Flores see Parrilla García ("Introducción" 3-24; "Cronista olvidado") and Gwara. The verse portions of *Grimalte y Gradissa* are a contribution of Alonso de Córdoba (Matulka 415; Parrilla García, "Introducción" 25-35). Weissberger speculates that Flores's *Grimalte y Gradissa* was a reaction to the success of the *editio princeps* of the Castilian translation of *Fiammetta* in 1497 ("Authors" 74-75).

[219] Ms. E.III.9 and Ms. P.I.22 of the Real Biblioteca de San Lorenzo de El Escorial are described by Vozzo (13-15).

[220] French poet Maurice Scève realized a translation which was published in 1535 and 1536 (Parrilla García, "Introducción" 38).

posed the literary artifice, the "fabric of illusion" (68). Hence, according to Weissberger, *Grimalte y Gradissa* is, as it were, a self-conscious allegory of new writing techniques and reading habits. With few exceptions,[221] newer studies on *Grimalte y Gradissa* either acknowledge or focus in some way on the metafictional dimension of the work. Isabel de Sena, for instance, sees in *Grimalte y Gradissa* a fiction "sobre el proceso de llegada a la escritura" (335). Brownlee traces a development that leads from Ovid's juxtaposition of the universality of myth and the individuality of the subject in the *Heroides*, to Boccaccio's fusion of the two epistemological spheres in the figure of Fiammetta, to *Grimalte y Gradissa*, where Flores underscores "the need for action to guarantee the truth status of speech so that symbolized event and signified utterance correspond" ("Counterfeit Muse" 126-27). The author thus demonstrates and dramatizes the "irreducibly narcissistic nature of language" (*Severed Word* 190). In a feminist reading, Louise M. Haywood holds that Flores achieves the subversion of traditional gender roles and courtly love by merging different narrative levels and breaking down the boundaries between fiction and reality ("Gradissa" 93-95). Patricia Grieve also acknowledges the importance of Gradissa as a reader of *Fiammetta*. Gradissa "avoids the pitfalls of mimetic desire and shows herself to be the ideal moral reader, one who benefits from the example of another's misfortune" (92).

Thus Grieve calls attention to the perspective a contemporary reader would adopt, facing Flores's text. It is important to realize that *Grimalte y Gradissa* is not essentially a text about epistemology and literature; the concern of the author, the characters, and the readers is evidently love–to be more precise, the consequences of passionate love. This thematic focus in the context of late medieval notions of love is at the heart of the following analysis. The study of this topic must, of course, take into account the narrative structure of the text. Yet I will restate and address the question of the metafictional dimension of the text, concentrating not on the innovative potential but on contemporary, traditional reading habits. I will show that in *Grimalte y Gradissa* Flores, like earlier writers of

---

[221] Bayardi contends that Fiometa's final suffering in Hell is a result of her suicide. Her disregard for the narrative structure and intertextual aspects of *Grimalte y Gradissa* distorts her analysis; see below.

the genre, scrutinizes a conflictual love relationship. He uses narrative techniques which are the hallmark of the first generation of sentimental fiction: prosimetrum form, imaginative reenactment of subtexts in the process of literary creation, (pseudo-)autobiographical point of view, epistolary discourse, and cyclic closure by way of incorporating the reader. [222] Yet *Grimalte y Gradissa* differs markedly from *Siervo*, *Sátira*, and *Triste deleytaçión* in that Flores denies his protagonists the sublimation of emotional frustration in ennobling loyal amatory servitude and redemption of the rejected lovers as writers of praiseworthy love literature. [223] In other words, Flores exposes the fatal long-term consequences of courtly love; to the reader familiar with *amor hereos*, *Grimalte y Gradissa* is an unmitigated treatise against passionate love.

a) Libro de Fiameta

Grimalte y Gradissa is, as it were, a sequel to Boccaccio's *Elegia di Madonna Fiammetta* in which Flores merges the subtext with autobiographical elements. *Fiammetta* was well-known among 15th-century Castilian writers (Arce); it was translated into Castilian and printed in 1497 in Salamanca with the title *Libro de Fiameta* (Vozzo 17). Among modern critics Boccaccio's *Fiammetta* is appreciated as a forerunner, if not a prototype, of the modern psychological novel. Yet a look at the text from the angle of faculty psychology reveals that *Fiammetta* is firmly couched in terms of premodern models of the human mind. The frontispiece of the 1523 Seville edition of the *Libro llamado Fiameta* clearly states the main concern of the book: "Da aentender muy particularizadamente los effectos que haze el amor enlos animos ocupados de pasiones enamoradas" (qtd. in Vozzo 18). [224] *Fiammetta* is essentially a book about the effects of passionate love. [225]

---

[222] See above chapter II.
[223] Rohland de Langbehn includes *Grimalte y Gradissa* in the second generation of sentimental fiction, which she sees related to the *converso* question, particularly engaging in the debate of the moral value of women ("Problema de los conversos").
[224] The frontispiece of the 1541 Lisbon edition reproduces this text (Vozzo 18).
[225] In a comparison of Chaucer's *Knight's Tale* and Boccaccio's *Teseida*, Ciavolella shows that Boccaccio was familiar with the medical notion of lovesickness, although his "description of the physical effects visible in the lover are more poetically imaginative and less scientifically precise than Chaucer's" ("Mediaeval Medicine" 235).

Fiometa, as she is called in the Castilian translation, [226] presents her autobiographical account as an *exemplum* ("casos míos") to other ladies in love: "nobles señoras, en los coraçones de las quales amor, más que en el mío, por ventura prosperadamente mora [...]" (77). Fiometa, celebrated for her beauty, is happily ("razonablemente contenta"; 80) married to a virtuous and caring husband. Her fortune changes when she discerns an attractive stranger in the crowd in the temple. She judges the youth to be very handsome, not yet in love, and virtuous.

> Por cierto yo hove fuerça de retraer los ojos de remirarlo algún tanto, mas la imaginación de las otras cosas ya dichas y estimadas, ningún acidente forçándome, ni yo misma me la pude quitar. E ya en mi voluntad seyendo la emplenta de la su figura quedada, no sé con qué callado deleite comigo la oteava y quasi con muchos argumentos afirmadas verdaderas las cosas que d'él me parecían, contenta d'él ser remirada, alguna vegada ascondidamente si él me oteasse remirava. (86)

Fiometa gives a rather detailed account of her *philocaptio*: the species of the handsome man is associated with promising *intentiones*, resulting in an enticing image that is imprinted upon the soul. The desired response to her gaze has fatal effects.

> Mas toda consideración a lo final pospuesta de seguir el apetito prestamente dispuesta fui a poder ser presa; por que, bien como el fuego a sí mismo en otra parte se embía o lança, que una luz por un muy delgado rayo trascorriendo, partiéndose de los suyos hirió en los ojos míos; ni en ellos contenta quedó, antes, no sé por quáles vías ocultas, súbitamente al coraçón penetrando me fue [...]. Consigo un calor truxeron, el qual, la amarillez lançada, a mí muy bermeja y calurosa hizo como fuego, y yo, en aquello mirando donde aquesto procedía, sospiré. Y de aquella hora adelante ningún pensamiento en mí pudo sino de complazerle. (87)

---

[226] All quotes to Boccaccio's *Fiammetta* refer to Vozzo's edition of the 1497 printing (*Libro de Fiameta*). Flores could not have based *Grimalte y Gradissa*, which appeared two years earlier, on this edition. Though the possibility that Flores became familiar with the 1480 Naples printing via his connection with Aragón cannot be discarded (De Sena 335, n. 2), it seems more likely that his source was a manuscript of the Castilian version.

The stranger's spirit emits through the eyes a pneumatic ray, mixed with very fine blood, which resembles itself. Upon striking Fiometa's heart the vapor of the spirit causes agitated disturbances (Couliano 29-30).[227] Hence Fiometa's encounter with the stranger results in a severe case of *amor hereos*, aggravated by fascination. The rest of the *Libro de Fiameta* is a corollary to this initial *philocaptio*.

It is important to realize that Fiometa is not "a helpless victim, for her falling in love is a kind of justice; while she was trying to capture others with her beauty, she was captured herself" (Smarr 134). As Smarr points out, she "shows herself damned from the start" (132). In the introduction the narrator presents herself to the enamored ladies as a patient of *amor hereos* in an advanced stage: "los tempestuosos y temerosos pensamientos, los quales con tormento contino molestando o afligéndome, en uno el comer, el sueño, los alegres tiempos y la mi beldad han de mí quitado" (77). The *Libro de Fiameta*, then, is an analepsis to this initial self-characterization as a lamentable *exemplum* of lovesickness.

As indicated in the prologue, the bulk of the *Libro de Fiameta* consists of amorous and desperate "imaginamientos" (91) and "cogitaciones" (88) of the lovesick heroine. The action recounted is only secondary, and it is also organized around Fiometa's *amor hereos*.

Right after the *philocaptio* Fiometa's Ama recognizes her affliction and appeals in vain to her reason to rebuff the "falsos deleites prometidos de la suzia esperança" (96). Fiometa is delusional; Venus pays her a visit and Fiometa gives up resistance. The two lovers, who adopt the aliases Fiometa and Panfilo to fool the clueless husband, enjoy for a while their adulterous liaison. Panfilo leaves Fiometa with the excuse of having to take care of his family affairs and the promise of returning shortly. Fiometa busies herself with amorous "imaginaciones" (137, 140-51, passim). Yet, as she realizes in retrospect, Panfilo's feelings towards her might have changed with his departure: "No me vino una sola vez en el ánimo haver leído en los versos de Ovidio que los trabajos quitavan a los mancebos amor de las voluntades [...]" (139). When Panfilo fails to return Fiometa's suffering becomes apparent. Unconfirmed rumors that he has married or has fallen in love with another woman increase her desperation and the effects of her disease. Sleepless-

---

[227] See above chapter I.

ness and poor appetite weaken her body, leading to "diforme flaqueza" (182-83). The husband, worried about the "manifiesta malinconía" (183), tries to cure her by moving to a lush country resort with diversions like merrymaking and hunting, music and "baños muy sanos" (184). As the medical writings on *amor hereos* state, these measures should indeed alleviate her suffering.[228] Yet, since Fiometa spent time together with her Panfilo at this place, she is permanently reminded of her lost beloved: "mas, del recordarme allí muchas vezes haver seído de Panfilo acompañada, amor y dolor, veyéndome sin él, sin duda cada uno se acrecentava" (186). Further attempts of the Ama to cure Fiometa through logotherapy fail too, though at least she is able to prevent Fiometa's suicide. Fiometa makes plans to search for her lover disguised as a pilgrim ("tomar ábito peregrino con alguna fiel compañía, y en él visitar las sus tierras"; 268); again she is incapable of executing her idea. For a moment her hope rises as the Ama reports that Panfilo is back; it turns out that it is only a stranger of the same name. In a long soliloquy Fiometa refers to heroines of ancient mythology, who suffered similar amorous pain. At the end of the *Libro de Fiameta* the narrator addresses her "little book" which should be an "enxemplo [...] a aquellos que biven prosperados, por que ellos pongan mesura a sus bienes y huyan de se hazer semblantes a mí [...]" (310-11).

The narrator of *Libro de Fiameta* presents an autobiographical narration about a case of lovesickness which oscillates between an *exemplum* for enamored ladies, a diatribe against the absent lover, an apology for her conduct,[229] a self-accusation (236-38), and a persuasion of the potential reader Panfilo (109).

This unresolved case of *amor hereos*, with its complex discoursive structure and pragmatics, is taken up in Flores's "continuation" in *Grimalte y Gradissa*.

---

[228] See above chapter I.
[229] According to Schnell, Fiammetta presents herself as the victim of a superhuman power (Venus), but is reminded by the Ama that it is her libido which has led to her desperate situation (442).

b) *Flores's Fiometa*

After years of unrequited courtship, Grimalte, alter ego of Juan de Flores, bestows on his beloved Gradissa Giovanni Boccaccio's *Elegia di Madonna Fiammetta*. Moved by compassion, Gradissa puts her admirer to the test, demanding that Grimalte reconcile Fiometa with her disloyal lover Pamphilo. When Grimalte finds Fiometa, who is in search of Pamphilo, they find lodging in a monastery near Pamphilo's native city of Florence. An epistolary exchange between the lovers does not soften Pamphilo's rejection. Grimalte intervenes personally and convinces Pamphilo to meet Fiometa. Pamphilo perseveres in his refusal to satisfy Fiometa's desires. Soon afterwards Fiometa dies of grief. Grimalte erects a lavish tomb in commemoration of Fiometa. He challenges Pamphilo to a duel with the intention of avenging Fiometa's death, but Pamphilo decides to seek the wilderness to do penance. Upon notice of the tragic end of Fiometa's and Pamphilo's romance, Gradissa positively resolves not to take the risk of accepting Grimalte's advances. It takes Grimalte twenty-seven years and the help of hunting dogs to locate Pamphilo in a deserted place in Asia. Pamphilo has been transformed into a savage who does not respond to Grimalte's inquiries. Only after Grimalte imitates Pamphilo's animal-like life does he succeed in breaking Pamphilo's vow of silence. At night they witness the frightening apparition of Fiometa being tortured by devils. Pamphilo explains that he is haunted by these visions three times a week. In the concluding paragraphs Grimalte addresses Gradissa, reassuring and justifying his steady passion.[230]

Barbara Matulka (261) and Pamela Waley ("Introduction" 29) both point out that Flores takes up the story as it is left by Boccaccio: Fiammetta had promised in Boccaccio's work to go off in search of Pamphilo, who did not return to her after a mission to his native city. For the modern reader it is baffling how easily Flores integrates Boccaccio's protagonists into his own literary creation. There is the possibility that Flores was a naïve reader, who understood Boccaccio's fiction as a factual, autobiographical account, expecting his audience to do the same. Given Boccaccio's fame as a

---

[230] Haywood analyzes the complex narrative architecture of *Grimalte y Gradissa*, in which she discerns four diegetic levels (86-90).

writer and the popularity of his works this theory can be discarded. [231] Is Flores, then, deliberately violating the contemporary horizons of expectations, thus reflecting on the very process of literary creation?

The narrative structure of *Grimalte y Gradissa* unquestionably creates metafictional effects (Gerli, "Metafiction"; Blay Manzanera, "Metaliteratura"; Brownlee, *Severed Word*). It is, however, important to realize that the techniques used by Flores reflect traditional reading habits and modes of composition. The appearance of Fiammetta in *Grimalte y Gradissa* is foreshadowed by the concluding portions of Boccaccio's *Elegia*. The heroine addresses her "pequeño librico," instructing it to present itself "delante de las enamoradas dueñas" in order to provide them an *exemplum* (*Libro de Fiameta* 310-11). The technique of anthropomorphization was not uncommon in medieval works. Glossing on Thomasin von Zerclaere's *Der wälsche Gast*, Wenzel maintains that the author compensated for the absence of his bodily presence by way of making the book a representative of himself (205-06). Creating a simulacrum of face-to-face communication, which was the epistemological basis of medieval literature, the book acquires a life of its own, communicating and interacting with readers whom the author is unable to reach (207). Hence, Flores's alleged innovation resides in having dramatized a traditional notion of literature; from communicating with Fiammetta, the anthropomorphized book, it is only a small step to make her a character in his own work.

Furthermore, Gradissa indicates how a medieval reader reacted to Boccaccio's text.

> Venida su muy graciosa scriptura a la noticia de una senyora llamada Gradissa, las agenas tristesas tanto la apassionaron que ella no menos llagada que aquella otra se sentia. (3) [232]

Gradissa herself underscores the impact Boccaccio's text has on her own life: "en sus males pensando, quasi como ella las siento, en special que muchas vezes me veo temerosa que si por vuestra mi diesse, yo misma me daria al peligro que ella tiene" (4). Reading the text,

---

[231] A generation earlier, Íñigo López de Mendoza, Marqués de Santillana, mentioned in his *Proemio e carta* directed to the Constable of Portugal "Johan Bocacio" among the famous "romancistas o vulgares" (214-15).

[232] All quotes are taken from Waley's edition.

"scriptura," engenders in her "compassion" (12). I have demonstrated that for the premodern mind the process of reading involved the formation of mental images. Boccaccio's Fiammetta alludes in her introduction to the evocative power of reading.

> Ante los vuestros ojos, aparecerán las míseras lágrimas, los impetuosos o arrebatados sospiros, las tristes bozes, los tempestuosos y temerosos pensamientos [...]. Cada una por sí y todas en uno ayuntadas, soy cierta que los delicados gestos con lágrimas bañaréis [...]. (*Libro de Fiameta* 77)

This quote also illustrates that the images have an emotional ingredient. On the other hand, images stimulated by reading of fictional texts have the same ontological status as images resulting from sensory perception of empirically existing things. They are stored in memory and can be the material for literary creation in which the writer is free to use them in the process of literary invention.[233]

Flores is very well aware of the fictional nature of his pretext, and he does not make an attempt to conceal this from his readers. On the contrary, he emphasizes that Fiometa's story is a "scriptura" (3). He also designates his own text an "invention": "Comiença un breve tractado compuesto por Johan de Flores, el qual por la siguiente obra mudo su nombre en Grimalte, la invencion del qual es sobre la Fiometa" (3). Flores laconically states that he projected his persona, named Grimalte, into his creation consisting of new images and imaginary reenactment of his pretext *Fiammetta*. As Weissberger observes, he makes explicit the process of fictionalization of the first-person narrator, which was implicit in earlier sentimental fictions ("Authors" 68). To the modern critic this constitutes an "initial tear in the work's fabric of illusion, a tear that will gradually widen as the narrative unfolds" (68). Yet Weissberger's own characterization of the pragmatics of the text casts some doubt on this interpretation. If *Grimalte y Gradissa* was indeed conceived for the print medium, it seems only natural that the author could not rely on the competence of his readers. In the prologue he gives a précis of the *Elegia di Madonna Fiammetta* to the reader who might not be familiar with Boccaccio's text. He addresses an appar-

---

[233] See above chapter I.

ently diffuse audience, which embraces, as Flores supposes, uneducated or inexperienced readers. He deems the information that the author Flores becomes the character/narrator Grimalte pertinent to the instruction of these neophyte readers. At any rate, the fictional nature of *Fiammetta* is never an issue in *Grimalte y Gradissa*; in the diegetic universe of the text the reality of the subtext is taken for granted (Grieve 79).

Therefore, the prologue's metafictionality is possibly the outcome of the author's attempt to provide the reader with an overly clear introduction to a text that is inspired by another "famosa scriptura" (Flores, *Grimalte y Gradissa* 3). The question is, then, how Flores's continuation relates to Fiammetta's book. According to Kelly, the subtext's "principal types or characters [...] serve to designate the *matière* [...]" in topical invention ("Topical invention" 239).

> But, in conformity with Marie de France's method of illuminating obscurities in the source *matière*, the author could restate a given character's attributes and conduct in conformity with his understanding of the *matière* and the context he finds suitable to it. (239)

Hence the question is what attracted Flores's attention in *Fiammetta* and what "obscurities" he tried to elucidate with his own "invention."

The prologue of *Grimalte y Gradissa* refers to Boccaccio's heroine as a woman captured by love: "fue de amor presa" (3). As I have demonstrated, this reflects the thematic focus of the Boccaccian pretext. The narrator ventures no doubt about the intention Fiometa pursued with her text.

> Tomo por remedio manifestar sus males a las damas enamoradas porque, en ello tomando exemplo, contra la maldad de los hombres se apercebyessen; y asi mysmo porque en quexar sus fatiguas mas senzillas las sentiesse. (3)

The problem that *Fiammetta* poses, however, resides precisely in the fact that the narrator Fiometa tries to persuade her audience; *Fiammetta* is presented as an autobiographical text with a radical, subjective point of view. The readers of *Fiammetta*, in this case Flores and his characters Grimalte and Gradissa, have to determine whether Fiometa's story is indeed an *exemplum* against the falsehood of men. In order to resolve this query it is indispensable to learn about the circumstances of Pamphilo's abandonment of Fiometa; thus the obscurity which Flores explores in *Grimalte y Gradissa* is the question of why Pamphilo did not return as promised. The reader of *Fiammetta* can speculate that Pamphilo was hindered by external circumstances such as accident, captivity and the like. His passion may have died because he realized that the liaison was illegitimate, unreasonable and noxious, or because he fell in love with another woman. He may never have loved Fiometa, may have feigned love and deceived her. The resolution of Pamphilo's motives is essentially linked to his further course of action. The reader must know if Pamphilo is willing to fulfill his pledge to Fiometa to be a loyal lover; only then can he decide whether Fiometa's claim that her fate is an exemplary story about the dishonesty of men is valid.

In *Grimalte y Gradissa* Juan de Flores takes up *Fiammetta*, lending voice to Pamphilo and providing a *desenlace*. He links Fiammetta's *matière* artfully with Grimalte's and Gradissa's liaison. Grimalte is the catalyst to bring Fiometa's and Pamphilo's story to a conclusion. The mandate of his beloved makes clear that his task is to ease Fiometa's pain by reconciling her with Pamphilo or freeing her from her amorous captivity. Gradissa also wants him to judge the discussion and events he witnesses. "No menos me movio [Gradissa]," explains Grimalte to Fiometa in their first encounter, "ser iuez entre Pamphilo y ella, porque quiça son sus quexas iniustas o por ventura mayores" (12). Finally, Grimalte is the chronicler of events, who submits his report to the final verdict of Gradissa. Hence his own fate as a lover is linked with his performance as a go-between, a healer, a critic and a writer.

For this reason, if he wants to succeed in his courtship of Gradissa, Grimalte's mission is not only to save Fiometa but to take her side in the debate about the responsibility of the crisis. Flores made little modifications to the character of Fiometa as he found it in the Boccaccian subtext. She presents herself as an innocent victim: "¿Que persona tan cruel pusiera duda que Pamphilo a mi enganyosamente amava?" (15). She rejects Pamphilo's reasons for terminating the liaison, deeming herself worthy of being loved: "Y si tu verdaderamente amasses a mi, por todas razones conservarias lealdat mayor que yo merezco" (38). Reasonable arguments do not reach her: "Ahun que quiero no puedo tomar templança para que la razon me conseie! [...] Mas, Pamphilo, yo no se remedio con que te desame [...]" (37, 39). Like Boccaccio's heroine, Flores's Fiometa is obviously suffering from *amor hereos*. In spite of her accusations against Pamphilo and the realization of his deceptions, the view of his person continues to engender desire: "porque si los mis malditos oios, enganyados del amor y occupados en tus desseos, se deleytan en verte [...]" (44). There also are numerous indications that she has to pay the price of lovesickness: "Mayormente que si antes me conocierades, mi troquado pareçer os fuera testimonio de mis passiones" (14); "el lohor que hasta aqui de mas bella que otra he possehido, tu olvido me lo ha quitado." (19). Her mind and body are consumed by the psychosomatic effects of the continuous *cogitationes*.[234] No specific reasons for Fiometa's death are indicated: "Dando mil bueltas a unas partes y otras, con spantables senyales en la desfigurada cara, dio fin a su triste vida" (52). Although some critics argue that Fiometa actually commits suicide (Castro Lingl, "Fiometa's Suicide"; Waley, "Love and honour" 274; Bayardi), Flores's terse description evokes the image of an agonizing Fiometa tossing and turning in her bed. It is ultimately irrelevant whether she dies of the consumption of pneuma due to her mental activities or ends her life in the melancholic despair caused by burned humors.[235] Contemporary readers would certainly see her as a victim of *amor hereos*.

In spite of her accusations against Pamphilo, immediately before her demise Fiometa expresses her mortification and admits that she sullied her husband's and family's honor (43, 46). Grimalte witnesses Fiometa's confession, her stubborn rejection of reason and the fatal effects of her passion.

> Pocas o quasi ningunas de mis palabras tocaron en los oydos de Fiometa, mas antes en la turbada muerte todos los sentidos tenia occupados. Que la larga y muy enoiada vida que antes havia sostenida la tenia tan gastada que con muy pequenyo mal

---

[234] A further indicator of Fiometa's physical debility is her collapse after having sex with Pamphilo: "sobrado gozo derribo a ella en el suelo quasi muerta" (31).

[235] Boccaccio's Fiameta refers repeatedly to her "manifiesta malinconía" (*Libro de Fiameta* 183).

sobrevenido podria conocer muy estremo fin de morir, mayormente este de gran vigor, que luego muerta sin remedio la dexo. (51-52)

Nevertheless, he supports her position and ultimately condemns the "malvado Pamphilo," echoing Fiometa's verdict: "Pero ell, fingiendose el mas iniuriado, con la mala gracia affirmando entre si, se despide [...]" (44). In his intervention he never questions the validity of Fiometa's demands. He not only arranges a meeting with Pamphilo, but also tries to persuade him to reestablish the bond with Fiometa. He argues that Pamphilo is a fool not to seize his luck: "Mas esto pienso que plaze a Dios que asi sea, que los de poco iuyzio sean ricos de ventura, y los que sin ventura sean ricos de saber" (17). According to Grimalte it would be reasonable, a sign of discretion, to reciprocate Fiometa's love: "Y los que discreto conocer tienen, iuzgando vuestra crueza, os culpan de no claro conocimiento" (26). According to Grimalte, Pamphilo's rejection, not his initial affection for Fiometa, was based on a misjudgment. Grimalte insinuates that the *philocaptio* was not the result of an erroneous assessment typical of *amor hereos*, but a reasonable decision reflecting the beauty and valor of Fiometa.

He seeks with this reasoning to counter Pamphilo's central point and rhetorical gesture: Against Fiometa's discourse governed by Will, Pamphilo assumes the voice of Reason (Waley, "Love and honour" 269-70; Grieve 79).

> Pero yo, como desseo tu bien, me plaze condemnarte, pues ya es verdad que yo no esto preso en los lazos de amor, y la mi discrecion libre esta mas pruempta para dar conseio que para caher en los yerros tuyos. [...] Agora que enteramente conozco la razon, virtud y conçiencia me obligan desenganyarte de las cautelas que aquell cruel y tyranno amor enganya a los que lo quieren seguir. (Flores 35)

He claims that he has escaped the grip of passionate love and that now he is ruled by "discrecion." However, he still feels affection or compassion for Fiometa. "Por la larguesa del tiempo que no te vi," he explains his cure, "yvan cobrando algun reposo mis desseos, mas agora tu venida las viegas llagas me refresca" (21). The greater dominance of reason in males, he asserts, helped him.

> Pues deves pensar que yo no menos que tu me veo de amor aquexado. Mas como por la mayor parte los varones con cezo miran aquel reves que de tales cosas acaheçe cadaldia, y rehusan lo que la voluntad pide, queriendo mas al conseio de razon offerirse, yo, aquell mirando, mas de tu honra me duelgo; y en caso que tu, mal aconseiada, quieras perderla, yo quiero contigo en esto mostrar mayor amor en la conservar. (21)

He pretends not only to have mastered his feelings but alleges his concern for her *honra*.

In his first letter to Fiometa he assures her that he would have met his promise to return, "pero esto no con el desseo de tus desseos mas por quitar de ti pensamientos contrarios a tu salud" (20). It is patent that Pamphilo not only seeks to justify his actions, but lays emphasis on the fact that he is concerned about Fiometa's health: "¡Quanto muy mas obligado te soy agora que quando con nuevos oios y corazon encendido tus amores procurava!" (41-42). In his discourse, then, he conflates a palinode with a logotherapy.

The medical treatises on *amor hereos* advise that the healer appeal to the reason of the patient.

> Pues ¿como sera posible que persona de tal estado pueda con stranyo hombre en agenas tierras bevir sin que tus parientes y amigos no hayan de proveher sobre ti? Que si tu con amor demasiado te plaze perder honor, los otros no lo quieren. (21)

Repeatedly Pamphilo admonishes Fiometa to preserve not only her honor but also her family's. Pamphilo goes so far as to pretend that his abandonment was motivated by fear for his beloved.

> Y esto me hizo buscar maneras a mi partida, porque desto, segun nuestra continua conversacion, ya yvamos el secreto divulgando, y el temor del perdimiento tuyo, mas que el peligro mio, me causo absentarme. (22)

Nevertheless, the reasons Pamphilo presents to the mediator Grimalte cast serious doubt on his sincerity (Waley, "Love and honour" 270-71).[236] He postulates that love is a transitory phenome-

---

[236] Regarding the subversion of the traditional function of *exempla* and advice in *Grimalte y Gradissa* see Von der Walde Moheno.

non, easily changed by "nuevos deleytes" (28). He bluntly rejects the conventions of courtly love.

> Pero para conservar amor, no debria tener mas termino que hun anyo de seguimiento y medio de possession. [...] El hombre que gracioso y dispuesto se conoce, razon es que reparta sus gracias por muchas, que no es iusto que sola una le goze. (29)

Grimalte realizes the subversive potential of Pamphilo's conduct.

> Pues parece que *nuevas leyes usays en amor*, en querer y consentir que aquella tan sin errores moriesse por vos; que mas razonable cosa es, como suele acaheçer, a nosotros hombres morir por las mujeres. (58 [my emphasis])[237]

The reader of Grimalte's account is aware that Pamphilo's reasoning with Fiometa must be regarded with suspicion. However, his attempt to cure Fiometa is sincere, either because he feels for her, or because he wants to get rid of an unwanted pursuer.

In this attempt he meets the interests of Fiometa.

> La qual, si por a dexarte por otro, como tu a mi por nueva sposa hiziste, si tus conseios no bastaran, a lo menos puedan tanto que sean para darme olvido como tu a mi diste. ¿Y quien duda salvo que si como en aquell caso tus enguanyosas palabras hovieron effecto, que no menos en esto lo hayan? (19)

Even deceit would be acceptable if it eased her pain: "y si amor verdadero no puedes tener conmigo, a lo menos seame cauteloso, porque alguna vez creyendote mi bevir sea contento" (33).[238] At the core of *Grimalte y Gradissa*, then, is not the quest for a restitution of the order typical of romance, but a very novelistic attempt to prevent Fiometa's death of lovesickness. In this endeavor Fiometa,

---

[237] The Boccaccian Ama also accuses Panfilo of breaking the laws of love: "El hombre que tú [sc. Fiometa] amas, sin duda según las enamoradas leyes, como tú a él, te deve amar; si no lo haze, haze mal, mas ninguna cosa a hazerlo lo puede costreñir [...]" (*Libro de Fiameta* 249).

[238] Grimalte gives the same cynical advice to Pamphilo: "Y si no podeys tener verdadero amor, a los menos cauteloso lo mostrat, por no dar la temerosa muerte ad aquella que ya la veo" (27).

Pamphilo and Grimalte collaborate and, like the Ama and the Husband in the *Libro de Fiameta*,[239] they fail together.

The fictionalized first reader of Grimalte's narration is Gradissa, who had commissioned this report "por extenso scritas" (5): "Assi que ella [sc. Fiometa] me sera un speio de doctrina con que vea lo que con vos me cumple hazer" (5). Given the calamitous outcome of Grimalte's efforts as a go-between,[240] it comes as no surprise that upon receiving Grimalte's chronicle she rejects him positively.

> Y por ser Pamphilo tan cruel a Fiometa no podria yo a vos mostraros alegre cara, en special que con razon alguna culpa se os deve poner; la qual es, porque vos fuestes del malvado Pamphilo enganyado, que por no saber como vos escapasse de las armas, busco el mentir por remedio. Mas ¿quien duda salvo como vos vio partido de su tierra, que ell alegre, y mas que nunqua lo fue, a ella sea tornado, rompida la fe de su aspera vida como las iuras y promesas que fizo a Fiometa? [...].
>
> Y si agora yo me veo libre ¿querriades vos que en las redes de aquella Fiometa me lançasse? Por cierto, en quanto pueda, foyre de caher en ellas. (63)

Before he departed on his mission Grimalte had ventured the suspicion that his lady was using *Fiammetta* only as an excuse to dispose of her exasperating suitor (6-7). This raises the question of how Grimalte could think that Boccaccio's book would favor his courtship in the first place (11). According to Weissberger, Gradissa's reading represents "a characteristically feminine resistance to courtly love based on an awareness of its underlying depreciation and oppression of women [...]" ("Politics of *Cárcel de amor*" 317). Grimalte, the male reader, on the other hand, apparently interpreted *Fiammetta* not as an example proving that men must be generally mistrusted, but as an *exemplum ex negativo* for his case.

---

[239] See above. Waley observes that Grimalte seems to echo Pamphilo's "cynicism"; she argues that Grimalte is "taking over the role of Fiammetta's nurse" ("Love and honour" 273), yet does not account for the rationale behind the attempts to persuade Fiometa.

[240] Grimalte had conceded beforehand his ineptitude as a writer: "Esto hazeys por creçer pena en mi pena, que bien conoceys que la gracia con que Fiometa quexa sus males careçe de mi persona recontaros aquellos. [...] Pues a mi no seria possible que la memoria ni sentido me bastasse a recitar las cosas tan bien dichas como a ella las oyesse" (7).

> Y si dezys que los enguanyos de Pamphilo me han seydo enemigos, deveys pensar, si su hystoria leystes, quan pocas passiones recebio en el seguimiento de Fiometa, mas ella muy mas contenta que ell alegre, pocas dilaciones dieron a sus desseos. Pues todas aquellas cosas que con poco trabaio se alcançan, no duelen tanto perderlas como aquellas que con grandes affanes se reciben, y asi como aquell que ligeramente la hovo, ligeramente la dexo perder. (6-7)

Unlike Pamphilo, Grimalte has served his lady for a long time without receiving a *galardón*. The mental image is firmly engraved in his soul by the pain he suffered. Gradissa has demonstrated her virtue by her "cruelty," [241] becoming even more desirable. In short, Grimalte has proved to be a loyal lover and the hardship he has endured will assure that his beloved will be spared Fiometa's ill fate.

If we follow Grimalte's line of reasoning, his acceptance of Gradissa's tricky request to resolve Fiometa's problems is the definite proof of his valor as a lover. Again, his view of the text he composed, the *tractado* he sent to his beloved, is gainsaid by Gradissa's interpretation. Like any reader familiar with the concept of *amor hereos*, she understands Fiometa's story not so much as an example of male falsehood, as Fiometa wishes, nor as an example demonstrating the need to choose the right lover, as Grimalte wishes, but as a demonstration of the fatal and inescapable force of passionate love.

In terms of narrative technique Flores emulates earlier writers of sentimental fiction like Juan Rodríguez del Padrón, Pedro, Constable of Portugal and F.A.D.C. He inscribes in *Grimalte y Gradissa* a cyclic structure in which the narrator addresses a reader who establishes the narrative closure. While in *Siervo* and *Sátira* the narrator redeems himself in creating perpetual memory of his constancy in love, Flores denies Grimalte this remuneration for his amatory efforts. The radical divergence in the evaluation of loyalty in passionate love is emblematically expressed through the motif of the tomb which *Grimalte y Gradissa* and *Siervo* use. Ardanlier's and Liessa's sepulcher warrants the lover's "PERPETUA MEMBRANÇA" for

---

[241] Matulka studies the impact of the literary tradition of the *belle dame sans merci* (255-60). In my opinion, it is not necessary to postulate a direct influence of Alain Chartier because faculty psychology and mnemotechnique perfectly explain how Gradissa's cruelty contributes to the formation of a powerful mental image.

having "FALLEÇIDOS POR BIEN AMAR" (Rodríguez del Padrón, *Siervo* 197).[242] In Flores's *Grimalte y Gradissa*, Grimalte erects a tomb for Fiometa, who died of loyal love, but it is a monument to a wasted life.[243]

> Y puse alli sus senyales, que fuessen entero conocimiento con entera relacion del despendido y mal gastado bevir con que amor y porfia gualardonava los mas de su servicio. (55)

Pamphilo had warned Fiometa that she would not be remembered for constancy in love but for the dishonor she brought upon herself and her husband.

> Y si de ti no te dueles, duelete de la honra de tu marido, el qual ahun queda en el mundo por *memoria de perdurable desonra*, la qual mas que la muerte mata. Despierta pues el nuevo iuizio, y torna a cobrar tu vida. (35 [my emphasis])

In an emphatic self-accusation, which foreshadows her afterlife, Fiometa shows that she is aware of the danger her conduct will bring upon her reputation and memory.

> Tu eres oprobrio de las famosas duenyas, induzimiento de la singular favor, en exemplo de toda maldat, de malos y de buenos avorrecida; perdida de los spirituales bienes, entera sperança de las eternales penas, causa de lloros a tus amigos, complido plazer de tus enemigos, sepultura de peccados, ymagen de quien haze desonestat para el mundo y tierra que te crio. (46)

Even Fiometa's supporter Grimalte acknowledges that the lovesick Fiometa will not enjoy the admiration of posterity: "Veamos, vos moriendo ahora que stays tan alexada de todas virtudes, que gualardon abriays de la passada vida. ¡O quan fea quedaria vuestra memoria!" (51).

The treatment of the theme of a tomb of love is paralleled in the status Flores and Rodríguez del Padrón ascribe the respective exemplary tales they incorporate in their texts. As in the *Estoria de dos amadores* in *Siervo*, the story of Fiometa and Pamphilo is pre-

---

[242] See above chapter II.
[243] Matulka studies the color symbolism of Fiometa's *sepultura* (266-82).

sented as a macroexample with which the lover hopes to resolve his own problems. In *Siervo* the *Estoria* directs the way to salvation; in *Grimalte y Gradissa* the *exemplum* determines the lover's failure.

Grieve has called *Grimalte y Gradissa* "a study of reason and will, in which only one of the four protagonists, Gradissa, exercises an admirable use of reason" (134). To this we must add that Gradissa is exemplary also in her astuteness. Against the advances of Grimalte, who complains about her cruelty, she presents her request to save Fiometa as a *galardón*: "Mayormente que vos muchas vezes quexastes de yo no daros en que me pudiesseys servir; y por alevianar algunos quexos de mi, era razon contentaros" (Flores 5). Again, in her final rejection she uses the rhetoric which veils the carnal lust of the courtly lover to outsmart her pursuer: "Y si vos verdaderamente amays, gran partido vos sera passar el tiempo en amores, mayor que venir en la execucion dellos" (63).[244]

It is significant that only the reasonable and cynical Gradissa escapes the cataclysm of the lovers. She is, as Grieve points out, conceived by the author as an ideal, modelic reader "who benefits from the example of another's misfortune" (92). She does not succumb to courtly love but "reads like a woman" (Weissberger, "Politics of *Cárcel de amor*" 323).[245] Flores ironizes the conventions of courtly love by realistically playing out the consequences of *amor hereos* and taking literally the hyperbolic or euphemistic formulas of courtly rhetoric. In the corollary to Fiometa's story he takes up the threads of the first part and weaves a subtle web of ironies, which presents an even more devastating picture of passionate love.

Unlike Boccaccio in *Fiammetta*, Flores takes great pains to avoid obscurities in his story, eliminating the ambiguity always inherent in exemplary stories. Although Grimalte's report concludes the story of Fiometa and perfectly fulfills Gradissa's demand, it does not inform the reader about Pamphilo's motivations and destiny. Since Gradissa reproaches Grimalte's ingenuity for having

---

[244] See also Fiometa's first response to Grimalte's complaints about the cruelty of his lady: "¿Y qual mayor bien buscays que por ella sin galardon morir?" (14). In the Constable of Portugal's *Sátira*, Piedat seriously characterizes the cruelty of the lady as an act of pity (138-39); *Triste deleytaçión*'s S^a argues that the E^o should be content with having chosen a virtuous lady (75); see above chapter II.

[245] According to Weissberger, it is not the so-called feminist debate, but Gradissa's resistance to courtly love that qualifies Flores's work as feminist ("Politics of *Cárcel de amor*" 317).

been deceived by Pamphilo's feigned contrition (63), Grimalte's quest to locate him is a last desperate attempt to rehabilitate himself. When he finally hunts him down in the wilderness he discovers that the once handsome Pamphilo has become a "wild man."

> De tan desfigurado facion stava que si no lo hoviera visto denante, ningun humano iuyzio lo podria a ninguna difformidad comparar. Porque todos los senyales de persona racional tenia perdidos por muchas razones. [...] Y esta cosa lo havia mudado en salvaje pareçer, porque no solamente los cabellos y barvas tenia mucho mas que su statura crecidas, mas assi mismo era muy vieio por la continuacion de andar desnudo, y los cabellos de la cabeça y barva le davan cauteloso vestir. Y su andar era tal que soplian las rodillas a los pies, los quales pareçian en ell scusados miembros. Pues ell, por su andar y pareçer diverso, en todos sus senyales a hun fiero animal pareçia. (67)

Deyermond has suggested that that appearance of *hombres salvajes* is typical of sentimental fiction, expressing "la tensión y la violencia que produce tal código [sc. del amor cortés] en cualquiera que lo elija seriamente como guía" ("Hombre salvaje" 108). Pointing to the "diversity of alleged similarities," Waley cautions against generalizing the significance of wild men in sentimental fiction ("Introduction" 42). Certainly *Grimalte y Gradissa* shows that the complexity of this figure can only be comprehended in the context of a given narration.

Grimalte's description of Pamphilo and the way he treats him show that Pamphilo is closer to an animal than to a human being: "todos los senyales de persona racional tenia perdidos" (67). Theologians and physicians emphasize that it is precisely the loss of humanity that characterizes the patients of *amor hereos*.[246] Is Pamphilo as a wild man, then, a hyperbolic image expressing the outcome of lovesickness?[247] The answer is yes, but only if we take into account Flores's subtle use of irony.

---

[246] Burke analyzes the references to Calisto's "bestiality" in *Celestina*, relating it to his imagination which inclines him to sensual desires ("Calisto's imagination"). Since it is inconceivable that Sempronio has any knowledge of Calisto's grandmother's fantasies, Burke's contention that Calisto's corrupted imagination is hereditary seems implausible. The notion of *amor hereos* clearly indicates that damage to the interior senses is caused in the *philocaptio*.

[247] To the medical-sensitive reader the image evokes the semiology of lycan-

Pamphilo presents himself in the debate with Fiometa as cured of lovesickness. We have seen that there is at the same time strong evidence that he deceived Fiometa, feigning passionate love. Grieve contends that Pamphilo's decision to do penance is motivated by reason as he takes responsibility for her death (88). He is, however, emotionally most affected by Fiometa's death. He leaves his home and family, forsaking a reasonable life; his relatives notice "depues de la muerte de Fiometa [...] en ell senyales de gran dolor" (61). Contemporary medical treatises like Bernard de Gordon's *Lilio de Medicina* indicate that excessive sadness can induce a state of melancholy (104). [248] Melancholy is a mental disease, a madness, typified by a semiology very much like the advanced stage of *amor hereos*. The reason for the similarities between the two maladies is that pathological melancholy can be caused by "humor corrupto melancónico quemado" (*Lilio* 104). This adust melancholy can result from blood burned by the extreme heat the lovesick patient's heart produces when stimulated by amorous *cogitationes* (Babb 24). Melancholic vapors pollute the brain and impinge on the working of the interior senses. Imagination can be disturbed, leading to "hallucinations, usually of a fearsome character" (Babb 29). [249] Pamphilo is haunted by "spantables visiones" of the deceased Fiometa (Flores, *Grimalte y Gradissa* 71). Again, this symptom resembles the semiology of *amor hereos*: Pamphilo is not and possibly never was madly in love with Fiometa, yet he is now forced to contemplate her image.

Flores gives Pamphilo's suffering another ironic twist. Yet again he confronts his characters with the dramatization of utterances they have made. In his attempt to persuade Pamphilo, Grimalte had used the topos of *amor vincit omnia*.

> Y cierto, segund su valer la muerte no havia de ser poderosa de quitaros su membrança, quanto mas hazeros ageno de sus

---

thropy, a disease related to mental illnesses like *amor hereos* and melancholy. In Rodríguez del Padrón's "¡Ham, ham, huíd que ravio!" the lover suffers from lycanthropy (ed. Hernández Alonso, *Obras* 329-30). As Hayden White points out, the idea of the *wild man* in Western civilization was essentially related to "insanity" (5).

[248] See also López de Villalobos's chapter "De manja y melancolia" in his *Sumario de la medicina* (fol. 3ᵛ).

[249] Castells provides examples from fictional and non-fictional texts in which the lovesick characters' melancholic condition causes hallucinatory visions and dreams (*Rojas and Renaissance* 9-28).

> amores; que si puesto caso el morir entrevinyera vuestros speritos, vestidos con dulçe gloria, conservaran eterna companyia, con invenciones de muy alegre ymaginacion de su figura. (26)

His unconscious premonition comes true in a terrible way, and so does Pamphilo's announcement that he will retire from human company with the intention "con muy atribulada vida sostener su memoria" (60).

The reader of medical treatises on lovesickness will consider the nature of Pamphilo's visions as a particularly cruel trick Flores plays on his character Pamphilo and as a subversion of an idealizing courtly tradition in which the lover is faithful to the memory/image of his deceased beloved.[250] Devils, "gentes abominables" (71), torture Fiometa; toward the end of the apparition they expose in a finale, as it were, her horrifying physical condition.[251]

> La pusieron encima de un carro que levavan dos cavallos [...]. [...] Alli puesta, desnuda de sus vestidos, mostravan a Pamphilo quanto la havia mudado su desconocimiento de aquello que ser solia. [...] De tal manera que quanto su graciosidat en el mundo me era alegre, tanto que mas me dava pena el agora remirarla. (71-72)

Fiometa twice complains that her beauty is consumed by her passion (14, 19);[252] when she dies Grimalte observes "spantables senyales" on her "desfigurada cara" (52). Hence the attentive reader is hardly surprised about her condition; her tortured body is an adequate image for a woman who died of lovesickness.[253] It is, however, important to realize that Pamphilo, who explicitly renounced the admiration of her image when she was still famous for her awful beauty, is confronted with this vision. The irony in this

---

[250] See Castells's analysis of respective passages in Dante's *Vita nuova* and Petrarch's *Rime* (*Rojas and the Renaissance* 18-19).

[251] As William Allan Neilson's study of women suffering in Purgatory or Hell for sins of or against love shows, the exposure of Fiometa's body is an original idea of Flores.

[252] Again Flores proves an attentive reader of Boccaccio's *Fiammetta*, in which the narrator bewails the loss of her former beauty: "la mi beldad han de mí quitado" (*Libro de Fiameta* 77), "diforme flaqueza" (183), "agora huida la graciosa beldad" (219).

[253] Bayardi's analysis of Fiometa's *infierno* does not account for this aspect of the apparition.

consists in the fact that Pamphilo, the failed healer, is now incapable of ridding himself of this altered, now appalling image of his former beloved which is, according to medical treatises, the *ultima ratio* in the cure of lovesickness.[254]

In short, Pamphilo suffers from symptoms typical of lovesickness even though he believed he had freed himself of his passion or never was a real lover. His fate is even more cruel than that of an actual patient of *amor hereos*, because he is condemned to continuously contemplate not the enticing image of his beloved but a horrible vision. It is not altogether clear whether Pamphilo deceived Fiometa or, as Dudley has it, "takes the road of madness to authenticate his love [...]" ("Inquisition of love" 238). Either way, to the medical-sensitive reader the message is clear: passionate love cannot be controlled; it destroys even those who think that they can overcome it or use it for their purposes. To this reader, as Grieve points out, *Grimalte y Gradissa* is a *reprobatio amoris* (78).

The fact that Flores needed a chronicler to finish his story does not sufficiently explain Grimalte's presence in Pamphilo's martyrdom. Grimalte hopes to regain Gradissa's favor by proving that he was not fooled by Pamphilo's feigned contrition. Yet his quest results in a further humiliation of this courtly lover. His mission makes it necessary that he immerses himself in a setting antithetical to the courtly world, i.e. a remote wilderness. Here he does not only observe Pamphilo's debasing madness, he rather imitates it and participates.[255] There is no doubt that he also is a victim of passionate love.[256]

After many years of separation he addresses Gradissa in the concluding paragraphs of *Grimalte y Gradissa*: "Y no creas mis destierros sean causa de no quererte, antes mi desfigurada persona no sabe que es olvidarte [...]" (74). His body is wasted and his mind is still occupied by the memories of Gradissa's image.

> Alguno vyendo mi mal me reprehenderia de simple por comportar tan estremo dolor. Pero las causas de tu beldat y valer me

---

[254] See above chapter I.

[255] Weissberger analyzes the carnivalesque dimension in Flores's *Grisel y Mirabella* and *Triunfo* ("Role-Reversal").

[256] Matulka conjectures that the name "Grimalte" alludes to the 13th-century Provencal poet Grymauld, who lost his mind after his lady gave him a love philter to test his affection (253).

desculpan, las quales si me vencieron, no siento fuerte omenaie que delante de tu vista defienda su libertad. (74)

Grimalte still hopes, on one hand, to conquer the affection of his lady. On the other hand, he seeks to justify his passion. Yet twenty-seven years have passed in the meantime. He and his beloved are old by medieval standards. Gradissa's beauty has withered; were Grimalte not blinded by his passion he would question her valor. As Alfonso Martínez de Toledo's *Corbacho* demonstrates, the Middle Ages regarded passionate love among the old as repugnant and ridiculous. His addressee, the shrewd Gradissa, and with her the actual readers of *Grimalte y Gradissa*, will see his fate as a demonstration of the pathetic outcome of passionate, courtly love, and reprehend Grimalte, as he suspects, "de simple." [257]

2. 'SI PUDIESE REMEDIAR SU MAL SIN AMANZILLAR MI ONRRA': *CÁRCEL DE AMOR*

The first extant edition of Diego de San Pedro's *Cárcel de amor*, composed between 1483 and 1492 (Parrilla, "Prólogo" 42), is dated 1492 (Sevilla [imp. Cuatro compañeros alemanes]). The next year the text was translated into Catalan (Barcelona [imp. Johan Rosenbach]). In 1496 (Burgos) Fadrique Alemán de Basilea published *Cárcel* together with Nicolás Núñez's continuation. In this format, *Cárcel* enjoyed an extraordinary popularity in 16th- and 17th-century Spain. Translations into French, Italian, English and German and the reprints of these versions made *Cárcel* an international success (Corfis, "Catalogue of editions" 21-47; Whinnom, "Introduction" 7-9; Parrilla, "Prólogo" 73-79). Among the texts grouped under the lemma sentimental fiction, San Pedro's *Cárcel* is outstanding not only as a best-seller of the 15th to 17th centuries (Whinnom, "Problem of the 'best-seller'") like his *Arnalte y Lucenda*, but also for the role it has played in modern scholarship.

In his pioneering work *Orígenes de la novela* (II, 38), Menéndez Pelayo celebrated *Cárcel* as the greatest achievement of the genre. Since then it has been received as a paradigm of sentimental fiction

---

[257] Kany points out that the last letter of Grimalte could never be sent to Gradissa from the lost wilds (46).

(Parrilla, "Prólogo" 52).[258] Although this view is not shared by all scholars of the text (Grieve 27), *Cárcel* is without question the most studied and edited work of sentimental fiction.[259] Particularly the formal aspects of the text have been well analyzed; while Menéndez Pelayo criticized San Pedro's prose as "demasiadamente retórica" (*Orígenes* II, 38), more recent scholarship appreciated his mastery of rhetoric on the level of *elocutio* (Whinnom, "Stylistic Reform"; Whinnom, "Introducción" II, 44-66; Whinnom, *Diego de San Pedro* 65-70, 84-87; 101-05, 113-16), the *dispositio* of the letters (Corfis, "Dispositio"; Miguel-Prendes; Battesti Pelegrin, "Tópica"), and as an overarching structuring device which defines *Cárcel* as a classical oration (Chorpenning, "Rhetoric and feminism").[260] The narrative analysis has focused on the figure of El Auctor, the first-person narrator of *Cárcel*. Various critics understand the puzzling interaction of the author-persona and the figments of his creation as a sign of the authorial self-consciousness and metaliterary dimension of the text (Rey; Mandrell; Gerli, "Metafiction" 58). Peter Dunn, for instance, goes so far as to label *Cárcel* "an allegory of authorship" (198). Taking into account medieval reading habits, Lisa Voigt argues that the most salient metafictional aspect of *Cárcel de amor* is the textualization of the concept of "ethical reading."

Three recent studies have opened new perspectives for *Cárcel* scholarship. From the angle of René Girard's socio-anthropological concept of triangular love, Grieve interprets the text as a "study of desire as the impulse of a chain of events" (44). Brownlee analyzes the discoursive structure of *Cárcel*, ascertaining a systematic violation of the cooperative principles of speech situations ("Imprisoned Discourse"). Weissberger ("Politics of *Cárcel de amor*") elaborates on Francisco Márquez Villanueva's proposition to read *Cárcel* as a

---

[258] See, for example, Wardropper ("Mundo sentimental" 170).

[259] See Whinnom, *Spanish Sentimental Romance* (39-55) and Parrilla ("Prólogo" 50-73). In her edition of *Cárcel*, Parrilla provides the most complete bibliography available today (161-81). Corfis first established a reliable text in her 1987 critical edition; all my quotes are taken from the most recent edition by Parrilla.

[260] Severin ("Structure and Thematic Repetitions") divides *Cárcel* into three sections, which are characterized by the oscillation between Leriano's and Laureola's changing fortunes. Moreno Báez asseverates that *Cárcel* was influenced by the *zeitgeist*, the *gótico florido*, structuring the text like a gothic cathedral (18-35). In an ingenious yet forced interpretation, Nepaulsingh claims that the organizing principle of *Cárcel* is the Wheel of Fortune (174-92).

"political novel."²⁶¹ She argues that the plot is driven by an aristocratic, patriarchal ideology which clashes with the institution of monarchy and its claims to power.

The recent discussion about the discursive structure and strategies of *Cárcel* has to some extent dehistoricized or overshadowed what is universally accepted as the thematic and pragmatic core and "modalidad enunciativa" (Funes 333) of sentimental fiction: the analysis of emotional and psychic processes and thoughts.²⁶²

Although most studies of *Cárcel* address the underlying conception of love when discussing the "allegorical" portions of the text, they tend to neglect San Pedro's initial description of the phenomenology of love in their analysis of other facets of the text.²⁶³ I contend that this "forgetfulness" of modern readers distorts possible contemporary readings of *Cárcel*; San Pedro used mnemonic images which would direct the reading of the 15th- and 16th-century reader not primarily to an analysis of the obvious political subtext, but to an exegesis of love.

Even modern critics, like Waley ("Love and honour" 259-63), who focus on the role of love in *Cárcel*, impose the notion of "courtly love," synthesized from *cancionero* poetry, on the text. Leonardo Funes, however, in a gloss on *Cárcel*, cautions against equating the love conceptions in essentially heterogeneous textualities like narrative prose and lyric poetry (334). The problem resulting from the lack of awareness of the shift in discourse is illustrated by Van Beysterveldt's reading of *Cárcel*. He discerns in *Cárcel* a new theory of love which he considers a link ("eslabón de enlace") between 15th-century courtly poetry and Renaissance literature ("Nueva teoría" 71). Although I do not want to argue here that *Cárcel* does not share features with later expressions of amatory literature,

---

²⁶¹ See also Santiago Tejerina-Canal, who emphasizes the amorous and political tyranny as a recurrent motif in *Cárcel*. Nepaulsingh argues with Márquez Villanueva that San Pedro expressed criticism against the oppression of the *conversos*, conceiving *Cárcel* as a "prayer for help." For an opposing view see Whinnom, who holds that there is neither in San Pedro's biography nor in his work an indication that the author of *Cárcel* was of Jewish origin (*Diego de San Pedro* 17-28).

²⁶² Also Sears, Howe, Mandrell, Chorpenning ("Loss of Innocence") and Ihrie focused recently on the discursive structure and strategies of *Cárcel*.

²⁶³ Nepaulsingh's claim, for example, that *Cárcel* is a "gospel of secular love consonant with the tenets of Christian love" (178), is only loosely connected to his analysis of the compositional principals of the text and the intention San Pedro pursued.

it is too reductive to insert San Pedro's works into a genealogy of innovative texts; it is hermeneutically more productive to relate *Cárcel* to contemporary horizons of expectations. In other words, instead of postulating a "new theory of love" we must consider the possibility that "courtly love" was contaminated with other traditional notions of love. The horizons of expectation I have in mind, of course, are medieval medicine and psychology.

Cárcel de amor is a text spiced with references to lovesickness. Various students of the text have noted the presence of *amor hereos* without elaborating on this aspect of San Pedro's work (Whinnom, "Introducción" II, 13-15; Nepaulsingh 175; Grieve 44; Gerli, "Señora" 243; Weissberger, "Politics of *Cárcel de amor*" 316).

Cárcel, then, directs its readers to an exegesis of love which is conceived as essentially "courtly" but imbued with *amor hereos*. In the following reading of the text I will adopt the perspective of a medical-sensitive reader, taking into account contemporary reading habits and psychological principles. In light of the global interpretations of Grieve, Brownlee and Weissberger, this reading might seem reductive. It is, nevertheless, justified by the fact that it will approximate the view of a group of contemporary readers, however small it might have been. I shall also show that *Cárcel* is by no means an "exceptional" text but, like Flores's *Grimalte y Gradissa*, relates to the earlier specimens of sentimental fiction in terms of narrative technique. [264] It is grouped together in this chapter with *Grimalte y Gradissa* because both texts play out the fatal consequences of passionate love implicit, yet to varying degrees sublimated, in *Siervo*, *Sátira* and *Triste deleytaçion*. While Flores cunningly rejects passionate love, San Pedro conceives of an equally subtle re-semantization of love-as-sickness. His ultimate failure is documented by a contemporary reader troubled by *Cárcel*'s denouement: Nicolás Núñez, whose rewriting of the last paragraph made San Pedro's unsettling text more palatable to the male reader.

San Pedro's *Cárcel de amor* is a first-person eyewitness account

---

[264] Hernández Alonso holds that San Pedro "imitó, absolutamente, la forma y técnica del *Siervo* en la *Cárcel de amor*" (*Siervo libre de amor* 84). Conversely, Whinnom points out that "it is by no means demonstrated that either Diego de San Pedro or Juan de Flores knew or was influenced by any of the 'sentimental novels' written by their Peninsular precursors [...]" (*Diego de San Pedro* 78). The question of "influences" and "imitation" is ultimately obsolete; the intertextual relations, however, between *Cárcel* and earlier sentimental fiction are evident.

directed to a "virtuoso señor" (3). The narrator, identified by the paratexts as El Auctor, recounts to his addressees what happened to him one day in winter shortly before sunrise. In a dark valley of the Sierra Morena he has an encounter with a savage knight, Deseo, who is dragging along a captive. The prisoner beseeches El Auctor to help him. El Auctor follows Deseo and his prisoner until finally arriving at a mysterious castle on the top of a rock. He gains access into the building where he finds the prisoner being bizarrely tortured. The captive identifies himself as Leriano. He confesses to El Auctor that he has fallen in love with Laureola, the daughter of Gaulo, king of Macedonia. He explains that the fantastic building is the Prison of Love representing his amorous predicament. Leriano implores El Auctor to speak to Laureola on his behalf. At the Macedonian court El Auctor succeeds in persuading Laureola to answer Leriano's letter, overcoming her initial rejection. Upon receiving the letter, Leriano quickly recovers and sets out for the court. Persio, a former friend and equally in love with the princess, notices the emotional tension between Leriano and Laureola and suspects a secret love affair. He untruthfully reports to the king that he has certainty of an adulterous relation between Leriano and Laureola. A duel between Persio and Leriano is arranged to put the allegation to the test.

Although Leriano defeats Persio and cuts off his hand, the King is convinced of Laureola's guilt by three false witnesses, and sentences her to death. Since efforts to change the King's mind fail, Leriano liberates Laureola from her prison and has Persio killed. He leaves Laureola in the custody of her uncle and seeks refuge in a fortified city. The King's siege of the place brings Leriano to the edge of defeat, when the defenders capture one of the witnesses, who confesses his perjury. King Gaulo rehabilitates his daughter, yet orders Leriano to stay away from the court until a reconciliation with Persio's powerful family is reached. Leriano instantly falls back into his state of amorous agony. After Laureola, who fears for her honor, refuses to meet with him, Leriano decides not to fight his fatal affliction any longer. An anti-feminist diatribe of his friend Tefeo incites Leriano to a long eulogy on the virtue and excellence of women. His mother arrives and bursts into a pitiful lament. Leriano, completely unaffected by this expression of grief, tears up Laureola's letters, dissolves them in a cup of water, and drinks them. His eyes fixed on El Auctor, he utters the words "Acabados son mis males" (79). El Auctor then resumes his way to Peñafiel, from where he sends his missive to the addressee, "besando las manos de vuestra merced" (79).

The incipit of the text explains that Diego de San Pedro compuesto *Cárcel de amor* at the request of "Diego Hernandes, alcaide de los donzeles, y de otros cavalleros cortesanos" (3). Nepaulsingh has ventured reservations regarding the authenticity of the paratexts: he argues that the incipit which assures us that the title of the work is *Cárcel de amor* and the epigraphs which identify the narrator as El Auctor are editorial additions, which may not necessarily conform to the *voluntas auctoris* (174-75). The modern critic, however, dismisses all too easily the hermeneutic value of the early readers' comments. There is no reason to doubt that San Pedro did indeed envision a powerful magnate and some courtiers as his readership. Moreover, San Pedro's "authentic" introduction is addressed to a "muy virtuoso señor" (3). Both incipit and salutation indicate that the inscribed reader of *Cárcel* is, unlike in *Siervo*, *Sátira*, *Triste deleytaçión* and *Grimalte y Gradissa*,[265] a male knight with relations to the court, a man of arms with a taste for courtly love.

This might, on one hand, account for the space San Pedro dedicates to the narration of chivalric adventures of his hero. On the other hand, and more importantly, his prospective audience most certainly shaped *Cárcel*, if San Pedro complied with the rhetorical maxim he expressed in the introductory lines of his *Sermón*.

> Para que toda materia sea bien entendida y notada, conviene que el razonamiento del que dize sea conforme a la condición del que lo oye [...]. (173)

In *Cárcel* this principle gains even more significance since the text was written at a specific request of Diego Fernández de Córdoba.

> Porque de vuestra merced me fue dicho que devía hazer alguna obra del estilo de una oración que enbié a la señora doña Marina Manuel, porque le paresçía menos malo que el que puse en otro tractado que vido mío. (*Cárcel* 3)

The chastised text is most certainly San Pedro's *Tractado de amores de Arnalte y Lucenda*; the model of the *imitatio* can be identified as

---

[265] See above chapter I and II.

his *Sermón* (Whinnom, "Introducción" I, 41). Given the important similarities between *Cárcel* and *Arnalte y Lucenda*, which San Pedro himself acknowledges in his prologue (*Cárcel* 4), the question arises in which respect he thought to imitate the *Sermón*.

There is the stylistic level, on which *Cárcel*, according to Whinnom, the greatest authority in these matters ("Introduction" I, 63), clearly surpasses *Arnalte*. Nevertheless, the stylistic differences are not as remarkable as the diverging notions of love put forward in both texts. Rohland de Langbehn draws attention to the discrepancy between Arnalte's courtly rhetoric and his pathetic, at times absurd and comic actions (*Interpretation* 127-28).[266] Conversely, she and the majority of critics see in Leriano a modelic idealistic lover (127). Hence, it is not too far-fetched to relate the courtly knights' implicit criticism of the "estilo" which San Pedro used in Arnalte to the "uncourtly" conduct of his protagonist.

San Pedro's *Sermón*, on the other hand, is an *ars amandi* for the perfect lover.

> The most important consideration is that he is suffering in a good cause. He should think of the excellence of the lady who has caused his passion; if he is unhappy it is because that is her wish, and he should be glad to suffer for her sake. (Whinnom, *Diego de San Pedro* 89)

According to Rohland de Langbehn, sentimental fiction narratively expands the normative content of San Pedro's *Sermón* (*Interpretation* 30). In Leriano, San Pedro apparently intended to create a character that embodies the most important qualities of the courtly lover. Yet, as I have been arguing, the shift from the discourse of courtly love literature, in which we may include the *Sermón*, to such longer narrative forms as sentimental fiction, releases the destructive potential of passionate love which the momentary lyric expression keeps in stasis. In spite of its idealizing character, the *Sermón* itself contains the seeds for the tragic denouements of sentimental romance.

---

[266] Whinnom calls Arnalte's love conception Ovidian, yet questions whether San Pedro was aware of the absurdity of the character Arnalte when he composed the text ("Introducción" II, 59). Whinnom also points out that the 16th-century French and Italian translators sympathized with Arnalte and condemned Lucenda (58; see also Whinnom, *Diego de San Pedro* 82).

San Pedro appeals to the Señoras to have pity on the courtly lovers.

> ¡O cuántas vezes les acaesce tener el manjar en la mano entre la boca y el plato por gran espacio, no sabiendo de desacordados quién lo ha de comer, ellos o el plate! Cuando se van [a] acostar preguntan si amanesce, y cuando se levantan preguntan si es ya de noche. [...] E como vean los que os sirven su poco remedio, traen los ojos llorosos, las colores amarillas, sus bocas secas, las lenguas enmudecidas [...]. (181)

What Whinnom calls a "ridiculous picture of the lover" (*Diego de San Pedro* 89) is a reflex of the semiology of lovesickness. To a reader familiar with the concept, the traces of *amor hereos* are even more tangible in *Cárcel de amor*'s use of allegory.

a) *Opening icons: "La imagen femenil" and the prison as soul*

In his analysis of *Cárcel* as a profeminist oration, Chorpenning has grouped together the portions following the proemium and preceding El Auctor's departure for Macedonia on behalf of the suffering Leriano as the *narratio*, which he defines as "a brief statement of the facts of the case" ("Rhetoric" 4). The "brief statement" is, as a matter of fact, interspersed into a highly sophisticated allegorical framework which, if seen as a *narratio*, violates the rhetorical imperative of *brevitas*. The analysis of the imagery and its connection with the "realistic" narration of the events in Macedonia shows that San Pedro achieved with his allegory much more than a mere exposition. He created a powerful mnemonic picture of lovesickness which he resemanticized in a courtly framework.

At the outset of the narrator's account he is placed in a perfectly "realistic" environment. It is winter time, and the war, most likely the campaign against the Moorish Granada, is put off. The narrator tries to traverse the Sierra Morena. In a dark, deep valley he encounters the fierce knight Deseo and his prisoner, Leriano. The clash of "realistic" and allegorical modes is startling for the modern reader, but it was most likely not to the contemporary reader.

The narrator is identified by the editors as El Auctor, establishing a link between him and the historical Diego de San Pedro. The question is whether they are participating in San Pedro's supposed metafictional enterprise, his conscious exposure of the workings of fiction, or whether they are naïve readers who regarded *Cárcel* as an autobiographical account. I think that we have to consider a *tertium quid*: as readers trained to think in images, they assumed that the historical San Pedro projected a persona of himself in an imaginary landscape in which "imaginary," allegorical elements coexist with "realistic" images of contemporary southern Spain and equally "realistic" yet distant figments of the kingdom Macedonia.[267]

Therefore, El Auctor does not emphasize his bewilderment about the apparition itself but about its nature.

> Por unos valles hondos y escuros que se hazen en la Sierra Morena, vi salir a mi encuentro, por entre los robledales do mi camino se hazía, un cavallero assí feroz de presencia como espantoso de vista, cubierto todo de cabello a manera de salvaje; levava en la mano isquierda un escudo de azero muy fuerte, y en la derecha una imagen femenil entallada en una piedra muy clara, la qual era de tan estrema hermosura que me turbava la vista; salían della diversos rayos de fuego que levava encendido el cuerpo de un honbre que el cavallero forciblemente levava tras sí. (4)

Most commentators of this passage focus on the figure of the "caballero salvaje" (ed. Parrilla, n. 2). Little attention, however, has been paid to the key image, i.e. the figurine carved into a crystalline stone. However, the iconographic presentation of the initial encounter, as it first appears in the Catalan translation by Bernardi Vallmanya (Barcelona, 1493 [imp. Johan Rosenbach]),[268] shows the figurine as the focal point of the artistic arrangement, connecting the savage knight, Leriano and El Auctor. It shows the "imagen femenil" nude with a belt, an object in her hand, and flames radiating from her body.[269] Harvey L. Sharrer demonstrates the debt of

---

[267] See above chapter I. As Funes has suggested, a shift in chronotopes is the most adequate theoretical concept to describe the transition from the mountain castle to Macedonia. I disagree however with Funes in proposing an ontological difference between San Pedro's Spain and Macedonia on a diegetic level (340).

[268] The only extant exemplar of the Library of the British Museum in London was reproduced in a facsimile edition by Societat Catalana de Bibliófils. The text is without pagination. See also Whinnom's edition (83).

[269] In Sharrer's interpretation the flames represent the aureoles associated in the iconographic tradition with Venus and the Virgin (989-90).

the woodcut artist to medieval representations of Venus and the Virgin. His findings suggest that the "imagen femenil" is an expression of widespread late medieval conflation of the sacred and the profane in Spain. Yet, as Sharrer points out, unlike other religious references in *Cárcel*, the image was not censored in later editions (995). He cautions that the details in the woodcut, like the nudity and the belt, which are not mentioned in the text, might represent the interpretation of the engraver or printer, and do not necessarily tell us about "la figura que se imaginaba el autor de la novela" (985).

The uncertainty as to the identity of the figurine derives from the fact that the figurine is apparently not identified in the text. Addressed by El Auctor, the knight explains to him that "con la hermosura desta imagen causo las aficiones y con ellas quemo las vidas [...]" (*Cárcel* 5-6). Two questions arise: First, why is it that Venus serves Deseo and not vice versa (he holds her in his weapon hand)?; second, why does he not identify her clearly? The failure to name the figurine is the more remarkable as San Pedro painstakingly explains the allegorical meaning of all the other key images in the text. The answer to our two questions is that the figurine does not represent Venus/Mary and that she is, in effect, clearly identified.[270] The confusion about the latter aspect arises from the fact that the modern reader, unlike his medieval counterpart, does not recognize that the "imagen femenil" is not a *res significativa*. In other words, the "imagen femenil" is not an allegory, but only signifies what it denotes; it is "an image of a woman." The implications of this reading take clearer shape if we look at the subtext for the scene under consideration.

Erich von Richthofen has pointed to Dante's *Vita nuova* as a source for El Auctor's encounter with Leriano and Deseo in *Cárcel*.[271] In the Dantean text the narrator describes the effect of an encounter with a beautiful woman.

---

[270] With this I do not question Sharrer's conclusions that the representation of the image in the Rosenbach print takes up iconographic tradition that relate to Venus and the Virgin. On the contrary, in the absence of a medieval tradition of nude portrait, it seems only natural that the wood-cut artist, who obviously recognized the model of Dante's *Vita nuova* (see below), resorted to other iconographic traditions.

[271] Parrilla's arguments against Von Richthofen's suggestion are not convincing (ed. *Cárcel* n. 4.2, p. 125-26): the "figura d'uno segnore di pauroso aspetto" (Dante 48) cannot, as Parrilla claims, clearly be identified as Love. Furthermore, there is no

> And thinking of her, I was overcome by a sweet sleep, in which there appeared to me a marvelous vision: I seemed to see in my room a cloud of fire, within which I discerned a figure of a master, of an aspect frightening to whoever might behold him; [...] I seemed to see in his arms a person asleep, naked except that she seemed to me lightly wrapped in a crimson cloth; one whom I, regarding with great attention, recognized as the lady of the salutation, who the day before had deigned to greet me.

> (E pensando di lei, mi sopragiunse uno soave sonno, ne lo quale m'apparve una maravigliosa visione: che me parea vedere ne la mia camera una nebula di colore di fuoco, dentro a la quale io discernea una figura d'uno segnore di pauroso aspetto a chi la guardasse; [...] Ne le sue braccia mi parea vedere una persona dormire nuda, salvo che involta mi parea in uno drappo sanguigno leggeramente; la quale io riguardando molto intentivamente, conobbi ch'era la donna de la salute, la quale m'avea lo giorno dinanzi degnato di salutare; 48-51)

After this dream the narrator composes a sonnet "To every captive soul" ("*A ciascun'alma presa*"; 50-51). Dante is most explicit about the effects of his *philocaptio*.

> From this vision onwards my natural spirit began to be hindered in its operations, for my soul was wholly given to thoughts of this most gentle lady; hence I soon became of so frail and weak a condition that many friends worried about my appearance.

> (Da questa visione innanzi cominciò lo mio spirito naturale ad essere impedito ne la sua operazione, però che l'anima era tutta data nel pensare di questa gentilissima; onde io divenni in picciolo tempo poi di sì fraile e debole condizione, che a molti amici pesava de la mia vista; 52-53)

In the *Vita nuova* the sight of his beautiful beloved leads to the narrator's amorous captivity, which is cast in terms of faculty psycholo-

---

reason why San Pedro should not have transformed Dante's dream vision into an imaginary landscape. The details of the wood-cut of Rosenbach's print demonstrate that the artist recognized the *Vita nuova* as a pertinent subtext. Sharrer acknowledges the subtext of the *Vita nuova*, yet conflates the Dantean image of Laura erroneously with the apparition of Venus on Boccaccio's *Elegia di madonna Fiammetta* (990-91).

gy. The powerful image of the beautiful woman becomes the object of incessant recollection ("pensare"), disturbing the operations of his mental faculties and affecting his bodily health.

Equally, the "imagen femenil tallada en una piedra muy clara" which *Cárcel*'s Deseo holds in his hand, causing Leriano's amorous captivity, is a mental image formed in the *philocaptio*. It emanates fiery rays which make Leriano's body burn. In other words, the obsessive *cogitationes* of the beloved's mnemonic image produce *appetitus concupiscibilis*, i.e. desire, which stimulates the captive's heart to emit hot pneuma.[272] Thus San Pedro transformed Dante's image of Laura, who causes his lovesickness, into the image of Laureola, who captures Leriano.[273]

In short, to the reader familiar with principles of medieval medicine El Auctor's initial "vision" is a striking image which presents the etiology of *amor hereos*.

Yet Leriano is not quite the patient of lovesickness as presented in the medical treatises. The difference is embodied in the image of Deseo. Deseo responds to El Auctor's inquiry about his person in a way we would not expect from his fierce and scary exterior.

> Mi oficio más es para secutar mal que para responder bien; pero como siempre me crié entre los onbres de buena criança, usaré contigo de la gentileza que aprendí y no de la braveza de mi natural. Tú sabrás, pues lo quieres saber, yo soy principal oficial de la casa de Amor; llámanme por nonbre Deseo (5).

According to Deyermond, the "wild man," a traditional figure in medieval literature and iconography (Bernheimer), represents in sentimental fiction the tension and violence which courtly love causes in the follower of its precepts ("Hombre salvaje" 108).

However, in *Cárcel* the savage is not just a man, but a knight who has internalized courtly values. Rohland de Langbehn is surely right in asserting that his "buena crianza" restrains him from pursuing his passion ferociously (*Interpretation* 148). Hence the courtly savage knight Deseo, in conjunction with the *amor hereos*-inflicting mental image, emblematically expresses the intriguing interplay of

---

[272] See above chapter I.
[273] As Von Richthofen observes (32), paralleling Dante's derivation of the name Laura from Daphne (=Laurel), San Pedro might have derived Laureola (Crown of Laurel) from Laura.

passionate love and altruism advocated by the authors of the first generation of sentimental fiction:[274] The lover is only a real lover when suffering from lovesickness without succumbing to the lower orectic impulses which result from the incessant contemplation of the mental image; ideally, he is constant because he is in the grip of *hereos*, and pure because he is a hero of self-mastery.

Nevertheless, from the angle of faculty psychology *Cárcel*'s Deseo is an oxymoronic figure. In his classification of the emotions Thomas Aquinas conjoins love, represented in *Cárcel* by the *imagen femenil*, and desire, represented in Cárcel by Deseo, and enjoyment.

> For love is precisely such a favourable attitude to some good, such a sense of its attractiveness; the movement or impulse towards that good is desire; and the repose in it once possessed is enjoyment or pleasure.
>
> (Ipsa autem aptitudo sive proportio appetitus ad bonum est amor, qui nihil est aliud quam complacentia boni; motus autem ad bonum est desiderium vel concupiscentia; quies autem in bono est gaudium vel lætitia seu delectatio; *Summa* vol. 19, p. 50-51; 1a2æ. 25,2)

Love generates desire, here called concupiscence, which ultimately aims at enjoyment. Furthermore, faculty psychology accounts for another key concept of courtly love: "for where the objective is some good, orectic movement begins with love, passes into desire and ends in hope" ("nam respectu boni, incipit motus in amore, et procedit in desiderium, et terminatur in spe"; *Summa*, vol. 19, p. 56-57; 1a.2æ. 25,4). Passionate love cannot be separated from hope for reward which has its manifestation in courtly rhetoric in the plea for a *galardón*. However, since the ultimate goal is enjoyment of love's object the *galardón* will never suffice until it reaches consumption.

The rationale behind *Cárcel de amor* is the impossible reconciliation of an idealistic conception of ennobling, altruistic love and a realistic psychology. Were Leriano, as virtually all students of *Cárcel* assure us, the real ideal lover, he would not ask El Auctor for help. His hope to change something about his amorous captivity, as in-

---

[274] See above chapter II.

significant as it may appear at first sight, sets the plot in motion. He is not content with suffering his martyrdom in the Prison of Love, which would, as the cataclysm of events in *Cárcel* shows, best serve Laureola.

The further plot development is a metonymic expansion of the complex initial image of *Cárcel*. Leriano, the prisoner of Desire, is brought to the Prison of love. At dawn El Auctor discerns a strange high tower. It is founded on a strong, transparent rock. Four pillars support a three-cornered tower. On top of each corner human images tightly hold a chain. At the pinnacle of the tower he notes an eagle whose beak and wings are lit by the rays emanating from within the tower. The hesitant El Auctor finally decides to climb the stairs to the entrance where he is received by a guardian who demands that El Auctor lay down his weapons; Ease, Hope and Content.

In the main hall of the tower he finds Leriano seated in a chair of fire, confined by the chains that reach down from the images on top of the building. The prisoner is attended by two women who place an iron crown of thorns on his head, piercing his brain. Against the repeated attack of a black man with a halberd, Leriano defends himself with a shield that issues from his head. He is served his meals at a black table by three attendants. There is an old, sorrowful man seated at the table. The whole scene is illuminated by the bright light radiating from the prisoner's heart.

El Auctor is puzzled. Only once the prisoner discloses his identity and the reasons for his captivity and torture is he able to make sense of his observations. Leriano explains that the rock is his faith, "fe, que determinó de sofrir el dolor de su pena por bien de su mal" (9). The four columns are his Understanding ("entendimiento"), Reason ("razón"), Memory ("memoria"), and Will ("voluntad"), who consented to his captivity (9). The three images on the roof are "Tristeza," "Congoxa," and "Trabajo," which do not allow his heart to rest. The eagle at the pinnacle of the building is Leriano's "Pensamiento." "Desdicha" and "Desamor" are his guards, which keep out "esperança" which might come to his help. The stairway is "Angustia." The doorkeeper is Desco, called "Tormento" in the Prison. The seat of fire is his "justa Afiçión," whose flames burn forever within him. The ladies who put the "corona de martirio" on his head are "Ansia" and "Passión," rewarding his fidelity "con el galardón presente" (11). The black man who threatens his life is "Desesperar." His blows are deflected by Leriano's "Juizio." He is eating at the table of "Firmeza," being attended by "Mal," "Pena" and "Dolor" (11).

The Prison of Love was a conventionalized image in love literature by the time San Pedro composed *Cárcel*. In *De amore* Andreas Capellanus provides an etymology of the word "amor":

> *Amor* is derived from the verb *amo*, meaning catch or be caught, for the lover is caught in bonds of desire and longs to catch another on his hook (*hamo*).
>
> (Dicitur autem amor ab amo verbo, quod significat capere vel capi. Nam qui amat captus est cupidinis vinculis aliumque desiderat suo capere hamo; p. 36-37; bk. I,3) [275]

From this it is easy to understand why a poet would conceive of imaginary prisons to express his emotional state. It is by no means conclusive that San Pedro was influenced, as Von Richthofen ventures (35), by De *Amore*. His *Cárcel*, however, can be related to the tradition of the allegorical edifice in which Barbara E. Kurtz includes not only French castles and prisons of love, but also theologians who used the castle as an image representing and analyzing the human soul ("Castle Motif" 41-43). [276] San Pedro's *Cárcel* is an analytical exposition of a lovesick soul, imbued with the psychological lore of his time. [277]

The Prison of Love is a cluster of images that requires from the reader, as it does from El Auctor, interpretive effort. The components interact with each other and the prisoner, constituting not only an assembly of personifications but a "real" allegory. [278] The pivotal point of the cluster of images is Leriano's heart; it is connected with the three images of sorrow who do not let it rest, and

---

[275] The editor Walsh notes that this false etymology is derived from Isidor's *Etymologiae* (10.1.5).

[276] Kurtz argues that San Pedro makes an "ironic counterpoint" to the Christian tradition ("Castle Motif" 40); I doubt that contemporaries perceived the prison-as-soul as ironic. Kurtz's article is a slightly revised version of her study "Diego de San Pedro's *Cárcel de amor* and the tradition of the allegorical edifice." The continuity of the soul as castle image is attested by Saint Teresa's *Castillo interior*.

[277] For an opposing view see Nepaulsingh, who argues that the *Cárcel* is meant to be justifiable in Christian terms (178).

[278] See above chapter I.

the eagle which is lit by the light it radiates and in turn illuminates the gloomy scene. The eagle/"Pensamiento" is a source of "clara luz por quien está en él [...]" (San Pedro, *Cárcel* 10); there is no doubt that the object of the amorous thoughts is the beloved–her image, to be precise. Hence Whinnom rendered the word "Pensamiento" correctly with "Imagination" in his translation ("Prison of Love" 9). The contemplation of the image leads to orectic movements, represented by "Tristeza," "Congoxa," and "Trabajo," which stimulate the heart to produce hot pneuma, whence the fiery seat of Leriano, who is aflame but not consumed by the fire. Medieval medicine explains that pneuma emitted by the heart is refined into luminous spirit, which operates in the sensitive soul. The light in San Pedro's scene is reminiscent of this quality of refined spirit. The impression of incessant, repetitive torture aptly expresses the continuous *cogitationes* of the lovesick soul and their devastating bodily consequences.

Although San Pedro's allegorical edifice evidently has a medical subtext, it cannot be reduced to an allegory of the semiology of lovesickness. There are distinctive elements that strike a medical-sensitive reader as odd and ring a bell to the reader familiar with contemporary lyric poetry.

The description of the Prison of Love is essentially static, representing Leriano's confinement and isolation. Interspersed in this description is an analepsis of the *philocaptio* which focuses on the role of Leriano's mental faculties. Leriano explains to El Auctor that when he fell in love, which equates to when he first conceived Laureola's image, he did not reject the "primeros movimientos," which "no se puedan en los honbres escusar [...]" by applying reason, but embraced them willingly (9).[279] According to Leriano, only the consent, if not collaboration, of the faculties of his rational soul made his *philocaptio* possible.

---

[279] See Thomas Aquinas: "An emotion urging us towards wrongdoing lessens our guilt if it precedes rational judgement; but if it comes after it, in either of the ways just noted, it either makes the sin a more grievous one, or it is an index of its being so" ("Passio tendens in malum præcedens judicium rationis diminuit peccatum, sed consequens aliquo prædictorum auget ipsum, vel significat augmentum ejus"; *Summa*, vol. 19, p. 40-41; 1a.2æ. 24,3). Most medieval theologians regard the "first movements" or sexual appetites as unavoidable and excusable as long as they are immediately quenched by reason (Müller, Michael). Siervo also claims that "los primeros movimientos que son fuera del humano poder" (Rodríguez del Padrón, *Siervo* 164); later he descends in his search for Entendimiento to the dark valleys of his "primeros motus" (203).

> Los cuatro pilares que asientan sobre ella [sc. la piedra] son mi entendimiento y mi razón y mi memoria y mi voluntad, los quales mandó Amor parescer en su presencia antes que me sentenciase; y por hazer de mí justa justicia preguntó por sí a cada uno si consentía que me prendiesen, porque si alguno no consentiese absolvería de la pena. (9)

Leriano reports the statements which the faculties made when summoned before the judge Love. Understanding approves the pain resulting from the *philocaptio* "por el bien de la causa" (9-10).[280] Reason goes one step further.

> Yo no solamente do consentimiento en la prisión, mas ordeno que se muera; que mejor estará la dichosa muerte que la desperada vida, segund por quien se ha de sofrir. (10)

Given the consent of Understanding and Reason, Memory promises never to forget so that Leriano will only be freed in death (10). Will adds that she will be the key to his prison, forever loving. Understanding, the higher faculty of judgment, backs up the *estimativa*'s operation which assigns utmost positive *intentiones* to the image, expecting a "good" that is greater than the foreseeable pain. This is ultimately the rationale behind Leriano's decision and the foundation of his Prison: "deves saber que aquella piedra sobre quien la prisión está fundada es mi fe, que determinó de sofrir el dolor de su pena por bien de su mal" (9).[281] In a startling twist, Reason not only agrees, but also condemns the lover to death. Memory offers herself as an executioner; the incessant recollection will lead to death.

Cárcel reflects the medical assessment of *amor hereos* in the etiology and semiology of the disease, even acknowledging it as a fatal disease. However, the crucial difference lies in the evaluation of the operations of the faculties of the sensitive soul. Physicians consider the formation of the obsessive mental image a malfunction of the lower faculties (*imaginativa*, *estimativa*, *memorativa*), unremedied by the negligent faculties of the rational soul. Following *Siervo* and

---

[280] Entendimiento echoes here, as Chorpenning points out ("Rhetoric" 4), the imperative of San Pedro's *Sermón*: "soffrid el mal de la pena por el bien de la causa" (178).

[281] Parrilla glosses that "La *fe* es aquí el compromiso según el cual Leriano se entrega al Amor" (ed. *Cárcel*, p. 9, n. 13).

Sátira, [282] *Cárcel* presents the lover's suffering from lovesickness as the result of a reasonable, premeditated decision (Whinnom, *Diego de San Pedro* 104). The resemanticization of *amor hereos* undertaken here hinges on the person who causes the disease; her beauty, virtue and nobility are worth dying for. In turn, this noble love ennobles the heroic patient of *hereos*.

This ideal love is projected into the image of Leriano's Prison of Love. However, the same image reveals that at the heart of his love lies a paradox. It becomes manifest in Leriano's interpretation of the black man's life-threatening attacks.

> El negro de vestiduras amarillas que se trabaja por quitarme la vida, se llama Desesperar; el escudo que me sale de la cabeça con que de sus golpes me defiendo, es mi Juizio, el qual, viendo que me vo con desesperaçión a matarme, dízeme que no lo haga, porque visto lo que merece Laureola, antes devo desear larga vida por padecer que la muerte para acabar. (San Pedro, *Cárcel* 11)

On one hand, his explanation echoes the ideas expressed in the faculties' verdicts at the trial of love: he is protected from despair and death by his Juizio, Judgment, or *vis estimativa*, which reasonably assigns to the beloved Laureola utmost positive *intentiones*; hyperbolically exceeding the idea that she is worth dying for, Juizio claims that the long suffering is preferable to a suicide. [283] Yet the question arises: why is suicide equated here with desperation?

The attacks by Hopelessness and Leriano's defensive actions imply that the lover does have some hope. From the perspective of faculty psychology, it can be argued that his exuberant love and powerful desire are necessarily linked to hope.

> Hope causes, or increases, love: sometimes by virtue of the emotion of pleasure, which it arouses; and sometimes by virtue of the emotion of desire, which it intensifies: for without some hope there is no strong desire.

---

[282] In Rodríguez del Padrón's *Siervo* the "reasonable" decision to love and pay the toll of *amor hereos* is also followed by the imaginary interaction between the ultimately responsible faculties of the rational soul (173-74).

[283] In Rodríguez del Padrón's *Siervo* it is Entendimiento which asserts that the real lover embraces the suffering, rejecting suicide (171).

(Spes causat vel auget amorem, et ratione delectationis, quia delectationem causat: et etiam ratione desiderii, quia spes desiderium fortificat, non enim ita intense desideramus quæ non speramus; Thomas, *Summa*, vol. 19, p. 86-87; 1a.2æ. 27,4)

The fact that Leriano's hope is linked to his desire becomes patent in his invitation of El Auctor into his ideally solipsistic confinement. At the end of his interpretation Leriano finally states his reasons for involving El Auctor: "no te pido otro bien sino que sepa de ti Laureola quál me viste [...]" (11). The role of El Auctor, then, is that of a herald of his heroic love. In a letter to Laureola, Leriano is more explicit about his intention: "será mi memoria, en quanto el mundo durare, en exenplo de fortaleza [...]" (41). It is an echo of the "perpetua membrança" which redeems via literature the frustrated lover in *Siervo* and *Sátira*.[284] Yet, as the further development of the story shows, in spite of the repeated affirmation that love in itself is the greatest reward, Leriano is not content with his fame as an ideal lover. Accepting the role of go-between, El Auctor also implicitly assumes the role of the healer, who wants to liberate the lovesick Leriano from the prison of love by kindling and satisfying his hopes.

El Auctor is initiated into his multiple roles in *Cárcel* as an observer of an elaborated allegorical image. His reaction is awe, confusion, and amazement once he becomes aware of the meaning of what he is witnessing. In this he resembles the inscribed reader of the text. The difficulty of a text was perceived by the medieval reader as aesthetically superior to "realistic" narration (Robertson 52-64). Moreover, as Whinnom (*Diego de San Pedro* 105) and Bruno M. Damiani (33) remind us, the use of allegory signals to the reader that *Cárcel* is an edifying, "serious" work as opposed to the pathetic picture of the failed courtly lover Arnalte.[285] Finally, the striking image of the Prison of Love achieves what most scholars generally consider the most important function of "allegory" in sen-

---

[284] See above chapter II.
[285] In works of sentimental fiction which present a critical, if not cynical, picture of courtly romance, for instance San Pedro's *Arnalte*, Flores's *Grimalte y Gradissa*, and *Grisel y Mirabella*, allegory as a means of revealing the protagonists' emotions is conspicuously absent. In *Siervo* and *Sátira* the authors make use of imagery in their apology for constant ennobling love. Regarding an evaluation of *Triste deleytación*'s allegory, see above chapter II.

timental fiction: it is a means of representing and analyzing the emotions and psychic conflicts which the love-stricken protagonist experiences.

The analysis of the initial allegory in *Cárcel* shows that the first part fulfills multiple functions. To consider it merely a "vision or dream of the author" (Cvitanovič, *Novela sentimental* 154) misconstrues its importance for the following "realistic" narration. It is significant that the image of the Prison in *Cárcel* is far more complex than the use of imagery in any other sentimental romance. Kurtz argues that San Pedro used the architectonical image of the Prison as a "convenient organizational scheme" in his "analytical exposition" of the lover's state of mind ("Castle Motif" 45). Did, then, San Pedro only perfect Rodríguez del Padrón's, Pedro de Portugal's and F.A.D.C.'s primitive means of "psycho-analysis," i.e. the loosely connected personifications or *abstracta agentes* in his complex allegorical imagery? If we consider the crucial importance of images in medieval culture it becomes obvious that he achieved in *Cárcel* more than just refining an analytical tool.

Anticipating the studies of Kolve, Whinnom holds that it is necessary to visualize *Cárcel*'s allegory in order to appreciate it ("Introducción" II, 51; see also Cvitanovič, "Alusión" 46). As the woodcuts to the Rosenbach printing demonstrate, the contemporary reader trained to think in images would find San Pedro's allegory particularly appropriate to the formation of mental images. In contrast with the scarce ekphrasis of the imagery in earlier works of sentimental fiction, the rich and organized description of *Cárcel* is striking. First to mention is the image of the ferocious knight, dragging the prisoner along with the rays emanating from the figurine in his hand. In its surprising, unsettling strangeness, medieval theorists of the *artes memoriae* will not hesitate to classify it as an *imago agens*.

Bearing in mind that since antiquity buildings have been the preferred organizational scheme of memory systems,[286] the mnemotechnical aspect of the Prison is even more obvious.[287] The *Cár-*

---

[286] Regarding the tradition of architectonical mnemotechniques see the classic study of Yates. More recent studies on medieval mnemonic culture have demonstrated the crucial importance of locational, not architectonical, memory systems for the medieval *épistémè* (Carruthers, *Book of Memory*). Gerli convincingly argues that Teresa de Ávila's 16th-century castle-as-soul image in the *Moradas* was indebted to the traditional *artes memorativae* ("Castillo interior").

[287] Wardropper remarks that the prison "remains as only a memory" ("Allegory" 43).

cel provides a set of clearly articulated, striking images. El Auctor scans the building from bottom to top, from where his attention is directed by the rays of light to the central room where he later finds Leriano in another set of mnemonic images. The reader can easily recover the complex image and its meanings by repeating mentally the movements of El Auctor's description.

The mnemotechnical function of the *Cárcel*, I suspect, has had its effect on critics like Wardropper, who holds that the "allegory is never lost sight of, from beginning to end of the novel" ("Allegory" 42); Walter Pabst, who argues that Leriano never "really" leaves the Prison of Love because he is suffering his amorous torment at each and every moment of the narration (45);[288] and Damiani, who makes the case that the "allegorical vision at the beginning [...] is maintained throughout" (34). More recent studies of medieval reading habits provide an adequate hermeneutical frame for Wardropper's, Pabst's, and Damiani's observations.

In Chaucer's *Knight's Tale*, based on Boccaccio's *Teseida*, a prison is at the same time a real confinement and a figurative prison of love. Kolve explicates that as the narration advances "the opening icon of the prison/garden–now left behind as a literal place, but lodged in our memory as a mental image–is redefined through a series of metaphors and used to illuminate the significance of the action in new and deeper ways" (91). Similarly, in San Pedro's *Cárcel de amor*, the initial images will leave a powerful mnemonic image in the mind of the reader trained to visualize literature. Thus the image of the doomed Leriano as a prisoner of love will be associated in the reader's mind with the narration of the events in Macedonia, guiding his interpretation of the "facts."

The medical-sensitive medieval reader, who finds plenty of evidence of Leriano's lovesickness in the description of his capture by Deseo and his solitary incarceration, will scrutinize the diverse rhetorical set pieces and genres that San Pedro worked together in *Cárcel* in the light of the protagonists suffering from *amor hereos*, embodied in the "opening icons" of *Cárcel*.[289]

---

[288] For an opposing view see Rohland de Langbehn, who contends that San Pedro uses allegory exclusively as a means of expressing emotion (*Interpretation* 199).

[289] El Auctor only alludes to the "images" of "Contentamiento y Esperança, y Descanso y Alegría y Holgança" who accompany him when he liberates Leriano from the Prison (28). The lack of visualizing aides, and thus memorability, effect that his imprisonment, not his liberation, foregrounds the subsequent narration.

b) *Leriano's failed salvation*

With his promise to remedy Leriano's suffering, El Auctor assumes the role of a healer of the lovesick prisoner; the cure he devises to thwart Leriano's desperation, by assuring Leriano that his love is reciprocated or to persuade Laureola to give in to his desire, hinges upon an assessment of the princess's emotions. He is, however, badly equipped for this task, as he himself admits.

> La moralidad de todas estas figuras me ha plazido saber, puesto que diversas vezes las vi, mas como no las pueda ver sino coraçón cativo, quando le tenía tal conoscíalas, y agora que estava libre dubdávalas. (San Pedro, *Cárcel* 12)

El Auctor, who was not able to discern the meaning of Leriano's prison and needed the interpretive help of the prisoner, is equally helpless in understanding Laureola's reaction to his revelation of Leriano's love.

> Mirava en ella algunas cosas en que se conosce el coraçón enamorado; quando estava sola veíala pensativa; quando estava aconpañada, no muy alegre; érale la conpañía aborrecible y la soledad agradable. Más vezes se quexava que estava mal por huir los plazeres; quando era vista, fengía algund dolor; quando la dexavan, dava grandes sospiros; si Leriano se nonbrava en su presencia, desatinava de lo que dezía, bolvíase súpito colorada y después amarilla, tornávase ronca su boz, secávasele la boca; por mucho que encobría sus mudanças, forçávala la pasión piadosa a la disimulación discreta. Digo piadosa porque sin dubda, según lo que después mostró, ella recebía estas alteraciones más de piedad que de amor. (17)[290]

He mistakes the indications of Laureola's pity–in terms of medieval psychology, also a "passion" that affects body and soul–as symptoms of passionate love.[291] His medical incompetence and misjudgments trigger a cataclysm of events that compromises Laureola's honor, damages the reputation and authority of the king, and causes civil war and ultimately Leriano's death.

---

[290] The importance of the passage is emphasized by a similar diagnosis later on (17).
[291] Various critics have discussed the medical subtext of the passage quoted; see the respective footnote in Parrilla's edition.

From the angle of contemporary medicine and psychology it is obvious that El Auctor is not qualified to play physician to the lovesick Leriano. He is not only incapable of detecting real, passionate love, but also chooses a cure that necessarily leads to disaster: Unless he hopes to remedy Leriano's suffering by luring Laureola into sexual intercourse, his plan to free Leriano from the Prison of Love by giving him hope that his love will be reciprocated is badly devised; although new hope temporarily dissipates the melancholic condition of his soul (Desesperar's onslaughts), the contact with Laureola will only reinforce the *cogitationes* of her image, consuming pneuma and wasting the body.

In spite of Leriano's explication of the components of the Garden of Love, El Auctor has failed to recognize the nature of Leriano's love. Ultimately, Leriano charges El Auctor with the responsibility of evaluating the situation: "Si te parece que soy bien servido, tú lo juzga; si remedio e menester, tú lo vees" (11). He also trusts in El Auctor's "juizio" in evaluating Laureola's feelings (23). According to Whinnom, El Auctor is "an outside observer, if not a completely impartial one. He can stand aside when Leriano's judgment is impaired by rage and offer cool counsel" (*Diego de San Pedro* 107). It is obvious, however, that El Auctor's judgment is impaired; Leriano has misjudged El Auctor's shrewdness. In the initial encounter with Deseo, his sensory functions are disturbed by the image: "era de tan estrema hermosura que me turbava la vista" (4). He spends a night despairing ("desesperava de toda esperança"), with "tristes y trabajosas contemplaciones" (6). At the entrance to the tower he admits that he himself is devoid of "Descanso," "Esperança" and "Contentamiento" (7). Leriano feels that he must console the disturbed El Auctor: "mi habla te será consuelo [...]" (9). Hence El Auctor resembles Leriano, regarding the symptoms pertaining to *amor hereos*. Although he is not passionately in love with a woman, he is also driven by love: "tanta afición te tengo," he assures Leriano before his departure to Macedonia, "y tanto me ha obligado amarte tu nobleza, que avría tu remedio por galardón de mis trabajos" (12). El Auctor is a *Doppelgänger* of the lovesick Leriano;[292] as such his judgment is impaired, causing damage to himself and those around him.[293]

---

[292] Battesti Pelegrin analyzes the relationship between El Auctor and Leriano, arguing that San Pedro conceived of El Auctor as a "double" who gives psychological depth to the characterization of the Leriano character ("'Je' lyrique" 13-17).

[293] Peter Dunn (195) and Elisabeth Teresa Howe (18) point out that everybody

THE SECOND GENERATION OF SENTIMENTAL FICTION 217

It is the paradigm of misjudgment out of passion that propels the plot of *Cárcel de amor*.[294] Because of his love for Leriano, El Auctor is unable to recognize Leriano's and Laureola's feelings and takes counterproductive measures. Moved by compassion, Laureola erroneously hopes to remedy Leriano's pain by responding to his request. Persio does not betray his former friend Leriano because he is genuinely wicked.

> Persio, hijo del señor de Gavia, miró en ellas trayendo el mismo pensamiento que Leriano traía; y como las sospechas celosas escudriñan las cosas secretas, tanto miró de allí adelante las hablas y señales de él, que dio crédito a lo que sospechava, y no solamente dio fe a lo que veía, que no era nada, mas a lo que imaginava, que era el todo. (30-31)

Like Leriano, Persio is in love with Laureola. For this reason he is able, unlike El Auctor, to discover Leriano's passion for the princess; he is, however, like El Auctor, mistaken in interpreting Laureola's excitement as symptoms of *amor hereos*. His own passion weakens his discernment and makes him inform the king on events which are merely the result of his aroused imagination. The King in turn rules unjustly against Laureola:

> Verdad es que la respuesta del rey no fue tan dulce como deviera, lo qual fue porque si a Laureola dava por libre segund lo que vido, él no lo estava de enojo, porque Leriano pensó de servilla, aviendo por culpado su pensamiento, aunque no lo fuese su entención. (37)

The King's ire impedes his judgment and makes him neglect the evidence of the ordeal in which Leriano prevailed, proving Laureola's innocence.[295]

---

misinterprets Laureola's signs of conduct, guided by their own passions. Mandrell argues that El Auctor's inexperience and confusion create Laureola's "ambiguity" (110).

[294] Santiago Tejerina-Canal suggests that the motif of tyranny establishes the unity of *Cárcel*.

[295] See also the Cardinal's admonition: "Y si qualquiera pasión enpedidos se hallan, no sentencian [sc. los sabios] en nada fasta verse libres [...]. [...] Assí, buelve en tu reposo; que fuerce lo natural de tu seso al accidente de tu ira" (45).

Finally, Leriano and El Auctor miscalculate Laureola's and the King's reactions after she is freed from her prison: he restores Laureola to her rightful position as heiress to the throne, yet denies Leriano access to the court until the feud with Persio's family is settled; Laureola, instead of granting the expected *galardón*, refuses to further compromise her honor by giving in to Leriano's pleas. From the angle of the reader knowledgeable of contemporary medicine and psychology, we must add the starting point of the chain of events: Leriano's lovesickness is the result of a misjudgment of his *vis estimativa*.

San Pedro conceived in *Cárcel* of a plot of events that rival, if not exceed, the bleak pictures of passionate love which Flores projected into his *Grimalte y Gradissa* and *Grisel y Mirabella* and which San Pedro painted in his own *Arnalte y Lucenda*. In this respect *Cárcel* meets part of San Pedro's proposition to write a text similar to his earlier work, yet improving on its "style" (*Cárcel* 3). As I have been arguing, the difference in "style" refers to the vision of passionate love. In spite of the tragic aftermath of Leriano's obsession for Laureola, *Cárcel* does not attempt to criticise or ridicule his love. On the contrary, San Pedro conceives of Leriano as a tragic hero, [296] an ideal knight and courtier conquered by his *hamartia*, the love for an unreachable woman.

Leriano's temporary recovery from his amorous pain gives him the opportunity to prove his prowess as a knight, to excel as an "héretier du héros arthurien" (Battesti Pelegrin, "'Je' lyrique" 11). He defeats Persio in single combat, proves to be a master of military strategy (Rohland de Langbehn, *Interpretation* 67-68), and demonstrates with his absolute obsequiousness and loyalty the qualities of the ideal courtly lover.

The most intriguing aspect of *Cárcel*, and San Pedro's greatest achievement, is the reevaluation of pathological love. El Auctor responds to Leriano's interpretation of the "moralidad" (12) of the Prison of Love with admiration.

> En tus palabras, señor, has mostrado que pudo Amor prender tu libertad y no tu virtud, lo qual se prueba porque segund te veo, deves tener más gana de morir que de hablar. (11)

---

[296] As Gascón Vera points out ("Anorexia eucarística" 65-68), *Cárcel* meets the 15th-century definition of tragedia and contains "embrionic" elements of the classical tragedy (67).

Leriano's resistance to the temptation of suicide is proof of his virtue. El Auctor repeats the idea that only the endurance of his suffering makes him an ideal and heroic lover.

> Esto te digo porque de tu pena te veo gloriar; segund tu dolor, gran corona es para ti que se diga que toviste esfuerço para sofrirlo. (23)

In his letter to the imprisoned Laureola, Leriano is most explicit in what he expects from his demonstration of strength in the face of a fatal disease: "será mi memoria, en quanto el mundo durare, en exenplo de fortaleza" (41). His love-death, finally, is an insuperable expression of this idea.

The statements of Deseo and Razón make the reader aware that Leriano is moribund (6, 10). The effects of *hereos* on him are alleviated by the hope sparked by El Auctor's misinterpretation of Laureola's feelings. Furthermore, the martial distractions ensuing from Persio's intrigues function as a momentary *remedium amoris*. As soon the fighting is over and Laureola dispels Leriano's hopes, he falls back into his former state of love-agony: "viéndose apartado della, dexadas las obras de guerra, bolvióse a las congoxas enamoradas" (59).

Faced with Laureola's adamant opposition, El Auctor changes his mind and ceases to encourage Leriano to fight his fate.[297]

> Y quando llegué a Leriano dile la carta, y como acabó de leella díxele que ni se esforçase, ni se alegrase, ni recibiese consuelo, pues tanta razón avía para que deviese morir. (63)

All hope gone, Leriano suffers the full impact of *amor hereos*.

> Todo lo que podié acabar su vida alabava; mostrávase amigo de los dolores; recreava con los tormentos; amava las tristezas; aquellos llamava sus bienes por ser mensajeros de Laureola; y porque fuesen tratados segund de cuya parte venían, aposentólos en el coraçon, festejólos con el sentimiento, conbidólos con la memoria, rogávales que acabasen presto lo que venían a hazer

---

[297] According to Mandrell, *Cárcel* is, as it were, a *Bildungsroman*, in which El Auctor develops his own authority; from this point of view, the now-experienced author brings the narration of a case of a fatal disease to its logical conclusion.

> porque Laureola fuese servida; y desconfiado ya de ningún bien ni esperança, aquexado de mortales males, no podiendo sustenerse ni sofrirse, uvo de venir a la cama, donde ni quiso comer ni bever ni ayudarse de cosa de las que sustentan la vida, llamándose sienpre bienaventurado porque era venido a sazón de hazer servicios a Laureola quitándola de enojos. (64)

After the "services" Leriano has performed for Laureola, he can now claim that his death is the ultimate sacrifice for his beloved. In the light of earlier declarations of El Auctor, who had emphasized that Leriano's suicide would mean defeat, the possibility that he commits suicide, as most critics argue, can be eliminated. Melancholy, fatigue, lack of appetite reflect the semiology of lovesickness (Nardi 14-15); Leriano has entered the terminal state of his malady. As El Auctor explains, the moribund Leriano "se dexava morir" (64) which hardly qualifies as suicide (Wardropper, "Mundo sentimental" 176; Sears 273; Parrilla, ed. *Cárcel* p. 64, n. 3). This interpretation is buttressed by the earlier reader Nicolás Núñez: his specter of Leriano acknowledges that the beginning of his love, i.e. his *philocaptio*, sealed his fate: "ni yo, según el principio levava, podía escusar de llegar a este fin" (93); he only stopped fighting against an imminent death: "dexéme morir, pues ya la vida quería dexarme" (94).

Yet not everybody is content with Leriano's decision. His friend Tefeo recognizes the nature of Leriano's suffering and tries to help.

> Viendo que su mal era de enamorada pasión, puesto que quien la causava él ni nadie lo savía, díxole infinitos males de las mugeres; y para favorecer su habla truxo todas las razones que en disfamia de ellas pudo pensar, creyendo por allí restituille la vida. (64)

As Parrilla (ed. *Cárcel*, p. 64, n. 5), Vigier ("Remèdes" 159), and Weissberger ("Politics of *Cárcel de amor*" 321) note, Tefeo has the intention of curing Leriano via logotherapy, by altering or dispelling the positive image of the beloved that occupies Leriano. In contrast with the fatal "cure" administered by El Auctor, Tefeo meets the medical standard of his times. However, his cure fails, possibly because he cannot focus his logotherapy on the image of the beloved whose identity is, inexplicably,[298] unknown to him.

---

[298] Parrilla comments that the respective lines "parecen totalmente incongruen-

Moreover, in spite of his agony, Leriano finds the strength to rebuke his friend with a lengthy speech about the excellence of the female sex. The diatribe reflects the contemporary "feminist" debate on the Iberian Peninsula (Ornstein), and certainly appealed to the readers of *Cárcel*; the fact that Tefeo's slander is silenced and Leriano's praise of woman given ample space leaves no doubt about the position of El Auctor in this dispute. More importantly, Leriano is not only irresponsive to the treatment, but actively fights the cure that would save his life and kill his love.[299] A further subversion of the medical discourse on lovesickness is obvious in the final death scene.

Leriano has Laureola's letters dissolved in a cup of water and drinks it immediately before passing away with the words: "Acabados son mis males" (79). The parallels to Jesus Christ's passion and the Eucharist have been pointed out early by Anna Krause (269-70) and by Wardropper, who sees in Leriano's "perfect" love a reflection of Christ's perfect love ("Mundo sentimental" 176).[300] Recently, Chorpenning suggested sources from the Old Testament which refer to rites of purification ("Leriano's Consumption"). This idea has been rejected by Gerli, who sees the influence of related motifs in *cancionero* poetry and connects the death scene with medieval *ars moriendi* ("Leriano's Libation").[301] The intertextual spectrum of the denouement of *Cárcel* was considerably broadened by Domingo Ynduráin, who points out parallels with ancient and contemporary texts. Under his examples of the motif of "beber cenizas," the drinking of the physical remnants of a dead lover, we find libation as a means of establishing the union between the lovers, and as a remedy against destructive love. The latter point leads Ynduráin to the medical subtext (307). The use of what the inquisitors called

---

tes en la narración, pues nadie podría ignorar la causa del duelo" (ed. *Cárcel* 64, n. 4). San Pedro might have chosen in this case to sacrifice narrative coherence to the verisimilitude of the failed cure.

[299] Disregarding the importance of Leriano's reaction to Tefeo's cure, his last speech is often viewed as an unconnected and unnecessary digression; see, for instance, Waley ("Love and honour" 48), Rohland de Langbehn (*Interpretation* 172) and Brownlee ("Imprisoned Discourse" 197).

[300] See also Whinnom (*Diego de San Pedro*, 101, 109). Despite acknowledging the Christian subtext ("Cardona"), Whinnom rejects the idea that Leriano is a figure of Christ ("Introduction" 16).

[301] See also Gerli's recent Lacanian reading of Leriano's last drink ("Leriano and Lacan").

"nóminas diabólicas," sacred texts written on papers and dissolved in water, were used in popular medicine as a cure for a range of afflictions (García Ballester 168; Solomon, *Literature of Misogyny* 103). Hence, with Leriano's libation and death San Pedro creates a conceit worthy of an ingenious *cancionero* poet: the drinking of the "sacred words," a medical treatment, does not cure his physical ailment, lovesickness, but is the ultimate confirmation of his loyal love; rejecting the "real" cure, the logotherapy, he embraces death, gaining eternal life as an ideal lover who is remembered as an "exenplo de fortaleza" (San Pedro, *Cárcel* 41).

This exemplarity is founded in his voluntary, yet "natural" death. He does not commit suicide, but literally dies of love. His death is proof of his lovesickness, which in turn confirms his sincerity and insuperable loyalty as a lover.

We find the concept that real love is passionate (pathological, in the medical perspective) love, that real love is love that altruistically defies death in the sentimental fictions of Rodríguez del Padrón, Pedro de Portugal and F.A.D.C. San Pedro, however, goes beyond the first generation of sentimental fiction. While Leriano's death bears witness to his constant and sincere love, the narrators of *Siervo*, *Sátira*, and *Triste deleytaçión* only invoke and contemplate death and threaten their ladies with the fatal consequences of their passion. *Sátira*, whose narrator ends his account presenting himself with the sword in his hands, illustrates best how these texts approximate the verge of death without being able to surpass it. The typical point of view of early sentimental fiction, the first-person autobiographical narration which is a heritage of the Ovidian *Heroides*, sets an absolute structural limitation regarding the presentation of the death of the protagonist (Rey 96). With El Auctor, San Pedro creates a narrator who has, on one hand, the insight into the lover's soul needed to produce the emotional intensity and authenticity. On the other hand, El Auctor is a reliable chronicler of the unavoidable death of this ideal lover.[302]

With Leriano, Diego de San Pedro conceived of an ideal yet realistic lover: ideal, because the Prison of Love materializes a psychological state of "real" passion and his death proves his value and sincerity; realistic, because he plays out the consequences of *amor*

---

[302] Regarding the problem of the unreliable, lovesick narrator in first-generation sentimental romance, see above chapter II.

hereos, a fatal disease. Transforming the lyric concept of love-as-fatal-sickness as an ennobling and empowering force into an extended realistic prose narration, San Pedro attempted to circle the square–and nearly succeeded.

Without conflating El Auctor and San Pedro, it is safe to assume that the picture of Leriano as a perfect lover comes close to the *intentio auctoris*. Nevertheless, in spite of San Pedro's efforts to resemanticize the realistic tendency of *Cárcel*, it still is a disconcerting text. As I have pointed out above, *Cárcel* consists of a series of fatal misjudgments, which El Auctor tries to sublimate in Leriano's death for a good cause. Yet to the attentive reader there are obvious scratches in the picture of the ideal lover and his heroic death.

I agree with Gerli in relating Leriano's death to the medieval *ars moriendi*. However, from the angle of this tradition the circumstances of his death are distressing. Leriano is not only irresponsive to his friend Tefeo's logotherapy but also rebukes his effort to help him. Moreover, the agonizing lover's defense of womanhood does not generate understanding for his position.

> Turbada la lengua y la vista casi perdida; y los suyos, no podiéndose contener, davan bozes; ya sus amigos començavan a llorar; ya sus vasallos y vasallas gritavan por las calles; ya todas las cosas alegres eran bueltas en dolor. (76-77)

The relatives recognize the symptoms of a terminal disease, expressing their sorrow. Leriano's mother, in particular, experiences his death as senseless: "¡O lumbre de mi vista, o ceguedad della misma, que te veo morir y no veo la razón de tu muerte; tú en edad para bevir" (78). Contrary to Leriano's judgment, which is, of course, seriously impaired, she perceives his death as a defeat: "ni te valió la fuerça del cuerpo, ni la virtud del coraçón, ni el esfuerço del ánimo; todas las cosas de que te podías valer te fallecieron" (78). To all this emotional turmoil around him Leriano is utterly unsympathetic: "como él sienpre se acordase de Laureola, de lo que allí pasava tenía poca memoria [...]" (79). The fact that he chooses to drink Laureola's sacred words instead of receiving the last rites further contributes to his alienation from his family. If the *ars moriendi* prescribes that the expiring person is amidst "his family and loved ones," receiving consolatory advice and the last rites (Gerli, "Leriano's libation" 416), then Leriano's death is a *contrafactum* that appeals to the reader coming from the tradition of courtly poetry, but most certainly violates contemporary religious sensibilities and expectations. Moreover, even though the disturbed Leriano is confident to have established a union with his beloved through the libation of the letter and his continuous memories,[303] it is apparent that he is not surrounded by his "loved ones." The only person he is capable of loving, Laureola, has rejected him and is far away, unaware of his "heroic" death.[304]

The attentive reader will also realize that Leriano's love is not as "ideal" as El Auctor and he himself try to present it. We have seen that the *raison d'être* of *Cárcel* is not Leriano's patient, solitary suffering, which, at any rate, would have been a true service to Laureola, but Leriano's hope for a *galardón*.[305]

He first assures El Auctor that the only "bien" he requests from El Auctor is that Laureola becomes aware of his love (11). Upon receiving the news that Laureola might reciprocate his feelings, he begins to approach her with letters, assuring her of his altruistic motives.

> Que muy mejor es morir por tu causa que bevir sin tu esperança; y hablándote verdad, la muerte, sin que tú me la dieses yo mismo me la daría, por hallar en ella la libertad que en la vida busco, si tú no hoviesses de quedar infamada por matadora. (19)

The argumentation is, of course, flawed, because at this point nobody but Laureola and El Auctor know about his passion. Leriano and El Auctor, however, convince Laureola to write to Leriano again, claiming that this will be the last request: "Solamente pedí tu respuesta por primero y postrimero galardón" (26). Once she has demonstrated her "piedad," Leriano immediately seeks her physical presence at court. After having freed her, he asks his go-between El Auctor for another favor: "y deseoso de saber en lo que Laureola estava, rogóme que le fuese suplicar que diese alguna

---

[303] It should also be mentioned that Leriano does not incorporate love letters, but Laureola's letter in which she denies being in love and complains about the trouble Leriano's passion has caused her.

[304] In the Prison Leriano confesses that his love for Laureola makes it impossible to feel for others (8).

[305] Critics like Cvitanovič, who label Leriano's behavior as "masochistic" ("Alusión" 20), misconstrue the nature of his desire regarding the ennobling, empowering force of love and its very "practical" motivation.

forma onesta para que la pudiese ver y hablar" (59). A progression in Leriano's demands from awareness, epistolary exchange and "pity," to physical presence to conversation is apparent; if the narration were to continue, Leriano's aim ultimately would be the hand of Laureola (Whinnom, "Introducción" II, 42), and/or physical possession (Van Beysterveldt, "Nueva teoría de amor" 78).[306] Persio, who is also in love with Laureola, is mistaken in informing the King of the illicit meeting between Leriano and Laureola that he fantasized, but he understands the nature of Leriano's desire very well. In order to save the image of the perfect courtly lover, San Pedro, as it were, must pull the emergency brake, and let Leriano die of lovesickness.[307]

A crucial role in establishing a tragic, heroic ending is the figure of Laureola. Leriano can only be the ideal, memorable lover if he loves in spite of not being loved.[308] Too much emphasis has been placed on the social differences that separate Leriano and the princess;[309] Leriano is well aware of his eminent social status. He appeals to the King: "devieras acordarte de los servicios que los míos te hicieron [...]; nunca hueste juntaste que la tercia parte dellos no fuese" (36). Since he is, presumably, a duke and the head of one of the most powerful families of Macedonia, his aspiration to the princess is not an entirely futile project. The obstacles are of a different nature: Laureola is smart enough to see the danger which the liaison would bring upon her, and she is simply not in love with Leriano.

In retrospect,[310] El Auctor is certain that Laureola granted Leriano a *galardón* not out of love, but out of pity (17). Her reluctance to give in is well-founded.

---

[306] Rohland de Langbehn points out that El Auctor manifests the "uncourtly" tendency of *Cárcel*, because his role as *medianero* necessarily foments sensual love (*Interpretation* 185).

[307] According to Débax, the character of Persio already fulfills the function to interrupt "cierta lógica narrativa" which develops with Laureola granting a *galardón* to Leriano (282). In his *Desprecio de la fortuna*, San Pedro chastises *Cárcel* as a "salsa para pecar!" (*Obras* III, 276).

[308] This constellation also characterizes the "ideal lovers" in *Siervo* and *Sátira*; see above chapter II.

[309] Parrilla, for instance, claims that Leriano expresses in his last letter to Laureola "la distancia moral y social que les separa" (ed. *Cárcel* 60, n. 2). Leriano's modesty, however, cannot be taken at face value, but must be seen as an expression of courtly rhetoric.

[310] Rey and Mandrell analyze the conflation of point of view in *Cárcel*.

> Si pudiese remediar su mal sin amanzillar mi onrra, no con menos afición que tú lo pides yo lo haría; mas ya tu conosces quánto las mugeres deven ser más obligadas a su fama que a su vida [...]. (21)

As her last letter indicates, Leriano's "services" do not change her attitude. On the contrary, she has learned that even compassion is disastrous in her position.

> Lo que por mí has hecho me obliga a nunca olvidallo y siempre desear satisfazerlo, no segund tu deseo, mas segund mi onestad; la virtud y piedad y conpasión que pensaste que te ayudarían para comigo, aunque son aceptas a mi condición, para en tu caso son enemigos de mi fama, y por esto las hallaste contrarias. [...] No creas que tan sanamente biven las gentes que, sabido que te hablé, juzgasen nuestras linpias intenciones [...]. (62)

This is categorically the reasoning of a shrewd and reasonable woman untouched by the tribulation of *amor hereos*. Hence Laureola is, on one hand, the source of Leriano's empowerment as an ideal lover and *conditio sine qua non* of his final apotheosis; on the other hand, in order to make Leriano the ideal lover, San Pedro had to create a female figure who is not "cruel" (Damiani 39),[311] but unaffected by the force of passionate love, and, after a learning process, immune to the power of courtly persuasion and male prowess.[312]

As Nicolás Núñez's interpretation of *Cárcel* indicates, among the many bewildering elements in El Auctor's portrait of the perfect

---

[311] Rohland de Langbehn's observation that, with the exception of El Auctor all characters of the text correspond to "preexisting ideals" is certainly not applicable to Laureola (*Interpretation* 144): in contrast with the stereotypical *belle dame sans merci* she is sympathetic and offers Leriano a reasonable reward for his military efforts (San Pedro, *Cárcel* 62-63). For this reason also the distinction between late medieval "crueldad" and Renaissance "desdén" established by Van Beysterveldt misconstrues Laureola's character ("Nueva teoría" 82).

[312] Theresa Ann Sears discerns in *Cárcel* a loss of faith in the power of prowess related to a discoursive shift from the masculine to the feminine. San Pedro, however, expresses emblematically the crucial, and empowering, importance of female rejection:

> El mayor bien de quereros
> es querer un no quererme,
> pues procurar de perderos
> será perder el perderme.

(*Obras*, ed. Gili Gaya, 228).

lover, it is the character of the resistant Laureola that most troubled contemporary readers. Núñez's continuation and rewriting of *Cárcel* also shows that El Auctor not only failed on the diegetic level as a go-between and healer (Brownlee, "Imprisoned Discourse" 198), but also as a writer who tried to save the endangered species of the courtly lover.

c) *Nicolás Núñez's reading of* Cárcel

In 1496 Fadrique Alemán printed Diego de San Pedro's *Cárcel* together with a "tratado" by Nicolás Núñez, a man also known as a *cancionero* poet.[313] Núñez's work was reprinted along with all of the subsequent Spanish editions of *Cárcel* (Corfis, "Catalogue of editions" 21-47). Núñez's *tratado* was an integral part of what early readers received and, as we can infer from its editorial success, was appreciated as *Cárcel de amor*; nevertheless, modern scholarship has dedicated minimal attention to the text. In a scornful aside, Menéndez y Pelayo asserts "que nunca tuvo gran crédito, ni en realidad lo merecía, siendo cosa de todo punto pegadiza e inútil para la acción de la novela" (*Orígenes* II, 34). Later *Cárcel* scholarship denigrated Núñez's addition as well, often rivaling Menéndez Pelayo's depth of analysis. Whinnom earns the credit for having made the text accessible to a broader public with his edition, translation and pioneering studies.[314] His evaluation of Núñez's "continuation," however, is unfavorable: in stylistic terms Núñez achieved a "remarkable pastiche," but in placing blame on Laureola he "grossly betrayed or misunderstood his model's uncompromising feminism" ("Nicolás Núñez's Continuation" 361). Parrilla acknowledges Núñez as the first "discontent" reader of *Cárcel* ("Acrescentar" 242), whose reading of *Cárcel* permits the reconstruction of some literary norms of the epoch. Taking up a question raised by Whinnom

---

[313] A bibliographical history of the Alemán edition and a description of the only extant exemplar is provided by Whinnom ("Nicolás Núñez's Continuation" 357-58). For the little we know about Núñez see Whinnom ("Introduction" 30).

[314] Whinnom edited the Spanish *editio princeps* of Núñez's *tratado*. He was the first modern editor to publish San Pedro's text with Núñez's text together in his English translation of *Cárcel* (*Prison of Love*). This procedure was followed in Parrilla's recent edition of *Cárcel*; all quotes from Núñez's *Tratado* are taken from her edition.

("Nicolás Núñez's Continuation" 359), Parrilla suggests that Núñez's changes in the character of Laureola, her confessed love, and her loquacity contributed to the success of *Cárcel* ("Acrescentar" 252-53). Brownlee goes one step further, labeling Núñez's work an "insightful continuation" (*Severed Word* 174) in which El Auctor, who has evolved into a sophisticated writer, corrects his failure to effect a reconciliation of the lovers on a diegetic level (176).[315]

Núñez's *tratado* is indeed "insightful," because he perceived the subversive potential of *Cárcel* which is, as I have been arguing, manifest in the character of Laureola. As I will show, he conceived, in a way subtler than has been realized until now, of an interpretation of *Cárcel* that alters Laureola's dangerous invulnerability to passionate love, yet essentially respects San Pedro's characters and their motivations.

In the prologue Núñez explains the purpose of his *tratado*.

> Parecióme que quando en el cabo de él dixo que Leriano, por la respuesta sin esperança que Laureola avía enbiado, se dexava morir, y que se partió desque lo vido muerto para Castilla a dar la cuenta de lo passado, que deviera venirse por la corte, a dezir a Laureola de cierto como ya era muerto Leriano. Y ahunque le pareciera que al muerto no le aprovechava, a lo menos satisfaziérase a sí, si viera en ella alguna muestra del pesar por lo que havía hecho; pues sabía que si Leriano pudiera alcançar a saber el arrepentimiento de Laureola, diera su muerte por bien empleada. (83)

It is obvious that Núñez realizes that Leriano's love is not exclusively altruistic or "ideal"; his concern is that Laureola's unaffectedness by passionate love robs the "martyr" of love of his "deserved" *galardón*. His outspoken intention is to succeed where San Pedro's El Auctor failed, i.e. in the interpretation of Laureola's feelings. He obviously disregards El Auctor's retrospective, unambiguous declaration that Laureola felt only "piedad," not love, motivating her response to Leriano's advances (17). As we will see, this disregard of San Pedro's El Auctor's late insight is the only, and necessary, "misreading" of San Pedro's subtext.

---

[315] Voigt relates Núñez's continuation to the medieval practice of "ethical reading" (132).

Núñez sends El Auctor back to the Macedonian court, where he confronts Laureola with the news of Leriano's death.

> Que cierta te hago que si su muerte vieras, siempre tu vida lloraras, mira quánto le eres en cargo. [...] Te hago saber que si como yo le vieras morir, de compassión fizieras en presencia lo que absencia tu poco amor y mucho olvido hizieron que no hizistes. (85)

If Leriano's intention really was to do everything to Laureola's advantage, El Auctor cannot claim to act on his behalf: he apparently aims at causing remorse in Laureola, torturing her with the accusation that she, with her "mucha crueza y poca piadad," is responsible for Leriano's death (85). Hence he pursues what Núñez in the prologue calls "satifaziérase a sí" (83). This "satisfaction" has the form of revenge for what he perceives as Laureola's crime.

He is less successful in the second aspect of his mission. At first, Laureola exercises the self-control and prudence which confused San Pedro's El Auctor: "como discreta, sufriendo las lágrimas, disimulando el enojo" (86). Her justification echoes the argumentation of San Pedro's Laureola.

> Ni creas que el conoscimiento que yo de sus servicios tengo desconozco ni menos desagradezco; y si con otro galardón pudiera pagallos que la honra no costara, tú me tuvieras por tan gradecida quanto agora me culpas por desamorada. (87)

However, the attacks of El Auctor have an effect.

> Sin de mí despedirse, desatinada de mucho llorar, turbada la lengua y mudada la color, se buelve a la cámara do antes se iva, con tan rezios gemidos que, assí de miedo que no la oyessen como del dolor de lo que fazía, sin me despedir me fue a mi posada [...]. (87-88)

Once more, El Auctor has provoked an emotional reaction, a passion in terms of contemporary psychology, which manifests itself in bodily symptoms. Hence El Auctor has succeeded in causing emotional distress, which satisfies his thirst for revenge. Nevertheless, he has no answer to the question of the nature of Laureola's feelings: he is confronted with her reactions, which he was incapable of deciphering in the first place. It is important to realize that, up to this point, Núñez has painstakingly observed San Pedro's conception of his characters: the enigmatic Laureola defends herself with reasonable arguments, while the inept interpreter El Auctor can only guess her real emotions.

Exhausted, El Auctor lies down and addresses a lamentation to the dead Leriano.

> Tan cansado de enojo y menguado de consuelo quedé de mi fabla que, de desatinado, sin sentir que hazía, me traspassé; y entre muchas cosas que comencé a soñar, que más pesar que plazer me davan, soñava que veía a Leriano delante de mí [...]. (89)

El Auctor describes in detail the appearance of Leriano in his dream vision. The items of clothing are color-coded and embroidered with *letras*, brief, metrically-constricted epigrams. After Leriano's speech Laureola is introduced into the dream vision, also covered with embroidered *letras*. Given that these epigrams, as Brownlee points out (*Severed Word* 174), function "as a kind of anatomy of the affect," El Auctor is now in a position to resolve his predicament: instead of relying on evasive body-language, he now can literarily read the bodies by interpreting the *letras*.[316]

Surprisingly, Leriano presents an obstacle to the task Núñez set for El Auctor in the prologue; he denies him the satisfaction of being consoled by Laureola's tribulation.

> Pues sus mercedes ya no las quiero ni puedo gozar dellas aunque quiera; y si con arrepentimiento me satisfiziesse, de su crueza quedé tan quexoso que aunque más fiziesse no serié pagado. (Núñez 93)

He admits that it would have been better to "serve," although it is obvious that his desire was directed at "enjoying" her.

> Que no me tengas por tan vencido de seso que no sé que fuera bien vivir para serville aunque no para gozalla. Pero como nunca de su respuesta supe de lo que más se servía, como tú sabes, deséme morir, pues ya la vida quería dexarme. (93-94)

---

[316] With the insertion of the *letras* Núñez introduces a ludic element which might have further contributed to *Cárcel*'s success with contemporary readers.

Since Laureola had made clear that any kind of relationship would compromise her honor, Leriano's claim that he did not know how to serve her best is simply wrong.

Consequently, Laureola ventures doubt of his honest intention to serve her in her reply.

> Porque si, como dizes, servirme desseavas, más honra me fazías en bivir que en darte la muerte; y cierto te fago que más tu flaqueza que tu mucha pena, ni menos amor, me heziste creer. [...] Pues si los leales amadores los desconciertos del amor no saben soffrir, ¿quién será para padecellos? (97)

She points to the blind spot of Leriano's argumentation, the question of how he could be desperate if her welfare was his only goal. This is a point that could have been made by San Pedro's Laureola. However, Núñez's Laureola reveals at the same time that she loves Leriano. She even goes one step further.

> Bastarte deviera a ti, Leriano, membrarte en la desputa que estovo mi honra y peligro mi vida, y contentaríaste tú con saber que te quería y que tu mal más que el mío me penava aunque no te lo dezía. (97)

Not only does she finally meet Leriano's and El Auctor's hope that she reciprocates Leriano's feelings, but she also confesses that she was willing to give more than petty *galardones*.

> Pues te dezía que esperaras vencer al rey mi señor por días, para que vieras si ante no mereciera ser loada por de buen conoscimiento que culpada por desgradecida. (98)

Before being called back to the other world, Leriano asks for a last favor, which she implicitly grants by allowing him to kiss her hands: "Y assí me despido, suplicándote que del alma, como dizes, tengas memoria, pues el cuerpo posiste en olvido" (100). Laureola's unwillingness to accept his bodily love while alive is remunerated by her constant loving memory, the essential trait of passionate love.

Núñez's El Auctor, then, has not only achieved revenge by reminding Laureola of Leriano's death, but has also redeemed Leriano as a lover by proving that the power of his love had conquered Laureola. The sinister denouement of *Cárcel*, Leriano's death, which San Pedro conceived of as an inescapable price of passionate, ennobling love, is reinterpreted in the dream of Núñez's El Auctor as a tragic misunderstanding. This confusion is blamed on Laureola.

While critics have pointed out this rewriting of *Cárcel* and rebuked it as a misreading of the text, they have failed to realize that Núñez presents El Auctor's "revelation" as a "male fantasy." We have seen that before the dream Laureola reacted in exactly the same way San Pedro's Laureola did, frustrating El Auctor's persuasions and his attempts to decipher her. After the dream El Auctor leaves Macedonia without confirming the "insights" he has gained in his vision. The narration ends where San Pedro's *Cárcel* ended, in Peñafiel, "do quedo besando las manos de vuestras mercedes" (104). In narrative terms, what has been called Núñez's "continuation" is actually a perceptive rewriting of the last paragraph of *Cárcel*, which Núñez perceived as an ellipsis.

He took great pains not to distort his subtext: his Laureola is the resistant Laureola of San Pedro, his El Auctor is the same inept interpreter. Since he encapsulated Laureola's confession and her reconciliation with Leriano in a dream, a fantasy, he did not alter the ambiguity of San Pedro's *Cárcel* and his unsettling character Laureola, but presented an alternative "vision" that reflects male fantasies of power, female guilt and weakness.

Seen as a whole, as probably most early readers did, San Pedro's *Cárcel* and Núñez's *tratado* are characterized by a gender-specific polyphony which allowed reading the text, as Weissberger has suggested, "as a woman" ("Politics" 322),[317] and, at the same time, represented a male reading style which tried to eliminate ambiguity. I think there is reason to believe that without Núñez's augmentation *Cárcel* would not have reached as many readers in its time as it did.

What groups together San Pedro's *Cárcel* and Flores's *Grimalte y Gradissa* and what sets them apart from the first generation of sentimental fiction is that they play out the fatal consequences of lovesickness. In order to achieve this it was necessary that they alter the characteristic point of view we find in *Siervo*, *Sátira* and *Triste deleytaçión*. A first-person (pseudo-)autobiographical narration

---

[317] Culler discusses this mode of reading (43-46).

cannot recount the death of the protagonist or his suicide. In *Cárcel* and *Grimalte y Gradissa* the narrative focus is placed in a participant observer who chronicles the events. Whereas Flores creates the persona of the pathetic Grimalte, who unwillingly lays open the unredeemable outcome of *hereos*, San Pedro conceives of the persona of El Auctor, who presents himself as a reliable witness and capable chronicler of Leriano's heroic deeds. In both texts only the shrewd women, Gradissa and Laureola, who have the strength to resist the power of passionate love and courtly persuasion, escape the cataclysm of love, indicating a fading away of the discourse of courtly love in which the abject position of the lover is the basis of his self-aggrandizement.

Flores and San Pedro present different answers to the essential task which earlier sentimental fictions approached, i.e. the narrative expansion of cases of lovesickness as encapsulated in many manifestations of late medieval lyric poetry. The literary production of the 16th and 17th century indicates that this problem lost its central importance to writers. However, the long-lasting editorial success of sentimental fiction, and more importantly, the continuity of the psychological horizons of expectations,[318] indicate that in the Golden Age of Spanish letters there still existed the kind of medical-sensitive reader and reading styles which I have tried to reconstruct and emulate in this study.

Only a few scholars, most notably Teresa Scott Soufas (64-100),[319] have dedicated their attention to the traces of *amor hereos* in Spanish Renaissance and Baroque literature; I am convinced that they touched upon a field of research that is yet to be fully explored.[320] My choice of a Golden Age horizon of lovesickness as discernible in 15th-century sentimental romance is obvious: frequenting the commonplace in criticism that Cervantes incorporated and subverted a great many traditional literary forms, I will treat Don Quijote's lovesickness in an epilogue.

---

[318] See chapter I.
[319] For bibliographical references see Soufas (71).
[320] Pierre Heugas, for instance, presents evidence of the subsistence of the "old" *artes amandi, remedia amoris*, and, hence, *amor hereos* in the 16th-century imitations of *Celestina* ("La Célestine" 304-17).

Epilogue

'ESTO DEL MORIRSE LOS ENAMORADOS ES COSA
DE RISA': FACULTY PSYCHOLOGY AND
LOVESICKNESS IN *DON QUIJOTE*

a) *Don Quijote's* locura

REMARKABLE efforts have been made to explain Don Quijote's madness and his psychological make-up, relating it to the medical discourse of Cervantes's times. The key text in this endeavor has been Juan Huarte de San Juan's *Examen de ingenios para las ciencias*. Huarte's *Examen*, first published in two versions in 1575 (Baeza) and 1592 (Valladolid), is an attempt to classify the individual's aptitude for intellectual labor according to his humoral disposition. Though firmly couched in accepted Galenic humoralism and time-honored faculty psychology, Huarte's apparent medical determinism necessarily proved controversial in the epoch of the Counterreformation. While the enormous national and international attention of the *Examen*, which is attested to by the numerous editions and translations (Serés, "Introducción" 114, 119-22), is arguably due to its scandalous theological implications, modern historians of medicine celebrated Huarte's work as an important vestige of the beginnings of modern "differential" psychology (Iriarte; Halka 13).

The first to postulate an influence of Huarte's *Examen* on Cervantes's work was Rafael Salillas (1905), who emphasized the pathological aspect, the humoral imbalance of Don Quijote's brain. His line of investigation was taken up and elaborated in 1948 by M. de Iriarte who argued that Don Quijote's "pre-psychotic disposition" (324) resulted in the protagonist's particular "ingenio." Iriarte's study was the basis for Otis H. Green's influential 1957 article in which he argues:

> Alonso Quijano is a man primarily *colérico*; [...] his natural condition is exacerbated by a *passion* and by *lack of sleep*, which produce a hypertrophy of his *imaginative faculty*; [...] his madness follows a natural trajectory away from, and back to, normality; [...] his moments of temporary improvement after his first two *vueltas*, and his final return to sanity, correspond to relaxations in, or the removal of, the causes of his aberration. In short, [...] Don Quijote's adventures could have happened only to a *colérico*, a man by nature *caliente y seco*, and that such a man was, according to Renaissance psychology, of necessity *ingenioso*. ("Ingenioso hidalgo" 177)

According to Green, an "acute attack of melancholy" completes the gradual recovery of the diseased imagination and leads to the death of the protagonist (188).

Green's picture of the choleric Don Quijote became a topos in scholarship.[321] His thesis was reexamined by Chester S. Halka, who points out that Green did not have firsthand knowledge of Huarte's *Examen*. Based on a closer reading of the *Examen*, Halka refutes Green's claim that Don Quijote is gradually recovering from his cerebral malfunction after prolonged periods of sleep which, according to Green, restore the necessary humidity to his dried-out brain. Halka argues that Don Quijote's mind and *ingenio* is influenced by the so-called adust melancholy, as described by Huarte. Adust melancholy, the residue of burnt "natural" humors, can abruptly change from a cold to a hot state. According to Halka, Don Quijote's "dual humoral complexion" (11) accounts for his personality, which combines "*entendimiento*" and "*locura*" (9).

Halka's reference was anticipated by more than two decades by Harald Weinrich's analysis of the *Ingenium Don Quijotes*, which appeared shortly before Green's article. The reason for the relative disinterest scholarship showed in Weinrich's study was an "Addendum" by Green, in which he criticized the German scholar for dismissing the presence of medical aspects in Cervantes's conception of Don Quijote ("Ingenioso hidalgo" 190).[322] Nevertheless, Green's assessment is misleading.

---

[321] See, for instance, Juan Bautista Avalle-Arce (115-27). Soufas provides bibliographical references to studies which focus on humorology and Renaissance psychology in *Don Quijote* (18, n. 57).

[322] Green's stance is echoed by Avalle-Arce (115, n. 9); Halka and Soufas ignore Weinrich.

Weinrich dedicates much space to the discussion of Don Quijote's melancholic complexion (*Ingenium* 47-62). In accordance with traditional humoral physiology, drawn primarily from the pseudo-Aristotelian *Problemata*, he classifies Don Quijote's madness as an *insania melancholicorum* related to the dual nature of adust melancholy (51-56). While Salillas, Iriarte and Green postulate a direct influence of Huarte on Cervantes, Weinrich inserts *Don Quijote* in the broader context of contemporary conventional natural philosophy and literary traditions. As Green has pointed out ("Ingenioso hidalgo" 190-94), Weinrich's contention–that Cervantes originally conceived of his hero as a ridiculous madman devoid of *ingenium*, upon whom he gradually bestowed the qualities of ennobling "high mania" in the process of literary creation ("hoher Wahn"; *Ingenium* 34-47)–is certainly disputable; yet his analysis is unquestionably closer to Cervantes's conception of Don Quijote than interpretations which reduce the *ingenioso hidalgo* to, as it were, a Huartian case study.[323]

Apparently unaware of Weinrich's study, Teresa Scott Soufas also argues that Don Quijote is suffering from melancholy. On the basis of a thorough study of 16th- and 17th-century conceptions of melancholy in conjunction with contemporary faculty psychology, she holds, against Green, that Cervantes's protagonist is not a choleric.

> Quijano is much better understood as a melancholic whose adust melancholic condition is caused and/or intensified by an idle life and a fixation upon reading that alter his naturally melancholic system in an adverse way. (22)

In other words, Don Quijote is "presented initially as a standard case of unrelieved scholarly melancholia" (22). Soufas maintains that the melancholic dryness of Don Quijote's brain affects the proper working of his memory. His memory is deluged with persistent memories of his readings of chivalric novels, yet it is incapable of absorbing new data (26).

> His intellect begins to make connections between the sensory information (still provided efficiently by his imagination) and the

---

[323] Soufas argues that Cervantes in fact parodies Huarte's idiosyncratic and heretic interpretation of traditional humoralism (30-32).

abundant images preserved in his memory. This is the normal rational process for thought, according to faculty psychology, but in Quijano's case it is accomplished through the offices of two functioning faculties and one damaged one. (28)

Newly received sense impressions (like the sight of wind mills) are erroneously associated with mnemonically stored images of the *novelas de caballerías* (like evil giants). Prolonged periods of sleep and rest, continues Soufas, effect a steady moistening of Don Quijote's brain, which eventually dissipates his mania and brings about a fatal melancholic condition (34-35).

Soufas's rendition of Don Quijote's psychological disposition has the merit of presenting an ingenious model of "madness" in accordance with the humorology and faculty psychology of Cervantes's time. Yet it is only partially supported by textual evidence. As Halka points out, there is no convincing correlation between Don Quijote's phases of sleep and a waning of his dementia (5-6). More importantly, his memory is not impaired in the way suggested by Soufas. He possesses not only a precise memory of his "pre-psychotic" life and of the reading that caused his mental derangement, but perfectly remembers everything that he perceives during his *vueltas* as an errant knight.

A close look at the narrator's description of Quijano's mental accident reveals that memory is not the affected faculty.

> En resolución, él se enfrascó tanto en su letura, que se le pasaban las noches leyendo de claro en claro, y los días de turbio en turbio; y así, del poco dormir y del mucho leer se le secó el celebro de manera que vino a perder el juicio. Llenósele la fantasía de todo aquello que leía en los libros [...] y asentósele de tal modo en la imaginación que era verdad toda aquella máquina de aquellas sonadas soñadas invenciones que leía [...]. (I, chap. 1; p. 100)

Sleep deprivation and intense mental activity, which involves the consumption of pneuma, lead to the corruption of bodily humors or adust melancholy. Adust melancholy and its accompanying frenzy transform the naturally melancholic (and therefore introverted and passive) Alonso Quijano into the errant knight Don Quijote. The text indicates that this condition primarily affects his "juizio." In terms of faculty psychology "juizio" refers most certainly to the *vis estimativa*, or judgment. In the basic three-ventricle model of the sensitive soul the *estimativa* connects the imagination and memory which, respectively, store and produce mental images. Hence, the reason that Quijote's imagination is filled with images of fictitious accounts of *caballería* is that they are retrieved from memory and erroneously judged to be real. Furthermore, this lack of "juizio" or malfunction of the *estimativa* causes incoming sense data to be misinterpreted. In this respect, it is significant that, with the possible exception of his vision in the cave of Montesinos, Don Quijote does not experience hallucinations, properly speaking: he sees windmills and judges them to be giants, he sees an inn and judges it to be a castle, and so forth. There is always a "real" physical object present which Don Quijote misjudges and associates incorrectly with his readings of chivalric romances; he has indeed lost his "juizio."

The question arises how this malfunction of the *estimativa* can be explained. Huarte holds that the *entendimiento* operates best in a dry and cool environment. Since Don Quijote's brain is most certainly dry, it can be inferred that it is the excessive heat that makes him lose his *juizio/entendimiento*: "Y debe ser la causa," explains Huarte, "que el entendimiento ha menester que el celebro esté compuesto de partes sutiles y muy delicadas [...] y el mucho calor gasta y consume lo más delicado [...]" (chap. 5 [chap. 8 of the 1594 ed.]; p. 341). Following Huarte's model of human *ingenios*, it can be speculated that the working of Don Quijote's *estimativa* is impaired by pneumatic heat due to the excitement of his readings. According to Huarte, the extreme dryness itself may be the cause of Don Quijote's madness.

> Aunque no de cualquiera grado de estas tres calidades resulta una diferencia de ingenio, porque a tanta intensión puede llegar la sequedad, el calor, y la humidad, que desbarate totalmente la facultad animal [...]. (chap. 5 [chap. 8 of the 1594 ed.]; p. 341-42)[324]

Another possible scenario is that the adust melancholy, with its dual nature of cold and heat, causes a cycle in which mental pertur-

---

[324] In this instance Huarte's opinion conforms with the medical tradition; he refers to the Galenic *dictum*: "*omnis inmodica intemperies vires exsolvit*" (chap. 5 [chap. 8 of the 1594 ed.]; p. 341-42).

bation due to extreme heat alternates with lucid moments in phases of cold adust melancholy.

Disconcerting in this respect, however, is the fact that Don Quijote's *locura* pertains exclusively to questions of chivalry, while he is universally considered a wise man in all other matters. This condition amazes his friend, the priest, for example.

> Discurre con bonísimas razones y muestra tener un entendimiento claro y apacible en todo; de manera que, como no le toquen en sus caballerías, no habrá nadie que le juzgue sino por de muy buen entendimiento. (Cervantes, I, chap. 30; p. 376)

How can humorology and faculty psychology account for this strange mental condition? I think it can explain the Don Quijote character only partially. The explicit intention Cervantes pursues with *Don Quijote* is to "poner en aborrecimiento de los hombres las fingidas y disparatadas historias de los libros de caballerías [...]" (II, chap. 74; p. 578). [325] What better strategy to achieve this purpose than inventing a queer mental disease caused by chivalric novels, a disease that is able to corrupt the mind of the *cuerdo* Alonso Quijano in the way described above?

The author of *Don Quijote* took great pains to give his hero a psychological make-up that would strike contemporary readers as realistic. Yet, in hyperbolically asserting that chivalric novels cause a mental disorder, he took poetic license. After all, *Don Quijote* is not a medical study but a piece of literature which refers essentially to literary subtexts. Hence it is not surprising that the etiology and semiology of Don Quijote's madness is not only determined by the scientific, medical tradition but also by a literary genre.

b) *Lovesickness in* Don Quijote

Both Cervantes's persistent reference to fictional subtexts and his apparent medical knowledge make it very likely that he was acquainted with the concept of lovesickness. I contend that the con-

---

[325] A similar claim is put forward in the prologue: "no mira a más que a deshacer la autoridad y cabida que en el mundo y en el vulgo tienen los libros de caballerías [...]" (I; p. 84).

nection between Don Quijote's *locura*, an obsessive mental affliction of the *vis estimativa* that refers to images of chivalry, and *amor hereos*, a mental disease that is caused by the misjudgment and compulsive retention of the image of a beautiful woman, is crafted deliberately; a contemporary reader familiar with the notion of lovesickness and fictional texts which portray cases of lovesickness would realize that pathological, passionate love plays an important role in *Don Quijote*.

It has been pointed out that in *Don Quijote* Cervantes alludes to, parodies, or criticizes conceptions of love found in literary subtexts. Edward Dudley, for instance, argues that the characters of Grisóstomo and Cardenio are modeled after the literary prototype of sentimental romance's lovers ("Wild Man" 120, 127). Javier Herrero holds that, in his intercalated novels, Cervantes deliberately exposes and criticizes the dangers inherent in passionate love ("Arcadia's Inferno"; "Sierra Morena"). In the *novelas* he incorporated numerous examples of pathological, passionate love. Grisóstomo, for instance, commits suicide because of his unrequited love for Marcela. In "El curioso impertinente," Lotario becomes the victim of a *philocaptio* (I, chap. 33; p. 411). Fernando's obsession with Dorotea is quenched after sexual intercourse. A little later he is captured by the sight of Luscinda (I, chap. 24; p. 296-97).[326]

Generally, critics have focused on passionate love in the *novelas* of *Don Quijote* where they visibly fulfill a "serious" purpose. Hans-Jörg Neuschäfer understands that Don Quijote's "pseudo-love" ("Pseudoverliebheit") highlights the seriousness of passion ("ernste(n) Verstrickung in die Leidenschaften") in the intercalated episodes (50). However, no attention has been given to the subtle subversion of passionate love that centers in the relationship between Don Quijote and Dulcinea del Toboso.[327]

After Don Quijote has assembled everything he considers necessary for his knightly business, he realizes that horse, armor, and weapons are not sufficient to qualify him as a real knight-errant.

---

[326] In the second part, the most evident presence of *amor hereos* is Don Quijote's suggestion of some of the established *remedia amoris* to cure Altisidora's supposed obsession with him (II, chap. 70; p. 552).

[327] Soufas points out similarities between Don Quijote's "scholarly" melancholy and the "love melancholy" of Alonso, the protagonist of Lope de Vega's *El caballero de Olmedo*, yet does not elaborate on this insight (74, 77).

> Se dio a entender que no le faltaba otra cosa sino buscar una dama de quien enamorarse; porque el caballero andante sin amores era árbol sin hojas y sin fruto y cuerpo sin alma. [...]
> Y fue, a lo que se cree, que en lugar del suyo había una moza labradora de muy buen parecer, de quién él un tiempo anduvo enamorado (aunque, según se entiende, ella jamás lo supo ni le dio cata dello). (I, chap. 1; p. 102-03)

The "invention" of Dulcinea del Toboso is the culminating act in Quijano's transformation into Don Quijote. He chooses a pretty peasant girl with whom he has been in love for a while. Considering Don Quijote's attraction to the girl, it is startling that the narrator casts doubt on the sincerity of Don Quijote's love: "Luego volvía diciendo, como si verdaderamente fuera enamorado: –¡Oh princesa Dulcinea, señora deste cautivo corazón!" (I, chap. 2; p. 106). He obviously feigns passionate, obsessive love, imitating the heroes of chivalric romance.

> Toda aquella noche no durmió don Quijote, pensando en su señora Dulcinea, por acomodarse a lo que había leído en sus libros, cuando los caballeros pasaban sin dormir muchas noches en las florestas y despoblados, entretenidos con las memorias de sus señoras. (I, chap. 8; p. 149) [328]

His impersonation of a passionate lover is most striking in the "finezas que de enamorado hizo don Quijote en Sierra Morena" (I, chap. 26; p. 318). He decides to perform "locuras [...] malencónicas" like the ideal knight-errant, Amadís de Gaula. It is apparent that Don Quijote's passion is feigned, merely a parody of literary models. This seems to contradict the narrator's affirmation that Alonso Quijano was in love with the peasant girl. If we choose not to distrust the narrator in this respect, it can be inferred that the "lady of his thoughts" ("Dulcinea del Toboso, única señora de mis pensamientos"; II, chap. 58; p. 466) is not identical to the peasant girl mentioned in chapter one.

While Don Quijote firmly believes in the existence of knights-errant and the reality of his delusional knightly adventures, he never insists on the existence of Dulcinea. He explains to Sancho:

---

[328] See also: "Hízolo así, y todo lo más de la noche se le pasó en memorias de su señora Dulcinea, a imitación de los amantes de Marcela" (I, chap. 12; p. 180).

> Así que Sancho, por lo que yo quiero a Dulcinea del Toboso tanto vale como la más alta princesa de la tierra. Sí, que no todos los poetas que [alaban] damas debajo de un nombre que ellos a su albedrío les ponen, es verdad que las tienen. ¿Piensas tú que [...] fueron verdaderamente damas de carne y hueso, y de aquellos que las celebran y celebraron? No, por cierto, sino que las más se las fingen, por dar sujeto a sus versos, y porque los tengan por enamorados y por hombres que tienen valor para serlo. Y así bástame a mí pensar y creer que la buena de Aldonza Lorenzo es hermosa y honesta; y en lo que del linaje importa poco, que no han de ir a hacer la información dél darle algún hábito, y yo me hago cuenta que es la más alta princesa del mundo. [...] Para concluir con todo, yo imagino que todo lo que es así, sin que sobre ni falte nada, y píntola en mi imaginación como la deseo, así en belleza como en la principalidad [...]. (I, chap. 25; p. 312)

He acknowledges that Dulcinea, like the muses of many poets, is not a person "de carne y hueso," but a figment of his imagination. In part two, he takes a similar stance, in a conversation with the duchess. From her reading of the first part of the novel, Don Quijote's hostess infers that:

> Nunca vuesa merced ha visto a la señora Dulcinea, y que esta tal señora no es en el mundo, sino que es dama fantástica, que vuesa merced la engendró y parió en su entendimiento, y la pintó con todas aquellas gracias y perfecciones que quiso. (II, chap. 32; p. 272)

As a reader of the first part, the duchess realizes that Dulcinea is a creature of Don Quijote's *entendimiento*, which he conceived and shaped deliberately into a mental image. Don Quijote, fiercely insistent in the reality of all of his chivalric imaginations, does not dispute this.

> Dios sabe si hay Dulcinea o no [en] el mundo, o si es fantástica, o no es fantástica; y éstas no son de las cosas cuya averiguación se ha de llevar hasta el cabo. Ni yo engendré ni parí a mi señora, puesto que la contemplo como conviene que sea una dama que contenga en sí las partes que puedan hacerla famosa en todas las del mundo [...]. (II, chap. 32; p. 273)

As in the conversation with Sancho, he emphasizes that the ontological status of his beloved is irrelevant; what matters is how he imagines her to be, or "contemplates" her in his mind. In other words, he has consciously formed an enticing and praiseworthy mental image. To the reader familiar with the phenomenology of lovesickness the parody is obvious. The sentimental lovers and enamored knights in earlier literature are captured by the sight of a beautiful woman; misled by their *estimativa* they conceive of a powerful, potentially treacherous, mental image. Don Quijote's *juizio* is malfunctioning, and he also conceives of a mental image of an extremely beautiful and virtuous woman which does not correspond to the qualities of the beloved. Yet, while the sentimental lover, who is not aware of his misjudgment, is inescapably in the grip of a devastating affliction, Don Quijote, who is fully aware of the discrepancies between real beloved (Aldonza Lorenzo) and the "lady of his thoughts" (Dulcinea del Toboso), makes a continuous effort to emulate this condition. In this, he is indeed no different from the cited *poetas* who seek to ennoble themselves by feigning passionate love;[329] yet the *persona* Don Quijote which embodies these "amores platónicos,"[330] his folly and his mishaps, subvert the very claim that passionate love is an ennobling force and a serious condition.

Don Quijote's counterfeit lovesickness or passionate love is one motif among many in the first part of *Don Quijote*. However, as Dudley observes, the "search for a means to disenchant Dulcinea" becomes "the fictional vehicle" of the 1615 continuation ("Wild Man" 119). After embarking on his last *vuelta*, Don Quijote decides to pay a visit to his lady in El Toboso.[331] His squire Sancho faces the task of concealing from his master that he did not deliver his letter from the Sierra Morena, and that he never met Aldonza/Dulcinea. He devises a strategy that takes advantage of Don Quijote's peculiar frame of mind.

---

[329] See my analysis of the "feigned" love in Juan Alfonso Baena's *Prólogo*, in chapter one of the present study.

[330] The expression is used by Don Quijote as well as Sansón Carrasco (I, chap. 25; p. 310; II, chap. 32; p. 267). In the retort to the priest at the ducal court Don Quijote affirms that he is not "de los enamorados viciosos, sino de los platónicos continentes" (II, chap. 32; p. 267).

[331] The *primer autor* comments that "las locuras de don Quijote llegaron aquí al término y raya de las mayores que pueden imaginarse [...]" (II, chap. 10; p. 92).

> Este mi amo, por mil señales, he visto que es un loco de atar [...]. Siendo pues loco, como lo es, y de locura que las más veces toma unas cosas por otras, y juzga lo blanco por negro [...] no será muy difícil hacerle creer que una labradora, la primera que me topare por aquí, es la señora Dulcinea. [...] O quizá pensará, como yo imagino, que algún mal encantador de estos que él dice que le quieren mal la habrá mudado la figura por hacerle mal y daño. (II, chap. 10; p. 94-95)

When three peasant girls approach, he pretends to perceive the incomparable beauty of Dulcinea, and evokes her enticing features. Yet his master, whose madness, as I have pointed out, is strictly limited to his profession of knight-errant, interprets the sensorial data correctly: "Yo no veo, Sancho –dijo don Quijote–, sino a tres labradoras sobre tres borricos" (II, chap. 10; p. 96). Sancho, however, executes his plan successfully by listing Dulcinea's features that have been altered in Don Quijote's perception by the "encantadores aciagos y mal intencionados" (II, chap. 10; p. 99).

Sancho's hoax is a parody of the conventional *descriptio puellae* which, according to Pierre Heugas, expresses a critique of the concept of the lady in the courtly tradition ("Variation" 5). Ronny H. Terpening recognizes in Don Quijote's confrontation with the country girls a mockery of the Aristotelian principle of mimesis, the *stilnovistic incontro*, and the description in Petrarchan conventions.[332] Still, the contemporary medical-sensitive reader would distinguish a far more perplexing web of ironies.

In seeing what is to be seen, i.e. three unattractive *labradoras*, Don Quijote, the madman, first responds in a perfectly healthy way. Since his madness entails the wish to suffer from authentic lovesickness, that is, to conceive of a mental image that idealizes the sensorial data, his reasonable reaction thwarts his hopes. From the medical treatises on lovesickness we know that the confrontation with Dulcinea as a hideous peasant girl should alter the obsessive mnemonic image and cure the patient of *amor hereos*.[333] Yet Don

---

[332] It is worth noting that the medical tradition, in particular the notion of *amor hereos*, is an important subtext in the *stilnovisti* and Petrarch. Herrero reviews interpretations of the character of Dulcinea ("Dulcinea and her Critics").

[333] Another parody of a cure of lovesickness is Altisidora's "disenchantment" with Don Quijote: "La consideración de las crueldades que ha usado este malandrín mostrenco me le borrarán de la memoria sin otro artificio alguno." (II, chap. 70; p. 553).

Quijote has no desire to be cured; on the contrary, his "lovesickness" is the outcome of a rational decision, which he takes great pains to realize. By exposing his master to Aldonza/Dulcinea, Sancho assumes the role of a healer of a resistant "patient" who feigns and cautiously maintains lovesickness. However, he appeals to Don Quijote's "real" madness and convinces him that the image of the *labradora* he perceived has been altered by evil sorcerers. Don Quijote, then, has reached a state very much like *amor hereos*, in which the sensorial data does not correspond to the mental image, but with most undesirable effects. Finally, Sancho, the inadvertent healer, evokes in an inverted logotherapy the idealized image of Dulcinea which should counteract the "cure."

It is important to realize that Don Quijote, as a result of this encounter, is deprived of his idealized Dulcinea and becomes obsessed with a repulsive image. Hence the "search for a means to disenchant Dulcinea" (Dudley, "Wild Man" 119) is, from the perspective of Don Quijote, a struggle for the recuperation of a positive mental image of Dulcinea. Conversely, those around him constantly strive to rob him of his desired image. This dialectic is present in virtually every episode of the 1615 *Don Quijote*: from Sancho's initial assault on the image of Dulcinea in El Toboso, to Don Quijote's adventures in the cave of Montesinos, to the foretelling monkey, to the pranks at the ducal court, and so forth. Even Don Quijote's last battle with the *Caballero de la blanca luna*, in which he suffers the defeat that puts an end to his aspiration as a knight-errant, is fought for the "precedencia de hermosura" (II, chap. 64; p. 517).[334]

As the novel progresses, more and more of Don Quijote's efforts to "disenchant" Dulcinea are frustrated. This means that in his mind Dulcinea keeps being transformed into a hideous peasant; it is this image that he is now obsessed with. While the passionate lover's contemplation of the beloved's exceedingly appealing image may eventually be the occasion of melancholy, it causes a pleasurable experience at first. Real passionate love arouses *appetitus con-*

---

[334] To this we may add the feigned love of Altisidora, which is another attempt to divest Don Quijote of Dulcinea's image by enamoring him; furthermore, Don Quijote perceives the teasing of the ladies at Don Antonio's house as an effort to instill "pensamientos mal venidos," tempering with his constant love for the "sin par Dulcinea del Toboso" (II, chap. 61; p. 498). Neuschäfer observes that the Dulcinea episode actually prepares the denouement, because the obsessive thinking about the enchanted beloved makes the protagonist "depressive" (46).

cupiscibilis, an orectic impulse which stimulates the heart to emit hot vital spirit.[335] Don Quijote, on the other hand, is obsessed with an appalling image, which is prone to produce *appetitus irascibilis*, which causes the vital spirit to retreat to the heart. Moreover, the pain Don Quijote feels upon the transformation of his beloved, and his being unable to undo the spell, must produce melancholy.[336]

The "enchantment" Dulcinea, which is central to the second part of the novel, leads to a cooling of the brain and an increase of melancholy. Thus, one of the major effects of Don Quijote's excessive reading, i.e. the heat that hampers his *entendimiento*, is counteracted and he returns to his natural melancholic state and "juicio [...] libre y claro" (II, chap. 74; p. 572). Yet his natural melancholy is aggravated by the sorrows he felt during his madness because of the altered image of Dulcinea; Alonso Quijano ultimately dies from the excessive melancholy that only Don Quijote could engender in his madness.[337]

In the *novelas* of the first part of *Don Quijote*, lovesickness subsists as a life-threatening medical condition. Juxtaposed with this concept of love-as-sickness, Cervantes presents a parodic reworking of passionate love in Don Quijote's consciously feigned passionate love for Dulcinea; it is particularly in the 1615 *Don Quijote* "que esto del morirse los enamorados," as Sancho remarks, "es cosa de risa" (II, chap. 70; p. 552).[338]

Both aspects of lovesickness in *Don Quijote* call to mind the presentation of passionate love in sentimental fiction which I have analyzed in the preceding chapters. In first-generation sentimental romance, passionate love is depicted as a pathological yet ennobling and redeeming suffering. In the two texts of the second generation of sentimental fiction, this notion of love inherited from lyric poetry becomes contested. While Flores, in *Grimalte y Gradissa*, exposes

---

[335] See above chapter I.

[336] See above chapter III. 1.

[337] The fatal disease is diagnosed by a physician: "Fue el parecer del médico que melancolías y desabrimientos le acababan" (II, chap. 74; p. 573).

[338] Analyzing texts by Lope and Calderón, Soufas argues that Golden Age authors still recognized love melancholy as a devastating condition. Yet, at the same time, they subverted the literary conventions and expressed a conservative critique of the melancholy intellect (69-70). She interprets this dialectic as an indication of the "transvaluation" or resemantization of melancholy which reflected and breached the rupture between scientific discourse and literary expression (68).

and criticizes the devastating moral and psychosomatic effects of *amor hereos*, San Pedro conceives of a palinode that, nonetheless, plays out the fatal consequences of passionate love. *Don Quijote* seems to indicate that Flores's negative view prevailed. However, given the century that measures between Flores's and San Diego's and Cervantes's works, no valid argument on the historical development of the treatment of lovesickness can be made.

Nevertheless, it is suggestive to cast the texts analyzed into the theoretical framework Michel Foucault conceived of in his classic study on *Madness and Civilization*. Foucault argues that beginning with the middle of the 17th century, madmen, together with other kinds of deviants, became confined to institutions. He insists that the isolation of the mad did not pursue therapeutical goals, but was a reaction to their deviance from reason. Hence madness was not primarily seen as an illness, but as a model for other forms of "unreason" (*déraison*). Foucault classifies Don Quijote's madness as a *"madness by romantic identification"* (28). He argues that Cervantes testifies "more to a tragic experience of madness appearing in the fifteenth century, than to a critical and moral experience of Unreason, developing in [...] [his] own epoch" (31).

I think that his view must be revised if we do not focus only on Don Quijote's dementia but also consider the parody of lovesickness in the novel. If we follow Foucault's periodization, sentimental fiction and *Don Quijote* pertain historically to the same *épistémè*. The medical-sensitive reader would see the passionate love of sentimental romance's protagonists as a serious medical condition, a mental disease, a form of madness. In the absence of a cure, the disastrous denouements in these texts certainly reflect this reader's horizon of expectations.

A look at the medical tradition indicates that this horizon had not significantly changed in Cervantes's time: *amor hereos* was still considered a pathological condition, a form of madness. Yet in *Don Quijote* the relation between the protagonist's madness–which was easily recognizable to the contemporary reader as a pathological condition–and lovesickness associates Cervantes's work more with the "Classic Age" than Foucault realizes.

As I have been arguing, Don Quijote's lovesickness is not a mental disease, but a consciously feigned condition. His creation of Dulcinea results from a lucid decision, which is, as it were, bracketed in his folly. His love is not crazy but unreasonable, because it is based on premises conceived of by a lunatic. Although attempts are made to cure Don Quijote's madness, his mental disorder is not excluded from society, but welcomed as a source of amusement, particularly in the second part of the novel. Yet, as I have shown, constant efforts are made to deprive him of the "unreasonable" mental image of Dulcinea. It is the "unreason" within madness that is the target, not only of mockery and parody, but also of persecution. At the end of the novel Alonso Quijano is cured of his madness, restored to reason; with the never-disenchanted Dulcinea, Cervantes immortalized the ugly face of "unreason."

TEXTS CITED

Albertus Magnus. *De Anima. Opera Omnia.* Vol. 7,1. Ed. Clemens Stroick. Aschendorf: Monasterii Westfalorum, 1958.
———. *De Bono. Opera Omnia.* Vol. 28. Ed. Heinrich Kühle, et al. Aschendorf: Monasterii Westfalorum, 1951.
Andrachuk, Gregory Peter. "The Function of the *Estoria de dos amadores* within the *Siervo libre de amor.*" *Revista Canadiense de Estudios Hispánicos* 2 (1977): 27-38.
———. "A Further Look at the Italian Influence in the *Siervo Libre de Amor.*" *Journal of Hispanic Philology* 6 (1981-82): 45-56.
———. "On the Missing Third Part of *Siervo libre de amor.*" *Hispanic Review* 45 (1977): 171-80.
———. "Prosa y poesía en el *Siervo libre de amor.*" *Actas del Sexto Congreso Internacional de Hispanistas, celebrado en Toronto del 22 al 26 de agosto de 1977.* Ed. Evelyn Rugg and Alan M. Gordon. Toronto: Asociación Internacional de Hispanistas; Department of Spanish and Portuguese; U of Toronto, 1980. 60-62.
Andreas Capellanus. *On Love.* [*De amore*]. Ed. and trans. P. G. Walsh. London: Duckworth, 1982.
Arce, Joaquín. "Boccaccio nella letteratura castigliana: panorama generale e rassegna biblio-critica." *Il Boccaccio nelle culture e letterature nazionali.* Ed. Francesco Mazzoni. Florence: Olschki, 1978. 63-105.
Aristoteles. *De Memoria et Reminiscentia.* Trans. Richard Sorabij. *On Memory.* Providence, RI: Brown UP, 1972. 47-62.
Arnaldus de Villanova. *Tractatus de amore heroico. Arnaldi de Villanova opera medica omnia* III. Ed. Michael R. McVaugh. Barcelona: Universidad de Barcelona; U of North Carolina, 1985. 43-54.
Aubrun, Charles V., ed. "Un traité de l'amour, attribué à Juan de Mena." *Bulletin Hispanique* 50 (1948): 333-344.
Augustinus Aurelius. *Confessiones.* Ed. with an English translation by William Watts. 1912. Vol. II: Books 9-13. Loeb Classical Library 1631. London: William Heinemann, 1951.
———. *La Trinité (Livres VIII-XV): Les images.* [*De trinitate*]. *Œuvres de Saint Augustin* 16, 2ᵐᵉ Série: Dieu et son Œuvre. Trad. P. Agaësse, notes J. Moingt. Bibliothèque Augustinienne. Paris: Desclée de Brouwer, 1955.
Avalle-Arce, Juan Bautista. *Don Quijote como forma de vida.* Pensamiento literario español 1. Madrid: Fundación Juan March, 1976.
Avicenna. *De anima.* Venice 1508. Ed. George P. Klubertanz. Saint Louis: Saint Louis U, 1949.

Avicenna. *Kitāb al-najāt*; see Rahman.
———. *Liber Canonis*. Venice 1507. Rpt. (facs.) Hildesheim: Georg Olms, 1964.
Babb, Lawrence. *The Elizabethan Malady: A Study of Melancholia in English Literature from 1580 to 1642*. 1951. Repr. East Lansing: Michigan-State UP, 1965.
Baena, Juan Alfonso de. *Prologus Baenenssis*. Ed. Álvaro Alonso. *Poesía de Cancionero*. Madrid: Cátedra, 1986. 69-74.
Battesti Pelegrin, Jeanne. "'Je' lyrique, 'je' narratif dans *Cárcel de amor* (à propos du personnage de Leriano)." *Cahiers d'Études Romanes* 11 (1986): 7-19.
———. "Tópica e invención: Los lamentos de las madres en la *Cárcel de amor* de Diego de San Pedro." *Literatura hispánica, reyes católicos y descubrimiento: Actas del Congreso Internacional sobre Literatura Hispánica en la Época de los Reyes Católicos y el Descubrimiento*. Ed. Manuel Criado de Val. Barcelona: PPU, 1989. 237-47.
Bayardi, Citlalli. "El infierno de Fiometa y el purgatorio de Pánfilo." *Caballeros, monjas y maestros en la Edad Media*. Ed. Concepción Company, Aurelio González y Lillian von der Walde. México, DF: Universidad Nacional Autónoma de México y El Colegio de México, 1996. 537-48.
Beecher, Donald A. "Quattrocento Views on Erotization of the Imagination." Beecher and Ciavolella, *Eros and Anteros* 49-65.
Beecher, Donald A. and Massimo Ciavolella, eds. *Eros and Anteros: The Medical Traditions of Love in the Renaissance*. University of Toronto Italian Studies 9. Ottawa: Dovehouse Editions, 1992.
———. Introduction. *A Treatise on Lovesickness*. By Jacques Ferrand. Trans. and ed. Donald A. Beecher and Massimo Ciavolella. Syracuse: Syracuse UP, 1990. 1-202.
Bernheimer, Richard. *Wild Men in the Middle Ages: A Study in Art, Sentiment, and Demonology*. Cambridge, Mass.: Harvard UP, 1952.
Blay Manzanera, Vicenta. "La dinámica espacio-temporal como elemento estructural en *Triste deleytacion*." *Actas del III Congreso de la Asociación Hispánica de Literatura Medieval*. Ed. María Isabel Toro Pascua. Tom. 1. Salamanca: Biblioteca Española del Siglo XV; Departamento de Literatura Española e Hispanoamericana, 1994. 187-96.
———. "El humor en *Triste deleytaçión*: sobre unas originales coplas de disparates." *Revista de Literatura Medieval* 6 (1994): 45-78.
———. "El más allá de *Triste deleytaçión* y el mito de Verbino." *Bulletin of Hispanic Studies* 75 (1998): 137-52.
———. "Metaliteratura y reflexividad en la ficción sentimental: la primera generación." *Anuario Medieval* 6 (1994): 39-74.
Boase, Roger. *The Origin and Meaning of Courtly Love: A Critical Study of European Scholarship*. Manchester: Manchester UP; Totowa, NJ: Rowman and Littlefield, 1977.
Boccaccio, Giovanni. *De casibus virorum illustrium*. Ed. Pier Giorgio Ricci and Vittorio Zaccaria. *Tutte le opere di Giovanni Boccaccio* 9. Milano: Mondadori, 1983.
———. The text and concordance of Giovanni Boccaccio's *De casibus virorum illustrium*, translated by Pero López de Ayala. Ed. [6 p. + 6 microfiches] Eric Naylor. Madison, WI: Hispanic Seminary of Medieval Studies, 1994. [also in: Electronic Texts and Concordances of the *Madison Corpus of Early Spanish Manuscripts and Printings*. Ed. (CD-Rom) John O'Neill. Madison: Hispanic Seminary of Medieval Studies, 1999].
———. *Il Corbaccio*. Ed. Giulia Natali. Grande Universale Mursia, Nuova serie 219. Milano: Mursia, 1992.

Boccaccio, Giovanni. *Corbaccio or the Laberinth of Love*. Trans. and ed. Anthony K. Cassell. 2nd rev. ed. Binghamton, NY: Pegasus, 1992.

———. *Libro de Fiameta*. Ed. Lia Mendia Vozzo. Collana di testi e studi ispanici I, Testi critici 4. Pisa: Giardini, 1983.

Bolzoni, Lina. "The Art of Memory and the Erotic Image in the 16th and 17th Century Europe: The Example of Giovan Battista Della Porta." Trans. L Chen. Beecher and Ciavolella, *Eros and Anteros* 103-122.

Bornscheuer, Lothar. *Topik: Zur Struktur der gesellschaftlichen Einbildungskraft*. Frankfurt am Main: Suhrkamp, 1976.

Brownlee, Marina Scordilis. "The Counterfeit Muse: Ovid, Boccaccio, Juan de Flores." *Discourse of Authority in Medieval and Renaissance Literature*. Ed. Kevin Brownlee and Walter Stephens. Hanover, NH: UP of New England for Darthmouth College, 1989. 109-127.

———. "The Generic Status of the *Siervo libre de amor*: Rodríguez del Padrón's Reworking of Dante." *Poetics Today* (1984): 629-43.

———. "Imprisoned Discourse in the *Cárcel de amor*." *Romanic Review* 78 (1987): 188-201.

———. *The Severed Word: Ovid's* Heroides *and the* Novela Sentimental. Princeton: Princeton UP, 1990.

———. "The Untranscendent Vision." *French Forum* 14, sup. 1 (1989): 475-85.

Bundy, Murray Wright. *The Theory of Imagination in Classical and Mediaeval Thought*. University of Illinois Studies in Language and Literature 12,2-3. Urbana, IL: U of Illinois, 1927.

Burke, James F. "The Insouciant Reader and the Failure of Memory in *Celestina*." *Crítica Hispánica* 15 (1993): 35-46.

———. "The interior journey and the structure of Juan de Mena's *Laberinto de Fortuna*." *Revista de Estudios Hispánicos* 22 (1988): 27-45.

———. *Vision, the Gaze, and the Function of the Senses in* Celestina. Penn State Studies in Romance Literatures. University Park, PA: Pennsylvania State UP, 2000.

Canet Vallés, José Luis. "El proceso del enamoramiento como elemento estructurante de la ficción sentimental." *Historias y ficciones: Coloquio sobre la literatura del siglo XV*. Ed. Rafael Beltrán, et al. València: Universitat de València, 1992. 227-39.

———. "Reflexiones filosóficas sobre el amor cortés y el *De amore* de Andreas Capellanus." *Homenatge a Amelia García-Valdecasas Jiménez*. Ed. Ferrán Carbó, et al. Vol. 1. Quaderns de filologia, estudis literaris 1. València: Facultat de Filologia, Universitat de València, 1995. 191-208.

Carrillo, Elena. "Amor cortés y contexto social en la poesía de cancionero." *Proceedings of the Ninth Colloquium*. Ed. Andrew M. Beresford and Alan Deyermond. Papers of the Medieval Hispanic Research Seminar 26. London: Department of Hispanic Studies; Queen Mary and Westfield College, 2000. 165-74.

Carruthers, Mary. *The Craft of Thought: Meditation, Rhetoric, and the Making of Images, 400-1200*. Cambridge Studies in Medieval Literature 34. 1998. 2nd ed. Cambridge, New York: Cambridge UP, 2000.

———. "The Poet as Master Builder: Composition and Locational Memory in the Middle Ages." *New Literary History* 24,4 (1993): 881-904.

Carruthers, Mary J. *The Book of Memory: A Study of Memory in Medieval Culture*. Cambridge Studies in Medieval Literature 10. 1989. 2nd ed. Cambridge; London: Cambridge UP, 1992.

Castells, Ricardo. "Calisto and the imputed parody of courtly love in *Celestina*." *Journal of Hispanic Philology* 15 (1991): 209-20.

Castells, Ricardo. *Calisto's Dream and the Celestinesque Tradition: A Rereading of Celestina*. North Carolina Studies in the Romance Languages and Literatures 249. Chapel Hill, NC: U of North Carolina P, 1995.

———. *Fernando de Rojas and the Renaissance Vision: Phantasm, Melancholy, and Didacticism in Celestina*. Penn State Studies in Romance Languages. University Park, PA: Pennsylvania State UP, 2000.

———. "El mal de amores de Calisto y el diagnóstico de Eras y Crato, médicos." *Hispania* 76 (1993): 55-60.

———. "El sueño de Calisto y la tradición celestinesca." *Celestinesca* 4.1 (1990): 17-39.

Castro Guisasola, Florentino. *Observaciones sobre las fuentes literarias de La Celestina*. Revista de Filología Española, anejo 5. Madrid: Jiménez y Molina, 1924.

Castro Lingl, Vera. "Back to the text: Another look at Juan Rodríguez del Padrón's *Siervo libre de amor*." *Romanische Forschungen* 106 (1994): 48-60.

———. "The Constable of Portugal's *Sátira de infelice e felice vida*: A reworking of Rodríguez del Padrón's *Siervo libre de amor*." *Revista de Estudios Hispánicos* 32 (1998): 76-100.

———. "Fiometa's Suicide in *Grimalte y Gradissa*." *Journal of Hispanic Research* 1 (1992-93): 345-48.

———. "*Triste deleytaçión*'s *madrina*: Godmother or midwife?" *Anuario Medieval* 5 (1993): 13-22.

Cátedra, Pedro M. *Amor y pedagogía en la Edad Media: Estudio de doctrina amorosa y práctica literaria*. Salamanca: Universidad de Salamanca, 1989.

Cervantes, Miguel de. *El Ingenioso Hidalgo Don Quijote de la Mancha*. Ed. John Jay Allen. 2 vols. Madrid: Cátedra, 1989.

Chartier, Roger. *The Order of Books: Readers, Authors, and Libraries in Europe between Fourteenth and Eighteenth Centuries*. Cambridge, MA: Polity Press, 1994.

———. "Texts, Printing, Readings." *The New Cultural History*. Ed. Lynn Hunt. Berkeley, CA: U of California P, 1989. 154-75.

Chorpenning, Joseph F. "Leriano's Consumption of Laureola's Letters in *Cárcel de amor*." *Modern Language Notes* 95 (1980): 442-45.

———. "Loss of Innocence, Descent into Hell, and Cannibalism: Romance Archetypes and Narrative Unity in *Cárcel de amor*." *Modern Language Review* 87 (1992): 343-51.

———. "Rhetoric and feminism in the *Cárcel de Amor*." *Bulletin of Hispanic Studies* 54 (1977): 1-8.

Ciavolella, Massimo. "Eros and the Phantasms of *Hereos*." Beecher and Ciavolella, *Eros and Anteros* 75-85.

———. *La 'mallatia d'amore' dall'Antichità al Medioevo*. Strumenti de Ricerca 12-13. Roma: Bulzoni, 1976.

———. "Mediaeval medicine and Arcite's love sickness." *Florilegium* 1 (1979): 222-41.

———. "La tradizione dell'*aegritudo amoris* nel *Decameron*." *Giornale storico della letteratura italiana* 147 (1970): 496-517.

Cicero, Marcus Tullius. *De inventione*. With an English translation by H. M. Hubbel. Loeb Classical Library. London: William Heinemann; Cambridge, MA: Harvard UP, 1960.

———. *De oratore*. Books I, II. With an English translation by E. W. Sutton. Loeb Classical Library. London: William Heinemann; Cambridge, MA: Harvard UP, 1959.

Clasby, Eugene. Introduction. *The Pilgrimage of Human Life (Le Pèlerinage de la vie humaine)*. By Guillaume de Deguileville. Trans. Eugene Clasby. Garland Library of Medieval Literature 76, Series B. New York: Garland Publishing, 1992.

Cocozzella, Peter. "From lyricism to drama: The evolution of Fernando de Rojas' egocentric subtext." *Celestinesca* 19,1-2 (1995): 71-92.

———. "The Thematic Unity of Juan Rodríguez del Padrón's *Siervo libre de amor*." *Hispania* 64 (1981): 188-98.

Constantine the African. *Liber de coitu: el tratado de andrología de Constantino el Africano*. Ed. Enrique Montero Cartelle. Santiago de Compostela: Universidad de Santiago, 1983.

———. *Viaticum I.20*. Ed. and trans. Wack, *Lovesickness* 186-193.

Corfis, Ivy A. "Catalogue of editions." *Cárcel de amor*. By Diego de San Pedro. Ed. Ivy A. Corfis. London: Tamesis, 1987. 16-50.

———. "*Celestina* and the Conflict of Ovidian and Courtly Love." *Bulletin of Hispanic Studies* 73 (1996): 395-417.

———. "The *Dispositio* of Diego de San Pedro's *Cárcel de Amor*." *Iberoromania* 21 (1985): 32-47.

———. "Sentimental Lore and Irony in the Fifteenth-Century Romances and *Celestina*." Gerli and Gwara 154-71.

Textos y Concordancias Electrónicas del *Corpus Médico Español*. Ed. (CD-Rom) Mª Teresa Herrera y Mª Estela González de Fauve. Madison, WI: Hispanic Seminary of Medieval Studies, 1997.

Cortijo Ocaña, Antonio. "La ficción sentimental: ¿un género imposible?" *La Corónica* 29 (2000): 5-13.

Couliano, Ioan P. *Eros and Magic in the Renaissance*. Trans. Margareth Cook. Chicago: U of Chicago P, 1987.

Crohns, Hjalmar. "Zur Geschichte der Liebe als 'Krankheit'." *Archiv für Kulturgeschichte* 3 (1905): 66-86.

Cull, John T. "Irony, Romance Conventions, and Misogyny in *Grisel y Mirabella* by Juan de Flores." *Revista Canadiense de Estudios Hispánicos* 22 (1998): 415-30.

Cull, John and Brian Dutton. Introducción. *Lilio de medicina*. By Bernard de Gordon. Ed. John Cull and Brian Dutton. Madison, WI: Hispanic Seminary of Medieval Studies, 1991.

Culler, Jonathan. *On Deconstruction: Theory and Criticism after Structuralism*. Ithaca, NY: Cornell UP, 1983.

———. "Prolegomena to a Theory of Reading." *The Reader in the Text: Essays on Audience and Interpretation*. Ed. Susan Suleiman and Inge Crosman. Princeton, NJ: Princeton UP, 1980. 46-66.

Cvitanovič, Dinko. "Alusión y elusión en la novela española de los siglos XV y XVI." *Estudios sobre la expresión alegórica en España y América*. Ed. Dinko Cvitanovič, et al. Bahia Blanca: Departamento de Humanidades, Universidad Nacional del Sur, 1983. 3-68.

———. *La novela sentimental española*. Madrid: Prensa Española, 1973.

———. "El tratadismo de Juan Rodríguez del Padrón." *Cuadernos del Sur* 11 (1969-71): 225-36.

Dagenais, John. *The Ethics of Reading in Manuscript Culture: Glossing the* Libro de buen amor. Princeton, NJ: Princeton UP, 1994.

———. "Juan Rodríguez del Padrón's Translation of the Latin *Bursarii*: New Light on the Meaning of 'Tra(c)tado'." *Journal of Hispanic Philology* 10 (1986): 117-39.

Damiani, Bruno M. "The Didactic Intention of the *Cárcel de amor*." *Hispanófila* 56 (1976): 29-44.

Dante Alighieri. *Vita nuova*. Italian text with English translation by Dino S. Cervigni and Edward Vasta. Notre Dame, IN: U of Notre Dame P, 1995.

De Armas, Frederick A. "*La Celestina*: an example of love melancholy." *Romanic Review* 66 (1975): 288-95.

Débax, Michelle. "Motivos tradicionales y organización narrativa en *Tractado de amores de Arnalte y Lucenda* y *Cárcel de amor* de Diego de San Pedro". *Literatura Hispánica, Reyes Católicos y Descubrimiento: Actas del Congreso Internacional sobre Literatura Hispánica en la Época de los Reyes Católicos y el Descubrimiento*. Ed. Manuel Criado de Val. Barcelona: PPU, 1989. 279-84.

Delhaye, Philippe. *The Christian Conscience*. Trans. Charles Underhill Quinn. New York: Desclee, 1968.

De Man, Paul. Introduction. *Toward an Aesthetic of Reception*. By Hans Robert Jauss. Trans. Timothy Bahti. Theory and History of Literature 2. Minneapolis, MN: U of Minnesota P, 1982.

Deyermond, Alan D. "El estudio de la ficción sentimental: balance de los últimos años y vislumbre de los que vienen." *Ínsula* 651 (March 2001): 3-9.

———. Estudio preliminar. *Cárcel de amor, con la continuación de Nicolás Núñez*. Por Diego de San Pedro y Nicolás Núñez. Ed. Carmen Parrilla. Barcelona: Crítica, 1995.

———. "El hombre salvaje en la novela sentimental." *Filología* 10 (1964): 97-111.

———. "The lost genre of medieval Spanish Literature." *Hispanic Review* 43 (1975): 231-59.

———. "El punto de vista narrativo en la ficción sentimental del siglo XV." *Tradiciones y puntos de vista en la ficción sentimental*. México: Universidad Nacional Autónoma de México, 1993. 65-88.

———. "Las relaciones genéricas de la ficción sentimental." *Tradiciones y puntos de vista en la ficción sentimental*. México: Universidad Nacional Autónoma de México, 1993. 43-64 [also in *Symposium in honorem prof. M de Riquer*. Barcelona: Universitat; Quaderns Crema, 1986. 75-92].

———. "The Text-Book Mishandled: Andreas Capellanus and the Opening Scene of *La Celestina*." *Neophilologus* 45 (1961): 218-21.

Di Lorenzo, Raymond D. "The collection form and the art of memory in the *Libellus super ludo schachorum* of Jacobus de Cessolis." *Mediaeval Studies* 35 (1973): 205-21.

Dinzelbacher, Peter. "Über die Entdeckung der Liebe im Hochmittelalter." *Saeculum* 32 (1981): 185-208.

Dolz-Ferrer, Enric S. "'Ficçiones digo': Letra y alegoría de la *Estoria de dos amadores* en el contexto del *Siervo libre de amor*." *Proceedings of the Ninth Colloquium*. Ed. Andrew M. Beresford and Alan Deyermond. *Papers of the Medieval Hispanic Research Seminar* 26. London: Department of Hispanic Studies; Queen Mary and Westfield College, 2000. 121-34.

Dudley, Edward. "The inquisition of love: *tratado* as a fictional genre." *Mediaevalia* 5 (1979): 233-43.

———. "The Wild Man Goes Baroque." *The Wild Man Within: An Image of Western Thought from the Renaissance to Romanticism*. Ed. Edward Dudley and Maximilian E. Novak. Pittsburgh, PA: U of Pittsburgh P, 1972. 115-39.

Dunn, Peter. "Narrator as Character in the *Cárcel de Amor*." *Modern Language Notes* 94 (1979): 187-99.

Dunn-Wood, Maryjane. "Guillaume de Deguileville's *El pelegrinage de la vida humana*: New Interest in a Forgotten Work." *La Corónica* 15 (1986-87): 259-63.

Earle, Peter G. "Love concepts in *La cárcel de amor* and *La Celestina*." *Hispania* 39 (1956): 92-96.

Eco, Umberto. "An *ars oblivionalis*? Forget it!" *PMLA* 103 (1988): 254-61.

England, John. "'Testigos de mi gloria': Calisto's bestial behaviour." *La Corónica* 28 (2000): 81-90.

Fernández Jiménez, Juan. "La estructura del *Siervo libre de amor* y la crítica reciente." *Cuadernos Hispanoamericanos* 388 (1982): 178-190.

Fish, Stanley. *Is There a Text in This Class? The Authority of Interpretative Communities*. Cambridge, MA: Harvard UP, 1980.
Flores, Juan de. *Grimalte y Gradissa*. Ed. Pamela Waley. London: Tamesis, 1971.
———. *Grimalte y Gradisa*. Ed. Carmen Parrilla García. Santiago de Compostela: Universidade de Santiago de Compostela, Servicio de Publicacións e Intercambio Científico, 1988.
Folger, Robert. "Memoria en *Siervo libre de amor*: El papel de la psicología medieval en la ficción sentimental." *La Corónica* 26 (1998): 197-210.
Fonseca, Luis Adão. Introdução. *Obras completas do condestável dom Pedro*. By Pedro, Constable of Portugal. Ed. Luis Adão Fonseca. Lisboa: Fundação Calouste Gulbenkian, 1975.
Fontaine, Marie-Madeleine. "La lignée des commentaires à la chanson de Guido Cavalcanti *Donna me prega*: Évolution des relations entre philosophie, médicine et littérature dans le débat sur la nature d'Amour (de la fin du XIIIe siècle à celle du XVIe)." *La folie et le corps*. Ed. Jean Céard. Paris: Presses de L'École Normale Supérieure, 1985. 159-78.
Foucault, Michel. *Madness and Civilization*. Ed. Richard Howard. New York: Vintage Books, 1965.
Fraker, Charles F. "The Four Humors in *Celestina*." *Fernando de Rojas and Celestina: Approaching the Fifth Centenary: Proceedings of An International Conference in Commemoration of the 450th Death of Fernando de Rojas, Purdue University West Lafayette, Indiana 21-24 November 1991*. Ed. Ivy A. Corfis and Joseph T. Snow. Madison, WI: Hispanic Seminary of Medieval Studies, 1993. 129-54.
———. "María Rosa Lida de Malkiel on the *Celestina*." *Hispania* 50 (1967): 174-81.
Freytag, Hartmut. *Die Theorie der allegorischen Schriftdeutung und die Allegorie in deutschen Texten (besonders des 11. und 12. Jahrhunderts)*. Bibliotheca Germanica 24. Bern: Francke, 1982.
Frye, Northrop. *The Anatomy of Criticism: Four Essays*. Princeton, NJ: Princeton UP, 1957.
Funes, Leonardo. "Dos notas sobre *Cárcel de Amor*." *Journal of Hispanic Research* 1 (1992-93): 331-43.
Gadamer, Hans-Georg. *Truth and Method*. Trans. Joel Weinsheimer and Donald G. Marshall. 2nd, rev. ed. New York: Crossroad, 1989.
———. *Wahrheit und Methode: Grundzüge einer philosophischen Hermeneutik*. 2. erw. ed. Tübingen: Mohr, 1965.
Gallagher, Catherine and Stephen J. Greenblatt. *Practicing New Historicism*. Chicago: U of Chicago P, 2000.
Garci-Gómez, Miguel. *Calisto, soñador y alterano*. Kassel: Reichenberger, 1994.
———. "El sueño de Calisto." *Celestinesca* 9,1 (1985): 11-22.
Garcia, Michel. "Vida de Juan Rodríguez del Padrón." *Actas del IX Congreso de la Asociación Internacional de Hispanistas (18-23 agosto 1986, Berlín)*. Ed. Sebastian Neumeister. Vol. 1. Frankfurt am Main: Vervuert, 1989. 205-213.
García Ballester, Luis. *Historia social de la medicina en la España de los siglos XIII al XVI*. Vol. 1: *La minoría musulmana y morisca*. Madrid: Akal, 1976.
Gascón Vera, Elena. "La ambigüedad en el concepto del amor y de la mujer en la prosa castellana del siglo XV." *Boletín de la Real Academia Española* 59 (1979): 119-155.
———. "Anorexia eucarística. La *Cárcel de amor*: como tragedia clásica." *Anuario Medieval* 2 (1990): 64-77.
———. *Don Pedro, Condestable de Portugal*. Publicaciones de la Fundación Universitaria Española, Tesis 4. Madrid: Fundación Universitaria Española, 1979.
Genette, Gérard. *Palimpsestes: La littérature au second degré*. Paris: Éditions du Seuil, 1983.

Gerard of Berry. *Glosule super Viaticum*. Ed. and trans. Wack, *Lovesickness* 198-205.
Gerli, E. Michael. "El castillo interior y el Arte de la memoria." *Santa Teresa y la literatura mística hispánica: Actas del I Congreso Internacional sobre Santa Teresa y la mística hispánica*. Ed. Manuel Criado de Val. Tomo 1. Madrid: EDI-6, 1984. 331-37.

———. Introduction. *Triste deleytaçión. An Anonymous Fifteenth Century Castilian Romance*. Ed. E. Michael Gerli. Washington, DC: Georgetown UP, 1982.

———. "Leriano and Lacan: The Mythological and Psychoanalytical Underpinnings of Leriano's Last Drink." *La Corónica* 29 (2000): 113-28.

———. "Leriano's Libation: Notes on the *Cancionero* Lyric, *Ars moriendi*, and the Probable Debt to Boccaccio." *Modern Language Notes* 96 (1981): 414-20.

———. "Metafiction in Spanish Sentimental Romances." *The Age of the Catholic Monarchs, 1474-1516: Literary Studies in Memory of Keith Whinnom*. Ed. Alan Deyermond and Ian Macpherson. Liverpool: Liverpool UP, 1989. 57-63.

———. "The Old French Source of *Siervo libre de amor*: Guillaume de Deguilevilles's *Le Rommant des trois pèlerinages*." Gerli and Gwara 3-19.

———. "'Señora, fablar querría mas miedo he de errar.' Signs, Sense, and Courtly Culture: On Marina Brownlee's *The Severed Word*." *Journal of Hispanic Philology* 15 (1990-91): 237-49.

———. "*Siervo libre de amor* and the Penitential Tradition." *Journal of Hispanic Studies* 12 (1988): 93-102.

———. "Toward a Poetics of the Spanish Sentimental Romance." *Hispania* 72 (1989): 474-82.

———. "Toward a Revaluation of the Condestable of Portugal's *Sátira de infelice e felice vida*." *Hispanic Studies in Honour of Alan D. Deyermond. A North American Tribute*. John S. Miletich. Madison, WI: Hispanic Seminary of Medieval Studies, 1986. 107-18.

Gerli, E. Michael and Joseph J. Gwara. *Studies on the Spanish Sentimental Romance (1440-1550): Redefining a Genre*. London: Tamesis, 1997.

Gilderman, Martin S. "La apoteosis del amante cortés: Hacia una interpretación del *Siervo libre de amor*." *Boletín de Filología Española* 12 (1972): 37-50.

———. *Juan Rodríguez de la Cámara*. Twayne's World Author Series 423. New York: Twayne Publishers, 1977.

Gillet, Joseph E. "The Autonomous Character in Spanish and European Literature." *Hispanic Review* 24 (1956): 179-90.

Gómez-Fargas, Rosa María. "*Triste deleytaçión*, ¿novela en clave?" *Revista de Literatura Medieval* 4 (1992): 101-22.

González Rolán, Tomás y Pilar Saquero Suárez-Somonte. Introducción. *Bursario*. Por Juan Rodríguez del Padrón. Ed. Pilar Saquero Suárez-Somonte y Tomás González Rolán. Madrid: Universidad Complutense, 1984.

Gordon, Bernard de. *Lilio de medicina*. Ed. John Cull and Brian Dutton. Madison, WI: Hispanic Seminary of Medieval Studies, 1991.

———. Text and Concordance of the *Lilio de medicina*: Biblioteca Nacional I-315. Ed. (14 p. + 6 microfiches) John Cull and Cynthia M. Wasick. Madison, WI: Hispanic Seminary of Medieval Studies, 1989 [also in *Corpus Médico Español*].

Grafton, Anthony. "The Humanist as Reader." *A History of Reading in the West*. Trans. Lydia Cochrane. Ed. Guglielmo Cavallo and Roger Chartier. Amherst, MA: U of Massachusetts P, 1999. 179-212.

Granjel, Luis S. *Vida y obras de López de Villalobos*. Trabajos de la Cátedra de Historia de la Medicina. Salamanca: Universidad de Salamanca, 1979.

Green, Otis H. "The Artistic Originality of the *Celestina*." *Hispanic Review* 33 (1965): 15-31.

Green, Otis H. "El *ingenioso* hidalgo." *Hispanic Review* 25 (1957): 175-93.
Gregory the Great, Saint. "Epistola XIII". Migne *PL* 77. col. 1128-30.
Grieve, Patricia E. *Desire and Death in Spanish Sentimental Romance: 1440-1550.* Newark, DE: Juan de la Cuesta, 1987.
Guillaume de Deguileville. *The Pilgrimage of Human Life (Le Pèlerinage de la vie humaine).* Trans Eugene Clasby. Garland Library of Medieval Literature 76, Series B. New York: Garland, 1992.
Guillaume de Lorris and Jean de Meun. *The Romance of the Rose.* Trans. Charles Dahlberg. Hanover, NH; London: UP of New England, 1983.
Gumbrecht, Hans Ulrich. "Eccentricities: On Prologues in Some Fourteenth-Century Castilian Texts." *The South Atlantic Quarterly* 91 (1992): 891-907.
———. *Eine Geschichte der spanischen Literatur.* Frankfurt am Main: Suhrkamp, 1990.
Gwara, Joseph J. "The Identity of Juan de Flores: The Evidence of the *Crónica incompleta de los Reyes Católicos.*" *Journal of Hispanic Philology* 11 (1987): 103-130 and 205-222.
Hagen, Susan K. *Allegorical Remembrance: A Study of The Pilgrimage of the Life of Man as a Medieval Treatise on Seeing and Remembering.* Athens, Georgia: U of Georgia P, 1990.
Halka, Chester S. "*Don Quijote* in the Light of Huarte's *Examen de ingenios*: A Reexamination." *Anales Cervantinos* 19 (1981): 3-13.
Harms, Wolfgang und Klaus Speckenbach. *Bildhafte Rede in Mittelalter und früher Neuzeit: Probleme ihrer Legitimation und ihrer Funktion.* Tübingen: Max Niemeyer, 1992.
Harvey, E. Ruth. *The Inward Wits: Psychological Theory in the Middle Ages and the Renaissance.* Warburg Institute Surveys 6. London: Warburg Institute; U of London, 1975.
Haywood, Louise M. "Gradissa: A fictional female reader in/of a male author's text." *Medium Aevum* 64,1 (1995): 85-99.
———. "Narrative and Structural Strategies in Early Spanish Sentimental Romance." *Fifteenth-Century Studies* 25 (1999): 11-24.
Heffernan, Carol Falvo. *The Melancholy Muse: Chaucer, Shakespeare, and Early Medicine.* Duquesne Studies; Language and Literature Series 19. Pittsburgh, PA: Duquesne UP, 1995.
Heiple, Daniel L. "The 'accidens amoris' in lyric poetry." *Neophilologus* 67 (1983): 55-64.
Hermeneutics and Medieval Culture. Ed. Patrick J. Gallacher and Helen Damico. Albany, NY: State U of New York P, 1989.
Hernández Alonso, César. Introducción. *Obras completas.* Por Juan Rodríguez del Padrón. Ed. César Hernández Alonso. Madrid: Editora Nacional, 1982.
———. Siervo libre de amor *de Juan Rodríguez del Padrón.* Valladolid: Universidad de Valladolid, 1970.
Herrero, Javier. "The Allegorical Structure of the *Siervo libre de amor.*" *Speculum* 55 (1980): 751-64.
———. "Arcadia's Inferno: Cervantes' Attack on the Pastoral." *Bulletin of Hispanic Studies* 55 (1978): 289-99.
———. "Dulcinea and her Critics." *Cervantes* 2 (1982): 23-42.
———. "Sierra Morena as Labyrinth: From Wilderness to Christian Knighthood." *Forum for Modern Language Studies* 17 (1981): 55-67.
Herriott, J. Homer. "The ten senses in the *Siete partidas.*" *Hispanic Review* 20 (1952): 269-81.
Heugas, Pierre. La Célestine *et sa descendance directe.* Bordeaux: Institut d'études ibériques et ibéro-américaines de l'Université de Bordeaux, 1973.

Heugas, Pierre. "Variation sur un portrait: de Mélibée a Dulcinée." *Bulletin Hispanique* 71 (1969): 5-30.
Hilty, Gerold. "Liebe als Krankheit: Altspanische Texte des 12. und 13. Jahrhunderts." Stemmler 127-37.
Hollander, Robert. *Boccaccio's Last Fiction,* Il Corbaccio. Philadelphia: U of Pennsylvania P, 1988.
Howe, Elisabeth Teresa. "A Woman Ensnared: Laureola as Victim in the *Cárcel de amor.*" *Revista de Estudios Hispánicos* 21 (1987): 13-27.
Huarte de San Juan, Juan. *Examen de ingenios para las ciencias.* Ed. Guillermo Serés. Madrid: Cátedra, 1989.
Huot, Sylvia. *The* Romance of the Rose *and its Medieval Readers: Interpretation, Reception, Manuscript Transmission.* Cambridge Studies in Medieval Literature 16. Cambridge [England]; New York: Cambridge UP, 1993.
———. "Visualization and Memory: The Illustrations of Troubadour Lyric in a Thirteenth-Century Manuscript." *Gesta* 31,1 (1992): 3-14.
Hutcheson, Gregory S. "Cracks in the Labyrinth: Juan de Mena, *Converso* Experience and the Rise of the Spanish Nation." *La Corónica* 25 (1996): 37-50.
Ihrie, Maureen. "Discourses of Power in the *Cárcel de amor.*" *Hispanófila* 125 (1999): 1-10.
Impey, Olga Tudorică. "*Contraria* en la *Triste deleytaçión*: materia fundamental del Aborintio de Amor y Fortuna." *Proceedings of the Ninth Colloquium.* Ed. Andrew M. Beresford and Alan Deyermond. *Papers of the Medieval Hispanic Research Seminar* 26. London: Department of Hispanic Studies; Queen Mary and Westfield College, 2000. 145-64.
———. "Un doctrinal para las doncellas enamoradas en la *Triste deleytaçión.*" *Boletín de la Real Academia Española* 66 (1986): 191-234.
———. "Los enigmas del *Siervo libre de amor.*" *Actas Irvine 92, Asociación Internacional de Hispanistas.* Ed. Juan Villegas. Vol. V. Irvine, CA: U of California P, 1994. 107-17.
———. "The Literary Emancipation of Juan Rodriguez del Padron: From the Fictional 'Cartas' to the *Siervo libre de amor.*" *Speculum* 55 (1980): 305-16.
———. "Ovid, Alfonso X, and Juan Rodríguez del Padron: Two Castilian translations of the *Heroides* and the beginnings of Spanish sentimental prose." *Bulletin of Hispanic Studies* 57 (1980): 283-97.
———. "La poesía y la prosa del *Siervo libre de amor*: ¿'aferramiento' a la tradición del *prosimetrum* y de la convención lírica?" *Medieval, Renaissance and Folklore Studies: In Honor of John Esten Keller.* Ed. Joseph R. Jones. Hispanic Monographs: Homenajes 1. Newark, DE: Juan de la Cuesta, 1980. 171-87.
Iriarte, M. de, SJ. *El doctor Huarte de San Juan y su* Examen de ingenios: *contribución a la historia de la psicología diferencial.* Madrid: Consejo Superior de Investigaciones Científicas, 1948.
Iser, Wolfgang. *The Act of Reading: A Theory of Aesthetic Response.* Baltimore: The Johns Hopkins P, 1980.
Jacquart, Danielle and Claude Thomasset. "L'amour 'héroïque' à travers le traité d'Arnaud de Villeneuve. " *La folie et le corps.* Ed. Jean Céard. Paris: Presses de L'École Normale Supérieure, 1985. 143-58.
Jaeger, C. Stephen. *Ennobling Love: In Search of a Lost Sensibility.* Philadelphia, PA: U of Pennsylvania P, 1999.
Jakobson, Roman. "The Metaphoric and Metonymic Poles." *Fundamentals of Language.* Ed. Roman Jakobson and Moris Halle. Janua linguarum, Series minor 1. The Hague: Mouton, 1971. 90-96.
Jauß, Hans Robert. *Toward an Aesthetic of Reception.* Trans. Timothy Bahti. Theory and History of Literature 2. Minneapolis, MN: U of Minnesota P, 1982.

Jauß, Hans Robert. *Alterität und Modernität der mittelalterlichen Literatur: Gesammelte Aufsätze 1956-1976.* München: Fink, 1979.
———. "Literary History as a Challenge to Literary Theory." *Toward an Aesthetic* 3-45.
———. *Literaturgeschichte als Provokation.* Frankfurt am Main: Suhrkamp, 1970.
———. "Theory and Genres and Medieval Literature." *Toward an Aesthetic* 76-109.
Joset, Jacques. "'Dulcis amaritudo': Una isotopía descuidada de *La Celestina.*" *Historias y ficciones: Coloquio sobre la literatura del siglo XV.* Ed. Rafael Beltrán, et al. València: Universitat de València, 1992. 257-66.
Kany, Charles E. *The Beginnings of the Epistolary Novel in France, Italy, and Spain.* University of California Press Publications in Modern Philology 21, part 1. Berkeley, CA: U of California P, 1937.
Kelly, Douglas. *Medieval Imagination: Rhetoric and the Poetry of Courtly Love.* Madison, WI: U of Wisconsin P, 1978.
———. "Topical Invention in Medieval French Literature." *Medieval Eloquence: Studies in the Theory and Practice of Medieval Rhetoric.* Ed. James J. Murphy. Berkeley, CA: U of California P, 1978. 231-51.
Kilbansky, Raymond, Erwin Panofsky and Fritz Saxl. *Saturn and Melancholy: Studies in the History of Natural Philosophy, Religion and Art.* London: Nelson, 1964.
Knape, Joachim. "Mnemonik, Bildbuch und Emblematik im Zeitalter Sebastian Brants (Brant, Schwarzenberg, Alciati)." *Mnemosyne: Festschrift für Manfred Lurker zum 60. Geburtstag.* Ed. Hermann Jung und Werner Bies. Bibliographie zur Symbolik, Ikonographie und Mythologie, Ergänzungsband 2. Baden-Baden: V. Koerner, 1988. 133-78.
Kolve, V. A. *Chaucer and the Imagery of Narrative: The First Five Canterbury Tales.* London: E. Arnold, 1984.
Krause, Anna. "El tractado novelístico de Diego de San Pedro." *Bulletin Hispanique* 54 (1952): 245-75.
Küpper, Joachim. "(H)er(e)os: Petrarcas *Canzoniere* und der medizinische Diskurs seiner Zeit." *Romanische Forschungen* 111 (1999): 178-224.
Kurtz, Barbara E. "The Castle Motif and the Medieval Allegory of Love: Diego de San Pedro's *Cárcel de amor.*" *Fifteenth Century Studies* 11 (1985): 37-49.
———. "Diego de San Pedro's *Cárcel de amor* and the tradition of the allegorical edifice." *Journal of Hispanic Philology* 8 (1984): 123-38.
Lacarra, María Eugenia. "La parodia sentimental en *La Celestina.*" *Celestinesca* 13,1 (1989): 11-29.
Lacarra Lanz, Eukene. "*Siervo libre de amor*, ¿Autobiografía espiritual?" *La Corónica* 29 (2000): 147-70.
Lanfranc of Milan, Guido. *Cirugía mayor*: Madrid: Biblioteca Nacional 2147. Ed. Enrica J. Ardemagni. *Corpus Médico Español.*
Langbehn-Rohland, Regula; see Rohland de Langbehn.
Latini, Brunetto. *Libro del tesoro: Versión castellana de Li Livres dou Tresor.* Ed. Spurgeon Baldwin. Madison, WI: Hispanic Seminary of Medieval Studies, 1989.
Lázaro Carreter, Fernando. Estudio preliminar. *Teatro medieval.* Odres Nuevos. 3ª ed. Madrid: Castalia, 1970.
Lida de Malkiel, María Rosa. "Juan Rodríguez del Padrón: Influencia." *Nueva Revista de Filología Hispánica* 8 (1954): 1-38.
———. "Juan Rodríguez del Padrón: Vida y obras." *Nueva Revista de Filología Hispánica* 6 (1952): 313-51.
———. *La originalidad artística de* La Celestina. Buenos Aires: EUDEBA, 1962.

López de Mendoza, Íñigo, Marqués de Santillana. *Poesías completas, II: Poemas morales, políticos y religiosos, El proemio e carta*. Ed. Manuel Durán. Madrid: Castalia, 1980.
López de Villalobos, Francisco. *Anfitrion, Comedia*. Biblioteca de Autores Españoles 36. 1855. Rpr. Madrid: Atlas, 1950. 461-93.
———. *Sumario de la medicina con un compendio sobre las pestíferas bubas*: Madrid BN I-1169. Ed. María Nives Sánchez. *Corpus Médico Español*.
Lowes, John Livingston. "The Loveres Maladye of Hereos." *Modern Philology* 11 (1913-14): 491-546.
Lynch, Kathryn L. *The High Medieval Dream Vision*. Stanford: Stanford UP, 1988.
Mandrell, James. "Author and Authority in *Cárcel de amor*." *Journal of Hispanic Philology* 8 (1984): 99-122.
Márquez Villanueva, Francisco. "*Cárcel de amor*, novela política." *Revista de Occidente* 14 (1966): 185-200.
Martin, June Hall. *Love's Fools: Aucassin, Troilus, Calisto and the Parody of the Courtly Lover*. London: Tamesis, 1972.
Martínez Barbeito, Carlos. *Macías el enamorado y Juan Rodríguez del Padrón: estudio y antología*. Biblioteca de Galicia 4. Santiago de Compostela: Sociedad de Bibliófilos Gallegos, 1951.
Matulka, Barbara. *The Novels of Juan de Flores and Their European Diffusion: A Study in Comparative Literature*. Comparative Literature Series. New York: The French Institute, 1931.
McVaugh, Michael R. Introduction. *Tractatus de amore heroico*. By Arnald of Villanova. *Opera medica omnia* III. Ed. Michael R. McVaugh. Barcelona: Universitat de Barcelona, 1985. 11-39.
Mena, Juan de. *Coronación*. Ed. María Antonia Corral Checa. *La Coronación de Juan de Mena*. Monografías 206. Córdoba: Universidad de Córdoba, 1994.
———. *Laberinto de fortuna*. Ed. John G. Cummins. Madrid: Cátedra, 1984.
———. *Tratado de amor*. See Aubrun.
Menéndez Pelayo, Marcelino. *Orígenes de la novela II: Novelas sentimental, bizantina, histórica y pastoril*. Edición Nacional de las obras completas de Menéndez Pelayo 3. Ed. Enrique Sánchez Reyes. 2ª ed. Madrid: CSIC, 1961.
Menocal, María Rosa. Review of John Dagenais. *The Ethics of Reading in a Manuscript Culture: Glossing the Libro de buen amor*. *Speculum* 71 (1996): 148-50.
Michel, Paul. *Alieniloquium: Elemente einer Grammatik der Bildrede*. Zürcher Germanistische Studien 3. Bern: P. Lang, 1987.
Miguel-Prendes, Sol. "Las cartas de la *Cárcel de amor*." *Hispanófila* 34 (1991): 1-22.
Moi, Toril. "Desire in Language: Andreas Capellanus and the Controversy of Courtly Love." *Medieval Literature: Criticism, Ideology, and History*. Ed. David Aers. New York: St. Martin's P, 1986. 11-33.
Montaña de Monserrate, Bernardino. *Libro de la Anathomia del hombre*: Madrid BN R-3398. 1551. Ed. Mirta Alejandra Balestra y Patricia Gubitosi. *Corpus Médico Español*.
Moreno Báez, Enrique. Introducción. *Cárcel de Amor*. Por Diego de San Pedro. Ed. Enrique Moreno Báez. Madrid: Catédra, 1989.
Müller, Jan-Dirk. "Auctor-Actor-Author." *Der Autor im Dialog: Beiträge zu Autorität und Autorenschaft*. Ed. Werner Wunderlich und Felix Philipp Ingold. St. Gallen: UVK, 1995. 17-31.
———. "Transformationen allegorischer Strukturen im Frühen Prosa-Roman." *Bildhafte Rede in Mittelalter und früher Neuzeit: Probleme ihrer Legitimation und ihrer Funktion*. Ed. Wolfgang Harms und Klaus Speckenbach in Verbindung mit Herfried Vögel. Tübingen: Max Niemeyer, 1992. 265-84.

Müller, Michael. *Die Lehre des hl. Augustinus von der Paradiesesehe und ihre Auswirkung in der Sexualethik des 12. und 13. Jahrhunderts bis Thomas von Aquin*. Studien zur Geschichte der katholischen Moraltheologie 1. Regensburg: F. Pustet, 1954.
Myles, Robert. *Chaucerian Realism*. Chaucer Studies 20. Woodbridge, Suffolk: D.S. Brewer, 1994.
Nardi, Bruno. "L'amore e i medici medievali." *Studi in Honore di Angelo Monteverdi*. Vol. II. Modena: Società Tipografica Editrice Modenese, 1959. 517-42.
Naylor, Eric. Introduction. The text and concordance of Giovanni Boccaccio's *De casibus virorum illustrium*, translated by Pero López de Ayala. Ed. [6 p. + 6 microfiches] Eric Naylor. Madison, WI: Hispanic Seminary of Medieval Studies, 1994.
——. "Pero López de Ayala's Translation of Boccaccio's *De casibus*." *Hispanic Studies in Honour of Alan D. Deyermond. A North American Tribute*. John S. Miletich. Madison, WI: Hispanic Seminary of Medieval Studies, 1986. 205-15.
——. "Sobre la traducción de la *Caída de príncipes* de Don Pero López de Ayala." *Historias y ficciones: Coloquio sobre la literatura del siglo XV*. Ed. Rafael Beltrán, et al. València: Universitat de València, 1992. 141-56.
Neilson, William Allan. "The Purgatory of Cruel Beauties." *Romania* 29 (1900): 85-93.
Nepaulsingh, Colbert I. *Towards a History of Literary Composition in Medieval Spain*. University of Toronto Romance Series 54. Toronto: U of Toronto P, 1986.
Neuschäfer, Hans-Jörg. "Die verzauberte Dulcinea: Zur Wirklichkeitsauffassung in *Mimesis* und im *Don Quijote*." *Sinn und Sinnverstandnis: Festschrift für Ludwig Schrader zum 65. Geburtstag*. Ed. Siegfried Juttner, Rainer Stillers und Christoph Strosetzki. Berlin: Schmidt, 1997. 44-51.
Núñez, Nicolás. *Tratado*; see San Pedro, *Cárcel*, ed. Parrilla.
Oexle, Otto Gerhard. "Memoria und Memorialüberlieferung im frühen Mittelalter." *Frühmittelalterliche Studien* 10 (1976): 70-95.
Ornstein, Jacob. "La misoginia y el profeminismo en la literatura castellana." *Revista de Filología Española* 3 (1941): 219-32.
Ovid. *The Art of Love, and Other Poems*. Ed. and trans. J. H. Mozley. Loeb Classical Library 232. London: W. Heinemann, 1939.
Pabst, Walter. "Die Selbstbestrafung auf dem Stein." *Der Vergleich: Literatur- und spachwissenschaftliche Interpretationen. Festgabe für Hellmuth Petriconi zum 1. April 1955*. Ed. Rudolf Grossmann, Walter Pabst, Edmund Schramm. Hamburger romanistische Studien, A. Allgemeine romanistische Reihe 42; Hamburger romanistische Studien. B. Ibero-Amerikanische Reihe 25. Hamburg: Cram; De Gruyter, 1955. 33-49.
Parrilla, Carmen: "'Acrescentar lo que de suyo está crescido': El cumplimiento de Nicolás Núñez." *Historias y ficciones: Coloquio sobre la literatura del siglo XV*. Ed. Rafael Beltrán, José Luis Canet, José Luis Sirera. València: Departament de Filologia Espanyola, Universitat de València, 1992. 241-53.
——. "Un cronista olvidado: Juan de Flores, autor de la *Crónica incompleta de los Reyes Católicos*." *The Age of the Catholic Monarchs, 1474-1516: Literary Studies in Memory of Keith Whinnom*. Ed. Alan Deyermond and Ian Macpherson. Liverpool: Liverpool UP, 1989. 123-33.
——. Introducción. *Grimalte y Gradisa*. Por Juan de Flores. Ed. Carmen Parrilla García. Santiago de Compostela: Universidade de Santiago de Compostela, Servicio de Publicacións e Intercambio Científico, 1988.
——. Prólogo. *Cárcel de amor, con la continuación de Nicolás Núñez*. Por Diego de San Pedro y Nicolás Núñez. Ed. Carmen Parrilla. Barcelona: Crítica, 1995.
Paz y Meliá, Antonio. Introducción. *Obras completas*. Juan Rodríguez de la Cámara. Ed. Antonio Paz y Meliá. Sociedad de Bibliófilos Españoles 22. Madrid: Sociedad de Bibliófilos Españoles, 1884.

Pedro, Constable of Portugal. *Sátira de infelice e felice vida. Obras completas do condestável dom Pedro*. Ed. Luis Adão Fonseca. Lisboa: Fundação Calouste Gulbenkian, 1975. 1-175.

———. *Sátira de infelice e felice vida*. Ed. Antonio Paz y Meliá. *Opúsculos literarios de los siglos XV a XVI*. Sociedad de Bibliófilos Españoles 29. Madrid: Sociedad de Bibliófilos Españoles, 1892. 47-101.

Pérez de Guzmán, Fernán. *Generaciones y semblanzas*. Ed. Robert Brian Tate. London: Tamesis, 1965.

———. *Floresta de philósophos*. Ed. Raimond Foulché-Delbosc. *Revue historique* 11 (1904): 6-154.

Peri, Massimo. *Malato d'amore: La Medicina dei Poeti e la Poesia dei Medici*. Medioevo Romanzo e Orientale, Studi 7. Soveria Mannelli (Catanzaro): Rubbettino, 1996.

Peter of Spain. *Questiones super Viaticum*. Ed. and trans. Wack, *Lovesickness* 214-51.

Pietropaolo, Domenico. "Dante's Paradigms of Humility and the Structure of Reading." *Dante Today*. Ed. Amilcare Iannuncci. *Quaderni d'Italianistica* X.1-2 (1989): 199-211.

Post, Chandler Rathfon. *Mediaeval Spanish Allegory*. 1915. Harvard Studies in Comparative Literature 4. Repr. Westport, CT: Greenwood Press, 1974.

Prentice, Robert P. *The Psychology of Love According to St. Bonaventure*. Franciscan Institute Publications, Philosophy Series 6. St. Bonaventure, NY: Franciscan Institute, 1951.

Prieto, Antonio. Introducción. *Siervo libre de amor*. Por Juan Rodríguez del Padrón. Ed. Antonio Prieto. 1980. Madrid: Castalia, 1986.

Question de amor. Ed. Carla Perugini. Textos Recuperados 10. Salamanca: Ediciones de la Universidad de Salamanca, 1995.

Quilligan, Maureen. *The Language of Allegory: Defining the Genre*. Ithaca, NY: Cornell UP, 1979.

Rahman, F. *Avicenna's Psychology: An English Translation of* Kitāb al-najāt, *Book II, Chapter VI and Textual Improvements on the Cairo Edition*. London: Oxford UP, 1952.

Rey, Alfonso. "La primera persona narrativa en Diego de San Pedro." *Bulletin of Hispanic Studies* 58 (1981): 95-102.

Rhetorica ad Herennium / Rhétorique à Herennius. Ed. et trad. Guy Achard. Collection des universités de France. Paris: Belles Lettres, 1989.

Riquer, Martín de. "*Triste deleytaçión*, novela castellana del siglo XV." *Revista de Filología Española* 40 (1956): 33-65.

Robertson, JR., D. W. *Preface to Chaucer: Studies in Medieval Perspectives*. Princeton, NJ: Princeton UP, 1962.

Rodríguez de Lena, Pedro. *El passo honoroso de Suero de Quiñones*. Ed. Amancio Labandeira Fernández. Madrid: Fundación Universitaria Española, 1977.

Rodríguez del Padrón, Juan. *Bursario*. Ed. Pilar Saquero Suárez-Somonte y Tomás González Rolán. Madrid: Universidad Complutense, 1984.

———. *Obras completas*. Ed. César Hernández Alonso. Madrid: Editora Nacional, 1982. 151-208.

———. *Siervo libre de amor*. Ed. Antonio Prieto. 3ª ed. Madrid: Castalia, 1986.

———. *Siervo libre de amor*. *Obras*, ed. Hernández Alonso 151-208.

———. *Triunfo de las donas. Obras completas*. Juan Rodríguez de la Cámara. Ed. Antonio Paz y Meliá. Sociedad de Bibliófilos Españoles 22. Madrid: Sociedad de Bibliófilos Españoles, 1884. 83-127.

Rohland de Langbehn, Regula. "Novela sentimental: La cuestión genérica." *Ínsula* 651 (March 2001): 10-12.

———. "Desarrollo de géneros literarios: La novela sentimental española de los siglos XV y XVI." *Filología* 21 (1986): 57-76.

Rohland de Langbehn, Regula. [here as Langbehn-Rohland, Regula]. *Zur Interpretation der Romane des Diego de San Pedro.* Studia Romanica 18. Heidelberg: C. Winter, 1970.

———. Introducción. *Triste deleytaçión, novela de F.A.d.C., autor anónimo del siglo XV.* Ed. Regula Rohland de Langbehn. Morón: Universidad de Morón, 1983.

———. "El problema de los conversos y la novela sentimental." *The Age of the Catholic Monarchs, 1474-1516: Literary Studies in Memory of Keith Whinnom.* Ed. Alan D. Deyermond and Ian Macpherson. Liverpool: Liverpool UP, 1989. 134-43.

———. *La unidad genérica de la novela sentimental española de los siglos XV y XVI.* Papers of the Medieval Hispanic Research Seminar 17. London: Department of Hispanic Studies; Queen Mary and Westfield College, 1999.

Russell, J. Stephen. *Chaucer & the Trivium: The Mindsong of the* Canterbury Tales. Gainesville, FL: UP of Florida, 1998.

Salillas, Rafael. *Un gran inspirador de Cervantes: El doctor Juan Huarte y su* Examen de ingenios. Madrid: Eduardo Arias, 1905.

Salinas Espinosa, Concepción. "La Visión deleitable de Alfonso de la Torre y el viaje alegórico." *Actas del III Congreso de la Asociación Hispánica de Literatura Medieval.* Ed. María Isabel Toro Pascua. Tomo 2. Salamanca: Biblioteca Española del Siglo XV; Departamento de Literatura Española e Hispanoamericana, 1994. 905-13.

San Pedro, Diego de. *Cárcel de amor, con la continuación de Nicolás Núñez.* Ed. Carmen Parrilla. Barcelona: Crítica, 1995.

———. *Lo carcer d'amor.* Trans. Bernardi Vallmanya. Ed. facs. Barcelona, 1492 [imp. Johan Rosenbach]. Barcelona: Societat Catalana de Bibliófils, 1906.

———. *Obras.* Ed. Samuel Gili Gaya. Clásicos castellanos 133. Madrid: Espasa-Calpe, 1958.

———. *Obras completas I: Tractado de amores de Arnalte y Lucenda, Sermón.* Ed. Keith Whinnom. Madrid: Castalia, 1985.

———. *Obras completas III: poesías.* Ed. Dorothy S. Severin y Keith Whinnom. Madrid: Castalia, 1979.

———. *Prison of Love (1492) together with the continuation by Nicolás Núñez (1496).* By Diego de San Pedro. Ed. and trans. Keith Whinnom. Edinburgh: Edinburgh UP, 1979.

———. *Sermón. Obras completas I.* Ed. Keith Whinnom. 2ª ed. Madrid: Castalia: 1985. 172-83.

Schadewaldt, Hans. "Der *Morbus amatorius* aus medizinhistorischer Sicht." Forschungsinstitut für Mittelalter und Renaissance. *Das Ritterbild in Mittelalter und Renaissance.* Studia Humanitatis: Düsseldorfer Studien zu Mittelalter und Renaissance 1. Düsseldorf: Droste, 1985. 87-104.

Schevill, Rudolph. *Ovid and the Renascence in Spain.* University of California Press Publications in Modern Philology 4, part 1. Berkeley, CA: U of California P, 1913 [Rpr. Hildesheim: Georg Olms, 1971].

Schleiermacher, Friedrich. *Hermeneutik und Kritik.* Ed. Manfred Frank. Frankfurt a. Main: Suhrkamp, 1977.

Schnell, Rüdiger. Causa amoris: *Liebeskonzeption und Liebesdarstellung in der mittelalterlichen Literatur.* Bibliotheca Germanica 27. Bern: Francke, 1985.

Schütz, Alfred und Thomas Luckmann. *Strukturen der Lebenswelt.* 4. ed. Frankfurt am Main: Suhrkamp, 1991.

Sears, Theresa Ann. "Prisoners of Love: Love, Destiny, and Narrative Control in *Le Chevalier de la Charette* and *Cárcel de amor.*" *Fifteenth-Century Studies* 15 (1989): 269-82.

Seidenspinner-Núñez, Dayle. "Readers, Response and Repertoires: Rezeptionstheorie and the Archiprest's Text." *La Corónica* 19 (1990-91): 96-111.

Sena, Isabel de. "'Subita volvitrice delle cose mondane': De la *Elegia di madonna Fiammetta* de Boccaccio a Juan de Flores y Helisenne de Crenne." *Medioevo y literatura: Actas del V Congreso de la Asociación Hispánica de Literatura Medieval.* Tomo IV. Ed. Juan de Paredes. Granada: Universidad de Granada, 1995. 336-50.

Seniff, Dennis P. "Bernardo Gordonio's *Lilio de medicina*: A Possible Source of *Celestina*?" *Celestinesca* 10:1 (1986): 13-18.

Serés, Guillermo. "Don Pedro de Portugal y el Tostado." *Actas del III Congreso de la Asociación Hispánica de Literatura Medieval.* Ed. María Isabel Toro Pascua. Tomo 1. Salamanca: Biblioteca Española del Siglo XV, Departamento de Literatura Española e Hispanoamericana, 1994. 975-82.

———. "Ficción sentimental y humanismo: La *Sátira* de don Pedro de Portugal." *Bulletin Hispanique* 93:1 (1991): 31-60.

———. Introducción. *Examen de ingenios para las ciencias*. Por Juan Huarte de San Juan. Ed. Guillermo Serés. Madrid: Cátedra, 1989.

———. "La llamada ficción sentimental y el humanismo vernáculo del siglo XV: un ejemplo." "Novela sentimental: la cuestión genérica." *Ínsula* 651 (March 2001): 12-14.

———. *La transformación de los amantes: Imágenes del amor de la Antigüedad al Siglo de Oro.* Barcelona: Crítica, 1996.

Severin, Dorothy S. "Diego de San Pedro from Manuscript to Print: The Curious Case of *La pasión trobada*, *Las siete angustias*, and *Arnalte y Lucenda*." *La Corónica* 29 (2000): 187-91.

———. Introducción. *La Celestina*. Por Fernando de Rojas. Ed. Severin. 5ª ed. Madrid: Cátedra, 1991.

———. Review of John Dagenais. *The Ethics of Reading in a Manuscript Culture: Glossing the Libro de buen amor*. *Romance Philology* 50 (1996-97): 116-21.

———. "Structure and Thematic Repetitions in Diego de San Pedro's *Cárcel de amor*." *Hispanic Review* 45 (1977): 165-69.

Sharrer, Harvey L. "La *Cárcel de amor* de Diego de San Pedro: La confluencia de lo sagrado y lo profano en 'la imagen femenil entallada en una piedra muy clara'." *Actas del III Congreso de la Asociación Hispánica de Literatura Medieval.* Ed. María Isabel Toro Pascua. Tomo 2. Salamanca: Biblioteca Española del Siglo XV, Departamento de Literatura Española e Hispanoamericana, 1994. 983-96.

Smarr, Janet. *Boccaccio and Fiammetta: The narrator as Lover.* Urbana, IL: U of Illinois P, 1986.

Smith, Bruce R. "Premodern Sexualities." *PMLA* 115 (2000): 318-29.

Solomon, Michael. "Calisto's Ailment: Bitextual Diagnostics and Parody in *Celestina*." *Revista de Estudios Hispánicos* 23,1 (1989): 41-64.

———. *The Literature of Misogyny in Medieval Spain: the* Arcipreste de Talavera *and the* Spill. Cambridge Studies in Latin American and Iberian Literature 10. New York: Cambridge UP, 1997.

Soufas, Teresa Scott. *Melancholy and the Secular Mind in Spanish Golden Age Literature.* Columbia, MI: U of Missouri P, 1990.

Stemmler, Theo, ed. *Liebe als Krankheit: 3. Kolloquium der Forschungsstelle für Europäische Lyrik des Mittelalters.* Tübingen: Narr, 1990.

Sternberg, Robert and Michael Barnes, eds. *The Psychology of Love.* New Haven, Conn.: Yale UP, 1988.

Tachau, Katherine. "The problem of the *species in medio* at Oxford in the generation after Ockham." *Mediaeval Studies* 44 (1982): 349-443.

Tejerina-Canal, Santiago. "Unidad en *Cárcel de amor*: el motivo de la tiranía." *Kentucky Romance Quarterly* 31 (1984): 51-59.

Terpening, Ronny H. "Creation and Deformation in the Episode of Dulcinea: Sancho Panza as Author." *The American Hispanist* 3, n. 25 (1978): 4-5.
Thiem, Jon. "The Textualization of the Reader in Magical Realist Fiction." *Magical Realism: Theory, History, Community*. Ed. Lois Parkinson Zamora and Wendy B. Faris. Durham: Duke UP, 1995. 235-47.
Thomas Aquinas. *In Aristotelis libros De sensu et sensato, De memoria et reminiscentia commentarium*. Ed. Raymund M. Spiazzi. Roma: Marietti, 1949.
———. *A Commentary on Aristotle's De anima*. [*Sentencia libri De anima*] Trans. Robert Pasnau. Yale Library of Medieval Philosophy. New Haven, CT: Yale UP, 1999.
———. *Summa theologiæ. Volume 19: The Emotions (1a2æ. 22-30)*. Ed. and trans. Eric D'Arcy. New York: Blackfriars; McGraw-Hill, 1967.
———. *Summa theologiæ. Volume 11: Man (1a. 75-83)*. Ed. and trans. Timothy Suttor. New York: Blackfriars; McGraw-Hill, 1970.
———. *Summa theologiæ. Volume 36: Prudence (2a2æ. 47-56)*. Ed. and trans. Thomas Gilby. York: Blackfriars; McGraw-Hill, 1973.
Todorov, Tzvetan. "Reading as Construction." *The Reader in the Text: Essays on Audience and Interpretation*. Ed. Susan Suleiman and Inge Crosman. Princeton, NJ: Princeton UP, 1980. 67-82.
Toro Pascua, María Isabel. "Guevara y la teoría amorosa en el reinado de Enrique IV." *Actas del III Congreso de la Asociación Hispánica de Literatura Medieval*. Ed. María Isabel Toro Pascua. Tomo 2. Salamanca: Biblioteca Española del Siglo XV; Departamento de Literatura Española e Hispanoamericana, 1994. 1085-93.
Triste deleytaçión. An Anonymous Fifteenth Century Castilian Romance. Ed. E. Michael Gerli. Washington, DC: Georgetown UP 1982.
Triste deleytaçión, novela de F.A.d.C., autor anónimo del siglo XV. Ed. Regula Rohland de Langbehn. Morón: Universidad de Morón, 1983.
Tuve, Rosemond. *Allegorical Imagery*. Princeton, NJ: Princeton UP, 1966.
Van Beysterveldt, Antony. "La nueva teoría del amor en las novelas de Diego de San Pedro." *Cuadernos Hispanoamericanos* 349 (1979): 70-83.
———. "Revisión de los debates feministas del siglo XV y las novelas de Juan de Flores." *Hispania* 64 (1981): 1-13.
Vida del trovador Juan Rodríguez del Padrón. Juan Rodríguez del Padrón. *Obras completas*. Ed. César Hernández Alonso. Madrid: Editora Nacional, 1982. 383-97.
Vigier, Françoise. "Le *De Arte Amandi* d'André le Chapelain et la *Triste deleytaçión*, roman sentimental anonyme de la seconde moitié du XVe S." *Mélanges de la Casa de Velázquez* 21 (1985): 159-74.
———. "Fiction épistolaire et novela sentimental en Espagne aux XVe et XVIe siècles." *Mélanges de la Casa de Velázquez* 20 (1984): 230-59.
———. "Remèdes à l'amour en Espagne aux XVe et XVIe siècles." *Travaux de l'Institut d'Études Hispaniques et Portugaises de l'Université de Tours* II. Ed. Augustin Redondo. Tours: Publications de l'Université de Tours, 1979. 151-84.
Vives, Juan Luis. *Tratado del alma*. Trad. José Ontañón. 2ª ed. Buenos Aires: Espasa-Calpe Argentina, 1945.
Voigt, Lisa. "La alegoría de la lectura en *Cárcel de amor*." *La Corónica* 25 (1997): 121-33.
Von der Walde Moheno, Lillian. "De ejemplos y consejos en *Grimalte y Gradisa*." *La Corónica* 29 (2000): 193-204.
Von Moos, Peter. *Geschichte als Topik. Das rhetorische Exemplum von der Antike zur Neuzeit und die* historiae *im* Policratus *Johanns von Salisbury*. Hildesheim: G. Olms, 1988.
Von Richthofen, Erich. "Petrarca, Dante y Andreas Capellanus: Fuentes inadvertidas de *La Cárcel de Amor*." *Revista Canadiense de Estudios Hispánicos* 1 (1976): 30-38.

Vozzo, Lia Mendia. Introduzzione. *Libro de Fiameta.* Di Giovanni Boccaccio. Ed. Lia Mendia Vozzo. Collana di testi e studi ispanici I, Testi critici 4. Pisa: Giardini, 1983.

Wack, Mary Frances. "Imagination, Medicine, and Rhetoric in Andreas Capellanus' *De amore.*" *Magister Regis: Studies in Honor of Robert Earl Kaske.* Ed. Arthur Gross et al. New York: Fordham UP, 1986. 101-15.

———. *Lovesickness in the Middle Ages: The* Viaticum *and its Commentaries.* Philadelphia: U of Pennsylvania P, 1990.

———. "From Mental Faculties to Magical Philters: The Entry of Magic into Academic Medical Writing on Lovesickness, 13th-17th Centuries." Beecher and Ciavolella, *Eros and Anteros* 9-31.

Waley, Pamela. Introduction. *Grimalte y Gradissa.* Por Juan de Flores. Ed. Pamela Waley. London: Tamesis, 1971.

———. "Love and honour in the novelas sentimentales of Diego de San Pedro and Juan de Flores." *Bulletin of Hispanic Studies* 42 (1966): 15-31.

Walsh, J. K. *El Coloquio de la Memoria, la Voluntad, y el Entendimiento (Biblioteca Universitaria de Salamanca MS. 1763) y otras manifestaciones del tema en la literatura española.* New York: L. Clemente, 1986.

Wardropper, Bruce W. "Allegory and the role of *El Autor* in the *Cárcel de amor.*" *Philological Quarterly* 31 (1952): 39-44.

———. "El mundo sentimental de la *Cárcel de amor.*" *Revista de Filología Española* 37 (1953): 168-93.

Weinrich, Harald. *Lethe: Kunst und Kritik des Vergessens.* 2. ed. München: C. H. Beck, 1997.

———. *Das Ingenium Don Quijotes. Ein Beitrag zur literarischen Charakterkunde.* Forschungen zur Romanischen Philologie 1. Münster: Aschendorf, 1956.

Weinsheimer, Joel. *Philosophical Hermeneutics and Literary Theory.* New Haven, Conn.; London: Yale UP, 1991.

Weiss, Julian. "Álvaro de Luna, Juan de Mena and the Power of Courtly Love." *Modern Language Notes* 106 (1991): 241-56.

Weissberger, Barbara F. "Authority Figures in *Siervo libre de amor* and *Grisel y Mirabella.*" *Revista de Estudios Hispánicos* 9 (1982): 255-62.

———. "Authors, Characters and Readers in *Grimalte y Gradissa.*" *Studies in Honor of Stephen Gilman.* Ed. Ronald E. Surtz and Nora Weinerth. Newark, DE: Juan de la Cuesta, 1983. 61-76.

———. "The Gendered Taxonomy of Spanish Romance." *La Corónica* 29 (2000): 205-29.

———. "'Habla el Auctor': *L'elegia di Madonna Fiametta* as a Source for the *Siervo libre de amor.*" *Journal of Hispanic Philology* 4 (1980): 203-236.

———. "The Politics of *Cárcel de Amor.*" *Revista de Estudios Hispánicos* 26 (1992): 307-26.

———. "Resisting readers and writers in the sentimental romances and the problem of female literacy." Gerli and Gwara 173-90.

———. "Role-Reversal and Festivity in the Romances of Juan de Flores." *Journal of Hispanic Philology* 13 (1988-89): 197-213.

Wenzel, Horst. *Hören und Sehen, Schrift und Bild: Kultur und Gedächtnis im Mittelalter.* München: C. H. Beck, 1995.

Wetherbee, Winthrop. "The Theme of Imagination in Medieval Poetry and the Allegorical Figure 'Genius'." *Medievalia et Humanistica* NS 7 (1976): 45-64.

Whinnom, Keith. "*Autor* and *tratado* in the Fifteenth Century: Semantic Latinism or Etymological Trap?" *Bulletin of Hispanic Studies* 59 (1982): 211-18.

———. "Cardona, the Crucifixion and Leriano's Last Drink." Gerli and Gwara 207-13.

Whinnom, Keith. *Diego de San Pedro*. Twayne's World Author Series 310. New York: Twayne, 1974.
———. "Diego de San Pedro's stylistic reform." *Bulletin of Hispanic Studies* 37 (1960): 1-15.
———. Introducción. *Obras completas I*. Por Diego de San Pedro. Ed. Keith Whinnom. 2ª ed. Madrid: Castalia: 1985.
———. Introducción. *Obras completas II*. Por Diego de San Pedro. Ed. Keith Whinnom. 2ª ed. Madrid: Castalia: 1984.
———. Introduction. *Prision of Love (1492) together with the continuation by Nicolás Núñez (1496)*. By Diego de San Pedro. Ed. and trans. Keith Whinnom. Edinburgh: Edinburgh UP, 1979.
———. "Nicolás Núñez's Continuation of the *Cárcel de Amor* (Burgos, 1496)." *Studies in Spanish Literature of the Golden Age Presented to Edward M. Wilson*. Ed. R. O. Jones. London: Tamesis, 1973. 357-66.
———. "The marquis de Pidal vindicated: The fictional biography of Juan Rodríguez del Padrón." *La Corónica* 13 (1984): 142-44.
———. "The problem of the 'best-seller' in Spanish Golden-Age literature." *Bulletin of Hispanic Studies* 57 (1980): 189-98.
———. *The Spanish Sentimental Romance: 1440-1550: A Critical Bibliography*. Research Bibliographies & Checklists 41. London: Grant & Cutler, 1983.
White, Hayden. "The Forms of Wildness: Archaeology of an Idea." *The Wild Man Within: An Image of Western Thought from the Renaissance to Romanticism*. Ed. Edward Dudley and Maximilian E. Novak. Pittsburgh, PA: U of Pittsburgh P, 1972. 3-38.
Wolfson, Harry Austryn. "The Internal Senses in Latin, Arabic and Hebrew Philosophic Texts." *Harvard Theological Review* 28 (1935): 69-133.
Yates, Frances A. *The Art of Memory*. Chicago: U of Chicago P, 1966.
Ynduráin, Domingo. "Las cartas de Laureola (beber cenizas)." *Edad de Oro* 3 (1984): 299-309.
Zaderenko, Irene. "Dante en la ficción sentimental." *Dicenda* 17 (1999): 283-93.

NORTH CAROLINA STUDIES IN THE ROMANCE LANGUAGES AND LITERATURES

I.S.B.N. Prefix 0-8078-

Recent Titles

THE POETICS OF INCONSTANCY, ETIENNE DURAND AND THE END OF RENAISSANCE VERSE, by Hoyt Rogers. 1998. (No. 256). -9260-2.
RONSARD'S CONTENTIOUS SISTERS: THE PARAGONE BETWEEN POETRY AND PAINTING IN THE WORKS OF PIERRE DE RONSARD, by Roberto E. Campo. 1998. (No. 257). -9261-0.
THE RAVISHMENT OF PERSEPHONE: EPISTOLARY LYRIC IN THE *SIÈCLE DES LUMIÈRES*, by Julia K. De Pree. 1998. (No. 258). -9262-9.
CONVERTING FICTION: COUNTER REFORMATIONAL CLOSURE IN THE SECULAR LITERATURE OF GOLDEN AGE SPAIN, by David H. Darst. 1998. (No. 259). -9263-7.
GALDÓS'S *SEGUNDA MANERA*: RHETORICAL STRATEGIES AND AFFECTIVE RESPONSE, by Linda M. Willem. 1998. (No. 260). -9264-5.
A MEDIEVAL PILGRIM'S COMPANION. REASSESSING *EL LIBRO DE LOS HUÉSPEDES* (ESCORIAL MS. h.I.13), by Thomas D. Spaccarelli. 1998. (No. 261). -9265-3.
'PUEBLOS ENFERMOS': THE DISCOURSE OF ILLNESS IN THE TURN-OF-THE-CENTURY SPANISH AND LATIN AMERICAN ESSAY, by Michael Aronna. 1999. (No. 262). -9266-1.
RESONANT THEMES. LITERATURE, HISTORY, AND THE ARTS IN NINETEENTH- AND TWENTIETH-CENTURY EUROPE. ESSAYS IN HONOR OF VICTOR BROMBERT, by Stirling Haig. 1999. (No. 263). -9267-X.
RAZA, GÉNERO E HIBRIDEZ EN *EL LAZARILLO DE CIEGOS CAMINANTES*, por Mariselle Meléndez. 1999. (No. 264). -9268-8.
DEL ESCENARIO A LA PANTALLA: LA ADAPTACIÓN CINEMATOGRÁFICA DEL TEATRO ESPAÑOL, por María Asunción Gómez. 2000. (No. 265). -9269-6.
THE LEPER IN BLUE: COERCIVE PERFORMANCE AND THE CONTEMPORARY LATIN AMERICAN THEATER, by Amalia Gladhart. 2000. (No. 266). -9270-X.
THE CHARM OF CATASTROPHE: A STUDY OF RABELAIS'S *QUART LIVRE*, by Alice Fiola Berry. 2000. (No. 267). -9271-8.
PUERTO RICAN CULTURAL IDENTITY AND THE WORK OF LUIS RAFAEL SÁNCHEZ, by John Dimitri Perivolaris. 2000. (No. 268). -9272-6.
MANNERISM AND BAROQUE IN SEVENTEENTH-CENTURY FRENCH POETRY: THE EXAMPLE OF TRISTAN L'HERMITE, by James Crenshaw Shepard. 2001. (No. 269). -9273-4.
RECLAIMING THE BODY: MARÍA DE ZAYA'S EARLY MODERN FEMINISM, by Lisa Vollendorf. 2001. (No. 270). -9274-2.
FORGED GENEALOGIES: SAINT-JOHN PERSE'S CONVERSATIONS WITH CULTURE, by Carol Rigolot. 2001. (No. 271). -9275-0.
VISIONES DE ESTEREOSCOPIO (PARADIGMA DE HIBRIDACIÓN EN EL ARTE Y LA NARRATIVA DE LA VANGUARDIA ESPAÑOLA), por María Soledad Fernández Utrera. 2001. (No. 272). -9276-9.
TRANSPOSING ART INTO TEXTS IN FRENCH ROMANTIC LITERATURE, by Henry F. Majewski. 2002. (No. 273). -9277-7.
IMAGES IN MIND: LOVESICKNESS, SPANISH SENTIMENTAL FICTION AND *DON QUIJOTE*, by Robert Folger. 2002. (No. 274). -9278-5.
INDISCERNIBLE COUNTERPARTS: THE INVENTION OF THE TEXT IN FRENCH CLASSICAL DRAMA, by Christopher Braider. 2002. (No. 275). -9279-3.

When ordering please cite the *ISBN Prefix* plus the last four digits for each title.

Send orders to: University of North Carolina Press
P.O. Box 2288
Chapel Hill, NC 27515-2288
U.S.A.
www.uncpress.unc.edu
FAX: 919 968-3829

www.ingramcontent.com/pod-product-compliance
Lightning Source LLC
Chambersburg PA
CBHW030339240426
43661CB00052B/1683